# Voices from the Street

Truths about Homelessness from Sisters Of The Road

by

Jessica P. Morrell

Foreword by Genevieve "Genny" Nelson

# Voices from the Street

Voices from the Street

Truths about Homelessness from Sisters Of The Road

by

Jessica P. Morrell

Foreword by Genevieve "Genny" Nelson

"In here there are no strangers...
## Sisters Of The Road
...just friends we've never met."

Gray Sunshine
Portland, Oregon

Voices from the Street: Truths about Homelessness from Sisters Of The Road

Gray Sunshine Publishing
© 2007 Sisters Of The Road
All Rights Reserved

ISBN: 978097692616-0

Managing Editor: Linda M. Meyer
Editor: Laura Meehan
Associate Editors: Sara Freedman, Elizabeth Fuller, Bo Björn Johnson, Kylin Larsson,
Cameron Marschall, Cassie Richoux, Lauren Shapiro, Anna Stoefen, Jennifer Weaver-Neist
Indexer: Pamela Ivey
Assistant Publisher: Emily Phillips
Cover and Interior Designer: David Cowsert
Cover Photo: Buddy Bee Anthony
Director of Marketing: Allison Collins

Printed and bound in the United States of America

Gray Sunshine, an imprint of Ink & Paper Group, LLC
1825 SE 7th Avenue
Portland, OR 97214
www.graysunshine.com


11  10  09  08  07      1  2  3  4  5

Dedication

*To the men, women, youth, and children*
*who make up the community of Sisters Of The Road.*
*You are our truth commission.*

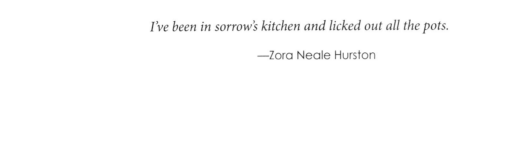

*I've been in sorrow's kitchen and licked out all the pots.*

—Zora Neale Hurston

# Table of Contents

*Foreword*

*Love and ever more love is the only solution to every problem that comes up. If we love each other enough, we will bear with each other's faults and burdens. If we love enough, we are going to light that fire in the hearts of others. And it is love that will burn out the sins and hatreds that sadden us. It is love that will make us want to do great things for each other. No sacrifice and no suffering will then seem too much.*

—Dorothy Day, *House of Hospitality*

In the fall of 1972, I began a college work-study job in Portland, Oregon's, skid row. I had asked the university I was attending for a position that had something to do with my major in Sociology, and this was it. Once there, I worked with conscientious objectors (COs) to the war in Vietnam. Each of them had been required to prove their opposition to war of any kind to the local draft board. For that they were given two years of civilian alternate service. These COs introduced me to the writings of Dorothy Day and the example of the Catholic Worker; a woman and a movement that believed offering hospitality to poor and homeless people was a personal responsibility, not one belonging to the state. Their clarion call to the works of mercy and to direct action as a response to social injustice was predicated on nonviolence. Dorothy Day's and the Catholic Worker's commitments would inform, inspire, and challenge every pursuit I followed for the rest of my life.

Through the '70s, I continued for a while to work in skid row, married one of the COs, helped open and for five years lived in a Catholic Worker House of Hospitality, adopted my son and daughter, divorced, and came back to the skids to once again find a job.

In 1979, my coworker Sandy Gooch and I, challenged to reinvent our CETA (Comprehensive Employment and Training Act) jobs, realized we could not make our own assumptions about what an entire poor and homeless community needed. We took the time to ask men and women in the all-night shelter, the women's day center, and at some of the missions and soup lines about the biggest issues in their daily lives. At the top of their list was the need for an alternative place to eat where they could gather as a community and dine with dignity. Later that year we opened Sisters Of The Road Cafe, with Sandy bringing the restaurant knowledge and me the Catholic Worker philosophies of gentle personalism and nonviolence.

Dorothy Day died in November 1980, a few weeks after Sisters' first anniversary. With a heart full of sadness and gratitude, I dug deeper into my work.

From the start, Sisters was guided by these beliefs: People are made up of heart, mind, body, and soul. When confronted with a problem, if the solution disregards this fact and only addresses one part of a person, it will fail in the end. Solutions must be as unique as the homeless man, woman, youth, or child who is asking for your help. Sisters would never do for anyone what they can do for themselves. We would all, customers and staff alike, assume the responsibility for ending homelessness. The reflection and action necessary to accomplish that would come from mutual aid and information, shared vision and power. Sisters would be a place where you could walk in with any number of problems (homelessness, joblessness, mental or physical health issues, etc.) and be welcomed, and recognize you still had choices left in your life. No one would be coddled and all would be held accountable for what they said and did. The best part though, was after you solved your problems, you would be equally welcome in Sisters. The meals would stay affordable, your success stories would educate and inspire others, and when mistakes happened you would be offered respect, tender mercy, consequences, and another chance. Sisters would be profoundly about love.

Our customers led me to the beloved community. Mo was one of them. Native American, he could speak truth to power with his poet's voice, and often enough I was the one he was talking to. He changed my thinking. A jokester too, his playful spirit softened the sharp edge of his lessons. As one customer put it, "He had strong medicine."

In a letter the staff received from Mo, he wrote, "I must give credit to the Sister's "family" for always being there to listen and support me in my recovery endeavors. Even after relapsing and coming into the cafe looking like some beat down animal, you all (past and present staff) always were there treating me as a human being. I know that it may not have been the most pleasant sight to see or experience; I know it's hard for me to handle when I see someone I care about hurting themselves. I just wanted to say thank you for always caring about your fellow human beings—you are an oasis in a land of despair to many people." What Mo experienced in Sisters was testimony to our beliefs. Mo's and all the rest of our customers' stories hold a precious place in my heart and mind. The web of our lives has taught me well.

Once I tried to tell Linda, a sweet and eight-months-pregnant woman sleeping nights in a shelter, what to do. I pushed her to sign up for low-income housing and be on time for her doctors' visit all in the same day. She looked at me like I had three heads. How the hell was she going to travel on the bus to both of these appointments, at opposite ends of the city, in four hours' time? I was designing plans for her based on my comfortable reality, not her impoverished one. She was not prone to change because of my ignorance, so I was compelled to walk a mile in her shoes and learn.

In our first year of operation, Sisters decided to open on the Fourth of July to point out the irony of "liberty and justice for all." But prior to opening that day, the ceiling fell in and almost knocked me out cold into a stockpot of boiling water. Instead of my head, the pot's enamel lid caught the debris. Its pummeled surface scared me. I didn't want to ask for help, I needed to be prodded by a friend. A lifelong introvert, still shaking from the near miss, I forced myself out of the cafe and into the neighborhood where I immediately found customers willing to join me in the cleanup. They brought their own tools and scrounged nails and a sheet of plywood to temporarily cover up the gaping hole. They changed what would have been "my" sorry story into "our" miraculous one.

Contractions and childbirth are as common as a cup of coffee in Sisters, and sometimes they come together. It happened one late January evening, the mom-to-be thought her baby would be born on the cafe's old green linoleum floor. As she cried out in pain, I timed her contractions while the rest of our customers looked confused and then dumbfounded by the imminent arrival of a newborn. They could sense her fear. She was penniless and not eligible for welfare until the first of the month, more than a week away. She was new in town, didn't have a place to live, and had nothing for her baby. Through her tears she pleaded with me to stay with her for the birth; a coworker drove us to the hospital. There was confusion to begin with because she had no doctor, no chart, and no history—a hundred questions consumed the first hour—then we were whisked away to a delivery room where they taught us both how to breathe. Within forty-five minutes, the head emerged and we heard the baby cry. There was so much care and concern and the longest few moments until all of this five-pound, fourteen-ounce baby girl was born. Her mother named her after me, moved her into a run-down hotel room, and swaddled her in an old wooden dresser drawer. The welfare worker took Genevieve within weeks and she was lost to her mother forever.

Then there was Hugh who died from the ravages of hypothermia, pneumonia, and alcoholism in the South Park Blocks. He was a faithful customer and barter worker who would scrub out pots with me for long hours after the cafe had closed for the day. His ancestors fished for salmon with nets or long poles at Celilo Falls before The Dalles Dam was built on the Columbia River. After Hugh died, I was invited to attend a Pipe Ceremony honoring him. Martin, the medicine man who led it, urged each of us to find a humble place within and bring forth a new habit sheltered in Hugh's spirit. It came to me. I would strengthen my will to be in this world; learn to love more fully; do the best work I knew how; let go of the anger; and not be complicit in feelings of low self-worth. Some of those have proved more difficult than the others.

Dorothy Day once said. "It is when we treat strangers specially that the world is transformed." All of our stories, mine and Sisters' customers woven together, have propped up my will to live in the world as if there already were life, liberty, and justice for all. It is a place of steadfast truth and extraordinary hope.

—Genevieve "Genny" Nelson

Genevieve "Genny" Nelson.

Photographer: Orion Gray

# Author's Note

*Author's Note*

*Suffering cannot be obliterated by the mere act of storytelling*

---

This book represents the work of a number of people who have tried to illuminate the disaster that is homelessness. I was asked by Genevieve Nelson, a cofounder of Sisters Of The Road, in Portland, Oregon, to write this book.

A team of several dozen people were involved in this project, which included field researchers, photographers, transcribers, and coders. A consultant was hired to help design the methodology, and an associate was hired to create and manage the database from the interviews.

When I was hired, the first transcripts were completed and the last of the interviews were still taking place as more than six hundred people stepped into a small office to tell the stories of their lives and how they came to be living without the benefits of shelter.

The project was designed not to gather statistics or to be quantitative, but rather as a means to gather in-depth, qualitative interviews. The team of field researchers was trained to ask a series of probing questions along with follow-up questions when the subject being discussed was especially important or the narrator was passionate about the topic. Each person was interviewed individually, a necessarily time-consuming process, with the interviews lasting approximately two and one-half hours. There were a total of six hundred and twenty-eight interviews, five hundred and fifteen of which were usable and supplied the pool from which this book is drawn. The narrators were mostly adult males. About one-third of those interviewed were women.

After several meetings with Genny, I was given a foot-tall stack of transcripts and began reading them and highlighting the sections I believed most revealed the truths of that person's life. As more interviews were transcribed, my stack grew and I found emerging themes and from them created a table of contents that seemed to reflect the major issues revealed in our interviews. By the time the last interview was transcribed, we had more than fifteen thousand single-spaced pages embedded with truth, pain, and surprising revelations. In these many pages, stark realities emerged along with sometimes practical and powerful wisdom.

While I was the author of *Voices from the Street*, this task was not mine alone, and I'd especially like to thank Genny Nelson, Orion Gray, and Gina Cadenasso for their support, early editing help, and insights. I'd also like to thank the rest of Sisters' staff, field researchers, and coders (most of whom were narrators) for their long hours of labor, and it is important to mention Carl Welch, Bob Caldean, and Dan Newth here for their tireless work with Gina. Additionally I'd like to thank Jamie Manuel for creating the database and managing the systems we used, the PhotoVoice photographers, the Board of Directors of Sisters Of The Road for understanding the importance of this project, Cecile Baril for her research, and the donors whose contributions made it possible, and finally, the men and women who stepped in from the streets to be heard. The late activist and Minnesota senator, Paul Wellstone once said, "Never separate the life you lead from the words you speak." And so here are the voices from the street.


Respectfully submitted,


Jessica P. Morrell, 2007

Photographer: Terry Prather

# Introduction

*Introduction*

*Only the truth is revolutionary*
—Graffiti, Paris, May 1968

## People need to understand
## we did not create this

On any given night in America, one to three and a half million people are homeless. Since they have no home or bed, they sleep under bridges, in parks, on cruel pavements, in doorways, alleys, in cardboard boxes, makeshift structures, or subways. Some sleep in bus or train stations, some are housed in shelters and missions. Often long before a person or family becomes a homeless statistic, a myriad of circumstances start teetering them toward it. These circumstances vary—the death of a caregiver; an abusive spouse, caretaker, parent, or stepparent delivers a blow that can no longer be tolerated; divorce; health problems; injuries; eviction; or a job loss. It is sometimes only a bit of bad luck, a missed pay check, or a shaky family situation shifting that pushes a person onto the streets. And then sometimes it's the result of a history of bad choices, or the long-term effects of mental illness, poverty, or addictions.

When you couple dire personal circumstances with the harsh realities of our current social, economic, and political climate, you create a collision course that can lead to disaster. Perhaps the homeless people among us are our proverbial canary in the mine shaft. But then perhaps not, since this isn't the first time they have been among us in America.

### Seeds of an Epidemic

The reasons for homelessness have never been that difficult to understand when you go to the root of the problem. First, there isn't enough adequate housing. For the purposes of this book, we define adequate housing as permanent, safe, decent, and affordable places to live. Affordable meaning rents at zero to thirty percent of median family income. A lack of such housing in this country stems from a number of elements including gentrification of urban neighborhoods nationwide that has resulted in an erosion or loss of preexisting affordable houses and apartments; cutbacks in local, state, and federal housing programs; and the demolition of seventy-thousand public housing units between 1995 and 2005.

Second, for decades earnings have lagged behind the real cost of living. According to the U.S. Bureau of Labor Statistics, the minimum wage has actually decreased thirty-eight percent since 1968. Higher numbers of unemployed workers are the shameful outcome of downsizing by companies and industries who are outsourcing jobs overseas. Our narrators consistently referred to the economy and the job market in our interviews, and the facts bear them out. Generally, good paying, secure jobs are becoming a scarcer commodity, which in turn creates more people at risk of homelessness. Walmart, often accused of exploiting its workers, is now America's largest employer.

Fewer jobs with livable wages translates into housing costs that are out of reach, especially for those earning $7.25 or less an hour. In a 1989 survey conducted in thirty American cities, it was found that twenty percent of homeless people work full time. But the mere factor of a job has not guaranteed housing for any of them.

Other issues contribute to the overall picture: In the '70s we removed people from state mental health institutions without adequate follow-up plans for their care or housing. We saw the return of thousands of Vietnam veterans, many of them suffering from Post-traumatic Stress Disorder or mired in drug or alcohol addictions. During the Reagan Administration the federal government's attitude about poverty and homelessness was dehumanizing and punitive, impacting public policy for years to come.

The Stewart B. McKinney Homeless Assistance Act of 1987, the only major federal response to homelessness to this day, is chronically underfunded and focuses on emergency measures, not systemic solutions. Although amended several times and introducing some good programs, it was meant to be merely a first step, and after twenty years it is woefully inadequate to tackle homelessness.

The '80s saw crack cocaine explode in urban neighborhoods like a thousand bombs, further shattering poor families and raising the levels of violence and instability. Add to this picture a much broader use of illegal drugs such as methamphetamines, an increase in single-parent households with low earning power, and thinning support networks such as traditional families. Health care costs are rising and are often out of reach of people who can barely pay the rent. An accident, illness, or heart attack can trigger the afflicted into a deadly downward spiral.

The concentration of wealth in America remains with a few instead of filtering throughout society. The welfare reforms signed into law in 1996 dropped nine million women and children from the rolls but their removal doesn't indicate that they're doing better or have secured work. Instead, it merely indicates that they are no longer receiving benefits. Along with countrywide cuts to social service programs, there are few resources available to the disabled and mentally ill. Then there are issues of alcoholism, drug addictions, and compassion overload. For all these reasons we leave our nation's most vulnerable members adrift on the mean streets.

More influences started piling on. In the months following September 11, 2001, a faltering economy, a plummeting stock market, a new national agenda, and looming war affected our most vulnerable citizens. The National Alliance to End Homelessness reported that in the year following September 11, there was a dramatic twenty-five percent increase of the homeless in major American cities.

Then a raucous hurricane named Katrina swept into the Gulf Coast in late August of 2005, and when the winds roared and waters rose, thousands were left without homes. America was forced to watch in horror as the poorest among us, normally invisible, were abandoned to suffer and die in the nightmarish, tropical heat.

When aid finally began to reach them, our tendency as a nation was to call them the "deserving poor." But if a similar tragedy had occurred in our city we would recognize them as low-income residents whose supplemental security income checks, Social Security disability checks, and welfare checks were not

## Numbers Tell a Story

Numbers tell a story that cannot be ignored. According to a report issued by the Urban Institute, from the late '80s until the late '90s, the numbers of homeless grew by 40 %. However, since this research is dated, chances are the number of homeless people is now far greater. The current numbers from cities provide the proof. In Los Angeles in 1990 there were an estimated 30,000 homeless; in 2005 an estimated 85,000. In Chicago in 2000, 3,000 families were in shelters; in 2005, 15,000 families were. In Phoenix in the early '90s, 6,000 to 8,000 people experienced homelessness every day; in 2005 the numbers were 8,000 to 10,000. In Houston in 2003, an estimated 20,000 to 25,000 people experienced homelessness; in 2005, the number rose to an estimated 34,000.

In New York, since 1988, the number of homeless has risen nearly 75 %. On July 3, 2003, CBS news correspondent Les Cowan reported that homeless families on the street are now the norm, not the exception. But the line in the broadcast that is especially noteworthy is: "New York City is just one example. The lines for soup kitchens are getting longer and longer. In fact there are more homeless families in Manhattan right now than during the Great Depression."

due to arrive in the mail until the first of the month. They were all without any resources. We would know them as the mostly poor, elderly, and infirm, unable to navigate on their own. And we would recognize some of them as members of our city's current homeless population. Can you at once be undeserving and invisible and then suddenly deserving when your nation observes you through the televised calamity of a natural disaster?

It is clear that just like the days following the terrorist bombings of September 11, 2001, we will witness an increase in the numbers of displaced and homeless people in this country from the hurricanes of 2005. That there will be more call for services, shelter and solutions. That poverty and homelessness are behind these many tragic stories. They exist within sight of wealth and abundance.

The prevalence of poverty and homelessness in the midst of an affluent nation is unnecessary. While the reality is overwhelming, these problems are solvable.

This book, which resulted from interviewing more than six hundred homeless people about their current lives, their histories, and insights, was undertaken for a variety of reasons. We wanted to go straight to the source: the people who have lived on the streets, who know firsthand the weaknesses of a system and the difficulties of survival without the most basic of safety nets—a place, a bed, a meal, a bathroom. We listened to them suggest over and over that politicians and policymakers should spend time on the streets in order to understand their reality. We heard them suggest solutions that are sometimes brilliant, sometimes obvious, and often simple.

We also wanted to uncover the underlying reasons for homelessness and to hear their suggestions for practical, community-based prevention. We wanted to avert another generation from entering this nightmare.

And make no mistake, despite existing programs and shelters, good intentions, missions and soup kitchens, life on the street is demeaning, dangerous, and sometimes deadly. Poverty has a body count as real as any hurricane, bombed-out building, or

## Sisters' PhotoVoice Project

Most of the photos in this book came from the PhotoVoice Project.

In the winter of 2005, Sisters began the PhotoVoice Project to empower their customers to photo-document their day-to-day lives and to share their unique perspectives through photographs and stories—including seeking shelter, food, healthcare, and community. Forty people began the project; ten participants completed the project and took over 500 photographs of their lives on the street.

The project aimed to promote critical dialogue and increase knowledge about personal and community issues through group discussion of photographs and to provide information to leaders and policy makers on the realities of the day-to-day lives of people experiencing homelessness.

Since its May 2005 premier, the PhotoVoice Project has raised awareness of homelessness and poverty issues—reaching nearly 15,000 community members through the sharing of the photographs and stories with youth, businesses, associations, and faith communities. It continues to inspire people from all walks of life to work together for a livable community for all people.

Sisters has created curriculum to accompany the PhotoVoice exhibit for use with children in grades K–12. The curriculum has been designed to incorporate activities, lesson plans, statistics about homelessness, and service-learning opportunities, and has emphasis on dispelling stereotypes. The materials are widely available for educators via the Sisters' web site.

battlefield. The cost is high for both those without a home and for a society that would like to sometimes ignore their growing numbers. Perhaps the mark of a great society is how it treats its most vulnerable citizens, especially those who are endangered, afraid, and humiliated by their circumstances.

There is a new sense of urgency to address the epidemic that is belittling and sullying this country. What began as an alarming trend in the '70s became a crisis in the '80s and has now grown to a full-blown calamity. Evidence of the homeless among us is everywhere—found in the haunted eyes of people who peer out from doorways, food lines, park benches, and the hollow and secret places of our cities. Evidence of their plight is revealed in the overcrowded shelters, the overburdened social service agencies, and the controversy swirling around them. Their numbers are growing. They're everywhere and they are everyone—veterans and the mentally ill, children and women, families and the frail.

Some of us see this invisible underground as a pestilence among us.

And some of us see their haunting presence as the failure of a society, of institutions, of policies gone wrong. We see heartbreak personified.

This book was created to talk back to heartbreak, misinformation, and seemingly hopeless circumstances. We all have a story to tell and the voices here, so eloquent and strong, come straight from the streets and shelters and hidden places. The voices here provide a home for the homeless and speak of prevention, solutions, and strengths.

You will hear voices that don't whisper, don't apologize or excuse, but instead cut to the bone with their need for dignity and safety, and an opportunity.

Photographer: Dan Newth

Photographer: Alan Shipley

# Chapter 1

*I never thought that I'd be homeless*

## Circumstances that Lead to Homelessness

*Compassion is not a relationship between the healer and the wounded. It's a relationship between equals. Only when we know our own darkness well can we be present with the darkness of others. Compassion becomes real when we recognize our shared humanity.*

—Pema Chodron

I learned something early on, and it has shaped the language that Sisters uses: you really can't say someone is dealing with homelessness. What they're dealing with are the calamities of homelessness. It could be just one, such as divorce or losing a job, or it could be a combination of things—but it's never just homelessness. It is hard luck, it is bad decisions, it is all the above.

Because Sisters' practice of nonviolence calls on us to speak the truth to each other, our narrators said they trusted Sisters' researchers and felt safe to reach down inside themselves and touch the depth of what had happened to them, down into the river of their emotions. They told us stories they had never told anyone, saying, "It's my fault; it's my bad choice," or "My mother had me turning tricks when I was 11 years old," or "I never had any place or group of people I could call home."

There were no surprises for me in this chapter, except one: the number of "military brats" we interviewed. They said they never stayed in any one place long enough to make connections, and this pattern continued for them as adults.

—Genny

Our interviews proved again and again that there is no such thing as a typical person who becomes homeless. We discovered that our narrators represented the rich diversity that exists in all parts of humanity and came from an array of backgrounds and circumstances.

Charles was 59 when he was interviewed. Once a married homeowner with four children, he became homeless after a series of catastrophes that began when he lost his job at Kmart. After his unemployment benefits ran out, he worked for a temporary service but then suffered a stroke that hospitalized him. After his stroke, despite his physical disabilities, he began looking for work again and filled out a reported nine hundred to one thousand applications without success. At the time of our interview he was consulting an attorney so that he could be declared disabled and collect Social Security benefits.

After Charles' stroke, he began living with a female roommate but his pride and need for self-reliance directly led to his current situation.

**Charles:** My roommate, she took care of me as long as she could, you know, and I did not want to impose on anybody. I have a lot of pride. And so, purposely, I got into an argument with her. One day around the end of February she told me not to be there any longer, and that is exactly what I wanted her to say because she would never put me out.

Tina, 33, explained that her homelessness stemmed directly from an eviction.

**Tina:** The eviction came up and my life just fell apart. I collapsed basically because I was not prepared for it. I could not find an apartment; that was obvious. My mother, still to this day does not believe it. She just cannot fathom it. When I came to Portland from Vancouver, I literally came with my little shopping cart and I did not know what I was going to do. I had nothing; I did not have friends.

Rhonda fled her grandparents' comfortable home in a coastal town of Oregon as an act of teenage rebellion and ended up on the streets of Portland begging for spare change. She managed to easily meet other young people and stayed at a shelter for teens and at friends' homes.

**Rhonda:** I really did not have a plan. I just kind of bounced from each house because they did not know each other, so they never really realized that all I was doing was like spending the night at each one's house once a week.

For most of those interviewed, Kathryn included, where personal choices led to homelessness, there was no pride in the choices or the results.

*Sisters: Tell me why you're homeless.*

**Kathryn:** Because I made wrong choices, and buying drugs and alcohol, and different situations that happened in my life. I was married for fifteen years, and everything was always taken care for me, you know. He even bought my clothing. He picked my friends. He did the shopping and I had three children by him. I never had to make choices. People did it, you know. It was like a mandatory thing and I was abused for…I was married to him for fifteen years, and I was abused pretty much most of the time. My children were abused. My daughter Miranda was sexually abused by her uncle, and her dad believed his brother over his own daughter, and what happened behind that is Miranda went to her school officials and they moved her out of the home. The reason I wasn't there is because I knew I had to get away because it was going to get harsh. And the wrong choice I made is, I should have taken my children with me even though they were going to be homeless, maybe, but, I didn't know how to make it out here. I didn't know what to do. What choices. Who to ask cause I was always fearful. And—is this what you want me to tell? This is it?

*Sisters: Yes.*

**Kathryn**: And I have three children. One is Miranda, 27, and Billy Joe, he's 21. He was hid on me for five years. My ex-husband told…well, before that, sorry…my family and his family would move me in and out of the house all the time, but, you know, from the old country, you marry one time and you go through thick and thin, you know? And that's the marriage thing. No matter what. And that's what I always thought. And he would say he was sorry and I'd believe. And, anyway, we had two children. We had a boy and a girl and, you know, that's a perfect family. A boy and a girl, a mom and dad and there were good times. But he was the alcoholic and you can really see in him that Dr. Jekyll/Mr. Hyde. As for me, I was so against alcohol. I always sold dope. We sold drugs. He had…and he worked at carpentry too, but there's a lot of money on the street. There's faster money. But that's also dirty money. And you always have good intentions to get a home or buy some clothes or get groceries and then you get this dirty money in your hand and, you know, you're feeling guilty or scared or your addiction would get carried away. And how I sort of look at it is: dirty money goes to dirty things. I always had good intentions and maybe once out of a hundred I would do the right thing. Not saying that during my time being a mother to Miranda and Billy I was a bad mama. I was a good mom. I thought if I got away that everything would be okay. And he wouldn't let me take my children with me.

Job losses, corporate downsizing, and general economic trends that were squeezing out jobs were mentioned often in interviews. Alex reported that he has been underemployed since 1994 and homeless about half the time during those years. His story followed a familiar progression. Alex's father had been in the military and so his family never lived in one place long. When he was 15, his family moved to Waynesboro, Virginia.

**Alex**: That is the first time I felt like I had any real home, where we stayed in one place for any length of time. Unfortunately, when I went to college, my family moved to Alabama, so I got uprooted one more time, actually. So, I have never really felt like I have had any particular place I could call home.

A college graduate, Alex entered graduate school at the University of Chicago, then worked as a quality manager in Luxemburg until his job ended. He returned to the United States and worked for a while, but when that job ended, the next job he had lined up fell through. With his finances dwindling, his wife divorced him. He traveled to Seattle where his brother lived. In Seattle he lived with his brother for six weeks, but because he was unable to find work, he ended up in Austin, Texas.

**Alex**: I stayed in the Salvation Army. I thought it was a terrible experience. I was embarrassed by the whole thing, surprised because I could not go in there when I needed to. I was supposed to know that I could not go in until five o'clock in the evening. It was a very bad experience for me having given to the Salvation Army for so many years. I did not know what to expect and I felt like the whole time I was there, that I was considered to be guilty of some kind of crime. Just because of the fact that I was homeless it is automatically assumed that I was a felon or a drug addict or an alcoholic, or something like that.

Simple accidents could lead to homelessness. At the time of our interview Justin had been living on the streets for a little over a year. He had broken both of his legs in a skateboarding accident and could not walk for almost six months.

**Justin**: I bounced around from friends' houses and family's houses and finally ended up on the streets after about six months because I got sick of living with people. I had been homeless a couple times before that. Usually it was just related to getting kind of fed up with my life, where I was living and what I was doing.

Loss was a recurring theme in our interviews. Beth Ann, 48, explained that she had lost her job, then both of her parents, and finally her home, all within a year. She had lived with her parents all her life and had few options when they died.

**Beth Ann**: I could not find a place to go into that I could afford. It was more or less part of my fault about getting homeless because I should have been looking longer for stuff and maybe putting money away towards an apartment.

I was kind of naïve, because I had never had to worry about things myself. I always had my parents there, and I was kind of sheltered when I was growing up.

Ralph was 41 at the time of his interview and had a grown daughter. He had been homeless the past five years after a divorce and the loss of his business.

**Ralph**: Basically, it happened because of the wrong choices I made. The divorce devastated me, so I gave up on everything in life, my business, and I turned to drugs and alcohol, unfortunately, which I have had problems with most of my life. But after that, I just…I had nothing. So, after that, I began to wander across the nation, trying to find myself and get back on my feet.

Simon, a Native American, cited losing his job as the factor that triggered his homelessness and a severe depression. His job was terminated after he had a kidney removed, then suffered from a series of chronic health problems.

**Simon:** I lost my job and I fell into depression big-time. I spent about a year living in my van in and around Portland.

He described the bleakness of that year:

**Simon:** Well, when you live in a van for a year and you have these panic attacks…sometimes I would just stay in there for days and not ever come out. I do not know how to explain that kind of feeling, but it is like impending doom, like something really horrible is going to happen. You just do not want to get out and on top of that depression. I have got kids and grandkids. And in this society, I have been brought up to believe that a dad and mom are supposed to be the example. But here I am, at the bottom of the rung, and that really bothered me, freaked me out.

Again and again, the people we interviewed explained that if a person is vulnerable to mental health problems, addictions, or alcoholism, these problems are likely to be aggravated by being homeless.

Alice, a 47-year-old mother of three with three grandchildren, grew up in North Carolina in an abusive home and spent time in prison as a teen.

**Alice:** I'd never really ever been homeless until the last three years when the company downsized and let me go, and I do not have any family here. My children are on the East coast. I never raised them per se; they were raised by their paternal family. And I lost my job, I lost a relationship, apartment, everything at the same time because I had to wait for unemployment [benefits] for eight weeks and I have been clean for fourteen years, doing great. I felt like I was a survivor and then I went back out, I started using again. I stayed out about a year, my health started going really bad, and then I woke up one day and said, 'this is it, I can't anymore,' and actually, I have been, I will be clean; tomorrow I will be clean twenty-three months.

Later in the interview Alice commented, repeating what came to be a familiar refrain:

**Alice:** I never thought that I'd be homeless, you know.

Ron, a 54-year-old recovering addict commented on the causes of homelessness based on his observations of the community around him.

**Ron:** There's so many variables. A lot of people are homeless because of drug or alcohol abuse, and that's a sickness anyway. But then there's just a situation that happens that people become unemployed, lose everything they have. Or medically; they get in an auto accident, or maybe they're waiting for an insurance settlement, or they broke a foot. You know a lot of things happen to people along the way.

A common theme in our interviews was that drug and alcohol abuse or addiction often caused a person's life to become unstable. Ben, who linked his cocaine use to his homelessness, stated simply:

**Ben:** I am from Brooklyn, New York, and I had a real good job. I worked at the post office like ten years and started abusing drugs, became irresponsible, undependable. It has been a downward slide ever since, and it is all related to drug abuse.

Roland, a 54-year-old veteran, was born in Colorado and has been homeless for extended periods of time, mainly living in vans and trucks for the past twenty years. Roland was blunt about his slide into homelessness.

**Roland:** When I got out of the army I just turned into a drunk, and I have been homeless ever since.

*Sisters: When was that?*

**Roland:** I got out of the army in 1972 so I have been homeless since 1972, mostly because I have spent more time going after booze and all that kind of stuff than it was everything else.

Although Roland was posted in Germany and didn't mention Post-traumatic Stress Disorder or ill effects from his army stint, he immediately ran into trouble when he left the service. He worked for about a year after being discharged, living in a "shack-like thing."

**Roland:** Then I started getting drunk too much to go to work and I resigned. Then I was just too damn drunk to even go to work or nothing.

*Sisters: And then what did you do? Where did you go? Where did you sleep?*

**Roland:** Well, I slept everyplace—cars, under bridges, tents—we were up in the mountains and we left home, that is Colorado. We went to California, same thing there…went to Nebraska, same thing there.

Eventually he ended up in the Portland area. Before being drafted he had never experienced homelessness, explaining,

**Roland:** I am from a middle class family type of thing. So I was always up in Mother and Dad's house until I got drafted.

Interestingly, at the time of our interview Roland had been sober for seventeen years.

Robin was not certain if he left home of his own volition or if his father had asked him to leave home when he was attending college studying music. At the time he was abusing methamphetamines and explained that he also suffers from manic depression. He described his descent that caused him to end up living on the streets:

**Robin**: I was not using when I started school, but I was using in my last semester at school and I moved into this apartment with a bunch of other people who were using also and managed to continue going to school and doing all that craziness. Eventually I just ended up on the street and I, of course, could not maintain going to school at that point. I was doing a lot of composition. I was spending probably five hours a day in front of the piano, writing my first piano concerto. I really want to do the music…

Robin explained that he was first homeless in southern California.

**Robin**: So I was kind of in survival mode on the streets of Riverside, California, for awhile. I ended up living in someone's spare room doing some housework and some work on the garage. Moved to the mountains in Colorado to kick addictions.

He credits his time spent in the mountains as lifesaving. He not only kicked his addictions, he found peace of mind. He now works as an activist helping other homeless people.

**Robin**: The price I paid for the purification of my spirit, for getting rid of the addictions and getting rid of judgment issues and really sort of becoming more at peace with who I am and what the world is. You know, it's a process of disintegration, and then you cannot put the pieces back together again, you have to build in pieces.

Brian's personal choice to become homeless is something he is pleased with. He first left home at 15.

**Brian**: I became homeless when I decided not to, per se, follow my parents' rules.

*Sisters: Were the rules out of line, did you think, or you just didn't want to…?*

**Brian**: I just didn't want to follow the rules. I was raised by a very strong Christian, Catholic, Italian, English parenthood, so…

*Sisters: Were the rules getting in your way of having fun, or…?*

**Brian**: Pretty much, yeah.

*Sisters: And when you were 15, the first time you went, where did you go?*

**Brian**: I went out to a friend's house. A couple of nights.

Brian returned home without notifying his family first.

*Sisters: What happened when you got home?*

**Brian**: My mom was in my room on my bed with my teddy bear crying. She was pale and hadn't eaten since I left. My dad had come to me crying, and my sister had come up screaming and crying, wondering where I had been, 'cause I didn't tell anybody where I was. And, I was on the news reported as missing and dead, 'cause nobody had heard from me.

*Sisters: Whoa. How'd that feel?*

**Brian**: You never know what you have till it's gone.

*Sisters: So, were you happy to be home?*

**Brian**: Yes.

*Sisters: And, how long did you stay?*

**Brian**: Couple of days.

*Sisters: Why did you leave again?*

**Brian**: Just because of the rules. I wanted to be grown and on my own, and maturing to see what life was really all about.

*Sisters: Which rules specifically sent you over the edge?*

**Brian**: Curfew 9:00. Bedtime 9:30. And, I was used to hanging out downtown, with everybody at the waterfront, and at the square. Realizing what life's really all about.

*Sisters: When you were hanging out with the people that were in those places, were they homeless at the time? Before you ran away from home, you were hanging out downtown?*

**Brian**: Yes. I've been hanging out downtown since between the ages of 13 and 15.

*Sisters: And, the people you were hanging out with downtown, were they homeless?*

**Brian**: Yes. Quite a few of them, and quite a few of them weren't.

*Sisters: Was it appealing to you?*

**Brian**: To be homeless? Yes.

*Sisters: What part?*

**Brian**: Just seeing what being on the streets really was, how dangerous it could have been or didn't have to be, what positions you put yourself in to do with the law, or not. It's really hard to explain, but I think homelessness was great.

*Sisters: Really? You thought that before you had your own experience, or you've had your experience and you think it was great?*

**Brian**: Having my experience throughout the past five to seven years has been great, being homeless on and off, because it's taught me that you don't know what you have till it's gone.

*Sisters: Would you say you enjoyed your homeless experience?*

**Brian**: Yes, very much so.

*Sisters: What part of it was enjoyable?*

**Brian**: Making friends who have become really strong family members. Just seeing…'cause everybody was like, well you know, "you have a house, you have a family to go home to, and we don't." And then, I got on the streets and I realized that pretty much the homeless people on the streets have become my family.

A number of people in our interviews cited a divorce as a precipitating factor leading to homelessness. Alex, another veteran, explained that he disbanded his small landscaping business following his divorce.

**Alex**: I just lost interest in my business. You know, when you are with somebody, you've got a house, you've got somebody to talk to, somebody you are with a lot, and that is a lifestyle. And then all of sudden certain things happen and you are no longer together. You just lose interest in things.

After his divorce Alex began picking up temporary and part-time jobs generating an income that sometimes reaches eight hundred dollars a month, but at other times far less.

*Sisters: So where do you live now?*

**Alex**: My van.

*Sisters: How long have you been living in your van?*

**Alex**: I have had it a year now, but basically I have been living in cars and trucks and vans and campers for pretty much twenty years.

*Sisters: What has that been like?*

**Alex**: You get used to it. It is safer than sleeping under a bridge because at least you have four walls around you and a roof and something underneath you. Nobody can come and bang your head in the middle of the night to rob you because you can always figure a way to lock the door. But the bad thing about that is that glass breaks easy and somebody breaks the glass, sticks a gun in your face…that has never happened to me, but I have heard of it with other people. They get broken into all the time like houses. Like if you are laying under a bridge or sidewalk or doorway or something, and somebody came by with a golf club or bat or something, just whack you upside of the head, take everything you got, and just leave; nobody will even know who it was. At least if they had to break a glass to get into your car it is going to wake you up. Might not give you much of a chance, but a little chance.

Alex went on to explain that he is not a target because of his size, but once when he had his truck and camper parked in the mountains, he came home from work and discovered that someone had tried to knock his camper off the truck by running it under a low tree limb.

The outcome was that his belongings were stolen and his truck wrecked.

*Sisters: You said you started drinking when you got into the army, so I wondered if the army had anything to do with it?*

**Alex:** I was drinking before because my mother and dad are alcoholics, so I have been around it all my life. It is just that when I got out of the army I went heavy duty on it.

Arnold was yet another veteran among our narrators. He had worked as a steel fabricator and made "a pretty good living." However, his life started plummeting out of control when he divorced his alcoholic, drug-addicted wife and became a single parent of three daughters because their mother was unable to care for them. While living in a small town on the Oregon coast, his family responsibilities were compounded by losing his job in a family-run business and having his driver's license revoked. A series of run-ins with the Department of Motor Vehicles resulted in a year in prison. After emerging from prison he scrambled for income, working odd jobs for people in the community and in his church and worked as a breakfast cook in his mother's restaurant.

After his mother opened a bed and breakfast he converted a garage on her property into an apartment for himself and his daughters. But a deteriorating relationship with his mother forced his family out of the apartment.

**Arnold:** I remodeled her whole apartment for her so she could rent it and so she had done that and I was living in the tent in the yard, using her electricity for my electric burners and stuff. I had electric burners and a little toaster out there. I even had a TV hooked up out there so that I could watch the news in the morning. Finally, I had a little bit of a falling out with my mother.

At this point Arnold found himself without options. His daughters moved in with his mother while he prepared to leave the area.

**Arnold:** I just packed everything up that I could get into the truck because I was so tired of trying to look for work down there. It seemed like I did not get any response from the applications that I put in for Fred Meyer [a local grocery and general merchandise store] and some of the other places. I had heard about Dignity Village, so I drove to Portland. All I had was a full tank of gas in the truck and a six-gallon canful in the back of the truck. And I had a big bag of clothes, a couple of chests, and a lot of hand tools and such.

After a few days of living in Portland he moved into Dignity Village, a community of homeless people living in tents and structures within the boundaries of Portland.

**Arnold:** Grandpa cleaned an area out underneath the table where we cook our food and set a little piece of carpet down in there. I got my sleeping bag and my bedroll down underneath there, I am sleeping under the table right now. I think the reason that I became homeless mostly is because not being able to drive for such a great period of time. That was embarrassing. Until I moved down on the coast I had always been independent. I have always worked and I like to work.

Some of our narrators became homeless after leaving prison or while they were involved with the criminal justice system. Randy, a native of Texas is one of our narrators who can

Dignity Village

Eight men and women pitched tents on public land in Portland, Oregon, in December 2000. Their site, initially called Camp Dignity, developed into Dignity Village. After months of moving from place to place, Dignity Village relocated to its current location far from the downtown area. Despite up-and-down relationships with government officials, Dignity Village has received broad support from many members of the local area and a number of important concessions and assistance from the City of Portland and other government and regulatory bodies.

Promoting themselves for true self-determination and an ecologically friendly development, Dignity Village continues its effort to establish a permanent site.

Dignity Village houses 60 individuals on a regular basis and offers limited overflow capacity.

Dignity Village is controversial for a number of reasons, but it is an interesting and important experiment in solving the challenges associated with homelessness.

trace his homelessness to the aftereffects of September 11 and complications of a criminal record.

*Sisters: Can you tell me a little bit about your background in regard to losing your housing?*

**Randy**: Okay. Let's see, I was…went to prison in Texas for a couple of years, got out—me and my brother already had a job working maintenance on corporate jet airplanes. And after the September 11th thing we just lost a lot of business, and I ended up getting laid off. And, although, I know I should have just got right out and gone job hunting, I don't know, I guess I went into kind of a depression or something. I couldn't make myself do it. So, I ended up…in a month and a half I lost my apartment but wasn't right out on the streets. I had a girlfriend, and I was staying with her most nights, just trying to wait it out until I got my income tax check. The reason I wanted to leave Texas and probably the reason I was so depressed was that I am on parole in Texas so, I just had a feeling I was gonna go back to prison, so that's one of the reason's why I left. I didn't want to go back. If I go back eventually, that's fine. I don't want to get another charge or anything, which is parole violation. And I've already had a parole violation because I couldn't pay the fees because I didn't have a job, so there's really no difference one way or the other. At least this way, if I can live up here and stay out of trouble, I think I'll be alright.

*Sisters: What fees couldn't you pay?*

**Randy**: Parole fees. They are charging my parole.

*Sisters: So once you lost your job you couldn't pay the parole fees anymore?*

**Randy**: Yeah.

Randy had met a man from the Northwest in prison, so decided to move as a fresh start and to escape the Texas parole system, thus ended up in downtown Portland.

A run-in with the law also led to homelessness for Conrad, who was 38 when interviewed.

*Sisters: So will you tell me a little bit about yourself and where you were raised?*

**Conrad**: Well, I come from a military family. I was born in Tacoma, Washington, and I was raised at various military installations. About every three to five years my family moved because of my father's military assignments. I went to high school in the area of Federal Way, Washington. I went to business college for a couple years after that, and I went into the military and also worked for Washington State government for a good number of years. I ran into some problems with driving while license suspended and ended up doing a long stretch in jail. I'm pretty much trying to reestablish myself in society after losing my job and losing my freedom for a couple months late last year.

Conrad went on to explain that he served seventy-five days for five warrants: Failure to Appear warrants from minor driving violations, and Driving While License Suspended.

**Conrad**: I was kind of relieved in a way. I knew that sooner or later I would have to go to court and resolve them, you know, and I was kind of relieved that I got caught and I could do the seventy-five days and be finished and done with all of them forever.

*Sisters: Did you have a job before going to jail?*

**Conrad**: Yeah, actually I had a real good job. I was a superintendent of an apartment complex, and I had a 15-year-old son that lived with me and everything and, of course, having to go to jail for seventy-five days I lost my job and lost my apartment. I didn't really have enough savings in the bank to weather an economic storm like that. I mean, no income for two and a half months, so here I am.

*Sisters: And what about your kid?*

**Conrad**: He went to live with my mom temporarily while I was in jail.

*Sisters: Is he with you now?*

**Conrad**: No, he's still staying with her.

*Sisters: Okay. And when you look at the consequences of an experience of homelessness, like the effects of not having a phone, or not having a stable noninstitutional address, in your experience, is there any other thing that you would say has affected your work, obtaining or maintaining work?*

**Conrad**: Yeah. I'd say mental depression. I'd say probably a lot of people that are homeless are severely depressed because of the situation. Not only do they need help with housing and phone resources, you know, and stuff like that, I'd say probably a lot of them need some type of counseling. Homelessness can be a traumatic experience if you're not used to it.

*Sisters: And has it been that way for you, a traumatic experience?*

**Conrad**: Yeah, it has. I'd say mentally it's been very hard. I never ever figured I'd find myself in the position I'm in.

*Sisters: Have you ever had to sleep out or in shelters?*

**Conrad**: I have had to sleep in an overnight shelter. I never have had to sleep out yet.

This chapter alone cannot describe the many reasons or circumstances whereby people end up homeless, but for many it has been a long road that led to our door and our interview rooms. We discovered that it's a road lined with tears and hardship, but also sometimes bad luck or mischance.

One of our narrators, Leonard, explained that he ended up in Portland after being deported from Japan.

**Leonard**: My father was in the military, so I've moved all around. And then I was in the military and moved around even more. And then, since I've got out of the military, I've lived fifteen years in Japan and I'm here now. I was deported from Japan.

*Sisters: You were deported?*

**Leonard**: Yeah.

*Sisters: How come?*

**Leonard**: I overstayed my visa and came back to Portland even though I'm not from here. Came to Portland with only one dollar.

*Sisters: One dollar?*

**Leonard**: And ended up in Salvation Army.

*Sisters: Tell me a little bit about the circumstances. Why were you in Japan?*

**Leonard**: I was teaching, and I have family over there. I'm divorced now.

*Sisters: So your visa ran out and they deported you.*

**Leonard**: Yes. My visa ran out and for almost a year, I was living illegally in Japan. I turned myself in because I didn't want to go to the Japanese prison, so the embassy more or less got me out of the country.

*Sisters: And did they bring you straight to Portland?*

**Leonard**: Yes, they did. They gave me a choice of cities along the West Coast to dump me. I've been through Portland before, a couple of times through Oregon. I didn't like Los Angeles, and San Francisco was a bit much. I've lived in Seattle before, too, but I have some bad memories. So, I said 'Okay, Portland.'

Then there were also a number of narrators who described that they became homeless because of a choice, rather than a crisis or circumstances forcing them into homelessness. Brent was such a case and described that he chose to become homeless when he was a college student. Our field researcher began the interview by asking him about his background leading up to his first experience with homelessness.

**Brent**: Well, I was a college student, I guess it started in 1997, spring of 1997. Homelessness was a choice for me because I was a student spending a lot of money on my accommodations and dorms and apartments, and it was not leaving me with a lot of money for college tuition. It was just draining my bank account dry. So I decided to live in my camper that I had on my truck—it was a cabover camper especially made for small pickups. I had seen a lot of other students living like that too. They just did it temporarily while they were at school, but for me it was a year-round thing and I liked it. I adapted to it and I did not have any problems with it. Sometimes friends would let me stay at their house just, you know, to get away from sleeping outside in the winter or the heat of the summer. And I did a lot of house-sitting. Actually it was working well for me because I was saving money. I was working on college campus and I was in my truck in the camper and I was actually saving money because I did not have to pay rent anymore. That was a kind of a unique experience to be able to save money after paying my tuition and books and all that, so I liked that aspect of it and I…I just thought I would give it a try and I liked it. Then when I get out of college in 1999, I was accepted into the University of Hawaii, master of public health program. I parked my truck at my relative's house in Washington, sold my camper, and went over to Hawaii.

After this he explained how his initial experiment in frugality turned into a more permanent lifestyle.

**Brent**: Then I turned down the offer at the University of Hawaii because the economic conditions there were not favorable for work. I did not want to go deep in debt for a masters degree. I came back to the mainland after a couple of weeks being in Hawaii and started looking for another college to do graduate work in. I found one back east in New Hampshire, so I bought a canopy to fit over the back of my truck and I have been living in that since then, probably for the last two and one half years, and it has worked out real well.

I put a heater in it, in the back, so in the winter whenever I get cold I just turn the heater on. That keeps me very comfortable. I found out that most of the time I am not in my truck. It is only for sleeping and to store a few things for my daily needs. I liked that aspect of it, especially when I was in college. I noticed that the only times I was in my truck or in my camper was when I was going to sleep, so the rest of the time I was either working or in classes or studying and now most of the time I am working or in a bookstore somewhere looking through books or in the *street roots* office or out selling papers and just taking life at a leisurely pace until I go back to college this summer. It saves me a lot of money and it does not bother me.

*Sisters: The first thing you said was that it was a choice. Can you talk a bit about how you adapted and if it has become a way of life?*

**Brent**: When I was a kid I spent many, many years in the Cub Scouts and Boy Scouts and then I went into the army. My dad was in the navy. I spent a lot of time camping, so it never bothered me to be outside, camping or roughing it. And what I have learned was you learn to adapt. I have slept in all kinds of different situations, climates. In the military we sleep outside in the subzero weather, you know, and I have had to sleep outside in the very extreme heat and humidity, so I have adapted and I learned, that it is not permanent. The weather changes and it is not that bad. In the Pacific Northwest all you have to worry about is having a heater. You only really need an air conditioner for maybe a week or so. It is not that hard, just a matter of adaptation, you know, and having a mindset that is saying, 'Well, this is okay.'

Brent went on to explain that he saw his living situation as temporary.

**Brent**: It is not going to be permanent for me, but right now it serves its purpose so I can save money for college. I save my money to go to college through *street roots* and I do not have to pay a lot of expenses that would deplete or diminish my funds, like rent and utilities and all that, so some day when I am through with college I would like to have a home again and I am sure I will after I get back into a profession and my life's work. But this is my choice; it is based on past experience with camping out when I was a kid, and then the military, and I learned that…that, you know, people can live in many different types of situations. They do not necessarily need the house or apartment or whatever to be happy. I would probably go into a shelter if I did not have my truck and canopy, but I do keep up on the maintenance on my truck and make sure that that stays in top condition.

*Sisters: You said if you ever had to sleep on the streets or in the doorways you would go into the shelters. Have you had any experiences with shelters or things like that?*

**Brent**: I stayed in the ShareHouse in Vancouver one time for about three months. I found that there are a lot of people who have drug and alcohol problems and along with that goes their personality and character problems. It creates a lot of conflict with other people. I do not drink, I do not do drugs, I do not smoke cigarettes, I do not even really like caffeine all that much. So I did not really mix well with a lot of the people that were in the shelters; they were using them only as squat houses.

*Sisters: You said conflict, what do you mean?*

**Brent**: It's just…I think it's the attitudes that I have and the attitudes they have towards life and how to live a life, how I live my life and how they live their lives, and I think a lot of them were envious of me because I had a vehicle and sometimes I would not accommodate them. I would not take them places and that would create conflicts. They could not accept no for an answer. I think a lot of it was because I am from a different world, my education and upbringing, I did not really mix well with people who wanted to just sit around and get drunk all day. I had different priorities, and so we were just from different tribes.

*Sisters: And when you say 'coming from a different world' what do you mean by that?*

**Brent**: My family, there are no alcohol addictions or alcohol abuse or drug abuse or addiction. So I was fortunate, I guess, in my family genetics or family tree that nobody really ever had any tobacco, alcohol, or drug addiction that passed down to anyone in my family genetically. When I was younger I did a lot of partying in college. I think that is typical with younger people when they are in college and a lot of that was twenty some years ago. But when I went to college as an older adult to finish my undergraduate degree, I felt differently about the party scene, so was a more serious student. While other students were partying at the fraternity houses, I was at Barnes & Noble reading through books and falling asleep in the chairs. Life changes for a lot of people when they get older and have different priorities.

Finally, there is the story of Diane. She arrived in our office at a time when she'd been housed for several months and was looking back on her complicated life. Like many of our narrators, her story is involved and sad and triumphant. We discovered that Diane is the consummate survivor and that the path that led her to our door zigzagged across the country and intersected with the lives of many other homeless people.

She was raised in a small town in Arkansas where her mother and grandfather were medical doctors. But her childhood was less than ideal, and after dropping out of college, she married at twenty and became the mother of three children and stepmother to six others. About ten years before our interview, her life, which included membership in the Junior League, unraveled to a point of no return.

**Diane**: In an eighteen-month period I lost my grandmother, my uncle who taught me how to do carpentry work, and my father; my mother was diagnosed with terminal lung cancer; and I lost a grandchild. My daughter, who had been through two miscarriages and a tubal pregnancy, she had had a baby and the baby was six weeks old and it was her first day back at work and somebody ran her off the road and killed the baby. She was in a coma for two weeks while my mother was in a terminal cancer ward in another city. My daughter was in Memphis and my mother was in Jackson, Tennessee.

*Sisters: And you say all this happened in an eighteen month period?*

**Diane**: Oh yeah. And I divorced my husband, too. Might as well throw that in…I finished my computer degree after I married him, while I had the nine children. I went through psychoanalysis and dealt with a Post-traumatic Stress Disorder while I was getting my computer degree and taking care of nine children and my grandmother, who had Alzheimer's, a heart condition, high blood pressure, and digestive disorders.

*Sisters: So when you say Post-traumatic Stress Disorder, what was that from?*

**Diane**: Oh, I had a lovely sibling relationship with my brother. He shot me when I was eight.

*Sisters: With a gun?*

**Diane**: Yeah. When I was…I can't remember whether I was 15 or 16 when he held me down for his friends to rape me. And I was physically and sexually abused by my stepfather.

After describing a horrendous childhood incident where her stepfather beat her until she bled, she returned to the events before she became homeless.

**Diane**: So I really didn't have a whole lot of life skills to cope with that year that was so bad. I'm strong. I'm intelligent. I taught Sunday school at the First Presbyterian Church. I was actually the officer of two different PTAs at the same time. And I was a member of the Junior League so don't think it can't happen to you.

Although during and after this difficult period she was attending classes in accounting, she came up with an unusual solution to her series of crises and also revealed a serious mental health condition.

**Diane**: I'm bipolar and I'd been on my medication and my daughter had left me and I had a long-term relationship that broke up and I was going to school and it was the semester after I took calculus. And that was ten years after I had taken college level algebra. And that was a little stressful. So I just couldn't take it anymore. I'm mostly Indian, and I set off for a vision quest. I set off to find my center. I had had dreams of the place and I found it in between Laramie and Cheyenne, Wyoming. That's where my center is. It's called Vedauwoo.

*Sisters: Vedauwoo?*

**Diane**: Yeah. It's been a spiritual place for Native Americans for a long time. It's a national park now. It's absolutely beautiful and you can feel the spirits there. So after I found it, I wound up working for a homeless day center in Cheyenne.

But of course, Diane's story doesn't end there. One day, when people she knew were about to ride a train, at the spur of the moment, she joined them. She continued hopping trains, often by herself, which is unusual, sometimes with a partner, for the next nine years, traveling around the country before settling in Portland with her two dogs. She met her current husband while riding the trains, and the two were married in a homeless shelter in Ogden, Utah.

---

Interviewer's Journal Excerpt: (A selection from the daily journals kept by the interviewers. These selections are not taken from journal entries directly related to narrators listed in the chapter.)

*Once we got started, it was fine. She pretty much told her story and didn't need much prompting from me. The biggest difficulty I had was in trying to listen and take notes simultaneously. Plus, I wasn't sure what exactly I was supposed to write down since it was being recorded as well. I remember us talking about writing down themes so that we would be able to quickly identify which themes came out of which interviews. I found myself writing down key words, phrases, even whole sentences. The problem was in deciding what was a "key" idea. It was all "key" and it was all important. I tried writing counter numbers from*

---

*the recorder and key words for really significant stuff, but again, I was imposing my values by deciding what was important. This whole process was infuriating and anxiety inducing. Mostly, it took away from the interview. I couldn't really listen. I eventually gave up writing— for the most part—and just listened.*

*Another difficulty was the background noise. It wasn't that the noise itself was distracting, but it made me worry about how much of it the recorder was picking up. Towards the end of the interview, when there was more room for questioning, I felt pretty comfortable asking questions to "get at" some of the categories on our sheet. It flowed fairly naturally.*

Photographer: Terry Prather

Photographer: Dan Newth

# Chapter 2

We were constantly hungry, but that was a long time ago

## Family Background and Childhood

*We first crush people to the earth, and then claim the right of trampling them forever, because they are prostrate.*

—Lydia Maria Child

After my first five years at Sisters, I worked for a while as a Child Advocate at the West Women and Children's Shelter, a couple doors down from Sisters. I brought so much of that experience back to Sisters.

The most startling thing I've learned from kids and moms both at the shelter and the cafe is this: we are reaping a whirlwind for not investing in babies and children with the care and services they needed twenty years ago. These children, now grown, will walk into the cafe and say, "Do you remember me?" And I do, and although sometimes they are doing well in their lives, the saddest thing is that they are often no better off than their moms were. They may or may not be on the street, but they haven't escaped poverty. Easily over half of our customers have suffered in their childhoods from homelessness, poverty, and abuse.

—Genny

Childhood influences were a large factor in the current circumstance of Mark, who was living in temporary housing at the time of our interview. Mark, an articulate 35-year-old whose parents had divorced when he was young, described a turbulent childhood. His father had a thirty-year military career and lived in Indianapolis and his mother lived in Portland. Mark mostly lived with his mother and stepbrother, but dropped out of high school after attaining a GED (General Equivalency Diploma), and then joined the army. He left the army after eleven months, returning to his mother's house until she kicked him out. Although he lived with his father for a while, his situation became unstable, and he sometimes lived on the streets.

When we met Mark he had recently been released from prison after serving a five-year sentence and had hopes of becoming a forest firefighter after receiving the training while incarcerated. His belief about the roots of homelessness was arresting.

Mark: It all really starts with bad parenting, in my opinion. There was never food in the house. I had a little brother, half-brother and, you know, he is not eating neither and, so, I got to worry about that too. I am a big brother and my little brother is not eating. He is not eating, he does not have any good clothes. I do not have any good clothes. You want to provide, you want to take care of that person, but you cannot because you just do not have it, you know, it is just a bad feeling, no good.

*Sisters: So, you were pretty much having to take care of your little brother?*

Mark: Right, yeah, but I could not because I did not have anything.

*Sisters: Where was your mother?*

Mark: Ah, she was probably out drinking, drinking with one of her boyfriends or something, that kind of thing.

*Sisters: She was gone all night?*

Mark: Going on constantly. I remember one time she was gone for three days and these people kept coming around. I did not know who they were, but I guess they were child welfare workers or something, and I told them, 'Hey, my mom has not been around, I don't know where she is at.' 'Okay, we'll be back.' They come back, mother is still not around, but okay, these people, obviously they are informed, they have been informed that we are by ourselves, but they are not doing anything, you know. Not one of them brought any scrap of food with them, ever.

*Sisters: Did you guys go hungry?*

Mark: Yeah, we were constantly hungry, but that was a long time ago.

At the time of our interview his mother had died the previous year. When our interviewer offered her condolences Mark answered:

Mark: I had not seen her in a long time. I do not even have any good memories of her so I really did not shed a tear.

*Sisters: You guys were not close?*

_____

**Mark**: No, not really. When you do not have one good memory of your mother then something is wrong, you know.

*Sisters: Not even when you were young or anything?*

**Mark**: No, I had more emotion when my cat died.

Both men and women had stories of impoverished childhoods, neglect, and abuse. And sometimes a simple statement or sentence spoke volumes. Andrea was 41 and trying to stay clean and achieve stable housing.

**Andrea**: From the time I was 5 years old, I can remember nothing but pain. I have been molested and all that, and it was not until a few years ago that I learned why my mother left my dad, and it was because he was like my husband.

Her mother who had six children by the time she was 19, ended up raising her children alone.

**Andrea**: We were without lights, we were without food, we just really had it bad.

Alice, another of our female narrators, was also 41 and also recounted painful memories and the long-term effects of an unstable childhood. A significant portion of our narrators spent part of their childhood living in foster homes, with relatives other than their parents, with abusive stepparents, or were moved in and out of varying living situations. Alice recalled for our interviewer:

**Alice**: My mother gets really depressed and moody and we would fight a lot. I just could not handle her and my aunt and uncle fighting and quarreling against each other to get me and my sister. And then we got separated and my sister stayed with my aunt and uncle and I had to live with my mother and stepfather and it was a bad situation all around, all my life.

Jane, a native of Massachusetts, cites childhood molestation and leaving home as setting her on the road toward drug use and ultimately, homelessness. She is clear about the road that led to homelessness.

**Jane**: Molesting and abuse going on at home. So when I was 18, I said, 'Up yours, see you.' I hitchhiked.

*Sisters: Where did you go?*

**Jane**: Stockton [California] is where I ended up.

*Sisters: Hitchhiked to Stockton, what was that like?*

**Jane**: Back then it was easy. Now I would not even do it if it was the last day on earth. I am not that irresponsible, especially being a girl.

*Sisters: But how was Stockton?*

**Jane**: Lot of heroin addicts.

It was the mid '70s and she got a job at a drug abuse center which included free housing.

**Jane**: I had a lot of problems from my childhood and dealt with a lot of them down there.

Eventually Jane moved to Portland because she had family members living here and missed them. She also is the mother of two children, now grown, who were taken from her by authorities. She reported that she suffers from seizures. At the time of our interview Jane had been recovering from heroin addiction, although she confessed to two relapses within the previous year. After living in shelters and camping out in the summer, she had been housed in an apartment for six months with the help from a local agency and was in an outpatient program for drug addiction.

**Jane**: I am just battling with being sober and not taking off for four or five days—not running from reality.

Jane described other homeless women she's met over the years.

**Jane**: A lot of women down here would prefer just not to be coherent. That is why they are all down here doing drugs. The men are too, but women, it seems like they are always breaking up with somebody because they have abused her. A lot of it is abuse, too much drugs, too much. They just want to get away, cannot deal with it.

Downtown has changed in the last five or six years. I mean, I cannot believe how many people are homeless down here now, especially women.

Jane mentioned that even if a woman manages to achieve housing, that it is still difficult to remain stable after years of using drugs.

**Jane**: It is kind of hard to get backing. And the thing with a lot of women down here is getting back to being stable. I cannot describe it. It's hard to get your mental organization.

Robert's story of childhood poverty and a family grappling to meet their basic needs is typical among the homeless we've met in Portland over the years.

Robert, 44, had the sort of multiple problems that are tragically common among the homeless. He's battled with drug addiction and alcoholism, has had lung cancer, and suffers from bipolar disorder. He recalled his childhood:

**Robert**: I have seen my mother and dad [struggle] a lot of times. We were almost homeless then, way back in the '60s, and cold, without heat. We got to cut down the firewood and we could not afford to feed ourselves; the people in the community would feed us all. I was never actually homeless as a child, but when I became an adult I realized we had been close to being homeless.

I used to watch my mother and dad struggle and strive every day to keep a roof over our head, clothes on our back.

Beth, a 22-year-old woman born in Alabama and raised in Arizona, also described a difficult childhood. During the interview she revealed that she is the mother of three and was pregnant with her fourth child.

**Beth**: I was raised in Arizona with my family—my parents and my two brothers—and I do not remember a lot about my childhood. A lot of what I remember is mostly bad things, and I kind of think that that has a lot to do with my life now. My parents used to abuse me a lot when I was a kid.

*Sisters: When you talk about abuses, what kind of abuse are you referring to?*

**Beth**: It was physical and emotional. I left home on my 17th birthday because I saw them doing the same thing to my younger brother, and that hurt more than me being hurt myself did.

Tina, a 33-year-old woman, tracked her homelessness directly to her childhood and her stepmother's abuse. She recounted:

**Tina**: I literally, honestly, truly have the Cinderella story. My stepmother—something was wrong with her. She did incredibly horrific things to me as a child, which I believe is why I turned out like I did as a teenager, a young adult.

So, basically when I went into puberty, my chemical system was shut down. I had no more natural pain relievers to endure the pain. I had no more happy center, no more pleasure center. All those chemicals that are naturally in your body were completely wiped out because I used them in protecting myself. So the first opportunity that I had to get high, I did. I went to treatment when I was 15 and I learned a lot. I think if I had not gone into treatment, I probably would have ended up killing myself.

For that two years of my drinking, it was desperation, it was pain, and I was drinking to numb because I was in so much pain because my mother was not there and life was just terrible.

Besides the trauma and pain of childhood, many of our narrators described the larger picture of their lives—how their homelessness had become their identity, and was ingrained in their worldview, their lifelong methods of coping, and their sense of not belonging. Recurring themes for many of the men and women we met told of a certain rootlessness, isolation, and a sense of abandonment.

**Tina**: I never thought about it until now, but I have never been in any one place long. This place that I got kicked out of (referring to an eviction), I was there almost a year. It was the first time I lived anywhere for that length of time. Then I got to the point where, 'Why bother?' You know, I mean, why bother going through all the changes and the troubles in getting a place when someone is just going to take it away from me anyway?

Like many of our narrators, Bob, a veteran who had been living on the street for twenty years and had not worked in eleven years, explained that it is nearly impossible not to be depressed when homeless, since it is simply a natural reaction to unnatural circumstances. However, many of the men and women we talked with can trace their depression back to years before they were homeless.

**Bob**: The same old thing will burn you out real quick and it did not help my depression, not one bit. But as far as I could go back and remember, I was depressed as a child.

James, another veteran, who at 48 had worked as a chef most of his life, described the instability of his childhood. In his story are woven many common themes shared by our narrators. The first theme was how he moved often as a child.

**James**: My mother was a piano player, so, like, my average was three schools a year. My record was nine schools in one year, and I never finished high school. I went two months to the eleventh grade out here. I did not graduate because I had already traveled around growing up, and it was hard for me to stay in one place.

Many of our narrators were also separated from their parents and family for varying reasons and lengths of time. About four and half years of James' childhood were spent in foster care, once because his mother was hospitalized for six months with skin cancer. He recalled an incident when they moved from California to Alaska because his mother had a job playing piano at the officers' club for an Air Force base. One night, when she was playing at the club after hours, her boyfriend showed up and pulled her outside and severely beat her. Mother and son fled to Portland, but still more relocations followed.

Later in our interview, he reflected on how a person's early history can impact his adult lifestyle.

**James**: I do not know; my whole life has been moving. I have had dynamite jobs, and I have made seven dollars for the whole week of work. I have been at the top of the mountain, and I have been definitely down in the bottom. I think if you have a person that lived in the same house, went to the same schools, same parents, it is almost guaranteed they will not be homeless, even if they lose their jobs and everything, there is something that is going to be there. Or, if you have someone who has been in a dysfunctional family or environment, then they are more likely to be homeless at some point in time than someone who has been in a stable environment. My situation is because of early instability. That is part of the cause, but not the only one.

James believes that this early impermanence strongly influenced his vagabond lifestyle, explaining that the longest he has ever lived in one place was eighteen months. Another impact from his childhood was that he began drinking when he was 14. At 17 he began working for carnivals until he was drafted in 1969, and was sent to Germany and Vietnam.

The track that leads from a crippling childhood most certainly can end in the streets of this country. What also became clear in our interviewing process was that people reported on childhoods where if abuse wasn't a factor, then instability was. Many of our narrators had lived in many places both as children and adults. For example, Randy visited our offices soon after he moved to Portland from Texas.

*Sisters: Do you know anybody up here?*

**Randy**: Not a soul.

*Sisters: That's very brave of you.*

**Randy**: I've met a few, but I don't know anybody. Yeah, I guess I've moved around all my life, as far as that goes. I've started my life over, I guess, basically a couple of times and I know I can do it. It's just a matter of getting out there and working at it.

*Sisters: How long did you live in Texas?*

**Randy**: Since '89.

*Sisters: Where did you live before that?*

**Randy**: Louisiana.

*Sisters: Are you from there?*

**Randy**: Well, that was where I graduated high school. My dad's in the service, so we moved around a lot. I was born in Mississippi. I have lived in Massachusetts, Germany, Ohio, New York, Kansas, Texas a couple of times, Louisiana a couple of times. I've just got gypsy blood in me.

In analyzing these stories, it was clear that Randy was not the only one of our narrators claiming "gypsy blood" or describing an unstable childhood.

One fact that surprised the staff who began analyzing the interviews is that many of the homeless are former "army brats" or came from military families. Military families tend to relocate often because of their temporary assignments to bases all over the world (typically lasting one to four years).

At the time of his interview, Simon had been homeless since 1993 and had grown up in a military family. He has worked at a number of temporary jobs. One position was as a cook at a Portland homeless mission. His story reveals some common patterns among people experiencing homelessness, particularly those who grew up in military families.

**Simon:** Actually I had learned to cook when I was 8 years old, self-defense. I'm an army brat. When I was a kid, traveling around the country after my father got out of the service, he had gotten divorced and we moved to the Carolinas, to a small town, and he lost his job there. We just kind of packed up and went around the country for about three months. I think about 1974. We just traveled all over the country. My father and mother had gotten divorced when I was about 5 and I did not get to see my mother again until that year. We had traveled from North Carolina up to New York, from New York to Oregon and went to see my mother because she was here in Oregon. We were basically homeless then. I remember a couple of times where we did not eat because my father just did not have the money, had not gotten his retirement check yet because he did not receive the monthly paycheck from the service. Basically we lived in the car. That would be my real first experience with homelessness.

We got back down to Lorton, Oklahoma. For some reason, my father just kind of gravitated toward where the military was, so he went toward the one place he knew well, which was Lorton. Some of it is a little bit foggy. I do not know how we ended up from a car to sleep in, to actually having a roof over our heads. But I know that he finally found a job working in a 7-Eleven food store and this was kind of humiliating to him compared to what he had been doing for years. But he worked in a 7-Eleven and then remarried a Jewish lady and we moved from Lorton to Cleveland, Ohio. That is the first time I ever lived in a city where a child could not walk [alone] at all because it was dangerous and that was in the '70s.

Simon's father divorced again and moved the family to Oklahoma City.

**Simon:** When I was 17, I did not leave home. I was asked to leave home. My father put me on the road with ninety-eight dollars in my pocket. I left.

His actual departure happened about a month before his 18th birthday. Simon's father handed him a sign lettered "Portland Oregon" and suggested that he visit his mother, so he set off hitchhiking from Oklahoma.

**Simon:** It took me four months to get here to Portland, hitchhiking. I would stop every once in a while because ninety-eight bucks did not go far—only a few meals and couple of nights at a motel and that was about it. I had to make money, so I was working on the way.

He arrived in Portland with fifteen hundred dollars and moved in with his mother for a while. However, Simon hadn't seen her since he was 12 or 13, and they had difficulties connecting after these years of estrangement. He explained that she also hadn't expected him to be sexually active although he was 18. After a few months, his mother gave him two hundred dollars and said, "Simon, go someplace; do something." So he traveled to Almyra, New York, where his grandmother lived.

**Simon:** I planned to hang with my grandmother, maybe she could do something with me.

---

When he reached her home he discovered that she had died while he was en route—this news told him by a neighbor.

**Simon**: I did not believe it. I broke into the house through the back window. Nothing. Everything was gone. So I am like sitting there in the middle of her empty house trying to figure out what am I going to do now. So I did go to my best friend's house, whose father was actually kind of the only authority figure I knew when I was a kid. My father was in Vietnam. He was kind of a surrogate. I went there and they let me crash there for a while. They got hold of my aunt who put me up for a while on the thing that when I got my inheritance from my grandmother…So, I decided at that time to join the army.

The people we interviewed came from all over and one 28-year-old man, Hector, was born in El Salvador and was adopted by an American family who also adopted four other children. Because of his father's job, the family moved often in his childhood—Vermont, Colorado, Idaho, and Minnesota. During Hector's last year in high school, he was "booted out" of his home because his parents were unhappy with his drug use. He spent many years living with friends "couch-surfing" and moved to Portland in 1996. He has also attended college several times, but dropped out and has worked as a maintenance man for apartment buildings, a position which included housing. Hector was living in Dignity Village at the time of our interview. Our interviewer asked him what it was like when he first landed on the streets of Portland with a backpack.

**Hector**: It was a study of a society.

*Sisters: How do you mean?*

**Hector**: Well, when you're on the outside, you are studying. When you are homeless, you are on the outside. It seems to me that when you're on the inside you are kind of more blind about things, so when you are on the outside you've got a three hundred and sixty degree view.

*Sisters: So, you used your time on the street to study society?*

Hector: Yeah. Who is real and who is not. That's what it's all about.

Based on our interviews, it appears that when people are cast out by their family, the trauma that results is not only emotionally devastating but life-changing. For many it was the first step in a decline that led to homelessness. A majority of our narrators reported that they did not have family members who they could turn to or that their family did not have the financial resources to help them. Many also reported that they were hiding their current living conditions from their families or friends. Shame and embarrassment about their circumstances is a recurring theme, as is the simple fact that they have few people or no one to help them when they need it most. Thus, homeless people often exist in a perilous place in a society that is rapidly becoming more fragmented—without a safety net or family ties to anchor them.

Drew, who was 41 when he was interviewed, had been homeless on and off for the past five years. Like many of the people from military families, he had moved often in childhood because his father worked in the oil industry.

Drew: It was pretty traumatic because I have never had long-term relationships with friends or gotten established in any one city for a very long period of time. You would always be the new kid on the block.

Sisters: *Do you feel like it had any effect on your experience with homelessness?*

Drew: I ran away a couple of times while I was living with my parents, so I guess I had it in my blood to travel or something. I think it did have something to do with it.

Being a stranger in the land, you are not welcomed as much as the people who have been there, are established or have roots there. I turned to drugs and alcohol because it made me feel a part of something. They were my friends because I had trouble moving, so I carried that to my relationships.

Sisters: *And how old were you when you started using?*

Drew: 13.

In analyzing the data from our interviews we discovered that many homeless adults left home at an early age. It was not uncommon to learn that the person we were talking with had been on his or her own since 15, 16, or 17. Curtis described how he had spent much of his life riding the rails, beginning in his teens. His interviewer asked him if he was running away at the time.

Curtis: Me and my mother never got along, so that had a lot to do with it. I do not know, I have always been independent, and I have always been pretty much antiestablishment and anti all of that. I kind of figured things out at an early age.

Brenda, a 25-year-old woman, had been homeless for about a year at the time we talked with her. She also had a difficult childhood framed by poverty and had been homeless with her mother, brother, and sister for a period when she was a teen. She recalled this period and how they had lived in a single-day rooming house that was infested by rats and roaches.

Brenda: We did not have any other place to go. And my mother, she did not have a house of her own and then we finally got an apartment, and that was in Columbia Villa. Then from there we were homeless again, and I stayed with my aunt. Then my mom finally got her place on Mississippi Street. We had a house, our first house to ourselves and we loved it. And the reason why we ended up having to leave from there is because our landlord passed away.

From there the family moved into a Section 8 house for two years, but were evicted because her mother was accused of selling drugs. With no place to go, the family ended up in a Salvation Army shelter. Brenda had always lived with her mother, and was in fact, extremely dependent on her. During our interview, she described the barriers that keep her from renting her own apartment as overwhelming. Without a high school diploma, and with few job skills, she's forced to work at low-paying jobs and cannot accumulate enough savings for the deposits and fees required.

Early intervention to provide skills and opportunities like those Brenda needs was a focus of Sylvester's thoughts.

**Sylvester**: America is in trouble. We have to solve any problem whether it be homelessness, alcohol and drug problems, anything, it all starts at home. Children as young as 5 years old, you got to instill good moral values and principles. You let it go further than 5 years old, you have lost them. We as a society are so caught up in our own adult problems that we are losing sight of the fact that we are going to have twice as many adult problems.

> ### Section 8 Housing
> The Department of Housing and Urban Development (HUD) administers a form of affordable housing established by Congress in 1974 commonly called Section 8.
>
> Section 8 housing is subsidized based on the tenant's ability to pay. The goal of the scaled payment plan was to encourage new construction for affordable housing and retention of existing affordable housing.
>
> This is one of a number of initiatives to create a larger pool of affordable housing. It has a number of drawbacks. While tax breaks and permit breaks given to new construction can increase the amount of affordable housing by requiring a percentage to qualify for the breaks, these limitations typically come with expiration dates. Since Section 8 subsidies rarely cover the full gap between the tenant's cost and the market value of the residence, landlords are hesitant to continue accepting Section 8 housing vouchers after restrictions expire. Section 8 housing also comes with a variety of restrictions for the landlord designed to prevent unsafe housing.

*Sisters: So, you think failing to raise our children well is contributing to homelessness?*

**Sylvester**: Oh! Yes, yes. I have seen so many young people out here on the streets too, kids. What are they doing out here? I do not know.

*Sisters: What do you think they are doing out here?*

**Sylvester**: Lot of them are out here because they were rebellious, but then there are some out here because of certain things that bother the kids. I have talked to several kids that were being sexually abused, molested in their homes and things like that. They did not want to bring society's attention to it so they just left. They'd (referring to the street kids who he'd met) rather live on the streets like an animal than be at home subject to that. Nice room and all, video equipment and all this, yet then my mother and my dad coming in and molesting me all the time. They would rather just be out here, risking their life everyday. That is another reason why these kids are around here. This is not a home. It is no place for them.

Nelson also can track his homelessness back to childhood origins although he wasn't driven from his home. Instead he dropped out of school and left home at a young age which began a pattern of travel and instability. He told our interviewer his history:

**Nelson**: I was raised in Arkansas. My family was basically normal. At the age of 17, I left Arkansas and proceeded to go around the United States to Michigan, Oklahoma, New York, just basically having fun.

He was now homeless for the fifth time and described the cause as "mental problems" that he was trying to solve. During the interview, Nelson revealed that he'd been in trouble for years for writing bad checks and other crimes.

**Nelson**: I have managed to screw everything after some time because of either lying, cheating, stealing, whatever and it has always gotten me into trouble. And I cannot do that anymore. I am 40 years old. It is not going to work. I do not want to be 55 years old and living out on the streets. I just do not, so I have to get this fixed. But I will figure out what is causing me to do this and I will stop it and I will get myself back on my feet and if I can, show my family that I am trying to help myself, not just by saying things, but by actually following through with them.

Sam, a 35-year-old, began our interview by talking about his childhood:

**Sam**: I was born in San Angelo, which is like the heart of Texas—a bunch of country roads, countrified people. Lived there with my grandparents until I was about 11 years old. My mother was more or less a flower child from the '60s. She was just not ready to raise her children. She had me, my sister, who is older, and my younger brother. She finally came back and brought us to New York where we lived for several years. My mother had been married numerous times—I had four brothers, and one sister; all of them have different fathers. It does not make her a bad person. Lived in Corpus Christi probably twenty years of my life. Did not graduate high school or anything, I was locked up a lot of my younger years as a juvenile.

Sam went on to describe how he lived in various juvenile facilities because he did not like following the rules. It turns out he was "turned loose" from his home at 13 then spent a year and a half in one facility, was sent to a halfway house where he "screwed up" and was sent to another Texas Department of Corrections institution until he was 17. He earned a GED, learned to weld while in the juvenile facility, then joined the Reserves as one means to further his welding career through the GI Bill.

---

**Sam:** I am lucky and fortunate. I have never been to prison, thank God.

Later in the interview Sam admitted that he's estranged from his family and doesn't want to burden them with his problems or reveal his homelessness.

**Sam:** We have just had problems over the years. I have been kind of resentful from all the things my mother has done. When we do see each other, it is for short periods of time and I do not ask her for anything. I do not tell her how I'm doing. I do not call her to say, 'Hey, Mom, stuck in Portland, send me money.' It is not like she would if I did.

Finally, the story of Barbara personifies how childhood trauma is inexorably linked to an adulthood of pain. With her mother a heroin addict, she was born with heroin in her system. But this was only the beginning of her problems. When she was 11 her mother began prostituting her to pay for her heroin habit and she also became addicted herself at this tender age. When asked for clarification she explained that her father had committed suicide and her mother died of an overdose.

**Barbara:** I did not have a home since I was 15 basically; I had to survive by prostitution. I was a heroin addict until about a year ago, I quit doing heroin a year ago.

*Sisters: And how has that recovery been for you?*

**Barbara:** It is very great, I have…I have a boyfriend now that…that is showing me a different side of life than prostitution. He showed me how to feel again, how to love, how to be a person, you know, and it…it scared me because I have never had that before. I have never, because when you are out on the streets you do not care about nothing or no one. You have no emotion, you have no feelings, you have no heart, you have nothing. You feel like a piece of meat and that is what you are, you know. He showed me how to care about somebody and showed me how it is okay to cry and how to be…how to feel about myself. It has got to the point to where I actually fell in love for the first time, 39 years old, because I did not know what it was. And it is scary, and I push him away sometimes because he took me really deep into a relationship to where it is scary, you are scared. So I fight with him just to make him leave me alone. I tried to push him away and stuff.

But her childhood still haunts her and she explained that it can accurately be described as a nightmare.

**Barbara:** It was real hard. It was very hard because when I was younger, my brother-in-law, he molested me, brutally assaulted me and tortured me. A psychiatrist said that I am very fortunate I pulled through it all because he said most women, especially from the time I was 6 till I was 16, said that I am very fortunate that I kept my sanity, you know, that I am very strong and I worked through it.

Barbara went on to graduate from high school while homeless—sleeping at a homeless shelter, on the streets, and under bridges. She worked as a CNA (Certified Nursing Assistant), a phlebotomist, and in a group home for troubled children. But her drug addiction and other problems constantly dragged her down, and she served several prison terms for robbery, prostitution, and selling drugs.

At the time of our interview, Barbara was on parole and sleeping under a bridge with her boyfriend. She described how she had been shot five times by a john who also killed her lover, who died in her arms. As Barbara's story unfolded, it seemed that she had dealt with more heartbreak and trauma than one person can possibly survive in a lifetime. And her story begs the question, what would her life have been if a safety net would have caught her a long time ago?

---

Interviewer's Journal Excerpt:

*The woman that I interviewed walked in with her boyfriend and 1-year-old daughter. I wished that we had a space for them to hang out and wait, but in our small office it would have been difficult. So the man and the baby went on their way back to Salvation Army where they have a childcare room, at least that was what the woman who I interviewed had said.*

*This interview was quite intense. There were many points where she was yelling and crying. The woman was extremely angry about her situation, which seemed rightfully so as she told me of her life. She has been homeless since she was 14 years old. She had been moved from one foster home to another before that time, where she had experienced a lot of physical and sexual abuse. She ran away at 14, came to Portland from rural Eastern Oregon, then moved to San Francisco. When she got to San Francisco, she said that there were no services to assist a young teenager. She turned to prostitution to get her basic needs met. After a while of prostituting, she turned to drugs to heal her pain and found herself in a deep addiction.*

*Now with her daughter she had found success in recovery. But that is the only success that she identified, since after she had graduated from recovery she was left with nowhere to go. She and her boyfriend moved back up to Portland in hopes of creating a new and better life with her daughter, of whom she said she doesn't know who the father is.*

*She has only been in Portland for two days and is already frustrated with the process of trying to get government assistance as far as Aid to Families with Dependent Children. All the while she was talking, I was doing my best to maintain some sort of emotional control because her story made me angry. She had gone through so much, truly feeling that she was trying, but was getting nowhere. I also had to fight that urge of trying to help her and advocate for her, although I did direct her to some resources that I knew of and someone who I know is an advocate for homeless families.*

---

# Chapter 3
## Chapter Three

I felt like I had no one

## Self-esteem, Aloneness & Estrangement

---

*Too often we underestimate the power of a touch, a smile, a kind word, a listening ear, an honest compliment, or the smallest act of caring, all of which have the potential to turn a life around.*

—Leo Buscaglia

Historically, our customers have said they feel painfully invisible to others in the larger society. When they come to the cafe they say, "Here, I feel visible. You know my name, you look at me." The other side is, because of being treated as if they are invisible, people attempt to make themselves be unseen. Last night I had this experience while carrying my own boxes across the city sidewalk as I was moving my belongings between apartments. I was alone, tired, and walking slow, with my backpack wrapped around me, and pushing a bunch of my stuff in a handcart. And I knew I wasn't, but at that moment I felt homeless, and I wouldn't look up at anyone.

One of our customers that I knew through Sisters' women's group once told me about an African tribe that greets each other by saying, "I see you." I'll never forget the smile on her face. It blew her mind: three little words that could change the way society looks at you.

In mainstream America, the phenomenon of not having enough money or things makes you hated. Being in homelessness or poverty makes you *hated*. That's what has to shift. For us to have a revolution of the heart, enough people have to decide that the money-and-things definition of success is not for them and they're going to change it.

—Genny

Victor was 40 at the time of his interview and hailed from Kansas City before he moved to Portland with his wife of one week.

**Victor**: [After eight months] things did not work out, and she threw me out. I knew no one and had no choice but to go into a shelter which was one of the most degrading things in the world.

*Sisters: Why was it degrading?*

**Victor**: I had always made over five hundred dollars a week because I always contracted, did side work, even though I had a full-time job. I always had money. I had a car and a truck and a motorcycle and nice furniture, and I never had to depend on anyone. I have asked my mother maybe three times for money since I have been 18. I have never had to worry about work; I can always find work. I also like to work. I do not like to sit at home.

*Sisters: Tell me about your perception of homelessness before you went into a shelter.*

**Victor**: I felt like I had no one. I felt so small. Besides everything, she threw me out, and I was really upset about that. I was pretty much crying every day. I was very lonely. I had no one, really, no friends, and I had nothing. That is what homelessness was to me, living outside and being ashamed of it. You duck your head when anybody drives by or walks by. I do not feel like anybody should have to experience it. I do not want anybody to know that I am living in a shelter.

*Sisters: What is the stigma that you see with living in a shelter?*

**Victor**: They might think I am a lower class person. They might think 'How did you get there?' I do not like to lie but I am not going to tell everyone, 'Because of drugs.' I am ashamed that I do drugs and I really wish I did not. I do not tell everyone.

Later in the interview, Victor revealed that his mother and brother do not know that he's homeless.

**Victor**: [My brother] knows I have been [in the past], but he does not know my exact situation. I cannot really talk to my brother about anything. He is not always compassionate and understanding. I really wanted to sit there and literally cry on his shoulder and tell how I feel, but he cannot always listen. My mother—I cannot talk with her about this. I do not know how to say this…it is kind of embarrassing and lonely and it kind of hurts to say, but my mother has not really been able to show love towards me. Maybe because of all the things that happened over the years and maybe because I have not been real close with my mother; she is not really loving.

Victor was one of many of our narrators who hid their homeless situation from their friends and family. Geoffrey was 44 when he came into our office and described his unusual situation. Although he receives income from Social Security, he lives on the streets or in shelters about half of each month because he gives money to his ex-wife and children and he doesn't have enough income to make it through the month. He also hides his homelessness from them and explains why he gives them his money.

**Geoffrey**: It makes me feel that I still have some value in my life, that I am worth something. I would give my ex-wife [money]; if the kids needed extra clothes and things like that I would buy those too, you know, that is above and beyond the child support I was giving them. I just…decisions that I made, decisions my wife—ex-wife—and I made together, set them back in their young innocent childhood. They were not responsible for it and they should not have to pay for it, so I did the best I could to try and rectify that. I talk to my kids and they do not see it in a negative way, but they talk about, a lot about things in the past I know scarred them in a certain way, you know, the reason why the break up and stuff like that.

*Sisters: But you have pretty good relationship with them it sounds like?*

**Geoffrey**: I have excellent relationships with my kids. Oh, yeah, oh, yeah, I love my kids. They love their daddy too. There is real love today too; it is not, 'Dad, I love you because you bought me this.' Where they love me just because I am Daddy again, the daddy that they always knew as little kids and as adults now they can enjoy the real me. Now they sit around and laugh and talk and they know when I give to them I am giving to them from my heart, not because I have to. My daughter, she is 23, and I give to her from my heart, you know, and, 'Daddy, could you loan me your [money].' 'Yeah, okay, yeah, I'll [loan you] twenty dollars.' I've been loaning her money for two years.

*Sisters: Loaning?*

**Geoffrey**: Yeah, now, if she wants to try to pay me back, fine; if not, I won't ask her for it. I will never ask her for that, you know, never. Another thing they do not really know, they do not really—it is probably interesting to you too—they do not really know that I spend half the time on the streets.

*Sisters: They don't?*

**Geoffrey**: They do not know that. It would not sit well with them because they care about me. It would hurt them, but then I do not think they would really understand why I put myself through this for them, so in order to keep any dilemmas, any feelings of sadness, 'Poor Daddy is just helping,' you know, and they are trying too. You know what I am saying? I pray to God I can go along and they can go along but until then, I do not let them know that two weeks of the month I am out here on the streets in unstable conditions just because of trying to help them. Because they think I got enough money to take care of myself too and my daughter. 'Dad, where do you stay?' I told her I stay in a cheap motel downtown. She knows there are a lot of cheap motels, and she said, 'Dad I'm trying to get a job.' I do not mind, but they do not need to know that I am down here most of the time, on the streets and have to go to the Rescue Mission for meals and stuff like that. If they happened to find out they'd be devastated.

*Sisters: It would devastate them?*

**Geoffrey:** Because, I do not know, in some way would show them how much I really love them.

*Sisters: Yeah.*

**Geoffrey:** But they would not want me to, especially my daughter. She is mature, and my son, 21-year-old son, they are mature enough to know that 'Dad, you went through all of this, all the years? Just like that, and you are still going through it today, and you are a better person. You do not deserve to continually go through this.' I know, but, you know what I mean? That is why I keep it from them.

*Sisters: What about your wife?*

**Geoffrey:** She does not know either; none of them know. My brother, none of my family here knows that since I have been here in June I have been spending half the time on the streets. After two years—it will be two years in June—perhaps I have had a roof over my head one year.

*Sisters: Wow! But your mother knows?*

**Geoffrey:** No, she does not know either.

*Sisters: Your mother does not know either?*

**Geoffrey:** She does not, no one knows.

*Sisters: No one knows.*

**Geoffrey:** No one knows.

Ralph is a military veteran who has lived in several places around the country and also mentioned that his family does not know he is experiencing homelessness.

**Ralph:** I do not talk with my family any more.

*Sisters: You have a family schism?*

**Ralph:** Yeah, we were just real bad, dysfunctional.

*Sisters: Has it affected your relationships, to be homeless?*

**Ralph:** I do not think it has had any effect on my relationships with people. I have never had a girlfriend whose relationship lasted over a year. I have learned to accept that. It is just the way it is going to be.

---

I am down at the bottom…[being homeless provides an opportunity] to look in at everything; you find out who is real and who is not. It is a total study on society.

Kenneth, who has four brothers and a sister, reiterated a common theme: many homeless people do not depend on their families for emotional or financial support. Often their families do not know that they are homeless or their true circumstances, and often family ties were severed before the person became homeless.

**Kenneth**: All my brothers and my siblings have their own lives. I do not want to burden them with mine.

As our narrators spilled out the stories of their lives, we heard that estrangement, aloneness, isolation, and desperation are common feelings for them.

Their self-concept was also affected by the difficulties in maintaining personal hygiene. They hated wearing dirty clothes and not being able to bathe, shower, or shave regularly, with women especially affected by a lack of facilities and hygiene supplies. Our interviewer asked Thomas who was 54 and a recovering heroin addict:

*Sisters: You said when you're not clean that affects your self-esteem. I was wondering if you could talk some more about that?*

**Thomas**: Well, you get embarrassed. I'd say maybe if you don't have deodorant on, you haven't showered in a week, you got to get on public transportation around other people, keep you from going out and looking for a job, or you wonder what people

Photographer: Buddy Bee Anthony

think about you. They look at you. You show that you're homeless. I mean, when you go out and look for a job or something, you want to present yourself. You don't want to let someone know that you're in a down and out position because they're going to want to know why you're down. All kinds of questions are going to arise and it's none of their business.

I basically disassociated, other than people who were on the streets and were doing the things I was doing. I only associated with people who were helping me in some way or another...now I got into church, get around different people. I don't hang around with anybody that uses drugs anymore. I stay away from them. I don't want to be around it.

Ivan, who was 40 and had a history of writing bad checks, was trying to change his survival methods and approach to life. He also revealed that he avoids relationships of all kinds because of his homelessness.

**Ivan**: I will keep to myself. I will do what I need to do, then once I get into a place of my own, then I will get to know people. It is not that I am ashamed of it. It is not a nice thing, but I do not want somebody to look at me, say, 'Okay he is homeless, we should pity him,' because that is not what it is about. You do not do that to somebody. If you feel you should help, then help. But do not make them feel like you are doing it because you feel sorry for them. You feel sorry for the situation itself, not them. I do not think a lot of people realize that.

Curtis, who had been homeless for about five months when he came into our offices, was asked, if he had the world stage and could offer one insight about his experiences, what he would want people to know.

**Curtis**: It is embarrassing. It really is.

*Sisters: What is embarrassing?*

**Curtis**: Well, it is embarrassing to myself because I have never been homeless, and it is kind of shameful in a way. It makes me wonder, how did I get here? What did I do wrong to be in these circumstances that I am in? I have always thought I lived a good life and I have helped people when I could. It just astonishes me that I have come to this.

Abdul, a Muslim formerly from New York, felt doubly isolated because he hadn't yet connected with Muslims living in Portland.

**Abdul**: I keep to myself a lot, which is good, but it is not good. I should be around people who kind of like believe the same things that I do.

He felt particularly estranged because there are few mosques in the Portland area offering a place for prayer and camaraderie.

*Sisters: So, the mosques in New York are always open, they provide a place of refuge?*

**Abdul**: If you are stuck at two o'clock in the morning you can bang on the door and get in one, you know. You are stuck out here at two o'clock in the morning. You are just stuck.

[Here] I am not around the people that I worship with. Most of my friends are back East. I do not know anybody out here. So I am just trying to be honest...I am just out here by myself. I do not have any support or anything.

Another of our narrators explained his situation simply but eloquently.

---

**David**: When you are homeless, you are on the outside.

Our narrators often described their sense of separateness from the rest of society. Tina, who was living in an apartment and participating in an outpatient program for addiction at the time of our interview, described living in a shelter before her current living situation.

**Tina**: I was kind of an outcast. Sometimes that is a good thing, especially there; it was just really strange being there. No TV. You are not connected to the news, what is going on normally.

Another narrator described homelessness this way: "It is being lonely, low self-esteem, not feeling like I am acceptable to society."

Brenda described how disorientated she had been by her new situation.

**Brenda**: I do not even know how to live on the streets, I do not. And without my mother being down here, I will follow her around, I am lost. I am like a little puppy lost, just wandering around, just wandering around the streets, do not know which way to go, do not know who to ask, do not trust nobody…

She described her intense fears about her situation.

**Brenda**: I think I will lose it if I stay down here too long. I will go crazy. All these cuckoo nut people walking around here, that is harmful to other people. You think they are talking to you, they are not. That is how a lot of people get killed, hurt, and they really should do something about them. I just cannot be down here much longer. I will go crazy dealing with these people down here.

Randy, who moved to Portland to escape a complicated legal situation, discussed solutions for escaping homelessness. Like many of our narrators, he was unhappy about his physical appearance.

**Randy**: It's so hard to stay clean and keep your clothes clean. If you're carrying around a backpack, you are limited on how much clothes you got to wear, and if you wear the same clothes day in and day out and someone expects you to go for a job interview…how can you have any self-esteem or anything if you look terrible? I think that's something that's very important.

*Sisters: So, having the ability to keep yourself and your clothes clean can help you maintain your hope?*

**Randy**: Your hope and your health. And, if you can't stand the way you smell or look to yourself, how in the heck are you gonna go and represent yourself to anybody else with any pride?

*Sisters: What is it that leads to the feeling of being overwhelmed? What was it in your case?*

**Randy**: It just seems like I couldn't do enough fast enough to even start. Just lost an apartment and I even lost my vehicle, which was crazy. My landlord towed my truck thinking it was my neighbor's truck. But at the same time this happened, I didn't have enough money to pay the rent, so I still couldn't get the truck. So, it was kind of a weird thing, but it happened anyway. No transportation, although there were buses. Little things just seemed to add up, and when it's all happening at one time, it hits you so fast, you just want to give up. I don't know, your brain…you can't gather your thoughts enough to know where to start and you just kinda let go.

*Sisters: Too many things at once?*

**Randy**: Yeah, and you always say, 'Well, if I had done this, that wouldn't have happened' or 'If I had been better at that.' So, you're kinda just blaming yourself; so you're lowering your image of yourself, and the more you do that, the easier it is to give up. If you don't care about yourself, then what are you gonna do? That's a complex process. So now you just got to force yourself. It all starts with yourself. As hard as it is, get out there and start doing something. After you get a job, whatever that job is, start going to work, you'd be amazed at how much better you feel about yourself. And once you start feeling better about yourself, it becomes easier to do more for yourself.

It works hand in hand. It snowballs downhill, but it can also snowball back uphill, with just getting started.

Some of our narrators explained that they moved to Portland or other cities to be near friends or family. At one time Joshua, an army veteran who has lived in several cities, had moved to Wichita to be nearer his family, but living near his family didn't work out because conflicts that had existed since childhood couldn't be resolved.

**Joshua**: I was kind of homesick. Most of my family was still together. I started my life over a couple of times. I don't know what it is. Maybe I got a mental problem myself. I seem to allow myself to hit bottom and then have to start over again. Maybe through drinking and drugs, but I don't really blame it on that, I think it's more of…getting lazy or something, not caring.

*Sisters: You seem to care a lot.*

**Joshua**: I kind of do, but, between thinking and doing it just doesn't happen sometimes.

*Sisters: So, alcohol and drugs created some disruptions for you?*

**Joshua**: Oh yeah. I've been busted for marijuana three or four times. Two public intoxess. I still think more than blaming it on the actual substance, it's more of a state of mind. I know better, but I still do it. I guess being selfish, I want to do what I want to do, when I want to do it. The rest of it can go to hell. That's why I wonder if it's more of a mental thing. I don't know if that's a common thread among homeless people or not.

*Sisters: I don't know. A desire to do your own thing and then the consequences.*

Joshua: I do realize that kind of thinking is indirectly related to moving around a lot. I've never had a steady life, and being disrupted periodically, over and over, I'm just so used to it, that's the only thing I'm gonna do.

*Sisters: So, you moved a lot when you were growing up?*

Joshua: I went to first grade in Mississippi; second and third grades in New York; fourth and fifth grades in Ohio; sixth grade in Texas; seventh, eighth, and ninth grades in Kansas; then graduated in Louisiana. My mom, she's a counselor and we talked about it a little bit, and having that much disruption in your early teen years can have an effect on you. I'm sure that's part of the reason.

*Sisters: You're saying moving around like that, it's hard to form deep connections?*

Joshua: Yeah, you never get a chance to, you don't know how.

*Sisters: That sounds rough.*

Joshua: When you're a kid it doesn't seem rough. It can be fun. But then when you get older and start wanting to keep your friends and say, 'I like this place and I don't want to leave,' then it starts getting hard. That's one of the reasons my sister ran away and got married without permission when she was 16 because my parents were moving to the other side of town and she was going to have to go to the archenemy high school and she was going to have none of it. I was already gone; I was in the service at the time, she was the next oldest. She wouldn't stand for it and she left. My dad was kind of an asshole, which I think is part of the reason why I am how I am. I think that's a reason.

*Sisters: Kind of like a rebellion.*

Joshua: Yeah, you are transient all the time.

Many of our narrators reflected on childhoods that had set up behavior patterns with far-reaching implications. Dean, 28, had been homeless on and off since he was 19. He had also dropped out of college and was in a drug treatment program during our interview. He described the factors that contributed to his homelessness.

Dean: When it comes right down to it, every situation we find ourselves in is a direct reflection of our attitudes and our beliefs, our values. But, it's been largely contributed to by alcohol and drug abuse. I chose to get into that and I got in way over my head, like everybody does. And at the same time, I have, like, some psychological problems that I've got to deal with. Even when I've been sober, I've had difficulty with social situations, especially the more pertinent ones like work, school. Never kept jobs very long. Very impulsive. More than willing to just flip the boss off and walk out the door and feel really great about being free, cutting out, running. It feels really good. But that's gotta change. It's time to grow up.

Later in the interview he was asked if he'd ever slept outdoors.

**Dean:** Not this last time around but before, like last summer, I did a lot of sleeping outside. I was underneath the Morrison and the Hawthorne [bridges]. It's getting sketchier and sketchier. I don't look forward to sleeping out. If I ever end up outdoors again, I'm getting myself a camouflage tarp and I'm going into the woods.

*Sisters: How come?*

**Dean:** To be honest with you, the downtown environment strikes me as being rather depressing and it's probably because of my perception. I see the town through the eyes of someone who's spanged [asked for spare change], gotten drunk and loaded, and hauled off [to detox], and it's just kind of depressing. There's a lot of addicts down here. People just scraping the bottom of the barrel; people that are mentally ill, disabled. I mean it's just a really depressing and dispiriting sight and I'm just done. I'm tired of it. I'm going to go back to college again in the fall; pay for it myself or get financial aid. It [homelessness] lost its appeal to me.

Dean described how he's primarily survived by couch-surfing at friends' homes.

**Dean:** Homelessness is very demoralizing and it can become a habit. Helping homeless people is a moral obligation that any civilized society would have, regardless of the causes. There's plenty of excess, [in our society] even in economically hard times, to feed the homeless. But I think ultimately homelessness, unless you have a significant mental illness, really ends up being the cul-de-sac that your decisions and your choices will have led you to, especially in terms of alcoholism or an addiction that's seriously going to get you down there.

It's very demoralizing because if you live in a habit of being basically a stigmatic element to a respectable society and having to be careful and watch out for your peers—because some of your peers are pretty shady and might screw you over—the longer you are homeless, the more socially challenged you become. If you're homeless for ten years, it's going to be difficult for you to keep a job, be able to handle yourself in society. When something goes wrong, you just feel the urge to cut and run and go out into the woods or underneath a bridge, to fall back on what you're comfortable with. Even if that in itself was not very comfortable.

[And] it's difficult to be clean and presentable in this town. And whenever I was homeless, I really liked not to look homeless because I'm a fairly proud person. I want to have some respect from mainstream society, even though mainstream society for the most part will ignore me. It just feels good; it feels good to be clean. When you're dirty that's really demoralizing, dirty and smelly. Being homeless can be demoralizing and dispiriting enough as it is. But if at least you feel presentable to the world around you, then you can kind of hold your head on an equal level with the people, the business people.

*Sisters: So your appearance matters, how you portray yourself to the world.*

**Dean**: I think so. When I get depressed, one of the first things that goes is my personal hygiene. Stop brushing my teeth, get all…I call it 'white trashin' it.' And so, it is. Hygiene is important. I think it's a good barometer of how you feel about yourself and it helps you to feel better, too. Clothes are fairly clean, you're pretty clean. You've got your stuff, your belongings. Say if you've been staying in a place for a while, you can keep some of your belongings there. You're not walking around advertising yourself as being what a large part of the world would call a derelict and a loser. Because a lot of people say that, myself included: 'I don't care what people think about me.' But you know what? We really do. And it's important to try to feel at least halfway decent about yourself because that's a good motivator for trying to elevate yourself and improve your lot in life. It's really worth it. It will help you to feel better about yourself.

*Sisters: And to you it seems like self-esteem is important.*

**Dean**: It really is. And it is important because if you don't feel good about yourself, then you're more inclined to slip into basically that whole cycle of getting your free food, spanging for your money. A person that has got better self-esteem, feels better about themselves, is more inclined to be motivated, more inclined to, you know, deal with the difficulties and the discomfort of the situation and try to improve on it rather than submit to it and succumb to it. It can be a very bad cycle that makes you feel worse about yourself. And so you give into it; you keep feeling worse, and before you know it, you do that long enough, and it's very difficult to pull out. Being homeless is kind of like a 747 plummeting down into the face of the earth. You only have so much time before you can pull back on that stick and pull out of that dive. The sooner you do it, the better.

Justin came into our offices for an interview when he was 30. Previous to living in Portland, he'd been homeless in Bend, Oregon, and before that, Clearlake and Los Angeles, California, and New Mexico. He described himself as alcoholic and said he'd been smoking marijuana since he was 9, began drinking at 12. He grew up in Prineville, Oregon, but when his stepfather died when he was 11, he began acting out and was placed in a foster home, then a juvenile institution, and became emancipated at 15. He's been through treatment programs several times and has worked at various jobs, mostly as a cook. He talked often about stabilizing his situation so that he could work again.

**Justin**: My main goal right now is to have an apartment. I don't want to be homeless. I'm trying to do what I can to not be homeless. My friend got beat up the other night and got his sleeping bag stolen, and his eye blackened. They didn't need his sleeping bag. They were high. That's the kinda shit that goes on, on the streets. The worst thing is I feel bad and ashamed. I feel bad that I don't have a job, or a house. I'm 30 years old. Most people my age do.

*Sisters: You are ashamed on your own, nobody shames you?*

**Justin**: I've had people yell, 'Get a job motherfucker!' and it's like, hey, give me one. I'll go to work. They don't realize that bad things happen, and that's why I'm homeless. I didn't wake up one day and say 'Fuck it, I don't need my house. I just want to be homeless.' It's no life to have. It's difficult. You are always having to hustle something up. I'm glad I'm not a drug addict.

*Sisters: What's the most challenging part of your life right now?*

**Justin**: The most challenging part of my life I would have to say at this moment would be wanting it the way it was. Like reminiscing during long nights. Because you can kind of keep yourself busy during the day doing this and that, you don't really think about it all that much and you don't really feel homeless when you're busy. But it sinks in when you go back to your squat every night and you're laying there and you remember how it was. I think that that would probably be—I guess dreaming of the way it was.

Adam had worked as a machinist in Ohio, and when he lost his job and was unable to find work, he began living in his truck and then sold it and moved to Portland in hopes of starting over. He'd worked at a few jobs since living in Portland, but hadn't found a steady job and was sleeping in shelters. It was his twenty-fifth birthday the day he spoke with our interviewer.

*Sisters: And what about the way it was do you miss the most?*

**Adam**: Being homeless you do have a schedule, but it's not *your* schedule. Everyone says that when you're homeless it's just because you're running from responsibility. And that's true. I believe that for some of the street kids, it's a big adventure and some people like that lifestyle. But it isn't really running from responsibility. You still have responsibility when you're homeless. You have to show up. During the day, you'll see the same people hitting up all the missions. It's kind of like a big family. If you stay in there for a while, people get to know you. And, it's like a big herd going from mission to mission. You know, you just kind of do this cycle throughout the day. So you aren't just doing whatever you want to do.

Richard had small but important suggestions for breaking out of the cycle of homelessness.

**Richard**: There are a lot of cycles in being homeless. And you try to change it and you try to kind of step out of the circle a little bit whenever you have the chance. Because mentally it will drive you crazy; it wears on your mind. You ask yourself, 'Will this ever end? Am I going to be living this life for a long term?' It starts playing with you a little bit, being homeless. I don't want to say to make yourself out to be better than the next person, but it is an advantage, if you can bust out and not do what everyone else is doing. It makes you feel better about yourself in that you're not stuck in that cycle.

You can get into that grind, and it's like a herd. If you ever followed me around, you would see the same people at different missions at certain specific times during the day. It's uncanny. It's like a migrating herd.

*Sisters: So you're saying to just remove yourself from the space periodically keeps you from becoming permanently homeless. So what kind of strategies do you have for getting out of the space?*

**Richard**: I would probably have to say go out, do your own thing sometimes. Go out to eat every once in a while, don't go to the mission sometimes. If you have an extra five dollars and you feel comfortable that you can spend it, go to McDonald's and act like everyone else getting off from work. Get into that attitude like you just got off from work. Or do your time at the library. Visit the employment office just like it's a job. Do it for eight hours or whatever. Make it like a job. Go in there, work when they open, get out at three or four o'clock. And it kind of makes you feel like you're back into society.

Marjorie described how sometimes anxiety coupled with feelings of low self-esteem wreaks havoc on relationships when a couple does not have stable housing. Our interviewer asked her about the consequences of her homelessness.

**Marjorie**: [describing intimate relationships] It's impossible to feel good about the other, and then you both feel like shit and you take it out on each other. It tears you down mentally. If you are by yourself it is okay; when you are with somebody it is…it is hell.

*Sisters: And if there was a couple-shelter available, you feel like that would ease that kind of tension?*

**Marjorie**: Yeah, because you are working together to improve. You are doing something together more positive. Some days if something does not work out for me, then I have to fall back on him. And if it did not work out for him, he has got to fall back on me. It is a pain in the ass, it causes us to fight. He has beat me up a few times because of it, and it is not him, you know what I am saying? It is just not him, but like I said, you take it out on the closest thing to you. We are the closest thing to each other, so we beat each other up, but we pull through it. I have left him a few times, he has left me, but we go back together. Sometimes we need to cool off, but I do not blame him for a lot of things. I shut my mouth and do not push it.

Charlie, who was in his 50s, talked frankly about how drugs and alcohol had interfered in his life. He was in recovery at the time of our interview and described how feelings of isolation had exacerbated his situation.

*Sisters: And, so looking back, what do you see are the things that helped you to get out of it?*

**Charlie**: After twenty-eight years I am tired man. I really am tired of this life, of that way of living, tired of losing things. I've lost relationships, marriages…I want my daughter back in my life. She is a beautiful girl. She is 21 now. I want my family back. I was beat down, mentally, physically, literally. I was beat down. I'm lucky to be alive. I want a life; I want a life again. I want to be part of the world, to give, put something back, be a productive member of society. Grow up. It is time to grow up.

*Sisters: And, when you talk about your family and relationships and how they were affected by your experience with homelessness, could you talk about that?*

**Charlie**: Basically, you are homeless if you do not have relationships, you cut all that off. You just cut the world off man, you just do. I was too proud to go to my sisters and ask for help. It was because of the condition I was in.

*Sisters: How do you mean?*

**Charlie**: I was just too proud to show what I had become, what my life had become. I felt like I was a big nothing in those five years. I did not amount to anything, I was not worth anything. I just could not reach out and ask for help anymore, although, I really did not ask them for help anytime before in my lifetime. It is just basically my parents, and since they are both deceased, I did not have anybody to call on. But I would not ask, 'I'm tired of this, I want out. Can you help me out of here?'

Brendan, 24, grew up in a home where his parents were drug addicts. In fact, his father died of a drug overdose, his mother had attempted suicide, and he began experimenting with drugs as a teenager with his cousin. When he first became homeless, he spent a night sleeping in a church doorway, then the following night was looking for a place to sleep.

**Brendan**: I was walking around trying to figure out where to go and the only place I could find was where me and my parents used to live. The garage was open. Someone was living in the house now, but the garage was open, and what is really strange about that was that is where my father overdosed and died. That is where I ended up, sleeping just a few feet away from where he died.

Brendan eventually ended up at a mission and started learning about services available in Portland. He had thoughtful insights into the psychological effects of homelessness, especially during the first weeks of homelessness.

**Brendan:** I was trying to explain the right word for it. It breaks down your spirit pretty much, just the whole experience. As the days progressed I was getting more depressed. Finally I had to leave the Rescue Mission because there you just lose hope really quickly. It just made me feel pretty worthless because…just the way that they, you know, shove you around. After you eat you got to run downstairs and then jump in the shower, then go to bed at like eight thirty. You get up at five o'clock, you are out the doors going, 'What do I do now?'

Brendan went on to wonder why he's only rented his own apartment once, saying that at 24 it was time to grow up and accept responsibility.

*Sisters: If you had your own place you would feel grown up?*

**Brendan:** I know I am capable of that, capable of a lot more than what I have been doing. I had gone numb but just recently, in the last two years, realized that I want to live again. I guess for a lot of years I did not have that. I was just kind of living without making a sound, sort of existing, coasting through life.

*Sisters: Why do you think that is?*

**Brendan:** Something really bad happened a few years ago. I will not go into any details about it, but it was quite traumatizing. And then after that my father died, my mother transferred all her anger, from my father dying, toward me…so our relationship just went out the window. And for a while I pretty much thought that why all those things happened in my life was because I deserved it, because I was a terrible person, I was just worthless.

Recently I have just really started to realize that I am not a worthless person. I am a good person, I am, and that I deserve a life, that I deserve to live and be productive and, you know, to be happy.

*Sisters: That is a big thing to realize. It is not easy either.*

**Brendan:** Yeah, and unfortunately, I think that is why a lot of people are trapped in the system of being homeless. A lot of the shelter programs and just the whole attitude towards homelessness that the mainstream society has keeps people in their mindset. Sort of, 'I'm not worth it,' or 'I'm just a homeless piece of trash. I'm not worth it.' So a lot of people are just stuck.

Brendan went on to describe how although he'd survived some dark times and had lost hope, he was now rebuilding his life and discovering hope through a drug treatment program, Narcotics Anonymous, and new friendships. At first he was intimidated and frightened by these interactions but is gradually becoming more comfortable.

*Sisters: Why did it scare you that they wanted to hang out with you?*

**Brendan:** It was unfamiliar, something that was totally alien, strange, so it took some time for me to get used to that but now I am. It has been so long since I had friendships like that, since I was a teenager.

He went on to describe his Narcotics Anonymous group as a second family and how speaking up in the meetings is transforming him.

**Brendan**: I have seen some tremendous acts of kindness on the streets, and oh, they are great. There are some great people out there on the streets, some gigantic hearts.

And talking to you, or just a smile, that can really lift someone's spirits on the street, because a lot of people just walk by and stick their nose up in the air. You try to ignore it but they look through you like you do not exist, and that is a terrible thing to do to a person.

*Sisters: What does that do to a person?*

**Brendan**: After a while that just accumulates and, you know, you start believing that you are invisible. You are just nothing, you are worthless and you do not have any right to be in society with the normals. God, if people would just realize how much a smile or a handshake or an honest 'How are you?' means. And then stand there and wait for a response and see how they really are, how much of a difference it can make in someone's day or an entire life.

---

Interviewer's Journal Excerpt:

*I see that in the people I interview—so many people are still harboring lots of pain from bad family relationships, etc., and they feel vulnerable and hurt. I hear talk of "hardened" drug addicts and criminals in the media, but I don't see anyone very hard, not really. Most everyone is tender on the inside, fragile. I don't know if it's me or the project or the questions, or what, but the veneer comes off almost immediately with almost everyone, young and old, men and women, chronic homeless and first-timers.*

---

# Chapter 4
## Chapter Four

*You get arrested for freaking sleeping*

# Interactions with the Criminal Justice System

---

*Let's not just transform those in need, we can also find ways to help transform those in power.*

—Unknown

In the end, none of these stories our narrators told came as a surprise to me, not the good ones and not the harsh ones, because they mirror what Sisters has learned from personal experience. It's our knowledge of both inappropriate and compassionate behavior on the part of law enforcement that's given us the courage to speak up when police brutality occurs. Here are three stories:

In the early days, we witnessed a mounted police officer immobilizing an inebriated man experiencing homelessness, by pressing him between the butt of his horse and the wall outside of Sisters. That incident birthed our Meal Coupon program. I ran out to the officer and said, "He's okay, he's welcome here." Sisters has never excluded people under the influence because we know they need examples to change their lives, like when they come into the cafe and see a former drinking buddy who's now working behind the counter. But at the time, shelters didn't admit people under the influence. Our cafe team envisioned something we could give to officers to hand out, with the message: if you see other guys like him, tell them where Sisters is. The Police Department bought our first thousand meal coupons!

About six years ago, I'd been invited to give a presentation about Sisters to a faith-based group. At the end I opened up the floor for questions, and a woman said she had a close friend she admired who was in law enforcement and was a good man, a family man, well respected, and all those things we believe make up a credible human being. But with tears in her eyes, she shared with us that he and some fellow officers had more than once come to Old Town/Chinatown to beat up people who were homeless. She felt safe enough to be honest because I'd been talking about nonviolence, not humiliating anyone, and about how behavior is inappropriate, not people. I was deeply moved by her courage and so, *so* disheartened to learn that what you always hope is a misconception of law enforcement can be true.

Community policing was introduced in Old Town in the early '90s. One morning the cafe was going to be late to open, and it was my job to apologize to the customers in line. As I was out front, an officer in a patrol car pulled up and got out. I was nervous, thinking, *Oh man, he's gonna tell me we have to move the line, or ask why it's not moving.* As if he read my mind, he smiled at us and handed me a flier announcing Old Town's first community policing meeting. We were all invited to this meeting, held in our own neighborhood, about how to transform the image of police, held for decades, from law officers to peace officers! That era for Sisters meant that for the first time, we forged authentic, lasting relationships of mutual respect sustained to this day, even leading to officers holding their wedding at Sisters.

—Genny

**Jamie:** You read the ASPCA rules; animals are treated better than we are. I would wish I could live in a Humane Society. They have a bed, they have both food and fresh water. They get bathed. Their excrement gets cleaned up, they keep themselves clean because they are lucky themselves, okay?

I like a shower, that will be fine. I can do my own self, but they are treated better than we are. I have slept on the street fifteen months before I came here, straight. Fifteen months on the sidewalk. I sit on the curb at night. I used a bathroom in the alley by the dumpster, it stinks, it is swill, it is filthy, it is degrading. You have to look all the time over your shoulder and it is two thirty in the morning you are in the alley or between cars on the street, watching for cops not to see you because unfortunately they do not understand that a person is born with these functions, and because I could not get help. I have to do it outside because that is my home. Now what? So you go to jail because you got a ticket. You have to go to court. Then you go to jail. I was there [on the streets] fifteen months. I did not get caught because I learned. I got taught by some of the best on how to do things. I do not shoplift. I do not do anything else except having to use the bathroom, drink a beer in a container, but I do not need a ticket. I do not like court, and I do not want to bother with it. What was the reason that you got a ticket for? Oh! Sleeping. That is my favorite one. You get arrested for freaking

Photographer: Brynne Athens

sleeping. 'You got to move.' Sorry, when I was born, I used the bathroom; I breathed air, it was fresh; and I slept; and I ate. You know what? I still do these things, and they are still human requirements.

Jamie was not alone in reporting feelings of persecution and alienation.

**Wally**: When I was sleeping on the sidewalks and stuff, I was kicked off. The cops would come and wake me up and tell me I could not sleep here, you know, and I felt like a piece of garbage and then I was upset. Where am I to go sleep? I do not know where to sleep, and I was not in the shelter, because I got this anxiety. I cannot sleep on the sidewalk because the mayor is saying that the public is complaining about the homeless people sleeping on the street and so, now they are telling them to move. Where do you go? You know, where do you sleep?

Simon revealed that part of the conflict with police starts with dismissive language.

**Simon**: I have seen one guy, one time being busted, this dealer, on the MAX [local light rail system]. They pulled him out. We were all sitting on top of the stairs. The detective that pulled the guy off the MAX, you know, this guy goes to get on the MAX, he is just, just a guy, I mean, he was not dressed up well, [being] homeless and this undercover cop just starts reading him the riot act. There were about seven or eight of us up there. We all started yelling at him, I mean, because it was so obvious that he was just being an asshole. Lots of times they, the homeless people, are not referred to as people, they are referred to as 'belligerents,' like a separate group of people, those unwanted individuals.

Edward was born in 1943 and served in Vietnam in a Special Forces unit that extricated soldiers who were imprisoned or somehow left behind. Now divorced and a grandfather, he lived for years on the Oregon coast and had worked as a logger, an iron worker, a carpenter and most recently traveled around the country installing telephone equipment. However, three years previous to the interview, a seizure landed him in a coma and he was unable to work by doctor's orders.

Like many homeless people, when he was interviewed he was in limbo: fighting so that he could be declared disabled and collect SSI (Supplemental Security Income) and receive help from Adult & Family Services, waiting to reach 65 so he can collect Social Security, and waiting for the medical attention he needs. He'd been on the streets for two years after being evicted without cause. (Oregon allows private landlords to evict tenants without cause. However, if the tenant lives in a mobile home, or in any kind of federally subsidized housing, the landlord cannot use a no-cause notice.) Consequently, Edward subsists chiefly by collecting cans and bottles to pay for food and cigarettes.

*Sisters: So, do you get enough to eat?*

**Edward**: Most of the time. The only problem I have is sleeping and getting kicked out from where I am all the time. I do not like it.

*Sisters: Tell me about that.*

**Edward**: That is when the cops come down and say, 'You got seventy-two hours to move out,' and you have no other place to go and wherever you go they will run you out in seventy-two hours anyhow. I do not make any mess. I keep it clean, but it is also hard sleeping in the dust and dirt and on the ground, especially at my age.

*Sisters: And the cops frequently roust you?*

**Edward**: Oh yeah, all the time. They come down and say, 'Time to move,' so we get up and move. So I hide my stuff, and they cannot find it, so they come down and sweep and take everything out of there and clean it up. Then they are gone for about maybe a couple of weeks, then they come back and do the same thing over again.

*Sisters: Sweep you?*

**Edward**: Yeah, I hate it, because we are not doing anything outside, nobody knows we are down there, and we do not make a mess. No notices [of sweeps], I do not think it is right, not a bit, I really do not.

According to our narrators sweeps with little or inadequate notice are a common occurrence. Many lamented how they lost all their belongings and were forced to start all over again not only to find a place to sleep, but also to collect blankets, tarps, tents, and hygiene necessities.

Edward described how difficult it is to become stable after you've lost both your health and housing, but also how the daily harassment wears on a person.

**Edward**: Sometimes if you are sitting in a park relaxing, and cops come down, harass you, 'Who are you?' 'What are you doing down here?' That is none of their business as long as you are not causing any trouble.

*Sisters: Why do you think they single you out?*

**Edward**: Not just me, everybody.

*Sisters: They harass everyone in the park?*

**Edward**: No, not everyone…a lot of the homeless people, they single out homeless people more than anything else.

*Sisters: How do they know you are homeless?*

**Edward**: Because you are sitting with a bunch of people, so they just figure you are homeless, so they come down and check out and see if you are. 'You're not supposed to be in a crowd. Go.' So we get up and move out of the park and soon as they are on the other side, we move back to the park, sit there. Why not? It is our right, but there are a lot of them that have warrants and stuff going on and they get picked up and hauled off.

All I want is a place over my head where I can do my cooking and relax. We do not even get a chance to sit down and relax anymore. They keep us running and going all day. We have no place to go.

*Sisters: So, what have been the effects of homelessness on you, mentally, emotionally, physically, spiritually?*

**Edward**: It is just stress. You can get stressed out more easy, wonder what is going to be the next day, what is going to happen, and where I am going to be. Because you cannot plan, I just get up the next morning, thank the Lord that I am alive and will try another day, see what comes up.

*Sisters: So, you cannot even plan where you are going to sleep at night?*

**Edward**: I do not know if I am going to come back and my sleeping bag is going to be down there or the cops are going to pick it up and have it hauled away.

This is supposed to be a free country but it is not anymore.

*Sisters: What do you think the difference is now?*

**Edward**: Cops.

*Sisters: The cops are worse?*

**Edward**: They do not treat you like they used to. We used to be able go talk to them and shake hands with them and I remember that when I was younger. Now they will not even shake your hand, they will not even talk to you, treat you rude.

Tim, a 35-year-old who had also been homeless in Las Vegas, expressed his frustration about the ordinances aimed at homeless people in both Las Vegas and Portland. Describing his experiences of being homeless in Vegas he said:

**Tim**: They have no mercy on homeless. They definitely will harass you and definitely will take you to jail. I was cited for interfering with the flight of a pigeon just because I kicked at some pigeons that were in front of me.

*Sisters: For interfering—*

**Tim**: With the flight of a pigeon. Yes, literally. What kind of a law is that? But obviously, they have it because they got ninety-five dollars on me.

*Sisters: Wow! That is bizarre.*

**Tim**: And, especially to a person who is homeless that has no income. I had to work day labor…and that really put me off, trying to pay that.

*Sisters: How long did it take in working day labor to raise ninety-five dollars?*

**Tim**: It would probably take me three days. I thought he was nuts when he told me, 'I'm going to write you a ticket for it.' But you do not really argue with them there because they will beat you down. Police there are nothing nice.

*Sisters: So, when you say 'beat you down', what do you mean?*

**Tim**: Oh! They will beat you, they will.

*Sisters: Physically?*

**Tim**: They will physically abuse you. They will put the nightsticks to you.

*Sisters: Have you seen it?*

**Tim**: Oh yeah, I have seen it a bunch of times. That is one place you do not mess with the police, especially in Henderson which is part of Las Vegas incorporated. They will write you a ticket, they will take you to jail if you do not have five dollars in your pocket, literally. They will consider you a vagrant, even walking down the sidewalk. You do not have to be stopped; you do not have to be anything. They will definitely take you to jail…you will spend a few days there. I do not know what the purpose of it all is. They just try to make sure you do not come back into their part of town and that is a deterrent, to keep what they consider undesirables, people who do not have enough money in their pockets, from walking down their streets.

Alex, who is 54 and a recovering addict struggling to get his life back on track, offered this opinion about how Portland's ordinances affect his livelihood. His comments point out the unique bind that a homeless person often finds himself caught in.

**Alex**: It's pretty much a crime to be broke. Everything you do is illegal when you don't have any money.

*Sisters: Can you tell more about that?*

**Alex**: If somebody wants to pick up cans, say to get recycling money, it's actually a crime to go through a trashcan. They can put you in jail for that. You don't have any money: it's called loitering. If you go down to the waterfront, you can't hang around or lay around there: it's considered camping. That's illegal. It seems like that not having money, there's a lot of laws that you fall into because of that.

Problems with police prior to periods of homelessness can make contacts with police while homeless more challenging. Sandra's first negative contact with police came during a domestic violence disturbance.

*Sisters: What options do women have?*

**Sandra**: Not much, Harbor Light, Jean's Place [local shelters for women], unless you go to Salvation Army if you are abused, what else is there? I cannot remember more, but if you do not fall under certain categories, you know, like saying you are abused. I did that before when I left my ex, the one that drank all the time because we would fight. I called the cops and guess who went to jail.

*Sisters: He did? They have to take one or the other now?*

**Sandra**: They told him to sleep it off.

*Sisters: What did they tell you?*

**Sandra**: 'You're getting arrested.'

*Sisters: What for?*

**Sandra**: I do not know what it was, guess because I punched him back, he got me into a corner and started calling me F&C word, him going around calling women that. That is the worst word. He has a scratch on his face because I [fought back]. Hell, I had a black eye, a bloody nose, a fat lip. Abuse is a really big problem down here, I think.

*Sisters: Are there other things about the police you wanted to talk about?*

**Sandra**: Hell, they used to stop me all the time.

*Sisters: Here?*

**Sandra**: Yeah. They would stop me all the time even when I was with my daughter thinking I was a prostitute because I lived by 82nd. Police are not nice, they jump to conclusions a lot of the times.

*Sisters: Oh! 82nd, is that one of the prostitution-free zones?*

**Sandra**: Yeah.

*Sisters: Did you live in that zone, in the prostitution-free zone up in 82nd?*

**Sandra**: Yeah.

*Sisters: So, they stopped you?*

**Sandra**: Constantly. I [would be] going to the store to get a pack of cigarettes [or something], so more than once.

*Sisters: Why do you think they stopped you? Why you?*

**Sandra**: I do not know. I was just there. They did it twice to me at five thirty in the morning. I think I was walking around picking up some cans or something like that, well, you do something, you know. If I was a prostitute, it is five thirty in the morning, come on.

There were occasionally stories from our narrators about exchanges with the police that were positive.

**Marla**: We set up another camp. We had a little tiny pup tent that we set up just barely off the beach. There was a wooded area we set it up in. It was a nice area, but then the water started rising eventually, you know. We decided it was time to move to higher ground so we moved to the other side of the road.

You know, in that first camp the police, for Christmas, they bought us a big box and left it at the end of the trail. They had some blankets in it and a little of this and a little of that, and four or five survival blankets. And when they had that homeless conference, they brought over their leftover trays. They brought over a huge meat tray with sliced meats and then a veggie tray. It was great.

*Sisters: Oh, that's wonderful.*

**Marla**: Yeah.

*Sisters: Now do the police know about your second camp so they can bring you presents?*

**Marla**: Well, they knew we were there.

Marla went on to explain she once ended up disoriented a mile from her camp after sleepwalking. A local resident called the police. She continued:

**Marla**: [I was barefoot] and it was raining of course. But here comes the police and he says, 'Oh Marla, we know where you live and we'll take you home.' And so they got me back to the parking lot where the beach was and they took their flashlights and got me over to our camp.

*Sisters: Oh, wow.*

**Marla**: I was, 'Honey, we got company.' Oh well, it's officers whatever their names were and it was kind of funny. So yeah, they knew we were there.

For Marshall, a police officer filled more than a law enforcement role.

*Sisters: Do you feel like you're treated differently?*

**Marshall**: I've been treated differently, yeah. It's like being treated as less. Then again, there's always those few that, you know, are kind and gracious, you know, considerate. It's like on occasions out and about, you know, and up over around part of time where I stayed, there was always offerings. You know, somebody actually directly asking me if there was anything that I needed. Not very often, but occasionally. When you talk to society though, immediately what comes to my mind is the police. You know, they're the enforcers of society and it was that the police didn't have any type of tolerance whatsoever. Now there is some but I don't think it's enough. I mean I could be grateful, like this one individual, he's a police officer that works up there in southwest, he was kind of instrumental in my starting to take a look at recovery as an answer because he was kind. He was considerate. You know, he was concerned. He's not just out to bust me, to take and make my life difficult. He showed humanity of what it is being a police officer is all about. He's not enforcing the law, he's just being a human being. Being a friend. I just seen him the other day. He's got a big issue with the grocery carts. You know, he wants to see me going towards Fred Meyer with a Fred Meyer grocery cart. He doesn't want to see me leaving Fred Meyer with a grocery cart.

*Sisters: Did he tell you that?*

**Marshall**: Yeah. I says, 'Well, I was going to take and leave it right there with that grocery cart right there.' You know, I was about 100 feet away from the bus stop. I was headed back to town.

*Sisters: Okay…*

**Marshall:** Oh, if I was doing something wrong, he'd bust my ass. But he just stops to talk with me and see how I'm doing.

Unfortunately, positive encounters seem to be less common, certainly less memorable, than negative ones. Rita, who was 42, a former homeowner, degreed accountant, and the mother of six- and eight-year-old sons, had a particularly distressing story to relate and was in the process of initiating a lawsuit against the Portland Police. Her problems began with postpartum depression after the birth of her second child, a condition exacerbated by her mother's death following a four-year illness. Her husband divorced her during her mother's last weeks, with the final decree awarding her less than three hundred dollars a month child support.

As her depression deepened, she was having increasing difficulties concentrating and working and then began using drugs to self-medicate and lost her job. Without steady income, her house was foreclosed and she moved into a rental house across the street. But she was unable to work steadily and was evicted, and then her husband sued her for custody of their sons. At the time of our interview, she was only allowed supervised visitations.

She was evicted in early January and spent the first night in her car. She related events of that first night:

**Rita:** And I was pulling over to go to sleep and then the cops came and put their lights on and asked me for all my ID. So I gave them what I had. I did not have an insurance card because I had left in rather a state of shock, and for some reason it was not in my wallet or I could not find it at the time. My car was full of things, and I started digging and she (a female officer) said, 'Oh it's okay,' and she took and ran my license and everything was okay, so she gave it back to me. I told her, 'I'm sorry, I'm a little disorganized. Tonight is the first night I had lost my home and I'm sleeping in my car.' And she said, 'Oh, I'm sorry, is there anything I can do?' And I said, 'I just want to know why you pulled me over.' She goes, 'Well, you made a U-turn right in front of us and we're just checking on things.' She was most polite and gave me all my ID back and said, 'Be sure you carry your ID. I understand that it's your first day on the street, so I'm not going to fine you, but it is a requirement to carry the insurance card.' I said, 'Okay, I'll try to find it,' and that was that and she drove away, I put my car seat down and went to sleep.

Two weeks later, Rita was in her old neighborhood again when a police car followed her for a few blocks then pulled her over. The officer became immediately belligerent and when she questioned the reason for stopping her, his response indicated that he had mistaken her for another woman. When she tried to point out his mistake, he became even more hostile.

**Rita:** And he said, 'Get out of the car,' so I got out of the car and he said, 'Get over to the curb,' and I tried to walk past and I said, 'Why are you being so rude?' and he said, 'Get over to the curb.' So I walked past him and he grabbed my shoulder, really rough and this was a big man. He stood at least nine inches taller than me and probably one hundred pounds heavier and he grabbed my shoulder and I flinched, it is just kind of automatic, so he took me, he grabbed both my arms and twisted them behind my back and broke them both.

And I screamed, 'You're hurting me,' at the top of my lungs and he slammed my face into the car, broke my glasses, lacerated my cheek, gave me a black eye, two fat, split lips and a concussion, and left me tied up in the back of the car for a couple of hours while he laughed with his friend waiting for backup. Five cop cars showed up. I was in the back of the car with my arms twisted up behind my back like I was some big bad criminal trying to get away from him. It was ridiculous. He had me pinned so that I could not move a muscle and left me back there while they went through each and everything I owned, all my clothing, because I was living in it [the car], so it took forever and they laughed and joked.

She was arrested for disorderly conduct but was not given adequate medical attention because there was too much swelling and her injuries were not believed to be serious. After her release, she was able to call a friend who drove her to a hospital where the true extent of her injuries was discovered and she was put into two full arm casts. When she was interviewed, she had been living on the streets for three months during the winter, struggling with basic daily activities like eating and using the bathroom because of her casts, and had just gotten temporary housing. Rita was able to find a lawyer through a social service agency, was on medication for depression, and was clean and sober.

**Rita:** I do not know much about the justice system except that it is not just.

When she was interviewed, Marla was in her early fifties and had been homeless for about fourteen years. She first became homeless when her live-in boyfriend beat her and she escaped by joining several friends who were camping in the woods near Newport, Oregon. She lived at various camps and near small towns along the coast for four years before moving on to other places. Her experience with the kind police who brought presents and later took her home were offset by a different experience in Georgia.

She awoke in their tent and found that she was covered in bites from fire ants. Meanwhile, as Luke [her boyfriend] went off in search of a better site, they had caught the attention of locals who called the sheriff, who then took Marla to the hospital for medical treatment. When she left the hospital she discovered that their property had been confiscated and Luke had disappeared. Two days later she was arrested for sitting on a park bench, the police claiming that it was private property although it wasn't posted as such. She was in jail for six weeks before she appeared before a judge.

*Sisters: What's Luke doing during all this time? Does he know where you are?*

**Marla**: Well no…I looked for him the next day and couldn't find him anywhere.

*Sisters: Have you seen him again?*

**Marla**: No…Luke and I had an understanding that if we were separated for any reason, he'd check the hospital and jail. That's just automatic. And I was in jail but never saw him or heard from him.

*Sisters: And the relationship was still good at that point?*

**Marla**: Yes, it was very good. We had said our vows to each other.

She was released from jail without a fine for time already served, and although she tried to claim her belongings, she was unsuccessful. Eventually a local church group raised money for a bus ticket back to Oregon. Meanwhile, Marla was calling her and Luke's family in Oregon, but no one had heard from him.

**Marla**: He was real close to his mom and his sisters. And so it's my feeling that while out looking for another camp for us, he either got mugged by a gang or eaten by an alligator.

*Sisters: So you think he's dead.*

**Marla**: Yes I do. And when I was in jail I had dreams of him laying in a gutter covered with maggots. It was awful. But that's my feeling, which breaks my heart.

Samuel, a 54-year-old veteran, has had few problems with the police, although he has been woken up and asked to move by officers. He explained that he tries to avoid confrontations.

**Samuel**: So I just get up, I do not argue with them, I do not fight with them, and they see that I am kind of a peaceful person. They just chase me off mostly, but I have not seen violence or nothing because I never gave them reason to. Some people, they want to argue…and I think that is what gets a lot of homeless into trouble instead of just swallowing your pride for fifteen, twenty seconds and leaving. They got to play all these other stupid little games. It is so much easier just to swallow your pride for a short period of time and just go somewhere.

Another veteran, Alan, is a Native American activist and described oppression on the streets and the unfairness of laws aimed at homeless people. He explained that too often homeless people become entangled in a legal system where they cannot win.

**Alan**: It is the rich against the poor with a well-to-do middle class sticking up for the rich because they know where their bread is buttered. They do not want to be on our side because we are not comfortable.

*Sisters: Sounds like a class war.*

**Alan**: It is war except our side is all beat to crap and given up.

---

*Sisters: How can we influence the legislation or the people that have the power to change things?*

**Alan**: I do not know. People power. It takes people power. I guess it would take a great leader, somebody that can make people believe in themselves because we cannot get anybody to do it. We tried and tried until our hearts were broken. People are so beat down they just do not care anymore. Who cares? I am going to die under the bridge.

*Sisters: You tried to….*

**Alan**: Tried to get people to stand up for their rights, but they are all running scared and they all got warrants now. See, the system just keeps grinding you up and crushing you down. You get a warrant because you cannot pay your fine. So you cannot go protest, because if you do, you are going to jail for your warrant. You cannot go to court and stick up for yourself.

*Sisters: So the people are afraid to speak up in protest because they have warrants?*

**Alan**: They are living in fear, not to mention all the cameras (referring to security cameras in downtown Portland). Most live in fear all the time, and they cannot apply for anything (social services and government benefits). You effectively shut your life off. They cut your life off until you do what they tell you to do. You cannot rebel in the society anymore without being punished.

*Sisters: If you have a warrant they cut your benefits?*

**Alan**: Cut everything. And the longer it takes them to get through cutting it, the more money you got to pay back if you ever do get it back. They make you pay to be in jail now. So if they throw me in jail for protesting then they are going to charge me sixty dollars a day. So if I get thrown in on Friday and I get out on Monday, I owe one hundred and eighty dollars. No more than that…If you are in for part of a day they charge you for the whole thing, so that is two hundred and forty dollars rent for protesting against what the government is doing wrong. So how am I going to pay that? I cannot afford to pay that…

*Sisters: This is to keep you from protesting?*

**Alan**: Sure. I cannot afford sixty dollars a day.

Samuel also questioned the efficacy of this practice.

**Samuel**: I do not know what the exact figures are or how much it costs to have a person incarcerated for any length of time on a per-day basis, but we are talking about turning jails into homeless motels at this point.

Sean, who was 24 and a native of California, had worked as an activist for homeless rights in Olympia, Washington, and had thoughtful assessments of the sort of catch-22 situation that many homeless people fall into when they're arrested. During his interview, he also discussed how the legal systems in Washington and Oregon hinder a homeless person's chances of becoming housed.

**Sean:** They want to make it illegal if you camp in your car. Now, if you have a car, that is an asset, that is a resource that can get you to and from work even if work is far away. They pass the ordinance: if you are sleeping in your car, you can be taken to jail and your car be impounded. If you cannot get your car out of impound because you have to pay this fee that you cannot afford, then you cannot get to work. If you have no car, maybe you are job hunting every day and your car is the way you job hunt. Well now, you cannot job hunt. You cannot get anywhere and you have no place to stay once you get out of jail.

*Sisters: So, by criminalizing sleeping in your car they are simultaneously taking away your housing and your—?*

**Sean:** Ability to work. And it is not a matter of just making life harder for the homeless; it is a matter of incarcerating the homeless and worsening their situations. You are going to create more homeless people with these laws, since they are provided with no way out. It is something called 'legislation of safety,' which is something I think is the biggest misunderstanding in city consciousness and in the city government—the idea that you can legislate public safety. That is the big buzzword in Olympia and in lots of places right now. The public at large feels very threatened by homeless people.

*Sisters: Why do they feel threatened by the homeless?*

**Sean:** Because they do the same activities that people do in their homes privately, but they do them in the only place that they have, and that is in public. They [the public] feel threatened by people who smell bad and who look ragged and who might be dangerous.

During the interviews we learned that a significant proportion of our narrators had been arrested or had a criminal record or outstanding warrants. For many in the homeless community, legal problems are directly tied to their homelessness and their inability to break free from the cycle.

Darren, who is a Chippewa Indian originally from the Midwest, was interviewed after he had served six months for driving with a revoked license and had been incarcerated four different times previous to this sentence. He discussed his most recent jail time with our interviewer.

*Sisters: Did that cause disruption in your life?*

**Darren:** You learn how to start over. You get out [of jail], you have nothing. Then you start to accumulate things. I don't worry so much about replacing things because I know I can. Nothing lasts forever. There are certain things people like to hang onto, memories, memorabilia, stuff like that. I, from going to jail, have gotten to the point where that's very limited in my scope of life.

*Sisters: And as far as your time sleeping out, what kind of experiences with the police did you have?*

**Darren:** I was not bothered by the police too much sleeping at night under the bridge. I was, however, bothered by the police if I tried to lay down on a bench during the day in the area [downtown Portland] regardless of whether I was just laying back reading or if I was laying back trying to nap.

*Sisters: If you could just give me an example or how many times that happened and what the exchange was like...?*

**Darren:** Usually they would come by on horseback, this was the month of May, it is getting warmer, lot of cops on horseback were there. They would come, wander in through the park and observe you, and I would be lying on a bench, usually with friends around me. And the cops would come over—and first they wake you up to make sure that you were not in a drug stupor, because if you were, then right away they could send you to detox and get rid of you—and if you were not, they'd tell you that you've got to sit up. And they do not let you ask them too many questions.

It is like asking your parents questions when you were a kid, you'd get answers like, 'Because I said so,' you know, 'Because I'm the law.' I see people sleep out on the grass that are not homeless, who are out there getting a tan with their family, and if somebody decides to nap on the lawn, cops do not hassle them at all. I have seen people that are homeless try to take a nap on the grass, same stuff except maybe they are resting their head on their backpack, cops come by and roust them. And the excuse always is, 'We wanted to make sure you were okay. Make sure you weren't passed out or dead.' Then they are just told to move along, often checked for their ID to make sure that they are not barred from the park, or have warrants for their arrest.

They ask for IDs all the time. I am tired of showing mine.

Kenneth questioned the definition of 'loitering.' He'd been living on the streets and in shelters for six months before we talked with him.

**Kenneth:** Then they have problems of people sitting on their business stoops or panhandling. They are trying to rest their feet, they've been walking around for six hours. I don't understand why you can't just sit down, why it's considered loitering. I've personally sat down to read a book; loitering is sitting and doing nothing. I was reading a book, but yet a policeman can come by and tell me to move because I'm loitering. I think it's time we changed the definition of the word 'loitering.'

*Sisters: Change it how?*

**Kenneth:** Well, the police officers come by and say you are loitering because you are on public property. Well, I've worked most of my life, I've paid taxes, I am the public. You may not like it, but I'm the public. Why can you harass me because I'm homeless, and you don't harass the guy that goes to college or works in the office building sitting over there on that bench?

I think a lot of homeless people get hassled by the police so often or even if it is not often, unnecessarily by the police that, and I hate to say this about myself, but you just reach an attitude where you say, 'Fuck the cops.' They are definitely not there to help. You see them only in the light of, 'Oh, here comes another hassle.' I have really lost a lot of respect for law enforcement in this town just because of that. I am so much more willing to want to please the police and abide by their wishes if I respect them than if I do not. Getting people to do what you want by threatening to arrest them or even police brutality is just not the right way. I think if the cops were to come through and just stop and say, 'Hey, what's up?' you know, 'How's your day going?' just talk to you for a second and move along without asking for your ID and calling in to see if you got warrants. If the cops were just like normal people there to protect the homeless people from crime as well as non-homeless people from crime—they are there to protect everyone, treat everyone equally—that would really get a lot of respect from the homeless people. And then the homeless people would really go out of their way to not cause any problems for the police.

Rick was 34 at the time of his interview and had moved to Portland from Detroit because he needed to start over after an eleven-year relationship ended. He was attracted by the low crime rate and beauty of the city. He had suffered from a severe panic disorder most of his life and admits to self-medicating with alcohol in the past. At the time of our interview he had obtained medication and his panic attacks were under control. As a gay man who had sometimes lived on the streets, he also had special concerns about possible violence that is aimed at gays.

But one incident he described toward the end of the conversation raised especially troubling questions. Rick was arrested at the Greyhound station because he was intoxicated and did not have a bus ticket. Three or four police vehicles responded with six or seven officers. They circled him and one policeman twisted his arm behind his back while the others combed through his belongings and pockets.

**Rick:** And the police kept asking me what I was shooting up and stuff, even though holding my arms they could see that I do not have track marks. I suppose I could have been shooting up somewhere else but I do not shoot up, never have. To make a long story a little shorter, they had directed my attention behind me while still holding my arms. I glanced over my shoulder and with nothing there I looked forward again and in the pile with my belongings that they had removed from my pockets, were not one but two crack pipes, used ones. And I just said, 'No, those are not mine, you guys put those there.' Their response was, 'Did you see one of us put those there?'

And, of course, they had just momentarily directed my attention behind me; they all agreed that they were found in my pockets, and they gave me a choice. They said, 'You can go to prison or you can get out of downtown for good.' I said, 'You guys can't do this to me.' They twisted my arms until I agreed in pain to leave downtown for good, and then took me off to detox. When I was released in the morning not knowing how to survive anywhere but downtown having been homeless nowhere else but downtown, I returned and kind of laid low for a while but anger built up inside of me because of that threat. I did not deserve it. I had been here almost a year and had never caused any problems for the police, so I could not understand the reason for that kind of threat, threatening me with prison, and it really angered me. That is really when I lost my respect for the police.

I have since walked around showing my face freely; I refused to hide my face every time a cop went by. You just cannot do that and there are way too many of them. I was angry. I walked around thinking, *Go ahead and stop me and try to pull this on me again.* It frightened me that they very well could pull this and I could go to prison. I let people know about it just in case it happened again. In fact, I tried to cover myself by leaving a record on the Internet of my experience with them planting the crack pipes on me so that if I needed to tell a judge that there would be some record even if I were imprisoned. But nothing has ever become of it since.

I could understand if there were two cops that decided to plant a crack pipe on me and try to scare the shit out of me, but they have six policemen and women, all agreeing that this stuff was found in my pockets…that really scares me. Something is wrong. They are either afraid not to go along with each other or they are all corrupt or having fun with these games. I have learned my rights. I know what I am required to do and what I am not required to do when a policeman asks me. I do not small talk with them. I do not even say hi to them anymore because I lost all my respect for them. And I do not know how long it will take to get that respect back. Or if it will ever come back.

Finally there is the story of Anthony, which illustrates that when a person has an adversarial relationship with the police or officials, the repercussions can be enormous. Anthony's story also demonstrates how a personal catastrophe can tumble an entire family into homelessness.

He began by describing how his childhood had been spent living in many places, including Europe, because of his stepfather's military career. Then he described how his path led to homelessness. Anthony formerly worked in the aerospace industry in California, along with construction jobs, and has an electrical contractor's license. Eventually the job market became tight in Northern California so he moved his family to Idaho and then Texas. The father of six, while in Texas he was severely injured on the job. For two years

Worker's Comp paid him thirteen hundred dollars a month and the family managed to get by. But then more health complications began and on top of those problems, he suffered five heart attacks. At the time of his injury, the family lived in a beautiful five-bedroom ranch home and owned three cars. After the bank foreclosed on his home he bought a mobile home, but the seller was unscrupulous and he lost the mobile home. By then, his two oldest daughters were married. With options running out, he, his wife, and four younger children began camping at various sites. Our interviewer probed into the details of these times.

*Sisters: What about your work at this time? Were you able to find work?*

**Anthony**: There was almost nothing I could do at this point. Like I say, I kept having heart attacks and I was in a real bad state of mind. By then the depression was really bad. Stress, anxiety, I was not dealing. I reached a point I wasn't coping very well at all.

*Sisters: And so what happened at this time? You said you were in and out of places. What do you mean by that?*

**Anthony**: We moved into a little place. Some little dump trailer house. We'd gotten enough money together to move in there. Right after one heart attack, my two boys went to work and they worked for about eight months. And they were able to keep the rent up there.

*Sisters: So tell me what it was like camping with your family and how did they react to that situation?*

**Anthony**: There were a few times it was pretty tough but, by and large, I think if you were actually to ask the kids, they'd tell you it was one of the happiest times of their lives. They loved it. We had a good time. We were very close. We played music. We sang a lot together. We were always together. We did our cooking and were always seeing new places. There was always time to talk about anything. And it was a real growing-closer time for our family. It was good. We've always been very close, but it was cool.

Eventually Anthony, his wife, and his two youngest daughters ended up in Portland and lived with his brother and his family for eight months. When that situation deteriorated, they sent their daughters back to live in Texas with their older sisters and Anthony lived out of his van for eight months while his wife had temporary housing, then he and his wife moved into a tent at Dignity Village.

Anthony has been a musician since he was a teenager, and with options for income dwindling, he began playing music on a street corner in downtown Portland. His earnings from playing varied, but he earned between sixty and one hundred dollars a day. However, his situation again took a turn for the worse when a retired deputy who works as a security officer in downtown Portland informed him that he was shut down because his music was amplified, and warned him that if he continued to play anywhere on the streets of Portland he'd be arrested, fined five hundred dollars, and his equipment would be impounded.

**Anthony**: He said because I'd been too loud, I had violated the noise ordinance so I have now forfeited my right to free speech. I have no right to play anywhere in Portland ever again in my life.

*Sisters: And how did you respond to that?*

**Anthony**: I told him he was crazy, and I got an attorney. I started sitting out there where I always played with my shopping cart with a great big sign that said 'Gagged by the Portland Police.' And I had my guitar in the cart and I had a big bandana tied around the neck of it. I gathered over one thousand signatures and we sent them to Mayor Katz.

*Sisters: And then what happened to that?*

**Anthony**: Well, they got a lot of phone calls. Anyhow, he [the security officer] got chewed out by his supervisor, but he wouldn't back off. The lawyer told me 'From now on don't even mess with him.' So [the security officer] would come up to me and tell me to stop playing, tell me to just shut up, I was supposed to just go away. I'd say, 'I'm not supposed to talk to you.' And I'd just start playing again, and he'd just get beet red. And I'd just ignore him. And he'd start making threats and all of this stuff. It was ridiculous. But he's a very childish man. In fact, he stole two shopping carts from me. They were my own shopping carts too, I had them legally. I had receipts for them.

Anthony went on to explain that he bought damaged shopping carts from a grocery chain, then added a chain and padlock for security. After the officer took his first two carts without returning them to the store or impound room at the police station, he bought another to replace them. He also explained that while he was seeking legal advice and gathering signatures, he didn't work as a musician for two weeks. During that time he estimated that he lost at least five hundred dollars in earnings. Anthony, who carries a copy of the ordinance with him, also explained that the ordinance stipulates that if a citizen is too loud, that the officer's appropriate response is to ask him to lower the volume, not to threaten with arrest and fines. For Anthony, the civilian status of the security officer is less important than the fact that, like a police officer, the security officer wore a uniform and tried to use the law to make Anthony's life difficult.

Like many issues involving those experiencing homelessness, the problems with police relations and the legal system have many layers and complications. But this doesn't mean that the situation is unsolvable or intractable. Perhaps the first step toward solutions is to acknowledge homeless people as citizens first and foremost. And perhaps the heart of the problem lies in this comment from Joseph who at 41 was without a home or job:

**Joseph**: Homelessness is a crime. That is the way they treat you.

> Interviewer's Journal Excerpt:
> *I hate this city sometimes, this country. I want to scream and shake people. I want the truth to come like a burning brand out of my forehead and smite bureaucrats and the public alike. If he dies in the cold, if any of the people I interview do, I don't know how I'll deal with it. I know I can't "save" people, but these people are dying out there, and I feel like I'm one of a few people who even knows they are down there. They tell me things their own families don't know. I have hope, maybe even faith, that this study will make a difference, but it's such an abstract thing. I know how things work. It may make a difference, but so slowly, so little, at least at first. I want radical change. I feel desperate sometimes, like the only person who notices a car accident about to happen.*

Photographer: Jeremy Johnson

# Chapter 5
# Chapter Five

Homelessness is like a cancer they haven't found a cure for yet

## Homeless Veterans

*How far you go in life depends on your being tender with the young, compassionate with the aged, sympathetic with the striving and tolerant of the weak and the strong. Because someday in life you will have been all of these.*

—George Washington Carver

Sisters opened four years after the Vietnam War ended. In the early days, not only were a lot of our customers vets, but volunteers were too.

One man comes to mind. Like lots of guys on the street, Rob was a Marine, which means he signed up, he wasn't drafted. He said what I heard so many Vietnam vets say again and again, that when Democratic Republic of Vietnam President Ho Chi Minh died in 1969, many US soldiers realized they'd been lied to by their government because the whole country of Vietnam, North and South, was crying.

Another customer, David, came back with physical ailments caused by Agent Orange. He, too, was a Marine and signed up thinking he was doing the right thing for his country. I'd find him curled up in a ball in Sisters' doorway in an alcoholic stupor, self-medicating from the oozing sores on top of his head and other pains. He felt angry, hurt, and used. The Veteran's Administration was lying about the consequences of Agent Orange. They just weren't prepared for what veterans came home with: the physical damage, Post-traumatic Stress Disorder, and addictions; and they were in denial. David soon died from complications of Agent Orange. Many other vets "made it" and lived healthy lives, but we didn't see them at Sisters.

One of Sisters' early supporters who taught in high school said there was only one paragraph on the Vietnam War in his students' history books. Some of the veterans at Sisters decided they wanted to do high school presentations. They would work on them together in the evenings in the cafe, discussing what stories they wanted to tell, what ones would be too frightening, and how they wanted to say, "You think hard and long about entering the military under this government." The school visits never panned out, but just getting together was so valuable for them and for me—for their healing and my education.

Those days, those guys…they'd help me clean up the cafe late, as late as eleven o'clock because there was no dishwashing machine; they were really stellar. Sometimes a song would come on the radio, like a Helen Reddy love song, and we'd waltz out in front of the cafe. Can you imagine, waltzing out on the sidewalk? It was an earlier time. And the word went out among the vets that Sisters was a safe haven, and the truth about the war was known in the cafe. You could share your nightmares and people would hear you, and you could heal your nightmares, too.

—Genny

Thomas is a Vietnam-era veteran who has been living on the streets for years.

**Thomas**: I have been homeless for twenty years of my lifetime, most of my adult life, and it is a belittling experience. I was the type that traveled, I would take off and hitchhike and would either sleep under a bridge or find a mission for the night. I have seen a lot of things happen to people, like for instance their eyes yanked out of their head and then stabbed right before my eyes. It is not a very pretty picture. Most of my homelessness, I kept by myself because I didn't want to fit in with the rest, the way of the street. It is not the way I liked, so I try to keep myself clean all the time. I would go from one job to the next. I never could hold a job. I did as much as possible to stay out of any fights and trouble and most of the time I was homeless, I was more or less depressed.

*Sisters: How did you first become homeless?*

**Thomas**: Everything seemed to be okay, then all of a sudden the bottom just dropped down. I have no particular trade to speak of. I have done several different jobs without having an education in that field, but my biggest problem is that I have a temper.

After many problems in the work place, he was classified as disabled by the VA because of his mental health problems. He regularly uses the VA hospital, although he describes it as difficult.

**Thomas**: I have had, like, seven labels put on me and I have been through various types of medications. At one time I was on eight or more, twelve, and I kept talking to the doctors until I have gotten on a medication that is not as bad as it used to be. They've got me on an extra medication because I am having problems sleeping. The Veterans Administration had

Photographer: Melissa Howells

me down for one hundred percent disabled, but they turned around and put down seventy percent disabled because I can walk and talk and move. But I have a delusional disorder.

Things move, color, I have heard a voice once. It was on the outside of my head, not on the inside and I looked everywhere just to make sure that there was nobody around. I hear what I heard. It [his mental illness] could have been since I was a child, but when I went into the marines, they did not pick up on it.

Thomas has hitchhiked often as a means of travel and has seen many parts of the country in the past twenty years.

**Thomas:** There have been times when I've been caught out in the rain, snow, ice, and I'd be out that night because you don't know if you are going to have a place to stay. You do not know what is going to happen, you do not know who you are going to run into when you're hitchhiking, neither. After I left the military, and I was released too soon with an honorable discharge, it had a lot to do with me going into the streets because I was depressed about that. I did not want to be released from the marines, but I was, and the childhood I had was not too great.

He described the toll of chronic homelessness:

**Thomas:** It gets to the point that your mind will not stop, when you are trying to go to sleep. It is running full turn and you are taken…You cannot go to sleep because your mind is still going, racing, racing, racing.

*Sisters: How did your experience with homelessness affect your mind?*

**Thomas:** I believe it made it worse.

*Sisters: How?*

**Thomas:** A lot of them [fellow homeless] never really stayed on the street as long as I had because the same old thing will burn you real quick and it did not help my depression, not one bit. But as far as I could go back and remember I was depressed as a child.

You know, homelessness sucks, homelessness is not meant for anybody. Homelessness is like a cancer they haven't found the cure for yet.

James, 48, a former Vietnam vet, was given a dishonorable discharge. (Eleven percent of homeless vets were awarded dishonorable discharges, thus denying them benefits from the government, no matter their circumstances.) James was introduced in chapter two describing his difficult childhood. In the years previous to our interview he had been living in low-income housing, in missions, under freeway overpasses, outdoors, and from 1993 to 1996 in his car before it was stolen. He also lived for two and a half years in a teepee in Montana before moving to Oregon.

A high school dropout, James has been divorced twice. He's worked in carnivals, cooked in restaurants in a dozen states, and owned a restaurant in Montana near Glacier National Park which failed after a winter of heavy snowfall. His history also points out the everyday vulnerabilities of homeless people—he was robbed twice, mugged three times, and had his car stolen.

Like many young men of that era, he was drafted and then served eighteen months in the 82nd Airborne between 1969 and 1971. In Vietnam he ran into problems when a friend was severely wounded.

**James**: I had about a month to go. We were in Danang and a friend and I were sitting on the bunker when a mortar-rocket attack started. We jumped out, ran around to get in the bunker and one [rocket] landed about ten feet from us. I got cut with some of the shrapnel…and I was holding my friend in my arms calling for a medic. We called him a 'ninety-day wonder,' the second lieutenant…and I picked up my gun and I pointed it at him and said, 'Go get me a medic.' Well, he goes off running and the next day two MPs came and got me and led me to Saigon.

The second lieutenant, the son of a colonel, had run from the scene, never called for a medic, and James' friend died in his arms.

**James**: I spent three months in jail. They shipped me back here and court-martialed me for assaulting a senior officer. No benefits. No nothing.

James has also had problems with alcohol and began drinking at 14. At the time of his interview he'd been sober for seven months, with his health severely affected by years of heavy drinking.

**James**: I admit that alcoholism is the main cause of my homelessness, because I have had opportunity and good paying jobs and then blew it on a drinking binge.

    As long as there is some addiction problem, there is going to be homelessness, you know, those two go hand in hand.

Peter, another Vietnam-era veteran, worked as an accountant before he became homeless. He spent five years in the Navy's Submarine Corps and five in the Merchant Marines. The death of his fiancé and a series of financial calamities forced him to sell his business and home. These events brought on depression for which he's being treated. At the time of our interview he was 48 and living in temporary housing that is part of a job-search program. However, he's finding that being self-employed for years is a barrier to finding work. He's also new to the region and has few contacts because he was born in New York and he lived in Tampa, Florida, for twenty years. After the setbacks already mentioned, and with no family ties, he decided to move to Oregon for a change of scenery.

**Peter**: The day I left Tampa, it was one hundred and ten degrees and I got here that particular night, it was about forty degrees. And Greyhound lost my luggage, lost all my clothes, and all I had was a pair of pants and a T-shirt on. I fell asleep in a doorway.

At the time of the interview there were funding cuts in the job program he was enrolled in, and he was anticipating being evicted and starting over looking for a job. He expressed his frustration with the system and the current job market.

**Peter**: Ten years in the service and ten years in my own business, they are telling me I do not know what I am doing. It is a bit much, don't you think?

When asked for suggestions to change things for homeless people, Peter answered:

**Peter**: It starts with the person if they want to get off the streets. They also have to have the programs or facilities in order to do that. They actually need somebody to help them along and give them a chance with employment. You know change starts with yourself; like anything else, the ultimate decision to do something or not lies with that person. I remember when I was in the service in Vietnam…I and a few other people in the unit came along this opium field and actually we burned it. We had to get out of the area. But the point is, how easy it would have been for us to get on drugs in Vietnam, but [I] chose not to go that particular route.

Peter is unable to receive benefits from the Veteran's Administration because he is not disabled. During the interview it became apparent that he's reeling from the events that have landed him in his present situation.

**Peter**: Because you are always on the move, you are moving here, moving there, people who might be on the street, they just have to keep on moving, so there are no real friendships, so it kind of isolates you.

A recurring theme among our veterans was that they had been introduced to drugs and heavy drinking while in the service. And these habits often started them on a devastating downward spiral that ended with homelessness. Here is a typical exchange with one of our narrators, as the interview opened.

*Sisters: Can you just start by telling me a little about your background with homelessness. How you first became homeless? How old you were? What was the situation in your life?*

**Conrad**: Well for me, it was drugs. And I was introduced to drugs while I was in the military. I was stationed in Long Beach, California. I am from Portland, and it was a kind of a shock to go into the LA area and be from Portland, Oregon. This (LA) is a much bigger city. I got involved with a relationship and we were considering marriage, and when she asked me to leave my career in the military, I told her no, and we broke up. And after that I began to go out with the guys and drink, almost every night. And then slowly I was introduced to other females that were more loose, and hanging out with them to try to ease the pain and slowly got introduced to drugs. And then from there I went downhill real quick.

Not all of our veterans described their war experience, but Todd went into detail about his past, including his childhood. He described himself as having emotional problems since his mother died of cancer when he was 3. After his mother died he was placed in a Catholic orphanage, then foster homes, but began running away at 7, and ended up in juvenile facilities because he was a chronic runaway. The youngest in a family of eight children, he saw his siblings once a year at Christmas.

---

**Todd**: I loved seeing my brothers and sisters once a year. It was the finest part of my year to see them, and it was the hardest part to leave them and go back to the home.

The interviewer asked him about his siblings, and he replied that when he was a child some were married, some were homeless, and some in foster care.

**Todd**: My brother is two years older than me. He was with me [in the orphanage] but then we were separated. After that, as I was really unstable, they said that I was definitely emotionally disturbed. And I was, and still to this day I struggle, but not as bad as when I get hurt inside. I don't know how to deal with it. I just turn into a real mess.

He then went on to discuss his problems with alcohol and how he began drinking and smoking marijuana and cigarettes when he was 8. He was also 8 when he hitchhiked to San Francisco and began selling newspapers to survive. He was picked up and returned to a juvenile facility in Oregon. He dropped out of school at 16 and began working full time, then ended up in the military at 18.

In Vietnam Todd added opium and heroin to his repertoire of drugs. He was running into problems in Vietnam because of his heavy drinking and was switched to a new unit.

**Todd**: We were called the duster crew and were wasting way too much ammo and we were partying hard and drinking hard and we didn't give a damn and we weren't communicating, but we were just wasting all that ammo.

Because he was known for substance abuse he was assigned to a new detail that burned enemy corpses.

**Todd**: When you're really screwed-up they give you a real shitty job and teach you a lesson.

Next, he was beaten badly by a group of fellow soldiers for saving a Major in a fragging incident [fragging refers to using a hand grenade to attack someone on the same side, usually an officer, who is disliked or considered dangerously incompetent] and ended up in the hospital with serious injuries. He described the aftermath of this incident.

**Todd**: I went to get my own M-16, I'm still hurt bad, but I wanted to kill. Just open up the full automatic…I went back to the hospital and this time the sergeants were extremely pissed off because now it turned into a really big mess. So they got rid of me. They sent me to South Vietnam, two hundred miles outside of Saigon. A long way to Saigon and this time I am getting really frustrated and upset and pissed off and feeling like I didn't know what I was gonna do but maybe it's good I didn't. I was so pissed off about what happened 'cause it's twice they said that I almost died when I was in hospital. And then I went to a whorehouse AWOL for two days.

Todd went on to explain that he was almost court-martialed for this AWOL incident until a sergeant approached him and suggested that he become a demolitionist.

**Todd**: I said okay. So they trained me. It was easy, and then I started to smoke the channel away.

*Sisters: What's that?*

**Todd**: Heroin. That's the purest heroin. Channel is white and it's like ninety-eight percent pure. I wasn't shooting it, I was smoking it.

Todd went on to explain that he'd insert heroin into cigarettes in capsules that he'd buy.

**Todd**: Most of the people on that base were smoking pot or channel. We were smoking five or six pounds a day and that's a lot of channel…but we shared with one another. More than half the base was strung out. We had a real big drug problem on that base. Very bad.

Todd described how he'd fake a clean drug test by finding a rare non-drug user to give him a urine sample. However, one time while pulling this ruse he was caught and was placed in a military hospital to detox.

After his military stint, he worked at times, but continued heavy drinking and resumed his drug use, eventually becoming addicted to meth. Todd's background since he left Vietnam is difficult to piece together, because of his drinking and prison stints for various crimes including bank robbery. At times he was able to hold down jobs and even owned a house for a while. After a relationship went sour, he quit working and his housing became unstable.

**Todd**: I just gave up on everything.

When he was interviewed, Todd was sleeping in a dumpster near a loading dock. He spent his days obtaining free meals, visiting friends so he could shower, and hanging out in parks. He no longer drinks because of liver problems, but he still uses drugs.

In this country there is often a romanticized vision of the military, coupled with the knowledge that these Americans make sacrifices that most of us would rather avoid, and that many of them cannot leave behind. The realities of military life, including low pay, physical and psychological trauma, and a culture of addiction are rarely mentioned. Also what goes unspoken is how when a person first slips into addictions, he is sometimes sealing his fate for life.

Jack, who served in the Marine Corps and who has had lifetime struggles with alcohol and drug addiction, was asked if serving in the marines affected his substance abuse.

**Jack**: Yeah, you did while you was in there, drink or use.

*Sisters: So, you are saying it was commonplace?*

**Jack**: Pretty common in the military.

*Sisters: Did you start drinking or using more when you were in the Corps?*

**Jack**: More than I used to. I was just a weekend drinker when I was home. I was drinking every day up there.

Alex described how he went from a fifteen-year relationship and a middle-management career to living on the streets. It happened after he was laid off from his job and his girlfriend turned 40 and began dating a 19-year-old, and asked Alex to move out.

**Alex**: To be dragging down fifty, sixty Gs a year to nothing, living on the street, that is a big jump for somebody mentally. How do you adjust to all these people because some homeless need help really bad. The mentally ill ones, it just does not seem like there is enough room for them in the institutions. They cannot take care of themselves. That is kind of sad to see but there are a lot of homeless vets. I had no idea at the amount of homeless veterans. It is astronomical.

*Sisters: Before you found yourself without stable housing, was your perception of homeless people different?*

**Alex**: When I would drive by the mission I felt, 'God, those poor guys, that's so sad.' We used to give them money and stuff, and then I turned out to be one of those guys. That is a pretty harsh reality, from working for Xerox and General Motors to sleeping under a bridge. That is kind of harsh, but I think I adjusted pretty good.

Alex was also a recovered heroin addict. He explained that he started using drugs when he was in Vietnam and continued when he returned home. He was in the marines from 1974 to 1975.

*Sisters: Is there a connection there?*

**Alex**: Oh yeah, 17-year-old kid, come on, with all those guys coming back.

*Sisters: You were 17 when you started?*

**Alex**: Yeah, in the Marine Corps.

*Sisters: So, did the culture of the Marine Corps affect your drug use?*

**Alex**: Oh absolutely.

*Sisters: How?*

**Alex**: 'Try this, you won't believe what this will do to you.' You are a kid and you have smoked a little weed before and you are like, 'What is that?' 'Oh, this is opium, man.' 'What's opium?' I did not even know what it was at first, I knew what heroin was but I did not know what real opium was, that is, that heroin is, through a process, extracted from opium. These guys were all addicts already, so walking into that was a lot of peer pressure to do what everybody else was doing, to be one of the guys.

*Sisters: They are handing it to you and saying, 'Hey, we're marines.'*

**Alex:** They are all doing it. 'Come on kid,' they always called me kid. I was in at the [two hundreth] anniversary of the Marine Corps. I was the youngest marine in the country and they were going to send me to Washington in dress blues, go through this parade but I was too fucked up and then finally I didn't do it.

*Sisters: You were too high to go?*

**Alex:** Yeah. I had my dress blues. They were going to fly me on a military plane and my commander looked at me and he said, 'No way, take this guy back to the barracks will you?

*Sisters: So, they were going to honor you as the youngest marine?*

**Alex:** Too bad, instead they took the second youngest. I do not know where he came from.

Our interviewer asked him what boot camp was like.

**Alex:** Was real typical, boot camp was not as bad as I thought it would be. But after I got out, I ran into a lot of abusers. Mentally, physically, these guys were real strange, like warmongers. I mean they wanted to hurt people, some of those guys were real twisted.

*Sisters: Are you talking about your superiors?*

**Alex:** No, just guys…some of those guys came back and they were pretty bad off.

*Sisters: Are you saying the most difficult part of your service was the other soldiers in some ways?*

**Alex:** They were roommates. There were four of us in this one room and they were all strung out. And, I do not know, one day I tried it and, like they say about all heroin addicts, when your brain gets that first one it just says, 'You're home, it's just where you wanna be.' It is really like a warm feeling and nothing bothers you then, you can just kind of let everything go, emotional, physical stress, everything.

*Sisters: How long did it work?*

**Alex:** Till I got addicted.

Alex used heroin for about twenty five years, but is now clean and sober.

Simon spent three years in the army and has been homeless since 1993 when he quit a job to enter into a recovery program. His parents divorced when he was 5 and he lived with his father who was also in the army.

**Simon:** I like to say, I was born in Germany, brought up in New York, bred in the Carolinas, and spent a whole hell of a lot of time in Oklahoma. I went to about four elementary schools, two junior highs and two high schools. The hardest part was friends. Eventually I became a very big loner, liked being more to myself than anything else.

Simon was staying with a friend when we talked with him, and was on a waiting list for a bed in a shelter. Since he'd existed on the fringes of society for years, he had a number of ideas for improving conditions for the homeless.

**Simon**: I think that if everybody looked at the reasons why people are homeless, if everybody worked together, the homeless people working with the person that has a home, the organizations that work with them; if they all work together as one body, then maybe something could happen. Unfortunately, until we become a world like what we see on *Star Trek*, homelessness is not going to go away.

Ryan was 35 when we met him and he explained during his interview that he's not considered a veteran by the Veteran's Administration because he's a reservist, having served in the Reserves from 1984 to 1986. He described sleeping outdoors in Portland.

**Ryan**: Oh! It is cold, it is miserable, you know, you freeze to death, and there are only a few places you can go where the police do not really harass you about where you are sleeping. And those are places, normally, where there is a lot of wind, and if you do not have something over your head it is going to be a rough night for you. And walking pneumonia is not an idea of mine as a fun time.

The father of two, he's been unable to find work.

**Ryan**: I am willing and able to work, so that is a big plus. If you want a job, I think you can find one. You know it's just a matter of being able to present yourself to an employer and looking halfway decent. They are not just going to hire anybody that looks all scruffed up. I have always had a job all my life, worked since I was old enough to work.

During his interview, his mood swung between optimism and despair.

**Ryan**: Mentally it is stressful, it is just a burden on you. You do not see the light at the end of the tunnel. I keep bumping my head on all these walls and it just gets so discouraging that you just do not look any more. It just gets to that point. But I am not going to give up…I am just going to go with the flow; whatever happens, happens for the better.

If I had a roof over my head and a place I could shower, I think I could become a productive member of a society again. It is a matter of just having a place to lay down at the end of the day.

Benjamin was one of our youngest veterans at 34. A former Eagle Scout who earned thirty-five badges, he had received a medical discharge from the Navy after serving on submarines. His story seems to especially reflect the tragedy of homelessness. He had been homeless for six months, was unemployed and looking for work when we met him and explained that his discharge was for being overweight. He was asked if this was his first time being homeless.

**Benjamin**: Actually this is the second experience I've been homeless. I was homeless two winters ago back in the winter of '01. After that I was able to get some employment briefly and moved home with my parents. I stayed with the parents a year or so, and they came down with a financial issue; I was unemployed, they live on a fixed income. So, I leave my stuff there, I stay on the street, I go visit them when I can.

Later in the session he was asked what could be done about the problems of homelessness.

**Benjamin**: Being a military vet, I'm really discouraged that the federal government hasn't gotten involved with more programs to help military vets. If it be buying a building, or programs to educate. There are no programs for homeless people. They say there are no funds available. Well, stop buying missiles and bombs and start buying buildings and educational programs for your vets so we don't have to be homeless. Cure the problem, just don't throw a bandage on it.

*Sisters: What kind of specific help would help you?*

**Benjamin**: If I had a place to stay, and didn't have to worry about being prosecuted for illegal camping or something like that. Being harassed is wearing me thin.

*Sisters: How long has that been bad for you?*

**Benjamin**: The whole time of the homeless experience.

*Sisters: Have the police been courteous with you?*

**Benjamin**: Only after they realize that I am not breaking the law and know who I am as far as my military experience. When they put the two together that I have no criminal record and that I'm a veteran they become respectful. Then I become Sir instead of Homeless Tramp.

*Sisters: Have you had hassles with anyone else on the streets?*

**Benjamin**: No. I'm a three-hundred-pound man. My physical demeanor speaks loudly so I don't really have to.

*Sisters: How tall are you?*

**Benjamin**: I'm six foot. I let my size do the speaking for me. I haven't really been put in a situation where I have to feel violent. I was violent in my younger years. But now I'm 34 and I realize that some things need to just be let go.

*Sisters: Have there been other times when you've been harassed by police?*

**Benjamin**: Yeah. They always tell you that you are illegally camping. They threaten to write you a five hundred dollar ticket. I always camp with other people.

*Sisters: Under a highway or something?*

---

**Benjamin:** Under an overpass when it rains. When it doesn't rain, we try not to camp under an overpass. It's hard when it's raining and they make you leave.

*Sisters: What do you do then?*

**Benjamin:** What can you do? You go out and get wet. If an officer tells you to do something, you do it, but you do what you can to avoid them. You try to lay low, because you can't win. You try to stay a step ahead of them.

Later the conversation turned to individual rights and responsibilities.

**Benjamin:** I feel as though it's not only a right but a responsibility to vote. I feel voiceless, speechless and powerless right now as a result of this homeless experience, frankly. It feels like after you're homeless, and the police see you, you become a target. People in society today demand that you have money in your pocket; if you don't, you are prosecuted as a criminal. As such, the business owners and homeowners have gotten together with the police and they want homeless people to move on.

He was asked how the police singled him out.

**Benjamin:** They stop because of where I'm camping or squatting. They will wake you up in the middle of the night and ask you to move. One time I asked, 'Did you stop and hassle me just because I'm homeless, or because I'm breaking the law?' It really makes you stop and think. It really makes you feel bad. I'm a high school graduate; I'm an Eagle Scout and a military veteran. I feel as though I'm a class A citizen but I've been treated like dirt because I'm down on my luck. It's very hard to climb out of a homelessness situation when you smell bad or look dirty. I'm lucky I have the resource to go to my parents.

He went on to describe how he cleaned himself up weekly at his parent's house and also uses the facilities at the Rescue Mission. He added that he camped with a group.

**Benjamin:** You find a group of people you trust, which is hard. You hang out, watch each other's backs.

*Sisters: How do you find people you can trust?*

**Benjamin:** In my 34 years, I think I'm a good judge of character. Being in the military, my life may depend on it.

Geoffrey came from a military family, as his father made a career in the Air Force. The family lived in many places, including Germany. Before moving to Portland he'd lived in Los Alamos and made a living as a computer technician and programmer. He has worked at various companies in Portland and also as an independent contractor.

**Geoffrey:** It's tough being independent because it's feast or famine. Because when you're in between jobs you've got no money at all, but when you've got a job, you're like in seventh heaven. At the same time, the alcoholism was creeping up on me where I got more and more into a cycle of work like mad, get a big stash of money, party my brains out, and then go back to work when the money's out. But, the problem is the damage built over the years until it got harder and harder to go get a job. I was gradually getting sicker and sicker until I was too sick to even bother looking for more work and that's when everything fell apart. I got behind on the rent, got evicted. And, welcome to the streets.

If there was a silver lining in his situation, when Geoffrey visited a medical clinic, a doctor diagnosed him with liver damage and he quit drinking. He has been able to mostly stay in shelters because of his veteran's status and because he's in a recovery program. When talking about the special services available to homeless veterans, he couched his explanation with a bit of gallows humor.

**Geoffrey**: As a matter of fact you get so many advantages it almost feels like you're cheating or something. At TPI (Transition Projects, Inc., a social service agency that offers case management, shelter, and transitional housing) they have two waiting lists: the veterans, and the ordinary scum. They do take good care of their homeless vets. It's wacky, it's weird. That isn't what the recruiter promised me. He promised me college, a house, and the GI bill. He didn't tell me that you do get bed preference in the homeless shelter.

Bernie, 55, was a native of Arkansas, a father of four grown children, and was also a Vietnam-era veteran who described how discouraged he was with trying to find a job after he was released from prison. He'd been homeless previously in 1988 and during that time went through drug and alcohol rehabilitation. When he had been applying for work, he'd been revealing his medical history, which was another barrier to finding work.

*Sisters: Did they give you reasons why they can't hire you?*

**Bernie**: No. I mean, it's enough to depress you. You know, I'm suffering with clinical depression and Post-traumatic Stress now and I'm under a lot of medication, you know, but the medication is only one solution. It's not the main one. It's not going to help me get employment. 'Cause I tell the employer that I'm taking medication for depression and Post-traumatic Stress and then they're gonna say, 'Now wait a minute, that's a time bomb just ticking right there. If we hire him in here and say the wrong thing, he's liable to go off.'

*Sisters: Tell me about Post-traumatic Stress Disorder.*

**Bernie**: What I'm suffering from is when I was overseas in Vietnam. I was over there in 1965 till '67 and I worked on aircraft. Being an aircraft mechanic, repairing an aircraft and then putting it back in service is a lot more stressful, I feel, or equal to those men that was out in the field because there's eight to ten people's lives you hold in your hand. And you stand more of a risk of dying falling out of aircraft if it quit working than you would in the bushes shooting at another person. So, the responsibility was on me because I was the senior repairman so everything I signed off had to be okay. And when you lay down at night you know you just got through repairing a couple of helicopters and they're getting ready to take out on a rescue mission or on an assault mission and the thing falls out of the air. The government is going to find me and they're going to give me a court marshal and I'm going to go to prison for the rest of my life.

*Sisters: Has that ever happened?*

**Bernie**: Not to me it hasn't. I made sure it didn't. I took my job very serious, and then I had a lot of love and compassion for my fellow soldiers there, too. I wanted them to come back. I never wanted anybody to get hurt, you know.

Like a number of our narrators, Bernie is trying to obtain a disability status from the VA and the Social Security Administration. He reflected bitterly on this process.

**Bernie**: I served my country, you know, honorably, and then to come out and they just totally neglect me. It can add to the depression. The anxiety and the stress that comes behind that right there, you know, you're fighting. You're fighting an endless battle and one you know over a long period of time you're never going to win it…I put my life on the line so they wouldn't have to worry about it back here.

But, my main concern now is not so much for myself but it's for those people that's out here. I know a lot of them is just not able to do anything for themselves. Like I say, I have a lot of medical problems, too, but I consider myself being blessed compared to some of them out here. Some of them out here is still pushing shopping carts and sleeping on the sidewalk. Where they going to sleep if you don't give them no place to stay? You know, it's really sad that the United States, probably one of the richest countries in the world, has the most highest population of unemployment, homeless people, but yet we send billions and billions of dollars overseas to aid other people. Yet they won't take care of their own.

While some of the vets we interviewed were in recovery, our sampling of narrators proves that a substantial proportion of them are still struggling with drug and alcohol abuse. Jordon began his interview by explaining that after his return from Desert Storm he went on a year-and–a-half-long "hero party."

**Jordon**: I maintained being married for about four years but right after that, about 1995, I had…some habits that were so bad I could not hold on to a job, I could not even think straight and so that has made the last six or seven years really…I have been all over the place, all over the country, one coast to the other, just doing odd work here and there just to basically make enough money to feed myself and live wherever I could.

Jordon, who described himself as an alcoholic, was discharged for substance abuse, having acquired his drinking habits while serving in the marines, and stationed in San Diego before shipping out to the Gulf War and Panama.

*Sisters: Were you with other men who were alcoholics?*

**Jordon**: Yeah, eighty percent of the military, especially the Marine Corps is alcoholic. You give all these kids free room and board, kind of a big fat paycheck, nothing to do…I was in San Diego at the time and it was nothing but a twenty- or thirty-minute trip into Tijuana where it was legal and we just tore hell out of that town.

*Sisters: So, you were in Iraq and Panama and then in California?*

**Jordon**: Yes.

*Sisters: How did all those men maintain while drinking so much?*

**Jordon**: A lot of them do not. The Marine Corps runs the highest alcoholism and domestic violence numbers in all the branches of the service. A lot of violent marines, they really do not handle it. You basically just do it [drink heavily] till you run yourself either into death or get out.

*Sisters: Do you think it is the culture or the stress or what?*

**Jordon**: The Marine Corps has an image, you know, we are the baddest of the bad and we live by a code that basically empowers us to do what we want and nobody is going to touch us. That has its good points but then it turns around and bites you too.

Jordon also talked about the psychological problems he developed because he killed while serving.

**Jordon**: There are certain physical things that happen. Your heartbeat accelerates, you experience an endorphin rush, and the first time I had to do it [was] in Panama. Then this partly led up to my dismissal. I liked it, you know, I have always been a hunter. There is a rush, it goes any time you are putting an animal down, there is a rush that you get, but I really liked killing the enemy. So by the time Panama was over and we found out months later we were going to do it again in Iraq, I was maybe a little too excited about it. Now, they can train you and tell you what it is going to be like all they want, but they cannot describe the way it actually feels. And the first time I did it I got sick in my stomach right there in the jungle. But after that it was different, it scared me. It scared me, the fact that I enjoyed it, and that really led to a lot of my use.

*Sisters: To your alcohol use?*

**Jordon**: When I came back I drank excessively heavy because I automatically thought something was wrong with me. I should not have enjoyed doing it. There is something sick and twisted and all that, and I still feel that way. Ever since then I have never physically touched anybody again, not even in a fight because I know I have the training and the capability to slit them open and let them die right there on the sidewalk. I will run from that scenario if I have to.

*Sisters: Was there any counseling after that or was there any care and were you able to talk to anybody about feeling sick and wrong?*

**Jordon**: I never said a word. By the time my COs (Commanding Officers) and XOs (Executive Officers) knew, they were all veterans from the jungle and they knew that you get a certain look about you, you get a certain look in your eyes. They call it the *thousand-yard stare*, and it is just where you are actually looking through people…They [commanders] are very good, they know that look. Right after the Gulf, it was such a one-sided victory that the government almost instantly decided, we can let go of at least almost half of our military service…I do not know, I still get all sketchy talking about it sometimes.

He went on to discuss the Marine culture and how it influences young people.

**Jordon**: It [would] be different if you were in the Air Force or something where there is not as much emphasis on honor and control and ability. But that is how the Marine Corps is. You come right out of boot camp, the most dangerous thing I have ever seen in the world is an 18-year-old brand-new marine because right there, as you are bullet-proofed nothing can stop you. They have you so brainwashed; after all, they have been doing it for over one hundred and fifty years, they know what they are doing. They know how to brainwash somebody, I mean, no different than Jones [Jim Jones and People's Temple cult].

*Sisters: Do you think that was true with you?*

**Jordon**: Oh! I guess you could say I was born for it. I fit so into it [the marines' culture] it just became my soul."

---

Interviewer's Journal Excerpt:

*My first interview told me when we were introducing ourselves (he was a walk-in appointment) that he was not homeless, he was just traveling. What he told me, actually, was that his parents were professionals, his family has money, he was raised well-to-do, and he was just traveling. But I could see that his face was tan, and his pack was huge and heavy, and here he was to be interviewed by a project that interviews homeless people. So, before we even started I had to verify that he was homeless by our definition, at least. To do so, I asked him if he had a home to live in, or the money to obtain a place to live, when he was done traveling, and he said no. So, for our study I told him, he was homeless enough.*

*It turns out that he had gone to jail for drug possession and thus lost his housing, tried to stay with family members (which did not work out), couch surfed with friends for months,*

---

and wound up deciding to ride a boxcar out of town to escape the drug scene there. This is a not dissimilar story to many other people I have talked to that do identify as homeless. I think what sets him apart in his mind is his large bank of job skills and ability to make good money, and the fact that he had his own business, house, and lots of money shortly before he became homeless. It was also his first time homeless.

What was interesting is that later on he brought up people who won't admit to being homeless. I gently reminded him that he himself had at first introduced himself as traveling, and asked about the distinction. Without directly referring to himself, he said that people don't want to be labeled as homeless, so they say they are traveling. I see that a lot; once people sit down and start talking to me, they realize that they have been homeless, at least according to our definition, more than they thought.

My second interview is a good example of this. I saw this person, an artist and an acquaintance of mine, at an art show last week, and got to talking to him about my new job. When he said he had just lost his place to live recently and was "crashing" in his mom's basement, I said he should come over and let me interview him. "I haven't really been homeless," he said. His friend who was standing nearby said, "What do you mean? When we lived at __ ____ we always had to hide our mattresses and stuff when the landlord came by, remember? He didn't know we were living there." "Oh, yeah," he said. And we booked the interview. So I remembered that conversation, and today I asked him, three quarters of the way through the interview, "How long has it been since you had stable housing, where you could call it your own and not worry about being caught living there or kicked out?" and he said "All my life—not since I moved out of my mom's house to go to college." It turns out he has been living illegally in art studios, etc., for the last twelve years! And this is a person who originally said he was never homeless.

So, it is important not only that I explain our definition of homelessness, but continue to define it throughout the interview and continue to probe about living situations. For instance, if someone says, "I was homeless and sleeping on the streets for about six months, and before that I was living at my sister's for about two years," then I need to follow up on that and ask about what it was like living at her sister's: "Did you sleep on the couch or have a room? Was it your mailing address? Were you welcome there? Were you able to stay consistently there for that nine months?" Because she may not identify it as homeless, and if you don't probe further, you won't learn that no, she was not welcome there, she slept on the couch, she couldn't receive mail there, and had to leave every time her sister's asshole of a husband came home. And that is not stable housing, and therefore, is homeless for the purposes of our study. So, without the probing follow-up questions, instead of identifying a two-and-a-half-year-long episode of homelessness for what it truly was, I would have only caught the six months she initially identified. And that's not getting the full story!

Photographer: Brynne Athens

Photographer: Jeremy Johnson

# Chapter 6

*It is very, very scary out there*

## Dangers and Violence in Street Life

---

*Bad is never good until worse happens.*

—Danish proverb

Since the first day the cafe was open, it became clear how vulnerable women on the street are, 24/7. Once in the early days, a woman came in hungry and I sat and talked to her. She told me she was turning tricks because she couldn't find work anywhere else. I served her a meal. Then the man who was pimping her came in and stood over her table and told her to leave. I introduced myself to him and said, "You can't sit with her, she gets to eat in peace. You are welcome to stay and eat over here." He came and sat down at the counter, and I got him some coffee, then he took two sips and left. Let me tell you, that story "walked" on the street so fast! The word was, "Something different goes on in that place!" For one moment that woman had some solace, a glimpse that she was more than just the tricks she had to turn.

And not just women…Years ago I interviewed customers about what nonviolence at Sisters meant to them. And every man said, "There's the streets and then there's Sisters. On the streets, I have to have eyes in back of my head because someone could have a knife. It's me or the other guy, always." There's a reason the idiom *what goes around comes around* is alive and well on the streets in Old Town. Is there a culture of violence on the streets? Actually, I'd say there's a culture of homelessness, and violence is a part of it.

How do people deal with moving off the streets and back into mainstream society? They transform. It's excruciatingly difficult and painful to cohabitate with violence on the street, and once offered an alternative, people rise to the occasion.

—Genny

**Darryl**: I am just scared, pretty scared.

Our narrators expressed concern that policymakers and the public view them as a nuisance, not as people who live in dangerous, life-threatening circumstances. Mike, who is 44, talked about the people he saw living on the streets.

**Mike**: Only the strong survive, a lot of the weak shall perish. A lot of them [people experiencing homelessness] are not bad people, it is just that sometimes mentally and emotionally, sometimes physically, they are not strong enough to endure what needs to be endured down there, to pull themselves up. Because it is a job being homeless. It is a job…

You know a lot of them have died. I will always say that if only they would have had a place to stay in a stable environment, they might be here today. Who knows? But I know some of them, and some of them died from pneumonia. Some of them died from hypothermia and stuff like that. The immediate cause of death is homelessness because if they had a place they would not have frozen to death out there.

*Sisters: So people are dying from homelessness?*

**Mike**: Dying, just literally dying. Too cold, laying down and dying. Dying from exposure and things like that. Just dying because when you are older, weak, and sickly in the winter, you lay down on the cold ground in winter. You are risking not waking up every night you lay on the sidewalk, or on cardboard, or under that bridge. They are literally dying just because they did not have shelter from the elements. That is sad. In America too. America is in trouble.

Howard is a homeless veteran who served during the Vietnam War, has had problems with substance abuse, and makes money going door to door washing windows and doing yard work. He described how he is surprised by the increasing number of homeless people he sees in Portland.

**Howard**: There are so many couples out there, or if not couples, there are, you know, males or females that have worked all their life and just recently lost their apartment or their house. And I have talked to them, and every week it seems like there is somebody new that has just recently become homeless, and it's just, it's terrible, because this is bad for the whole country. People that you never expect [to be homeless]…these people have never been homeless and now they are homeless, and my heart can't help but go out because it's ugly out there, it really is.

*Sisters: Ugly what way? I mean what happens to people around homelessness?*

**Howard**: Well, you got always the fear factor of the evils that lie out there and there're lots of them.

*Sisters: Like what?*

**Howard**: There're a lot of people out there that like to prey on homeless people.

*Sisters: Have you been preyed on?*

**Howard**: Violently? Yes. I have had the daylights kicked out of me.

*Sisters: This is here in Portland?*

**Howard**: Yes, here in Portland. You bet. Once it was by a group of, probably 16- to 18-year-old kids, a group of five kids, and there was me and another guy and we had no defense. We couldn't do anything. These were youngsters that were pretty healthy and they headed out for us because we were homeless. We were street tramps. We were walking alone and had taken a shopping cart.

*Sisters: What time of the day?*

**Howard**: It was later in the evening; I would say probably around eight o'clock in the evening both incidents occurred, and on a weekend. One was up in Howard district in northeast Portland, and the other time was downtown, on the northwest side of town. And both times I had a shopping cart. The one time I was by myself, but the first time there was myself and another guy. And the second time was what I call skinheads and they, they just beat me so I had to go to the hospital. I had my eye swell shut so badly that the eye doctor couldn't even open it up. I had to go back couple of days later.

*Sisters: Did they have weapons?*

**Howard**: They had, like, boards…two-by-fours I guess. I don't know what they were. I can't remember whether they were actually machine tools or what. And boots.

*Sisters: Did they kick you?*

**Howard**: Yeah, I mean these guys, like once I was down, they just didn't stop, and I actually feared for my life. In both groups, coincidentally, there were about five guys in each group. And the second time around, I really did actually think I was going, I was going to die.

*Sisters: This was the skinhead group?*

**Howard**: They were in their late teens or already 20 and, you know, just had shaved heads. And they had thick boots and their pants tucked into their boots. I had heard about them, and, you know, I had seen them run around, but I never encountered them before. Whatever you want to call these guys, because, you know, we had done nothing to them. I had never done anything to them, and these guys were just, were just punks that hurt people. I mean these guys were nuts.

*Sisters: Were you able to report it or anything like that or have you seen them again?*

**Howard**: No, I never saw them again.

He then went on to discuss this particular peril of living on the streets and said he knew of at least one homeless person who had been killed by a gang of skinheads. He described how another homeless vet was attacked by skinheads with baseball bats and managed to pull out his own weapon and chase them off. Howard also explained that skinheads tend to visit sites where the homeless live under bridges and freeway passes, and that some of the gangs that prey on the homeless are as young as 15 or 16.

Glen, too, described dangers he'd witnessed. Glen had been homeless on and off for years and was dreading being homeless again. He explained that he had lived for four years in an abandoned building that was crawling with roaches and now tried to stay in shelters whenever he could.

**Glen**: I know people that have gotten hit in the head with bats. All kind of stuff is happening out there.

Glen went on to describe a recent incident where a man was walking down the street late at night when he was jumped, beaten, and had his wallet stolen.

**Glen**: Guy stayed on the ground for a while, then he got up and walked off. That is the kind of stuff that makes you not want to be downtown sleeping around, because anybody could think that you have something and do the same thing to you, even if you might not have anything. They might have thought they have seen a lot of money or something that you had, but you only had a few dollars and that could take your life away.

## Victimization on the Street

People living on the street do not have the benefit of a locked door or access to a safe place; this combined with a lack of credibility with police and stereotypes against them can make daily life very dangerous. The National Coalition for the Homeless (NCH) annually studies hate crimes against people experiencing homelessness. From 1999–2004, including the period of Sisters' study, they "tracked [...] a disturbing increase in crimes targeting homeless people." Their report, *Violence and Death on Main Street USA: A Report on Hate Crimes and Violence Against People Experiencing Homelessness in 2004*, was based on data from news reports, advocates, victims' accounts, and homeless shelters. They report:

- "The number of homeless deaths has risen by 67% since 2002."
- "The number of non-lethal attacks against homeless people has risen by 281% since 2002."
- "These crimes occurred in 140 cities."
- "These crimes occurred in 39 states."
- "Age [...] of the accused/convicted ranged from 11–65."
- "Age [...] of the victims ranged from 4 Months old to 74 years."

(http://www.nationalhomeless.org/hatecrimes/pressrelease.html)

NCH reports that this violence has increased since the time of Sisters' study. In February 2007 NCH released an updated report. Attacks in 2006, included assaults, burnings, rape, and 20 fatalities. A number of attacks were by teens and young adults based on 'boredom.' Currently under federal law, housing status is not considered as a potential motivation for a hate crime.

Glen also explained that although he witnessed the mugging, he didn't dare help the man because then he might also be endangered because the mugger might "end up in the same shelter I am in one night."

Our interviewer asked Gary what problems, besides being arrested for loitering, do people on the streets face.

**Gary**: A lot of violence. A lot of drugs. A lot of guns, shootings. The whole time I've been homeless in Portland, I've seen a lot of shootings; people get killed or beat up. It's terrible.

*Sisters: Have you been a victim of violence on the street?*

**Gary**: Oh yeah.

*Sisters: Could you talk about that?*

**Gary**: I've been mugged, beat up, hit on, stabbed. I've been shot at; I've been in altercations with people on drugs. There for a while, it seemed to all stop, and things were getting better. I was working for a temp service but got laid off and got homeless again. Then I was staying with a friend of mine, went out with another person and had some beer and got intoxicated, went to a friend's house and a fight broke out; I was attacked by five people. When they attacked me, it was in the street, so I had three people in front of me and two people behind me and then they all attacked me. When they attacked me, I got thrown down on the ground and I had lumbar damage. I was on heavy pain medication and antibiotics.

He explained that although his injuries took nine months to heal, he still has relapses of pain and sometimes needs medication. He disliked the pain medication saying it made him feel "like a walking zombie."

**Gary**: I don't take drugs or anything, but after taking these prescribed medications from the doctor, I felt addicted. I almost got myself addicted to painkillers.

Douglas found street smarts and friends necessary. Douglas, 48, grew up in Pennsylvania but ran away from home as a teen and ended up in Washington, D.C. He had been living in Portland for thirty years and had been evicted by an unscrupulous apartment manager a year and a half before our interview, had undergone six surgeries, and suffered from cancer of the pancreas. He described how when he was evicted, he had nowhere to go and was still having health problems.

*Sisters: Were you in a wheelchair when you were on the street?*

**Douglas**: Yeah. For about three months and then they put me into the hospital and did another surgery on me. They fused my ankle together, and I started to walk without the wheelchair because I had no choice, really. He [my doctor] didn't want me to, but if you don't have a place to go, you really don't have a choice.

*Sisters: And how did being in a homeless situation affect your health and your recovery from the surgery?*

**Douglas**: It ruined my ankle to the point where they had to do more surgeries on me and put a plate and pins in. And then at one point they said I was on so much medication that the next step would be amputation and prosthesis, and I wouldn't let them do that. I just said don't give me no more pain pills. And I believe in God and I've been walking ever since. But I wasn't going to let them cut off my ankle. I wasn't going to let them do it.

He explained that after becoming homeless, he found an abandoned warehouse to sleep in with a number of other homeless people, then some of their extensive drug use led to it being boarded up by the police. Douglas elaborated on his survival techniques for living in the streets:

**Douglas**: You couldn't trust anybody to not touch it [your belongings] or take them. As far as that goes, I had a friend that we'd sleep next to each other and keep an eye on each other's stuff because if you were asleep and they really wanted to get your stuff, they'd get your stuff. So you don't get dumb and pull out any kind of money, if you happen to have money, or let people know that you have anything that you don't want taken away from you. You've got to be a little bit smarter than that or they'll take it away if they're bigger than you.

After the warehouse was shut down, he began sleeping outdoors in parks and under bridges, again accompanied by a friend.

*Sisters: And how come you want to have a friend with you?*

**Douglas**: For protection. Because you don't want to be alone. Even if you ain't got nothing, they don't know that, so people beat you up first and then see what you got.

*Sisters: Has that ever happened to you?*

**Douglas**: Yeah. Not here. Washington, D.C., it did once. I was pretty young then, just a kid.

Sammy was 34 at the time of his interview and admitted to a history of crime that included shoplifting and drug dealing. He had been living in Portland for nine years. A native of California, he became homeless when his father kicked him out of the house the day his mother died. He had been homeless on and off in the LA area when he met a young woman from Portland. He traveled by Greyhound to Portland to join her, but when he arrived in the evening, she wasn't there to meet him. Our interviewer asked him what that night was like.

**Sammy**: She was supposed to be there, be at the Greyhound station, and we were supposed to have a place to stay, and I got here and she wasn't there and I had no place to stay so I went to the bathroom and I started crying. I said 'Now what am I going to do? I am in a whole new city and I know nobody and what am I going to do?' and I started crying. So this old guy, he came up to me and he goes, 'You need a cigarette, don't you?' I said yeah. So I started talking to him. And he goes, 'Now don't worry, you just come with me and I'll show you the ropes around here.' So he started taking me to these places. The first place I went was the Blanchet House, 'cause they won't let you sleep more than one night at the Greyhound station. If you don't have a ticket, they boot you out.

*Sisters: But they would let you sleep one night?*

**Sammy**: Yeah, I slept there. I got there at nine and I got kicked out at ten o'clock the next morning, and then I went to Blanchet House for lunch.

*Sisters: And what time did this man find you in the Greyhound station?*

**Sammy**: It was about one o'clock in the morning.

*Sisters: And he was sleeping at the Greyhound station also?*

**Sammy**: Yeah, he stayed there with me; he didn't have to, but he did. You know, I was scared. I didn't know nobody. I was scared.

Sammy described how during his first meal at Blanchet House he found other homeless people to be friendly and helpful.

*Sisters: Did you know the homeless people where you came from—you came from the LA area?*

**Sammy**: Yeah, I had seen homeless people down there and they weren't so friendly; they were mean, evil, weren't nice you know, so it was a totally different world. I mean, it's a fast pace in California compared to Oregon. Oregon is not even up-to-date where California is.

*Sisters: In what ways?*

**Sammy**: Well where I grew up, there were shootings and everything—people stabbing and killing people and people fighting people. Dead bodies in dumpsters. Here you don't hear about those things. I mean, it's very rarely happening here, but everyday you hear about that in California, especially East Los Angeles and Compton. If you were in the gangs or something, then you were just probably put out. It's not good.

Sammy went on to describe an incident that happened to him in LA the first night he was on the streets. He had been sitting on a park bench when a man approached him, demanding drugs or money. When Sammy told him he didn't have anything, he stabbed him in the knee with an ice pick.

*Sisters: This was your first night on the street. Was it dark yet?*

**Sammy**: First night on the streets. It was like two thirty in the morning, and I think, wow, I don't know about the streets but this is really being on the street.

*Sisters: So did you sleep that night?*

**Sammy:** No, I stopped sleeping. I gave up sleeping that night and that's something real. That's why I started doing speed, you know, because I was scared to go to sleep. Yeah. 'Cause I can't sleep in peace after that.

Karen, 41 and a Native American, had a horrific family history that included her father committing suicide and a stepfather who had molested and raped her since she was 5, along with her two sisters and brother. Her mother, an alcoholic, was unaware of the sexual abuse until it was finally discovered when Karen was 15.

Because of her family background, Karen has a special awareness of the dangers that girls and women face, dangers that are especially heightened when women struggle to live without life's necessities and shelter. Our interviewer asked her if she had solutions or saw a need for changes.

**Karen:** They have more men's shelters than they do for women. I think we could use at least one more women's shelter. Because Jean's Place has a long waiting list and Salvation Army, you know, you have to check in by eight thirty and sign up each night. So they need to get another one for the women. And probably one more for the men, too, you know, because I'm still freaked about that Christine Lawson. She was my best friend.

Christine Lawson was found strangled in a doorway.

*Sisters: Do you want to say what happened?*

**Karen:** Well, they found her on 2nd and Couch… Her face was bashed in and she was strangled. She was a prostitute, a crack addict, and a heroin addict, but she was a sweetheart. She'd give you the shirt off her back. And when she found out I was into drugs and prostituting again, she about ripped my head clear off my shoulders. And when I was told what happened to her, I went ballistic. She was a good lady. Women aren't safe, you know. We all try to find a job and we can't, so we turn to hooking. We might have a problem with drugs, so selling your body is easier to do and get the money for that real quick and go get your fix than it is to wait for your paycheck or borrow money from somebody or what have you. It's scary because you don't know who you can trust anymore. Used to be you could look at somebody and know. You could look in their eye and say well, hey, I can trust that person; stay away from that person. Now you can't. And that's really scary. I mean, there's been six girls they found murdered in the last couple of months, you know. Pretty soon it's going to be guys. This is terrifying. And it's the homeless they're preying on, you know. Portland needs to wake up. They need to help these people. Get them off the streets.

Besides facing danger at the hands of others, the temptation of suicide is another danger people who live on the streets must deal with. Karen's traumatic upbringing, a serious car accident, and a destructive marriage contributed to a severe weight problem and then a drug problem. When her weight ballooned to four hundred and five pounds, she tried crack cocaine in a desperate attempt to lose weight.

**Karen**: It helped. Caused me to have a nervous breakdown, too. Caused me to go into prostitution. Tried killing myself a few times over it. Slept in doorways and back of people's trucks, under people's cars to hide. Using those porta-potties.

*Sisters: But you were 33 when you started using other drugs. How did you get the money for it?*

**Karen**: Selling my body.

*Sisters: And that was on the street? You didn't have a place to stay?*

**Karen**: Here and there.

*Sisters: Do you want to talk about that? What it was like?*

**Karen**: It was miserable. It was degrading. All I cared about was getting that next little rock, you know. I went from four hundred and five pounds down to one hundred and sixty. When my mom seen me she was glad I lost weight, but the way I went about it, I looked like I was going to die. I looked so pale. And I'm a big-boned woman anyways, so I looked really…I didn't do it properly and with my epilepsy it was even worse. And she packed me up and took me home. I cleaned up.

Karen explained that she used crack for five years and was clean for three.

**Karen**: Then I came back to Portland, and I was fine until I let somebody come stay in my room one night. They lit up a pipe and there I went.

At the time of our interview, she'd been clean again for thirty-eight days.

**Karen**: I'm doing it because it's for me. You know? I'm 41 years old. And not only that, couple of my friends died. One got murdered. It just was too much and I came to one day, I had my leg over the Burnside Bridge. I was getting ready to jump and somebody had their arm around my waist and they were pulling me for all they were worth. And I was trying to go and they weren't going to let me. And people look at me and they say, 'You don't look like a hooker. You don't look like an addict.' I said, 'Sorry to tell y'all, but guess what?'

When Gena, 22, was interviewed, she was living on the streets with a boyfriend and was on a list for Section 8 housing. She had a small income from SSI because of bipolar disorder and had a 5-year-old daughter who lived with her parents in Vancouver, Washington. She wanted housing so she could live with her daughter again and explained that she would never live on the street with her.

**Gena**: No, because then I will get her taken away from me. I see people out here all the time with children. I am surprised they still got their kids. It is cold out there.

Gena cited family problems for her homelessness. She left home as a teen to live with a sister and her husband for a while, but that situation didn't work out either. She expressed a common trait among the homeless people we interviewed—a fierce independence.

**Gena**: I would rather be here [living on the streets] than there. I do not like fighting with people. If anyone ever tells me to go, I would go. I do not stay around. I will go survive on my own. I do not even go to the shelters over here, I do not. I just sleep in cars and in doorways, buildings, anywhere. Anywhere I could stay out of the rain and stuff, I would find a place, my own little spot.

*Sisters: So you have been doing that since…?*

**Gena**: Summer. In summer, it was cool, but now that it is winter, you cannot really be outside no more, and that is why I am sick. I got a cold.

Many of our narrators preferred to avoid the shelters for various reasons, but a common reason is that the close proximity spreads disease.

**Gena**: Yes, it is scary because somebody coughed in my face down here. I have a cold, though I have a TB card. [To stay in shelters in Portland, Oregon, a person needs to get tested for tuberculosis and carry a card proving they're healthy.]

*Sisters: So, a homeless person coughed in your face down here?*

**Gena**: Yeah and that is scary too. I do not want to get that stuff. I was going to stay up at the Salvation [Army shelter], but I think it was too late because it was like two, three in the morning and what, they wake you up at five? I'd probably then only get to sleep for an hour.

*Sisters: So, where did you go?*

**Gena**: I just walked the streets in Portland all night because I was not trying to go anywhere if they were just going to wake you up in an hour. What is the point?

*Sisters: What is it like living on the streets?*

**Gena**: I am just always jumpy, you know, when I hear a sound because I don't want to die out there, you know, have somebody do something to you while you are sleeping. They can rob you, kill you, whatever they do to people who are sleeping out there. It is scary.

*Sisters: Have you experienced violence on the street?*

**Gena**: I see it every day, because everybody is crazy, or you know, a lot of mental people, because I am mental myself.

*Sisters: Have you ever been on the receiving end of that violence?*

**Gena**: No, I do not go out and look for trouble, no, but I see it everyday. Out in the street, everybody is…they are not happy with themselves, so they got to pick a fight with somebody. Because it is not fun being out here, so you can just imagine how they feel. And then to have somebody get into their business—now, that is why I tend to keep to myself. One time, we were sleeping in the park and these people came up to us and was all like, oh, trying to tell me somebody was going to kick my ass and then I woke my boyfriend up and he had a heart attack.

*Sisters: He got upset?*

**Gena**: Yeah, because I said, 'Are you are going to let somebody do that to me?' And he did not know what was really going on because he was sleeping. It is hard for me to get him up and by that time they were gone, and I do not even know the people.

*Sisters: Have you spent any time on the street without your boyfriend?*

**Gena**: I am always with him. I cannot go anywhere because I would be too afraid to be out there by myself. There is just too much going on. It is scary out there.

Gena went on to explain that another reason she doesn't use shelters is because she would be separated from her boyfriend and that he is in charge of their belongings. She carries things of value in a backpack, including a portable CD player.

*Sisters: What is it like carrying all your valuables with you all the time?*

**Gena**: I do not like carrying stuff. I have spots to put our stuff, but, you know, even when we put our blankets out somebody stole them. We had been stocking them up since summer. We had about thirty blankets, and when it had been raining, we were keeping warm until we went away and left our stuff for a couple of days in our hideout. We came back and they were gone. This is like, 'What are we going to do now?' So, we had to walk around until we found some blankets; it was late at night. We had to stand up there and wait till eleven by the mission. They gave some blankets and then they said they were not giving out none, then we had to go around and find us some blankets. That is nasty too, but it kept us warm for a minute.

*Sisters: Oh! You had to find it from another homeless person?*

**Gena**: Yeah, and I think the lady that we have got some blankets from, I think she has stole our stuff, but I wouldn't say nothing to her because she is like an old crazy lady. I was not trying to get into a fight with her.

Chuck, living on Andrews Air Force Base in Maryland with his parents in the '70s, was kicked out of his house as a teenager because of his homosexuality. As a result, he hitched to New York City and spent his young adult years digging food out of garbage cans on the streets and trading sex for food, a place to sleep, and drugs to numb himself. Chuck avoided social services at first because he was naïve and he had heard from other homeless people that they were dangerous, so he took his chances on the street.

*Sisters: So tell me a little bit about sleeping in doorways in New York City. How safe was that for you?*

**Chuck:** Not very safe. And it was worse in the middle of wintertime. And I was so naïve the first winter that all I had was a jean jacket to keep me warm. I'm surprised that I didn't get, like, frostbitten or anything.

*Sisters: Tell me about a good day and a bad day that you had on the streets in New York City.*

**Chuck:** Oh, a good day is if I could find somebody I could stay over at their house and everything. Even though I had to put out sex for it and everything, it was still a good day 'cause then at least I could, like, wash up and they would give me a clean change of clothing and everything. That was a good day.

*Sisters: And was that with women or with men?*

**Chuck:** Men mostly. And a bad day is when it's freezing cold in the middle of wintertime and you're standing on the street all alone and in your head you're like 'Well, everybody else has got a home and family that cares about them, that they're nice and warm and everything and here I am all by myself, with nobody giving a shit.' That was a bad day.

Chuck talked about the effect that living on the streets and avoiding fights had on his psyche:

**Chuck:** I still have a lot of wild animalism in me from being homeless because when you become homeless you have to basically become a wild animal for survival. You have to hone your instincts almost as close as some wild animal does. It's hell. In a nutshell, it's hell. Because you're always afraid. You're always afraid of everything.

---

Interviewer's Journal Excerpt:

*My interview today was with a woman who has had a very hard life. Instead of crying because of it, like many people do, she laughed sarcastically. I feel kind of cold, and like I can't breathe, like holding in so much pain rubbed off on me somehow in listening to it. I don't know which is worse, this, or being sad with somebody in an interview. The latter is more upsetting immediately, but less upsetting in the long run, perhaps. If we can cry about it and come out laughing at the end, like some of the women I have talked with, I am exhausted, but at least feel human.*

Photographer: Laura Brown

Photographer: Alan Shipley

# Chapter 7

*I am not a lazy person. I have worked all my life.*

## Barriers to Finding Work

*Philanthropy is commendable, but it must not cause the philanthropist to overlook the circumstances of economic injustice which make philanthropy necessary.*
                                                    —Martin Luther King, Jr.

One of the biggest myths is that homeless people don't want to work. I can name on one hand those who have fit that line during the last thirty years. Everyone else just wants the opportunity to earn their own meals. That's why our customers said to Sandy and me when we founded Sisters, "Don't be about free food; do this with dignity—either make it cheap enough that I can pay for it on my income, or give me the chance to work for my meal." We've never had to question the wisdom of why we made that choice. Over and over, people have come to us years later to say "thank you for not robbing me of my dignity."

The desire to work is part of being human. The desire for love and community is part of being human. When you become invisible to mainstream society, the myth is that you stop being human, that you're somehow made up of different stuff. But you're not. Your humanity doesn't go away just because society doesn't see it.

When Sisters first opened, day labor was operated by the state employment office. Now it's run by private corporations. Unlike the state employment office, which was only invested in people finding viable work, the corporations are interested in the profit they can make by sending people out. It's disgraceful.

It also angers me that we don't have enough places that afford people opportunities after they get their lives together. At Sisters we have always said that you get to walk into the cafe with no questions asked. Instead of punishing people, we build relationships and find out the whole story. While people have done some pretty inappropriate things in their lives, all they're saying is, "I'm not proud of what I've done, but I've done my time." They might have a ten-year hole in their job history because of drugs, jail, etc., but they shouldn't be punished twice by being denied work. This is not about feeling sorry for people or being a bleeding-heart liberal. It's about justice and human rights.

—Genny

**Logan**: I have always had a job all my life, worked since I was old enough to work. It's harder to get by nowadays. It seems like when I was younger, I had no problem getting work, never had no problem keeping work. Ever since September 11 it seems like a lot of things have gone awry. The workforce, the wages are going down. The workforce is not what it used to be. It is harder to get into a job.

*Sisters: And you feel like it is a direct result of the 9/11 attacks?*

**Logan**: Exactly, there is no doubt in my mind about it. I have definitely seen it affect what is going on firsthand. I even told [potential employers] I would take half my wage.

When it came to the connection between homelessness and looking for work, all our narrators described that keeping up grooming was essential to obtaining work. Some also talked about how landing a job was impossible when you have bad teeth or missing teeth, or other physical manifestations of homelessness.

**Logan**: I think keep your appearance up. And then actually people have to be motivated to want to go to work. I am a motivated kind of person. I want to work. I don't want to be in a situation where I am not working.

Dale was an ex-marine, and at 43 had been homeless for fifteen years when we interviewed him. He was part of a subculture of hobos who ride the railroads around the country. His lifestyle began when he left Idaho and became homeless after problems with his second wife who was an alcoholic. He was a dog breeder in his former life and since then he'd worked odd jobs and earned enough to get by but not [enough] to end his homelessness. He believed that there was money to be made if you're not too proud, and mentioned that he'd recently made forty-eight dollars in three hours by dumpster diving for aluminum cans. He also sold things he found in dumpsters and garbage cans and worked seasonally on a garbage detail for festivals and events. He said he preferred living on the streets to paying rent and stressed that optimism and a can-do attitude are necessary for survival on the streets.

Dale described how he observed many homeless people falling into their situation through a series of bad choices. He explained he chose this lifestyle.

**Dale:** Mine was planned. I escaped, my great escape.

*Sisters: What do you feel are the factors that have kept you in this experience?*

**Dale:** Seems like every time I try to get back into society I get kicked in the head for it. And renting or whatever, you got some jerk in a position above you that as you are stepping out, all of a sudden he is the nail on the next step that you are going to step on.

He referred to his survival strategies as his hustle and is proud of the energy and enthusiasm he applies to earning money. He also believes opportunity lies ahead for him.

**Dale:** I have got good jobs, big money, it is just…I got to wait for the open door again, the right door to open. And you got to be able to recognize it through patience, a little bit of vision in your head.

*Sisters: [Have you encountered any barriers to finding work?]*

**Dale:** Did you ever go look for a job with a backpack on your back? Boss says, 'What's your address?' [When he discovers the applicant has none]: 'Well, we'll call and let you know.' You are not getting the job when they see you are homeless; you got no telephone, you got a week bed [in a shelter]. If you got an address and someplace to leave your stuff, you can actually wear your best clothes and go there without a backpack on your back and make your best presentation to the person.

*Sisters: And what other solutions do you have for not wearing your backpack all the time?*

**Dale:** Oh, some places like JOIN [a Portland outreach program for homeless individuals and families], they will let you store your stuff, but now they want some of your time for allowing that. You got to work, volunteer so many hours to be able to store your stuff. But those hours you got to volunteer over there are the hours you want to go somewhere else, and there is the damper on that. The bus depot has a trap and you can store your stuff in there daily, three bucks a day.

Steve left his home in Washington state after a dispute with his family and has been homeless on and off since the '80s. He had been living in a friend's apartment for about a year when he was interviewed and often worked for day labor agencies. Like Dale, he believed that there was work available, but it required practical solutions and incentive to find it.

**Steve:** Do not tell me that there are no fucking jobs. I know there are…there have to be. And if there are not, it is because they are going to those who have an education or have the money or have connections or what have you. But it is impossible to find a job when you do not have an address. If you have an address downtown, especially in Old Town, any job you are looking for, you would hear, 'Oh, okay, sure, we'll take an application,' and then it goes in the garbage can. I have seen it happen a number of times. And yes, I have worked in a number of jobs, odd jobs, under-the-table…but when they find out that you are from that class of people [homeless], well, then either they assume that you cannot do it and they let you go, or some convenient excuse comes along.

*Sisters: What obstacles do you have getting a job?*

**Steve**: Besides not having an address? Having no place to sleep, having no place to change clothes, having no laundry. You cannot go to work in the same clothes everyday.

*Sisters: And there are no laundry services for you to access?*

**Steve**: Unless you have money, no. It all boils down to the big M.

*Sisters: So, if you were looking at solutions to ending individual homelessness and ending homelessness in general, what would make a real difference?*

**Steve**: I am not homeless now. But those who are homeless now, I would suggest laundry services, clothing services—and I do not mean clothing from the '20s, I mean, clothing that is appropriate for a job. The Downtown Chapel [of Saint Vincent de Paul Catholic Parish] has good clothing, but the sheer number of people who need clothes is overwhelming sometimes, and Downtown Chapel is about the only place that I know of that has good clothing. Other places have clothing, but you cannot go to work looking like you have stepped out of the '20s. It is just not feasible.

*Sisters: Okay, and you mentioned drop-in centers earlier. Is that something that you believe could help?*

**Steve**: More phone usage, more laundry services, more clothing—appropriate clothing—more showers perhaps. I am no longer in that situation; I do not have to worry about it anymore, but when I did I would have liked to have accessed those services, and I am sure that there are those who need them now.

Frances, 47, is from an upper-middle-class family and grew up in a small town in California. She became pregnant in high school and also started using drugs as a teenager. Her first experience with homelessness happened twenty-five years earlier when she was in her early twenties and her husband fled their home to escape arrest. They traveled in their truck for three months and began to enjoy the lifestyle.

**Frances**: We enjoyed it. I had never been out of the state and we were just driving anywhere. I had seen all the United States and I liked it. And we stopped and we worked for a few days or for many, and it was kind of interesting.

*Sisters: And did you live in your car?*

**Frances**: Or in a hotel if we could afford it. It wasn't what we intended to have, we intended to go to where my husband had family in Oklahoma and kind of situate near them and get a job and housing. But it just didn't end up that way.

*Sisters: Why didn't it end up that way?*

**Frances**: We just got carried away traveling. We were so young and our son was 4 years old and he was gonna start kindergarten the next year, so it was kind of like a last minute thing. And also a bad situation. My husband's dad passed away. But some of the life insurance money was his, and so his mom would send his money to him occasionally. And we still stayed on the road and just traveled and we thought, 'Well we will make it a learning experience for our son,' because we knew we would never have the opportunity to do it again until we retired, probably. So, you know, our son got to see all kinds of things and places.

She explained that they traveled extensively—Yellowstone, Lake Mead, Las Vegas, Reno, the Badlands, Atlantic City, and on to cities on the East Coast including Philadelphia. She explained that besides receiving occasional money from her husband's family, they worked at fairs and carnivals. The family eventually developed a more stable lifestyle and raised their son who married and became a father. Frances has worked as a waitress, housekeeper, painter, cake decorator, and on a road crew.

Six years ago, tragedy struck when her first grandchild drowned at ten months while she was visiting her son's family in Oklahoma. Because she felt partly responsible for the child's death, the trauma and guilt propelled her back into drug use although she'd been clean and sober for years previous to the accident.

When she was interviewed, she and her husband had been homeless for three months and sleeping in separate shelters each night. Their homelessness was directly tied to drug use, and hampered, in her case, by depression and panic attacks and by her husband, a carpenter, having suffered a back injury. They were both on methadone at the time of the interview and trying to get their lives back in order.

**Frances**: We are just tired. I am tired and feeling old. I don't want to hustle, I don't want to do drugs; I want to stay clean. I want a house. We have a cat that we've had for a long time, we got him in a foster home. It's too hard work trying to keep clean, shower, keep clean clothes. Nowhere to go to the bathroom. Thank God for Blanchet House, and the Rescue Mission, and the places that do it, but, you know, your life is governed by their offers, which doesn't leave much time for looking for work or working.

*Sisters: What would make this easier for you?*

**Frances**: Having somewhere to put my belongings for the day and dress appropriately for a job to where you don't go in and fill out an application carrying your belongings. Well, at least we have tried. We haven't gotten called back yet. And just being able to stay clean and presentable enough and have somewhere to keep your things, and have somewhere that you can be when there is nothing to do, or when you don't have appointments. You just kind of feel lost; I mean, we can go to Borders and read, and we go to the library. We've always been library people anyway. I just want to be normal with a roof over my head and enough food for dinner and my kitty and my husband, and that's all I want. It's always what's made me be happy. I don't want anything else. And it seems like there is so much housing, but everything is so slow, it's just so slow, I don't know if it's some red tape or what it is. Everything has become slow.

*Sisters: It takes a long time from when you sign up for something till you actually get it?*

**Frances**: Right. So many times over the years my husband and I have lived good and had money, had things, had a nice house and stuff, and it's just scary how fast you can lose it.

Another issue with our narrators is that if there are jobs available, they are for low wages, which makes ending their cycle of homelessness impossible.

Mack, 54, is a recovering heroin addict who feels shackled by minimum wage:

**Mack**: I don't want to spend the rest of my life at six dollars an hour. I can't do nothing with my life. I'd rather walk around on the streets, eat out here and there and have some time to myself and work a day a week than to get out there and kill myself and have nothing. Worry about losing your job, trying to maintain a roof over your head, from that kind of money? I don't even know how people pay rent for that kind of money. Do you? Six dollars an hour? Unless you live at home with your folks. I'm not really sure my folks are even alive. So, that avenue's over. The best you can do is get one of these agencies to give you low-income housing and have a million rules pounded on you and wonder if you're going to get thrown out. That's probably what's available for you, or you can rent a room somewhere.

*Sisters: And how does that affect your desire to want to go to work, if you're looking at a six- to seven-dollar-an-hour job?[At the time of our study, the minimum wage in Oregon was $6.50 per hour.]*

**Mack**: I'd like to have some goals in life, somewhere you can go forward, you can advance. If you have a real low paying job, more than likely you don't have any opportunity to make any more money. They just got you there because anybody that's hungry will take that spot. There's no room for advancement. There's no knowledge required for the job.

*Sisters: What relationship do you see? Having a six-dollar-an-hour job, how does that relate to homelessness?*

**Mack**: If you want a relationship with a woman you meet, and she says, 'What do you do for a living?' Oh, you know, 'I flip burgers over at McDonalds and I'm 54 years old and that's my career.' I mean you don't seem like a very ambitious person. If you're going to school and you're broke that's one thing. Because you will get somewhere with that or you're being trained. You got some ambition and drive.

*Sisters: And what do you think is the relationship between having a six-dollar-an-hour job and staying homeless?*

**Mack**: I think it makes it really hard to get out of that situation. You have to rely on some kind of assistance to have a place or anything. For instance, when I was doing carpentry work in 1975, you could buy a carton of cigarettes for about three and a half bucks. Cigarettes now cost thirty-five dollars a carton. A pack costs what you got a carton for then. Carpenter's wages were like seven dollars an hour back then. You know carpenters don't make seventy dollars an hour to match the inflation of the cost of living. It's like a general working person now, their buying power is half of what it used to be. It's why you see two people in a family working all the time. It's not the all-American dream—you're buying a new home and you got the car like in the '50s and one person works and the wife stays home. That's not feasible any more. So this homeless thing is just going to get worse unless there are some kind of changes made.

Other narrators expressed similar opinions and pessimism. Buddy, who has lived in other cities besides Portland, was frustrated trying to find work by using job programs created for those experiencing homelessness.

**Buddy**: It is just like a game. The guys that go in, they go through this [the job program], they leave, they go look for work, they cannot find work, there is no work.

If you are training people how to swim, but when they go out there is no water, what was the use of training them how to swim? And that is kind of like how it has been; there is no work.

A number of our narrators had additional problems with being older than typical job seekers. Frank, a 54-year-old army veteran who had been homeless for much of his adult life, had worked chiefly at temporary and part-time jobs. He once owned a landscaping business with his ex-wife but was looking for an office job since he believes he is too old for outdoor work.

**Frank**: I am too old. Nobody wants to hire me, it seems like. I am going to school. I got a three-year soldier's degree as a landscape technician, I got a certificate in computer science.

Ellen, 55, moved to Portland from Wichita, and had lived in many cities since childhood. Her homelessness was precipitated by a divorce and a series of problems including losing custody of her two daughters because they were molested by her boyfriend. She explained that one barrier to finding work was the lack of a day center where homeless people could rest and revive at all hours.

**Ellen:** They would be able to stay in on the hot summer days. They wouldn't have to be out walking the streets. They would have to go out at least three hours a day looking for a job. But, after they get done with this, then they would be able to come in and relax.

*Sisters: Why is that important?*

**Ellen:** Because, a person who has been out all day walking and carrying their junk around with them cannot concentrate on a job or anything else because they are too exhausted. If you have to carry ten pounds on your shoulders all day long, you don't sleep well at night. And if you don't have at least two meals a day, you don't get the vitamins you need. If you don't get the vitamins in the system that you need, you don't sleep at night. If you don't sleep at night, you can't go looking for a job because your mind is not in what you're doing. The vitamins keep your mind so that you can keep focused. Without those vitamins, you cannot focus, and you cannot fill out an application.

She explained that employers can tell if a person is homeless by their appearance, among other things.

**Ellen:** You can tell the difference. Two people go in to apply for a job and person A is just unemployed, but they have a home. They have a place to sleep. They have food. Person B is a homeless person who stays, unfortunately, at the Salvation Army. Person B has had to leave their junk outside the door when they go in to fill out their application, which is the number one thing they got on their mind: is it gonna be there when they come out? Person A has just gone in to fill out the application. Ok, they have probably only been laid off for a month or so. They don't have to worry about it. They've got money. Person B has no money. They're not only thinking, 'What about my stuff? Is it gonna be there?' but also, 'What am I gonna eat? Where am I gonna eat next? Where am I gonna sleep tonight? You know, am I gonna have to sit outside? Can I go in and relax?' When a person goes and applies for a job, he cannot put his best self forward if his best self is packed in a bag.

She returned to the need for building a day facility.

**Ellen:** And that's been my dream is to set up a situation, a program, where these people can come in and put their best self into what they're doing instead of what they've got left. I think that the homeless people, a great number of them out today, are homeless because they're in a situation where they can't fight back. And that's because of the shelter situation. Like I said, even the Salvation Army in Wichita before they got the new program, you could get in during the day. You didn't have to leave during the day. It was out in an area that was in a beautiful area. Peaceful, calm area; even if you were on the outside, there were picnic tables where you could sit. It was a nice place.

Trevor, a welder, was interviewed one month after he'd moved to Portland believing that what he'd learned on the Internet about a building boom going on was true.

*Sisters: You came up here for work and you have been here a month; have you found that work?*

**Trevor**: Actually, I have not been looking for work because I have not found a place over my head. I have been trying to do day labor as much as possible.

*Sisters: And how is that working?*

**Trevor**: Not very successfully because I have gone out a few days a week, but it is like I say, you have to clean up, you have to take showers, so you are only working, like, every other day if you can. So they do not send you out as frequently as they would anybody else because you are not there every day and it really makes it a burden to try even to find temporary work.

Trevor explained that some days he chose to miss work in order to get clean.

**Trevor**: The shower times are horrible. I mean you can take a shower at seven thirty in the morning, but you know what? If you are not at day labor at five thirty in the morning you are not going to go out. I would suggest an evening shower, like seven or something like that or something bright and early in the morning, four o'clock, or four thirty. And I would suggest a storage facility.

   If I had a roof over my head and a place I could shower, I think I could become a productive member of society. It is a matter of just having a place to lay down at the end of the day.

---

Journal Excerpt:
   *He had worked all of his life before his experience with homelessness. It seems so unfair that because he became sick he has not been able to get any help. After he left, I kind of lost it a bit talking with Shani and Genny about his situation. His loneliness and the lack of assistance for any real help just got to me in my heart at a place that I could not control. I let that out in some tears for a bit, which was good. It was great to have some support from the team.*

Photographer: Laura Brown

# Chapter 8

*It's hard enough being out here when you're healthy*

## Health Issues

---

*When there is no vision, the people perish.*

—Proverbs 29:18

If the chapter on "Barriers to Finding Work" makes me angry, this one breaks my heart. It's the number of customers we've met and come to know for twenty-seven years and the level of physical pain they've had to endure for lack of a health care system that even acknowledges them.

The day the Oregon Health Plan(OHP) began was a great day in our customers' lives—while it lasted. There were so many people who had not seen a doctor in decades and didn't know the myriad health issues they were walking around with on the streets had an easy cure, but a cure they hadn't been able to afford.

It's still the case out there that so many times, a pill could cure a person's conditions but because they can't get that pill, their illness becomes the thing that ate New York. That's a sin. Our customer, Nathan, endured physical pain for years because he couldn't get a hip surgery that you or I, with common health plans would have gotten in a month. Nathan taught himself how to navigate the ever-changing mazes within the OHP and Social Security medical policy system. After waiting two and a half years, Nathan now receives Social Security Disability and is scheduled for surgery.

And I think of all the women who (because of lack of access to hygiene on the streets) get chronic urinary tract infections and yeast infections. Untreated, yeast becomes systemic and makes your whole body sick. How do you apply for a job when you have a chronic yeast infection? And people who are diabetic can't access syringes and insulin. Insulin is a lifesaving drug; if you don't take it, you die, and it's up to thirty dollars a bottle now without insurance. Do health problems keep people on the street? Absolutely.

—Genny

Narrators typically reported having multiple health problems. In fact, often once narrators began describing their overall health situation, they would list their ailments as did Trina.

**Trina**: Pancreatitis, diabetes, osteoarthritis, asthma, I have a heart murmur, and on and on.

Hussain had a long history of health problems, dating back to infancy.

**Hussain**: I got a cracked skull in two different places. I was thrown against the wall when I was a newborn baby. I've got a dent in the back of my head, and plus I was in a very bad car accident. My back is partly broken. I was paralyzed from the neck down, but I had to learn how to walk again and I got my strength back up again. And my head went through the windshield and I was in a coma for six months. I lost my memory. I didn't know who I was. I didn't know my name. I had to start all over again to read and write. I used to be in eighth grade in math, fifth grade in reading before I got in that car accident. Now it's all gone in my head. Now I'm only in the second grade level and I gotta start all over again. That's why I'm learning-disabled and paranoid schizophrenic and dyslexic.

Warren, a Chippewa Indian, was applying for SSI benefits at the time of his interview, although he'd already been turned down twice. Besides suffering from depression, he also had physical health problems. He was taking five different prescription drugs when we talked with him.

**Warren**: I had a hip disease when I was a child, so I'm left with bone to bone, no cartilage between.

*Sisters: Okay, so this is a degenerative illness?*

**Warren**: Yeah. There are some days when sitting on a bus will cause me enormous pain, like a pinched nerve thing. If I walk too much, if I stand too long, things like that. So it does limit different types of jobs that I could do. I'm missing a finger on this hand. From the operation of that, it, like, it's not the hand it used to be, of course, but it's got more limitations on it than I had anticipated.

*Sisters: What happened to your finger?*

**Warren**: I lost it in a printing press.

*Sisters: Does being without stable housing affect your health and well-being, or would your health just be a problem anyway?*

**Warren**: Well, it's a problem anyway. The only difference would be the availability of time to where I elevate my leg, lay down. It's like, when I leave here I can go back to St. Francis [St. Francis Anglican Church], sit inside at a table, drink coffee. I could go out and lay in the park because it's a nice day. But when it's cold, wet, and windy, where do you lay down? You don't. There are no places like that for homeless people. That's a no-no. Homeless people don't get to lay down in the middle of the afternoon and take a nap.

*Sisters: Or put their leg up when it's sore.*

**Warren**: Exactly. And that I think is so wrong.

It was not uncommon for a narrator to describe a current or recent illness, nor was it uncommon to discover that our narrators had serious diseases while living without the benefits of shelter. For example, during her interview, Trisha mentioned being unwell. When pressed, she said:

**Trisha**: Everything. Everything. I lost almost sixty pounds having mono [mononucleosis]. I had to walk around with crutches. And then when I got the sexually transmitted disease, I couldn't really walk at all. I mean, I've gotten quite a few things, from asthma to full-blown diabetes.

*Sisters: You have diabetes now?*

**Trisha**: Yes, I do.

*Sisters: How do you manage it?*

**Trisha**: I don't eat much sugar at all, so I keep it pretty low. I don't use the injection at all. I check my blood, but I don't need the injection. I can keep myself under control.

*Sisters: You have the equipment to check your blood sugar levels?*

**Trisha**: Yes, but I can keep myself under control. I've come through a lot.

*Sisters: And you didn't have diabetes before?*

**Trisha**: I had borderline [diabetes]. I've also had asthma, and it's been almost two years now that I've kept it under control where I don't need to use my inhaler.

Tristan was a recovering alcoholic and one of many who described not only multiple health problems, but severe multiple health problems.

**Tristan**: I got coronary heart disease, I got pulmonary lung disease, I got degenerative bone disease, and if I had been still drinking the last couple of years, I would have probably been dead by now.

*Sisters: Wow! Have you lived your whole life with all of these illnesses?*

**Tristan**: No, I developed some and I have been run over by cars twice. I have had my body crushed by a big three thousand-pound automobile, twice.

Especially during the winter months, our narrators made comments about the weather and difficulties coping with rain, wind, and cold. Simon began his interview by urging the interviewer to get down to the nitty-gritty, the reality of everyday life on the streets.

**Simon**: If you want to hear the story of me being homeless, you should ask really specific questions about struggling, not where I get these clothes. Ask me something like what it's like, you know, at three in the morning when it's real windy and it's raining and you have just a shirt or something and you're sitting there in the cold. Stuff like that.

*Sisters: Okay. Let's start with that then. Tell me about that.*

**Simon:** Just for instance, after you go through a night like that, when the morning comes, your hands can get to a point where they have a blue look to 'em. And they're numb, right? And my personal thought was that I might have frostbite or something like that. And when you do get to a place eventually where your hands can get warm, it's like they unthaw almost, you know?

*Sisters: What does it feel like?*

**Simon:** Where you're so cold that—you know, I've never wanted to die or thought about suicide—but you're so cold that you just wish and pray that you could get warm. And that's all you want or need. People don't need a lot of things that they say you need. What you actually need are necessities for survival.

*Sisters: What are the necessities for your survival?*

**Simon:** Clothing. Food. Water. Shelter. Hygiene. Music.

Mary Beth's interviewer found some of her comments heartbreaking, especially when she talked about her health and how homelessness has long-lasting effects. At the time of her interview, she was 47 and married, had previously been homeless for six years, and had been housed for three months. She and her husband were renting a two-room apartment for which they paid five hundred and thirty-five dollars a month.

She explained that the shelter system and services for the homeless make it difficult to stay out of the elements. Most shelters in Portland operate only at night and insist that their clients leave early each morning, no matter the weather or time of year.

**Mary Beth:** They are kicking you out early in the morning—that is the saddest part, they kick the people [out] early in the morning, when it is freezing in the wintertime. There is nowhere to go and they are cold and they are getting sick. My body is still cold, after all these years, even though I am in a place. My arms are cold; I have to have four sweaters on, and it is from being homeless for so many years. My body is cold all the way through all the time. My hands are cold right now and I have, what, three sweaters on and a jacket.

*Sisters: And a hat and…*

**Mary Beth:** Then I got a hat. I am dressed like it is winter right now, that's what I am dressed for.

*Sisters: And when they kick you out and it is freezing and there is nowhere to go, what do you do?*

**Mary Beth:** You stay out in the cold and you get colder and you get sicker. We got people coughing there and that is the reason why people cannot sleep there, you got lot of people coughing. And that is because they are kicked out early in the morning. So I mean, it does not work. And where I am at right now, where I am living, the heater is turned off now; all the time we are cold, my body is not going to warm up and get well.

*Sisters: When you were sleeping at The Harbor Light [a Salvation Army shelter] for two months, you were saying you couldn't really sleep—there were people coughing, you were out early. How was that on a day-to-day basis, when you were released so early in the morning with all your belongings?*

**Mary Beth:** Your body eventually does not learn to relax anymore. You are uptight all the time. You are waiting. You are not supposed to be here, you are not supposed to be there. You are walking around to keep warm but your body is too weak, so it just stresses you out. And I think that probably causes a lot of people to get mentally ill. They cannot take the stress anymore, so they end up mentally ill because they keep wondering when it is going to change. And you start losing hope, too. A lot of them also do not want much to do with the people in society with money because they are too disgusted with the whole picture of it. I feel a lot of it brings on deep depression for a lot of them.

Mary Beth also had a history of medical problems. She had seizures beginning when she was a year old, and had brain surgery for the seizures, which affected her memory. She also suffers from depression, which she believes childhood sexual abuse contributed to. Finally, she believes she has adverse side effects from one of her medications.

Aaron, a native of Ohio, had thoughtful observations about homelessness, especially its effects on a person with a disease or chronic health problems:

**Aaron:** It's pretty rough; I'm diabetic so it is hard. And it's also hard because I take insulin and I have to take injections. And of course I'm carrying around rigs, which are syringes, and some people believe that I'm a junkie sometimes. I get those looks and sometimes people want me to sell them [needles]. But I don't want to get caught…I just tell them to go up to an exchange.

*Sisters: Where do you inject your insulin?*

**Aaron:** Sometimes a mission will let me go back into an office away from everybody, so people aren't looking and speculating or staking me out for like, after dinner: 'Man, hit me up man. Give me a rig.' But sometimes everyone at my camp knows I'm diabetic and they're cool with it. They know that I'm not using, or anything like that.

*Sisters: Now when you're injecting insulin, it looks different than when you're using, doesn't it? Maybe I watch too many movies, and I've never really seen people shooting up.*

**Aaron**: It depends on who's shooting and stuff but usually I inject into the stomach, and most users don't inject in the stomach. It just speeds up the insulin intake. It goes through my body faster if I go through the stomach rather than hitting a muscle, 'cause you can do it in your thighs, back of your arms, and your stomach. I prefer my stomach.

*Sisters: How do you get your insulin?*

**Aaron**: Sometimes there's programs out there that will help you but sometimes, like just this past month since I didn't have the Oregon Health Plan, I had to go into the hospital because I ran out. My blood sugars kind of went high so I had to go up to the hospital.

*Sisters: To the emergency room?*

**Aaron**: Yeah. I stayed there for a couple of days and then they hooked me up with, like, a thirty-day supply.

He went on to explain that he was attempting to register with the Oregon Health Plan, a state-sponsored program for low-income residents which would cover his need for insulin.

No matter the age of our narrators, most described that years, or even months of living on the streets had damaged their health. Randy is a diabetic and former drug user who explained:

**Randy**: Being a diabetic, sometimes I do not feel like walking around. I feel tired sometimes, just do not feel right. At least at the TPI (Transition Projects, Inc., a shelter and program) if I do not feel good, I can lay down. They do not chase you out during the day. You can lay in bed all day. Sometimes I have days where I do not feel good and I just want to lay down. It is clean over there. I could probably step in somewhere and check my blood sugar as opposed to going to the stinking bathroom.

During her interview, Liz, who lives in a tent at Dignity Village, was asked about her health.

**Liz**: I have the neck and back injury; with the cold, it hurts real bad. I have arthritis in my hands, so I cannot really use my hands and it hurts so bad. I have got arthritis in ninety percent of my body; the neck and back injury, there is arthritis in it. I was supposed to have surgery when it happened in 1998, and now five years from that point I can see how degraded my back has become. So, I know it will never go away. There are only certain points where I can move my neck. They only paid me thirty-seven thousand dollars, and I have to be like this for the rest of my life, and now I cannot work because my back pain kills me. I cannot do things I enjoy. I used to love to work but it is rainy now, and it is hard to grip things with my hands. I literally drop things out of my hands.

I can heat my tent and my arthritis does not hurt so badly, and with me getting hypothermia a lot it is—my feet will just go ice-cold, my hands go ice-cold, I start shaking and I cannot get warm.

*Sisters: So, you have experienced hypothermia out here?*

**Liz**: Yep, a lot. I can be under a stack of blankets but I have bad circulation and, you know, a lot of people out here get heaters because they are cold. I have PGE (Portland General Electric) assistance to pay half my electricity bill due to the arthritis. I get back spasms and neck spasms and it hurts real bad; I do not have any pain medication right now. I really do not want to be on it because it makes me not realize what is going on.

Leona was pregnant and living on the streets with her boyfriend when she was interviewed. She had moved to Portland a year and a half before we met her.

**Leona**: The main reason I moved up here was for my health. I have asthma real bad, and my asthma was just not permitting me to be able to live a life or even breathe back in Arkansas. I went from barely being able to breathe using my inhaler six to ten times a day to using it twice in two weeks and being able to walk everywhere.

In order to move, she was forced to leave her three children behind with her parents, who will not relinquish custody of them. After Leona and her boyfriend moved to Portland, they both found jobs and rented a home. But then he was laid off from his job and she began missing work because of health problems. In time they were evicted and forced to camp near downtown Portland and spend their time accessing services. Because Leona is also a diabetic, she spends much of her day traveling around to social service agencies and eating meals to help regulate her blood sugar levels.

Leona qualified for the Oregon Health Plan and food stamps because she is pregnant. However, she explained that since her pregnancy was not advanced and because she was not an addict, alcoholic, the victim of domestic violence, or a parolee, she didn't qualify for housing programs.

**Leona**: I'm just out there on my own again, and this time I have someone else to think about and to care about other than myself.

There were several reasons our narrators were not always able to access health care: they weren't enrolled in the Oregon Health Plan, they weren't aware of available services, they didn't have transportation, or they were afraid to visit a doctor. Chandler finally visited a clinic after he was unable to sleep because of asthma-related problems.

*Sisters: Do you wake up not able to breathe?*

**Chandler**: In the middle of the night when I lay down, it's hard to breathe and my throat feels real scratchy all the time. Then I start coughing a lot and she [a doctor who examined him] said that I cough like that 'cause my lungs are damaged from being out in the cold, breathing in cold air all night, it gives you asthma. And I didn't realize that, how serious asthma was, and she says, 'You could have died, you know.' I've had this cough for a few years. And I fear doctors you know, but I knew I wasn't healthy. I was scared to get a blood test. I was with some women I would normally not sleep with, so when I got my [HIV] test and it was negative, I was happy.

If there was a common factor among our narrators, it was a prevalence of health problems. Sometimes these very serious conditions were brought up in an offhand manner.

**Renee**: I have asthma. Did I tell you I had asthma?

*Sisters: You did.*

**Renee**: I didn't even know it. I get pneumonia every now and then. I have fibromyalgia. I hurt from head to toe, right now even.

Besides respiratory and degenerative diseases, many people had back injuries or back problems. In fact, back injuries were a common reason for losing the ability to work and thus losing housing. Rose was one of our narrators with chronic back problems.

*Sisters: Did your back get worse over time?*

**Rose**: Well, I used to do construction work, and the doctor told me originally that I had an old, old injury from childhood that did not even bother me when it happened, but as I got older the bones got harder, brittle, you know how that goes. In my late thirties or early forties, I had three back surgeries in one year and then it did not bother me again until, like, twelve years later; then it happened again, and now I think I have got arthritis, but I do not know. I have not decided to allow myself to ask my doctor, you know what I mean? You just do not want to think about a thing like that.

Alex described a work-related back injury.

**Alex**: I was working in Washington State for the Parks Department and I was cleaning up a park in a little all-terrain vehicle. There was one sheet of a newspaper laying in the park and I stepped out of the vehicle, bent over to pick up one sheet of a newspaper, and when I started to straighten up I just had this terrible shooting pain in my back, my whole spine. I thought I was struck by lightning at the time, I did not know what happened—I actually thought that lightning had struck me. So I laid there, I could not move and about a half-hour later one of my coworkers saw me over there kind of yelling for help and laying there, so they picked me up and took me to hospital. I had ruptured three discs in my lower back, so I went on physical therapy for about six months and the doctor told me I could not do any of my trades that I was skilled at, after that, and no bending, stooping, or lifting. They said they could do surgery but there was no guarantee the surgery would help and there was a slight chance of paralysis. So I did not want anything to do with that because I could still get around when my back was not hurting me or when I did not have back spasms, I could still get around pretty good. So that happened in 1989, that is when I first became homeless in Washington State.

Bradley described a similar circumstance that led to his homelessness.

**Bradley**: Basically, my first experience at homelessness was I was hurt on the job in Seattle. I was working as a chef and herniated two disks in my neck between fourth, fifth and sixth vertebrae. Labor and Industries did not pay me right off and did not take care of it. I ended up losing my apartment and everything else. I ended up sleeping in a sleeping bag with a bad back and then I got on welfare until Labor and Industries kicked in and then I eventually got off the street. It took almost a year before I got the operation because they cut off my money and they forced me to go back to work. I could work like maybe six or seven days, and that was it, I could not work anymore. So we set up the operation, the doctor would not do the operation right off the bat and I was really critically injured. It meant cutting nerves to my left side, my left arm, and I still have problems with it to this day. I got the operation, I was staying with my dad after the operation, sleeping in his trailer, and before I was even completely healed they cut off my money again and forced me back to work.

He went on to describe how the operation wasn't completely successful. He eventually received a settlement of twenty-five thousand dollars, obtained housing in Renton, and got another cook's job, although it wasn't as good as the one he had before. Since the injury and surgery, Bradley has been unable to work full-time at his profession.

Through conversations with our customers at the cafe over the years, we were aware of the many health problems that homeless people are prone to. But in analyzing our data, we found that the prevalence of serious diseases and life-threatening illnesses was greater than we had thought. This factor was especially notable when our narrators were being treated for cancer or had previously suffered from cancer.

Wayne was such a narrator. He explained why he was currently unable to work.

**Wayne**: Back in 1993, 1994, I contracted lung cancer and I went through a dilemma with that. Most companies, once they found out I was as young as I was—I am 44 now, but I was in my thirties [when he contracted cancer]. Doctors and specialists in lung cancer say if I contracted lung cancer early, there is an eighty to eighty-five-percent chance that it is going to reoccur in my life. So, when I go apply for certain jobs, they want to know your medical background. And when they find that I have had cancer, lot of them, their group insurance would not cover me, you know what I am saying? So, they have me labeled what they consider 'occupationally disabled' now.

Alicia moved to Portland from San Francisco with her mother in order to access better health care. She explained that she receives methadone, not because she's a heroin addict, but instead to treat pain.

**Alicia**: I am on that because I have degenerative rheumatoid arthritis and bone cancer—actually bone cancer plus a bone disease combined—as well as being hit by two cars. So I have been in a lot of pain, and there is no way that I could not be on any pain control because of the amount of pain I am in. My body could go into shock because your body can only handle so much pain. I was on opiate pain pills. I was on Percocet, Vicodin, morphine, Demerol, and at one point they were giving me Demerol shots. All those were killing my kidneys and my liver. They were doing blood tests every two weeks, one for my chemo to test and see how it was affecting my organs, and then two for the opiates to see how the drugs were affecting my kidneys and liver. Well, it started affecting them pretty bad, so they were like, 'We got to get you off of this.' So, they talked to me about methadone. They put me on methadone pills but you could only go up to a certain dosage on the pills and it was not working enough. So he referred me to a methadone clinic in San Francisco and I have been going there ever since and then we moved here. It…it really helped.

Alicia was also receiving chemotherapy at the time of her interview and was struggling with the side effects from the treatment and finding appropriate food for her condition.

*Sisters: You went to bed hungry last night?*

**Alicia**: Yeah, woke up hungry.

*Sisters: You were telling me about your chemotherapy making your stomach upset?*

**Alicia**: I am on chemotherapy, and my stomach is very, very sensitive and it got even worse after the accident. I can only eat certain foods, and I can only eat certain food at certain times. Yesterday, I could eat something and today I could not eat that…same thing today because my stomach is really weird, especially since they just took me from twenty-five milliliters to forty-two milliliters; that is a big joke.

*Sisters: So, they just increased your chemotherapy?*

**Alicia**: Yeah. Sorry, I am tired.

*Sisters: There is no hurry. I do not want to wear you out. So, have you gone to local places where they feed people and the food is not always something you can eat?*

**Alicia**: My mother will not eat if I cannot eat, you know. I tell her to eat, but she will not eat if I cannot; she says it just does not feel right. She just does not feel like quenching her hunger if I cannot, and it is so frustrating. I mean, you have no idea what it feels to be hungry and be nauseous, to be starving but not be able to eat. I feel like I'm running, in a circle like my cat is doing, chasing my tail.

Interviewer's Journal Excerpt:

*It's really hard to tell someone sick you can't do the interview. This man is on prescription drugs for a serious, chronic illness. He isn't going to stop taking them in the near future, just like the other guy without teeth I interviewed isn't going to get dentures anytime soon, maybe never, and the girl in the wheelchair isn't going to quit dying. So, do you not interview chronically ill people, because the quality of their interview isn't as good? Or do you take what you can get? That the perspective of a chronically/fatally ill person is interesting is very likely; but along with that, so is the chance that that person's on heavy meds, too.*

Photographer: Patrick Nolen

Photographer: Dan Newth

# Chapter 9
## Chapter Nine

It is a freakish, freakish feeling, a lot of anxiety

## Mental Health Issues

*Smiling is only a symptom of happiness and can be faked. Do not assume that everybody who smiles is happiness.*

—Jessica Albert

When Sisters opened in 1979, the truth of a broken promise had become obvious for folks who'd been released from mental health institutions into the community in the early '70s. The promise was, "We'll be setting you up in group homes." Some group homes happened, but many mentally ill people ended up on the streets.

Harris was an early customer, who, when his mental health issues were contained, did beautiful pen and ink drawings that to this day hang in Sisters. When he walked in the door with his mental health not under control, he had a different name, he'd talk in a different voice to himself or anyone who would listen, and would do things out of the ordinary. I'll never forget it. As clear as day, I can see Harris sitting at the counter and another gentleman sitting next to him. In those days you could smoke in the cafe. Harris lit a match and held it to this man's coat. Immediately I said, "Harris, remember you're in Sisters Of The Road. Blow the match out! You cannot set someone's coat on fire in Sisters Of The Road." He looked at me, blew the match out, and was "back."

Sandy and I got it then, and I mentor it to new staff and volunteers at Sisters even now: no matter what level of woundedness people have, we ask them to be accountable. Elsewhere, someone's mental health behaviors would immediately send people to the phone to dial 911. At Sisters, we speak the truth instead: name the behavior, call on them to remember they're in Sisters, and ask them to hold themselves together in the cafe and come back to a place where they won't hurt themselves or others. I'm not saying it's always successful; rarely, someone has crossed the line and become hurtful. But the constant practice of holding people accountable has created an environment where people dealing with mental health issues truly feel respected and safe. There have been a lot of customers' parents over the years who have introduced themselves to me at speaking engagements or who have come to Sisters to buy meal coupons for their son or daughter and said, "This is the only place my child feels free to be who they are."

—Genny

**Sandy:** I knew I was crazy, I asked for help a bunch of times, I went to the hospital once and four different psychologists, I went to a free clinic and the psychologist said, 'I'm sorry, I can't help you with your problems. You'll have to find someone that knows more.' That was really bad, I mean, that did not make me feel good. I am trying to get help, I am trying to ask for help, and no one knew how to respond to that. I tried to put myself in Sacred Heart Hospital and say, 'Look, I got a problem. I want to hurt the people; I think I may be a sociopath,' let in what I was, I was trying all the different mental illnesses I knew of, they had any information on, so I could try to figure out which one fit, then tried to diagnose myself from the inside out. And the hospital turned me out because they did not answer the one question of where to put me on, 'Are you suicidal?' I was not suicidal, no, I was mad. I was hurt, I was in pain, I was eaten up inside and I wanted to take it out on everyone else for not noticing.

You know, with the mental illness that I had, I wanted to punish them for it—the people that were being mean to me. They were the ones I wanted to hurt, and that is wrong. It is wrong that the system works like that. They have taken away the ability for people to go into a mental health organization to get treated; they have to go into individual emergency rooms. The second time I went in I had to threaten with malpractice because the first time they did not treat me, and so after I said malpractice and everything and this is what I heard the doctors say: 'If you're gonna threaten malpractice blah, blah, blah, blah,' he points towards the door, and there is a door, 'blah, blah, blah, blah, there is a door, blah, blah, blah, blah, there is a door,' he went on for like ten, fifteen minutes and I sat there and stared at him like, 'Are you done yet?' And finally he was done and sitting there and he said, 'Well, I'm gonna call an administrator at home,' and everything, get her to come in so she can make the decision. I said, 'Okay, thank you,' and he came a few minutes later, he says, 'Administrator's gonna come in to see you; she'll be here in a while.' I said, 'Well, thank you.' So I had to threaten malpractice, but I needed to be treated. I am really scared, and I need to have my mental illness, you know, issues taken care of and everything. That is the only reason why I am here. He asked, 'Why did you come here?' and I said, 'Well, I have a mental illness, I've bipolar I didn't get treated for at the first time in the hospital, I've lost the ability to cook food without burning, and I'm afraid I'm gonna burn down my friend's house that I'm staying at, I can't take care of myself, I'm not eating, I'm not sleeping, I'm not dealing with life problems right, and I'm homeless, and I haven't any place to live,' and he said, 'Homelessness isn't the reason to be in the hospital.'

A great number of our narrators suffered from depression, mental illness, and emotional problems. A third of them for whom the topic came up in the interview identified themselves as having a mental health issue or reported being diagnosed with one. Naturally this is a huge physical health risk, especially if they are psychotic or delusional while living on the streets. During our interviewing process, a number of narrators commented how dangerous the streets were for the mentally ill, and how inadequate the services were for them.

**Stan:** But the system itself, we're trying to look at rehabilitation, we're not looking at people trying to keep us down and lower our self-esteem. You walk into a food stamp office, I feel that I should be cared about. Show me concern, walk the path, you know, with me. If you burn out from your job, move on, give it to somebody else that cares. Go to another position, whatever. But don't just sit there and take it out on me or what Joe Blow did before I came in there, you know. You're just being treated in society, sometimes you're already down. You're depressed, you have low self-esteem. And you don't need anybody else beating you up. You know, show me what I need to do. And if you can't, lead me in the right direction where I need to go. And I'm seeing a lot of that not happening. It's like it just stops right there. It's like, 'Well, I don't know anywhere else,' just because they don't feel like giving you information.

And there are a lot of times when you feel like you just want to go to a park bench somewhere and just sit, and never wake up again.

The number of people living without shelter is linked to many factors, including policies that were changed in the '70s and '80s whereby many mentally ill people were inappropriately discharged from hospitals to the streets. According to the National Coalition for the Homeless, 20–25 % of homeless people suffer from some form of serious mental illness; however only 5–7 % of them need to be institutionalized. The National Coalition for the Homeless estimates that as many as 95 % could live in community settings if appropriate services and housing were available. However, the reality is that many homeless people who suffer from mental illness are unable to obtain supportive services such as case management, treatment (including medication), and housing.

It's also notable that homeless people with mental illness suffer more than the general homeless population because of their illness: they generally have more physical health problems, are often chronically homeless or remain homeless for longer periods of time, have less contact with family and friends, face more barriers to becoming employed, and are arrested or imprisoned more often.

When skilled and appropriate assistance is provided, the results can be effective.

*Sisters: What kind of disability are you talking about?*

**Jennifer**: Well, just depression and anger management and stuff like that, and I am in groups that help me to kind of…they show you how to kind of not call it, but kind of watch what you do and you are not as apt to have anger things flash out at people like I have.

I am not doing that as much as I used to. I am trying to be more, like if you get anxious with people or you get upset with people, you kind of feel like you count down to ten instead and let the other person kind of go off the deep end while you are sitting there kind of cool and calm and then the other person gets more or the less the looking-at than you do. You are not making of yourself as much if you kind of take it easy and just cool down and do not let the person get on your nerves. If I had not done that, I would have been up in the air yelling and screaming at the top of my lungs trying to and saying, 'I don't want to have to listen to you or anything,' you know, and I have got an awful lot out of my therapist. She has got one-on-one with me, and she also is my group leader that I go through on Wednesdays.

Being in the group kind of helps you to support people too that have even worse problems than you. But it helps you to kind of to be like a support to them and they also support you in some things that you might wanted to, and it is also like if you get into a better place like me and they are always happy that you…if you kind of get into a better situation. We have one lady in our group that has had a brain aneurysm or something and they said well, she was not going to get any better. She would start remembering things. She is doing a lot better than they think she is and she is always getting knocked down every time she says something stupid. She gets on the board and she is in like a care center or something and she is trying to get out of that situation because she feels like she is being knocked down every time she tries to do something, you know, and she is a lot better. She remembers a lot more things than she used to do and she would like to get into a better situation where she would not have to go through all that situation of being and every time she goes into the room, she needs to do things and because she says the rules is stupid, she gets put on the board and in fact she is on probation or something, and it is like they are talking down to her and saying she is not doing any better, she is getting worse, and she knows day one she is doing better, but they keep saying, 'No, you are not, you're getting worse.'

It is like they are treating her like a child instead of a grown person and that she can get into a better situation where she would not have to do that. She would probably feel a lot better too.

The more victories you get, you kind of feel better when you have, and then, in other case the therapist will help you do that if you need help in getting things like, if you need more, people will be more open to you to do things and they would help you, like with your medicine and stuff. I do not take that much medicine, but some people do; and it helps to get their meds and stuff and makes them be able to regulate their stuff better where they can do a lot more productive stuff that they would not be able to do if they did not get the medicine. And, like in her case, she is doing a lot better than she did, but they still do not think she is doing any better, so if we could have more [group leaders] like that, I would say it has helped me an awful lot because I am not as I used to be. I can be more productive in what I am doing and be more outgoing towards people than I was. I am not as apt to snap at people like I kind of did before.

Although almost a third of our narrators said they suffered from a mental illness, only fourteen percent reported Social Security payments (SSI/ SSD) as a source of income.[1] This statistic creates new questions. Why isn't a larger percentage receiving payments? The challenge of applying for services, lack of formal diagnosis, narrator's incorrect self-diagnosis, or some combination of factors?

Mental health naturally affects both the ability and the desire to work.

Kyle: I think they will want me to work, which is fine. I do not blame them. But I just want it understood that the mental health problem comes first, because if I do not get back taking care of, there is no sense in having a job.

Some of our narrators who suffered from mental or emotional problems were not formally diagnosed and were not on medication or undergoing treatment, but their words and stories spelled out their distress. Many narrators described how they were emotionally fragile and how a crisis could send them into a tailspin or relapse.

Tina: The eviction came up and my life just fell apart. I was just like, 'It was crazy,' so I had to relapse because I was not on my medication, so I was not stabilized.

The challenges faced by those experiencing homelessness make tasks most of society sees as routine difficult or even impossible. The difficulty of escaping homelessness conflicts with the desire to escape. Anxiety, frustration, depression, and other negative emotional and mental states may be understandable reactions, but they are still formidable enemies added to existing obstacles.

Kevin: You are already under pressure here, I mean, you are…when you are homeless like that, and it is a day-to-day thing about how you are going to, you know, make this appointment or get your clothes washed or just it is a constant battle to try to keep your head above water and stay clean. And, you know, and then, add to that the lack of housing and the places to sleep outside all are gone, you know, all those murders and all the…the crack and the

---

1. All narrators were asked about their income; discussion of mental illness was self-initiated.

violence on the streets, it is just, you know, it is hard. No wonder some of those people drink and do drugs, you know? People think, 'Why don't they just get out of it.' Well, until you have experienced it, you cannot really, you cannot really judge it. You cannot talk about it because it is like an evil monster.

Somehow when you become homeless, it is…I do not know, I guess it does something to your psyche, no matter how strong you are, no matter how…you know, it just, it does something to you that, the longer you are there the harder it is to get away from it. I wish I could explain it. It just, it is beyond words to explain it but it is real, I know it is real.

Proper attention to mental health issues can lift an individual's ability to respond to the rest of their environment.

**Mark:** I've been told that I have some mental problems like big depression and things like that, that I never really thought about before. And this all came about because I do have a physical problem. I have a bad hip. When I started getting medication for that and seeing the doctor, I had to do a psychological evaluation for SSI. That's when these other problems came out. My caseworker here in Old Town, she is a disabled person her own self, and she said that, herself included, that she never really thought about a mental problem stemming from the physical. I'd never really thought of it that way before either, but when you're not able to do something a hundred percent and you used to be able to, then there are mental aspects of it. I've been turned down by SSI twice, but it was my own fault because I didn't get everything that they needed to have a clear picture of what they're dealing with.

I've been seeing this one doctor since December for the physical problem, and I go out to the mental health place. I mainly went out there to find peace of mind because of the relationship problems between myself and my ex. I gave them the psychological evaluation. They put me on two different types of medication, which the only thing that I can say about the medication, if there is any change from me with the medication or me without the medication, is I am more able to take more BS from people. It doesn't bother me. I just kind of let it go, whereas, maybe one thing that used to bother me, it would sit there and be in my head all day. I'd be stewing about it. Now it's kind of 'Oh, well, that's your problem, not mine.'

Many of our narrators described how homelessness and depression are inexorably linked. John is a Vietnam-era veteran who was asked about the consequences of homelessness on his health. He explained that the Veterans Administration diagnosed him with depression.

**John:** I say, well, you don't have any money, you're living on the streets, should you be jumping for joy? Naturally you are going to be depressed. I got on Paxil and then I got off of Paxil and then I got on Paxil again and I got off of Paxil. I found that using that is not really working, what I need to do is to focus my mind on getting my life stringed out together.

Paul echoes the concerns about despair following homelessness.

**Paul**: I am 40 years old, I am not going to let this happen again…I am tired…After I first got up here [living on the streets of downtown Portland], I thought about suicide. But I thought a lot about suicide this last time, more than I have ever in my entire life…I would never follow through on it, but the thinking of it scares me.

Stephen was asked about the difference between living and existing.

**Stephen**: Well, I guess there's different kinds of living. To me, existing is when you don't have the money to go to the dentist.

Our interviewer asked Tim, a 35-year-old who had been homeless about five months, to describe how the experience has affected his mental health.

**Tim**: It is stressful. It is just a burden on you. You do not see any light at the end of the tunnel. I keep bumping my head on all these walls and finally it just gets so discouraging that you just do not want to look any more…hopefully my luck will change and somebody will feel sorry for me and give me a place to stay for a little bit. But something has got to change or it probably will work me down to where I just do not care. I do not want that to happen.

Brad, 38, was another of our narrators with a multiple diagnosis. He suffered from health problems along with depression and bipolar disorder. He was born in Turkey into a military family that moved every year. After his father retired, the family settled in Dallas. In the midst of a panic attack, he took the family station wagon and ended up in Los Angeles living on the streets.

**Brad**: When I left home at the age of 19, I had lived in, like, sixteen different places as an army brat. I have lived in about thirty different places since I left home, roughly. They are places I spent, like, three months and over; anything less than three months I do not even count.

Moving on became a lifestyle of jumping trains, hitchhiking, traveling, camping out, and staying in shelters. However, Brad has also managed to attend about two years of college, worked at construction cleanup, as a security guard, and as a circus jack.

**Brad**: I do not remember what it is like not to be homeless.

He explained that he was currently panhandling to get by and trying to figure out some means of getting more structure in his life or attaining a more mainstream lifestyle.

**Brad**: It seems like I forgot what it's like to be normal. Fifteen, sixteen years on the road is finally catching up on me. I got arthritis and I have gout, and heart problems. I am anemic and so I just cannot hitch…cannot do what I used to.

*Sisters: What do you think was really driving you from town to town?*

**Brad**: I was looking for a home.

*Sisters: A home?*

**Brad**: I do not really think I know what a home means. I have talked to people, and the closest I come is, a visible place that you love and care about and want to go back to and there is really no place like that for me…There has just always been this wall between me and other people. You cannot afford to have friends because down the road they are not going to be there, they are just not going to be there.

Brad receives medical care from the state and had cataracts removed under this plan. One of his big difficulties is taking his medication regularly. He hopes to return to school.

**Brad**: I got to get off the streets. The streets are killing me. I tell people I actually used to enjoy being homeless. Lot of people look at me funny, but it was fine. Freedom to go where I want, leave when I want, get up when I want, go to sleep when I want. There was a lot of freedom, there was a lot of fun. It is not fun anymore. It has lost its charm. It is like, I feel like I am racing the clock, like I am racing the clock.

Mental health issues do not arise out of a vacuum. Often the causes are horrific. As Melody points out, organizational failures can cause resentment toward all similar organizations, creating resistance to getting the help available.

**Melody**: It's hard for me to see sometimes that our voices make a difference. I'd like to see that change now, as part of me taking this survey. It was briefly explained to me on the phone what this survey consisted of, and on the flier also. I pretty much have been involved with homelessness now, I felt it was time for me to start voicing, and seeing changes. I'm not, by being homeless, it's so hard for me, sometimes, personally, to follow the news, and who's for this, and who's against that, and what politicians. If you were to ask me if I know who the Mayor is okay, but, if you were to ask me any other position of office, I wouldn't even know. And I know who the President is, but I can't even tell you, right off that bat, who the Vice President is, and it's because I just never cared.

And I think a lot of that stems from my past, too, not treating me fairly for the crime that I committed. I felt like it was self-defense. I felt that I had no way out, and I looked for the government itself, the judicial system, to protect me, to understand why I did what I did. My father was—I experienced abuse, when I was thirteen. My father watched my brother take my virginity and he did nothing about it. He just stood there and watched it. Nowhere to go, nowhere to turn. I was beat profusely, with belts and straps and water hoses, and hairbrushes, you name it. It was thrown at me, or whatever. And I've had nosebleeds, mouth-bleeds…my father's favorite thing to do to me was stretch my lips until they hurt. My ears, he'd hit me so hard, my ears would bleed. Dislocated shoulder, my ribs cracked, two of them. Just bruises everywhere. I've been put in cold tubs of water, and just sat, until I stopped crying. And the only reason I was crying, was basically because I wanted my mom, my mom gave me up when I was 7. And I was put in the tool shed, for two, three days at a time, in the dark, and just opened the door, just enough to get me something to eat. I've did my…how can I put it…I've urinated and had bowel movements on myself because, in this tool shed, because there was nowhere to use the bathroom. Just torture. Because I wouldn't go along with the plans of what he wanted me to do. And that was to hate people. And thank God, I'm working on those issues now, with the help of mental health and other agencies. And good ol' OHP, thank you! I'm allowed to get my life back together, back in order. More intense now than ever, but I think a lot of the government's stuff stems from my past and my feelings towards it.

Past victimization or feeling vulnerable can also create intense hostility, fear, and anger.

**Elizabeth**: They will get their ass kicked, fucking with me. I do not play that, men or women. I do not give a fuck, I will go off. I do not care, they do not know, somebody's going to the hospital. Yeah, see, and that is something that I will probably end up dead because of my attitude problem. It is not anger problem, because I do not have no anger problem, but if somebody put their hands on me or something like that—oh it is not going to be like I am just going to tell the police officer or something like that. I handle my situation the way I am handling, you know, they will want to watch out, but I will never, you know, use like a gun or knife or nothing like that towards anybody.

*Sisters: You do not carry a knife?*

**Elizabeth**: No, I do not carry no weapon. My weapons is my fist. My uncle taught me how to box.

Many of the interviews were unusable for research due to the narrators inability to focus on the questions. The interviewers tried to help narrators stay on track.

**Svenn**: I started my own commercial photography studio, doing advertising and graphic design in computers, marketing, promotion, communications, and media, mostly advertising and I was into entertainment but primarily marketing for like promo videos and, you know, I was doing real good. I think my highest year gross was one hundred and thirty thousand dollars so I used to be like, you know, I had…I had a normal life, I used to be a(n) okay guy.

*Sisters: You are still an okay guy?*

**Svenn**: No, not anymore honey, now I am a bad guy, so leading up to my first homeless experience: I would say I was living in McMinnville and owning my studio, been in business for about 10 years, and I was brought up to be successful, I had about a four-thousand square foot studio, hardwood floors, big photographer setup, I was making money. Yeah, I was, you know, a little bit off the kilter in the view of the McMinnville community, primarily with my mother and also the judge and the lawyers, and the mayor and everybody, they said, 'Oh, you know, he's just a little too wacky with the way he runs his business,' and so, one day, several things happened, I started to look at the homeless situation as being very dramatic, I thought, you know, 'This isn't right,' so I would come up to Portland and distribute blankets to the shelter, my nice, new truck, and one time I went to all these different hotels in Portland trying to get somebody to donate some blankets for the poor, homeless people and nobody would give me any blankets, it was very upsetting and I realized things were not so good. So, the point of my demise began when I took my checkbook out and I wrote like millions and millions of dollars of checks to people to I could not cover, it was like this crazy statement and people have often said that my behavior is bordering on manic or schizophrenic, I do not ever get depressed, so it is not really manic-depressive but I do have a very high-strung personality.

I had seen that movie, Rush Hour, by Eddie Murphy, and next thing, you know, I am running out of the theater thinking that the cats and the dogs are fed up with our sick society and they are going to attack their owners just like in the Bible, I thought it said that in the Bible but it is really more like Wizard of Honor or something. So I went around writing these checks to the homeless for millions of dollars, total stranger, I would just [hand] him money and I had some money at the bank so I just borrowed some money from some relatives but anyhow, the cops stopped me and said, "Oh you're crazy," and it was beginning to the end of, what I call, reality, for people and how they view me and they…they ended up locking me up in a mental institution within a couple of months after that, you know, and then they gave me some drugs that were really seriously bad for my brain, they deep-fried my brain for about twenty-four days, they held me in a mental institution, when I got out that was my first experience with homelessness and that is a very roundabout way to a long story and I really do not like talking about it or crying on anybody's shoulder but basically I was a pretty normal guy.

*Sisters: Can I stop you for a second and ask you questions?*

**Svenn**: I know, I want to backtrack but I am talking about the three issues that hopefully people, when they understand the three issues were covered in one: harm to others, harm to children, you know, harm to oneself. Now, when I say I will kill myself, that is basically a very true, true story. Forced with two choices, being illegally locked to a facility because some of the governmental facilities, some piglet or some citizen says that I scared them simply with my words, I just talk, I do not. I have a little theatrics. I talk I yell and scream and I get away with because I am not breaking any laws but they have shown me they could lock me up in this institution and I have experienced it once before and it is worse than jail, they medicate you, they tell you you are crazy, you are talking to a doctor like yourself and,

'We're sending you to psych ward,' and I am saying, 'Doctor, I'm not mentally ill, I'd like to go back to work, I have a window washing company, I have clients I need to serve, I got friends I wanna go see, I'm a normal person just like you punk, open the door.' Well, I told them that for five days in a row and they just wrote down little things: 'Oh, he's in denial.'

*Sisters: So, can we go back to this…? I am not a mental health specialist but I…*

**Svenn**: You know, I understand but please remember, the one statement I did not make about killing oneself would just have to be in a desperate time of hopelessness because anybody, if you experienced it before and it is a permanent.

It took me about four years to finally get clean with the whole city of Portland and McMinnville, get to where everybody said, 'Oh, I guess he's not really crazy, it's just his personality,' and it was a horrible, horrible, experience trying to rebuild my personality and I felt like I had my whole reputation was destroyed, I lost my company, I gave bankruptcy, lost my house, lost my girlfriend, and when that occurred, it was a dramatic point in my life that I should have handled more like a man, I should have said, 'Well, I can tough it out, you know, just because I get locked up and everybody says I'm loco, and they're spreading rumors about it that are not true, then I can make and I could,' I did not have the guts, the fortitude and another part of me said, 'Well, I'm just kind of left with nothing,' and that is what I have done, I have always said, 'Well, I can get back on my feet, you know,' it is much harder, easier to say than to do, but yeah, I just want to say…

*Sisters: Yeah, I think we are straying, and we need to stay recording, stuff like that is like…*

**Svenn**: Suicide would be avoidable thing to do, I did not know how to do it, I mean, a gun, I think a gun—always wanted to blow myself up, put dynamite, little pieces…hanging would be no fun, let us see…

*Sisters: You said that—because that was interesting. I wanted to get some more information about how you said that you went straight from the mental hospital onto the streets—so after they let you out that mental institution the first time, so was there any like help to get you back into your housing?*

**Svenn**: No.

*Sisters: I need you to talk about that process like what happened there.*

**Svenn**: It was really bad, I was strung out on a drug called Depakote, and Haldol, and lithium, and Ativan. They had put it in my system for twenty-four days, and the last ten days of my stay at, it is called Good Samaritan Hospital. The last ten days they just like doubled my dose of all the drugs because they wanted me to be so whacked out and, you know, fried in the brain that I was…they could release me because they knew that there was not anything wrong with me, and the doctor said, 'Well, it's possible that you don't actually have any mental illnesses.' This is after twenty-four days; that is a long time to be locked down, being pushed around, you know.

Hope, goals, dreams—they don't overcome mental illness but they help. Feeling that there are ways out can empower people to find those ways and seize them.

**Kelly**: I do not want to die like so many people that I know have died, especially in the last couple of years, never having gotten a grip and died in their addiction. I do not want to go out like that, I really do not. I want to have, you know, gotten a grip on things and, like I said before, be working in some kind of capacity, you know, helping other people who, you know, this sort of thing, just helping men and women who want to change their lives or, you know, who are homeless or suffer from mental health or something. I want to be one of those people doing that. I do not want to always be the victim, you know. I want to be a part of the solution, and I felt like because of my experiences, you know, I feel like I can offer, something when I get myself together of course. That is where I am right now, you know, trying to reverse all the damage I have done in my life again, get out of this hole I have dug for myself. And actually I am not as bad off as I have been in the past, you know, thank God.

---

Interviewer's Journal Excerpt:

*I felt dizzy and dirty hearing all that negative ranting from her, and when I tried to gently "call her on the truth" like Genny tells us to do with the mentally ill ("Maybe your stepmother wasn't involved. It sounds unlikely."), it didn't help; it just agitated her. So I have her emotional garbage to shake off of me.*

*Of course, this is the first really bad experience I've had; I've interviewed a couple of mentally imbalanced women and some impatient people, and had a hard time explaining some things to people. But this brings up all the fears we brainstormed in our training classes.*

*I am so tired and wiped out. This job is really hard. Tomorrow morning I interview a woman with multiple disabilities. Her speech is hard to understand. I worry about being able to understand what she's saying. I am worried my afternoon appointment will flake.*

---

# Chapter 10
## Chapter Ten

I have nowhere to go, I am in tears, I am trying to stay clean

## Recovery Issues

---

*I know what the great cure is: it is to give up, to relinquish, to surrender, so that our little hearts may beat in unison with the great heart of the world.*

—Henry Miller

Welcoming people under the influence, as long as they are not hurtful to themselves or others, is one of the clearest and most compassionate messages Sisters has ever put out. Over the years, services around us have changed; now, to stay at a shelter or get services people must often take a urine test; they have to be clean and sober. We believe you can't take away every point of entry into the system from substance users, because it's there that they get a glimpse of how they could change. It's important to be able to go in Sisters and see Joe, who they were drinking with two months ago, now working behind the counter.

Back when Latinos were the leading drug dealers in Old Town, we took down our sign, reworded it, and translated it into Spanish. It changed from "Drug dealers not welcome here" to "Drug dealing behavior not welcome here." One evening when we would normally have been closed, we held an event. A mariachi band volunteered to play in the cafe and we heated up Mexican hot chocolate. The Latinos weren't coming in, though. So we took the band and that good-smelling hot chocolate out on the sidewalk, and then they started coming in. The message was, "Jose, Juan, Hector, you are welcome. Don't bring in your drugs, don't be looking for it, don't do it in the doorway. But you as human beings are welcome." After that, they stopped doing drugs in our doorway. It worked.

The biggest thing to keep in mind about drug or alcohol addiction is that people are medicating a deeper pain, a bigger demon. Such was the case with Mo, whom I talk about in the Foreword, and from whom I learned so much about alcoholism. Can you be broken and be a warrior at the same time? He was. Shoshone-Bannock poet and friend Ed Edmo said to me once, "He has strong medicine." And he had just walked by him in the kitchen! I said, "Yeah, he does, and he's scared to death by it." When he died, there were hugely hurtful things that had happened in his life. In and out of recovery, he was an example of what it meant when people finally started talking about alcoholism as a chronic disease.

Mo said, "When I come in f'd-up, ask me what happened, engage with me about what the next step has to be. Don't wrinkle your nose because I smell bad. That's the compassion. But also say, "You gotta get yourself to detox." Talk to me about the mistakes and always offer tender mercy. Don't run or avoid saying the hard stuff, but do it without punishing me, ridiculing me, or making me feel less-than."

—Genny

Many homeless people develop an addiction after losing their housing. Following the harsh and daily grind of homelessness, they turn to alcohol or drugs for solace or to self-medicate untreated physical and mental pain.

Chad: I know that some people, when they start off being homeless, they are really cool people, but after a while when you are homeless, you got to have some kind of release, you know, and a lot of it comes from alcohol or drugs. Where I live it was big-time heroin use, lot of heroin. It is cheap, and a lot of people are using it. It takes the edge off.

No matter the statistics, or which came first, it is clear that addiction complicates a person's daily life. It often prevents people from holding down a job and an apartment, since employers and landlords don't want to risk involvement with them; taking care of their hygiene and health; and maintaining healthy relationships since many addicts have intentionally stopped or been denied contact with their families. The loss of these sustaining activities greatly increases a person's risk of becoming homeless.

Ivan was asked how he got started using heroin while in the service.

Ivan: [To] forget about things that happened over there, to hide your feelings, to hide yourself.

*Sisters: So, you kicked it when you got back?*

Ivan: Hardest thing I ever had to do. Fell back a few times and then I got out of it.

Our narrators also talked about traumas that triggered their addictions such as rape, physical abuse, an accident, emotional issues, or mental health problems. Bryce explained that he began using drugs after receiving bad news.

**Bryce**: The bad news that I got was my girlfriend was mugged by some person, severely beaten, then raped, and I found out that she was in a hospital in an intensive care unit.

*Sisters: So after hearing that you chose to do the drugs?*

**Bryce** I did not know how else I was to deal with it.

Many narrators talked about a lifetime burden of emotional trauma from abusive or unstable childhoods. They also described using drugs or alcohol to cope with the death of a loved one, a separation or divorce, or losing custody of their children.

Our interviewer asked Donald about circumstances that led to his homelessness and how he felt about losing his former lifestyle.

**Donald**: I sort of felt self-destructive. I went into self-destruct mode when I got divorced and so I really did not care that much about losing it all. And so almost maybe subconsciously I was doing it on purpose.

*Sisters: Kind of destroying your life?*

**Donald**: Yeah, as stupid as that sounds.

Many described being born into families with extensive drug use or alcoholism. In fact, our narrators mirror the evidence that alcoholism and addictive personalities run in families. For example, Perry, an identical twin, described how his twin brother Clark died. Clark was released from jail and was dead four days later of a heroin overdose. Perry was struggling with his addiction and had recently relapsed and ended up on the streets. He also had a wife in prison and an infant daughter who was living with his wife's family. Our interviewer asked him how he was affected by his twin brother's death.

**Perry**: I was definitely in shock. Grief is a hard thing to deal with. My family couldn't afford to pay for his cremation, so we couldn't get his ashes.

Their mother was an alcoholic and they had lived in foster care while she served time for armed robbery. Perry and his brother Clark had similar lifestyles.

*Sisters: Had you and Clark followed parallel paths as far as addictions and crimes?*

**Perry**: Yeah, we've both been involved with the criminal justice system since the age of twelve. And we started using at the age of 12—alcohol, pot, and acid. At 13, we were both snorting cocaine and crank and we still were smoking pot and drinking. Then, I don't know when he first started shooting dope, but I started at 15. I think he did too; it may have been 18 for him. We were both heavily into crime and drug use, and alcohol use. Both of us were primarily alcoholics.

*Sisters: That was your drug of choice?*

**Perry**: Yes.

*Sisters: What kind of alcohol?*

**Perry**: We started out with beer and Mad Dog [Mogan David 20/20 wine], and of course we drank whiskey and vodka, just experimenting. We primarily liked to drink whiskey and malt liquor, the strong stuff. We both used it to an extreme. All of our crimes were drug or alcohol related.

Recovery was a frequent topic in our interviews—the need to begin recovery, a person's shaky newfound recovery, or a person's long-term recovery. As one recovering heroin addict explained, "You have to get well before you can do anything." It was especially heartening to talk with men and women who had long since left their addictions behind and could look back with perspective and relief that they were no longer trapped in their addiction.

**Ignacio**: I don't look at me going back to drug use again. I had enough of that. I don't want to go through it anymore. If anybody beat me up as bad as I did myself…I'd kill them if they did the stuff to me that I did to myself.

We also heard about many different paths to recovery—one man camped in the Rocky Mountains as a kind of spiritual retreat to kick drugs. Many belonged to twelve-step programs or had gone through programs offered through social service agencies. One veteran who had been sober for seventeen years spends much of his time volunteering, because he believes in keeping busy as a key to sobriety.

**Dennis**: If you want to stay away from the drugs and whatever the case may be, you want to change your life. Find something to occupy your time.

What is clear is that addiction has enormous consequences. Paul, 54, had a particularly apt

## Homelessness and Addiction

In a report on addictions among people experiencing homelessness, the National Coalition for the Homeless (NCH) echoes an oft-heard sentiment that addictive disorders appear disproportionately among the homeless population, although they claim "there is no generally accepted 'magic number' with respect to the prevalence of addiction." (Addiction Disorders and Homelessness, NCH Fact Sheet #6, Published by the National Coalition for the Homeless, June 2006). They assert that such disorders cannot be blamed for the increase in homelessness, seeing that most drug and alcohol addicts never become homeless. This being said, they note that low-income people who become addicted are at increased risk for losing their housing.

National figures of addiction are echoed for our narrators. According to the Cities of Portland and Gresham/Multnomah County Consolidated Plan 2005–2010, "Approximately 30 % of Portland's homeless persons have chemical addictions, and 18 %have a mental illness…When people who are homeless are asked about the reason for leaving their most recent living situation, the most common responses are low income and unemployment, followed by drug or alcohol problems."

description of heroin addiction. He first became homeless in 1989, was a long-time heroin addict, and was using methadone at the time of his interview. He described addiction this way:

**Paul**: You can't mess with it at all. Some people can. It's like an alcoholic. Some people can drink and they don't ever get to be an alcoholic. And some people do. But most of the people that use heroin do get addicted. Most everybody uses it for the same reason. It's different from what people think. It's because it makes you feel good. That's why you like it. It's the best feeling you ever wanted to experience. It's the best feeling you ever had. You can't hardly describe it. Well, you can't really if somebody's never done it. But it becomes everything. After awhile, it's your wife, your life, and it won't leave you alone. And that's why they call it a 'monkey on your back.' And it's gonna beg, 'Feed me. Feed me.' And if you don't, it's going to kick you. You're sick until you feed it.

But I never liked being homeless. After awhile, I thought of it like camping in the city. And the worst part about it to me was not being able to take a shower every day. Because you can't present yourself, and your self-esteem gets lower. People naturally look at you different if you are not clean. Most people I've seen that are on the streets are either mentally incompetent in some way or they have a heavy alcohol or drug problem because they're in that situation, or that's how they got in that situation.

*Sisters: And as far as heroin use, I'm just wondering how it is affected by being homeless?*

**Paul**: I'd say I used more because I was able to always have the money. I mean, that's the first thing I would spend my money on. I didn't have to pay rent. My priority was the drug. I guess being on the streets, I used more drugs than I would if I had a place. Because the money that you would spend on rent, I spent on drugs. It's a sick situation.

*Sisters: And how would you get money to get heroin?*

**Paul**: In the end, I was a thief. I stole. Mostly stores, a lot of art materials…I'd take orders for what the art students wanted, and then I would bring it. I was making two hundred dollars a day if I really wanted to get after it. I'd just spend it though. The more money I had, the more I'd use. Just get a bigger habit. It's just a vicious cycle. Thank God I never died.

It was apparent in talking with our narrators that they were experiencing many levels of torment from their addiction. It was tied to guilt, regrets, low sense of self-worth, and self-loathing. They talked about the people they had disappointed, of friends and family who had given up on them. Charlie was asked about his state of mind after he lost everything and became homeless.

**Charlie**: Being a proud person, there is a lot of mental anguish that you go through because you cannot help being homeless and still see around you that life is going on, but without you. People are going to work in the morning, people are happy…they appear to be happy anyway, they are driving their vehicles to work. They got a life, you know. You think about what you had, think about your family, that they are going on with their daily routine…and this is what it was for me. I had that.

I went through a lot of mental torture. I torture myself bad mentally…I would kick myself daily for having the disease with alcoholism and drug addiction, for losing what I had. Those near and dear to me, my family, my daughter, wanting to get it back, but thinking that this is what I deserve, nothing better than where I am right now, homeless.

*Sisters: And, what made you feel like you deserved it?*

**Charlie**: I guess that is the drugs and alcohol talking. 'You are not worth anymore than where you are.' God! The alcohol and drugs and everything, they put you in a state of mind where you're just not worth it to yourself or to anybody else. It changes you around mentally, it does. It is a trap, man; it is a trap hard to get out of.

I am in recovery right now, and it is wonderful. I finally have arrived; I finally made it. Homelessness and drug abuse and alcoholism go hand in hand, I believe. It is hard to be in recovery and have no housing. It is really tough not to medicate in that situation. I have seen so many bad things being homeless and experienced bad things. I have been beaten, I have been in the area when people were being murdered, and it is just really a traumatic thing.

Recovery, for me anyway, means I have to have a safe place to go. Recovery and sleeping under a bridge does not work; it does not work at all. What is important about that safe spot is that I am not around drugs and alcohol, I am not around thieves, I am not around prostitutes, I am not around cheats, murderers, rapists. If they are not around me, I can concentrate on myself and on my goals, what I want to do as far as getting back on my feet and becoming a productive person in society again. If you do not have a place to go, that is the bottom line. There are a lot of places you can go as far as shelters and stuff, but it is just for the night. During the day what can you do? You wander around and that is all.

Later Charlie described how he had met other homeless people who were ten or twenty years older than him and recognized in them his future if he did not change.

**Charlie**: I want to experience life for what it is. I want to be excited for what life is and wake up like this morning—I woke up and thanked God for being alive again. And I was happy and clean and sober and I have a roof over my head and have got a life again. I actually heard the birds singing. Now I can appreciate life.

Fiona was a heroin addict at the time of her interview and had become homeless after she relapsed, lost her job, and then her housing. Like many of the addicts we interviewed, she represented a dual diagnosis, hers being addiction and depression. She is not atypical as she described how depression led to addiction and eventually to homelessness.

**Fiona**: I have been unhappy. I have always been isolated. I do not have anybody I really can call a friend. So, I am very lonely, and I have always suffered from deep, deep depression, always. When I do have a home, when I get my depressions I will stay in the house for weeks and months at a time. I will not answer my phone, will not answer my door, will not get dressed. Just watch TV or I will sleep a lot when I am depressed. I just close myself up from everything and everybody and I have done that my whole life.

Fiona, who had recently turned 41, expressed a common theme of those who are still using and living on the streets.

**Fiona**: I am really tired, and not only that, it is hard for me to even believe that all these years have gone by because I have spent so many years in a drug-induced state. I missed a good part of my life.

Many of the conversations between our interviewers and narrators became a search for answers, for finding cause-and-effect relationships and establishing truths.

Terrence, at 54, was a methadone user and understood the link between his drug use and homelessness. He echoed sentiments and regrets that we heard from a number of narrators.

**Terrence**: I ended up on the streets from that [heroin addiction]. I used because I put my priorities, rather than having a place to live, to buy drugs. So that's kind of how it affected the homelessness. And then I got used to it. In the beginning you're afraid. I think most people are afraid to be on the streets, a foolish place. You need a home in your life. You accept the thorn and you're not afraid of it. But you get tired of it, you know? The main thing is not having a shower and things. I think there should be a lot more available for people to get out of that situation of homelessness.

*Sisters: I was going to ask you about being afraid when you first get out on the street, and how then it changes and you get used to it. How does that happen?*

**Terrence**: You've never been without a place to stay, and it's like the world is all crumbling. 'It's over,' I think is how it felt to me a lot. Then once I went through it, I found out that it wasn't that bad and it is something that you can get out of. A lot of times I'd be on the streets and I'd quit using. There was a time I remember that I went from the streets to a halfway house. First, I went to detox for three days and then I went into a halfway house. In three and a half weeks, I had a thousand dollars saved because I didn't buy drugs. I didn't buy alcohol. All I had was cigarettes. I had food stamps, and they paid rental assistance. In Arizona they did that. They had General Relief. And then I started using again, and I threw it all away. And I kind of kept bouncing back like that a lot of times.

As Terrence testified, a recurring theme in our interviews was how difficult it is to get clean and sober, how the effort to stay clean and sober is ongoing, and how relapse is always a possibility.

Bobby, 44, had been addicted since he was a teenager.

**Bobby:** Once you become addicted to alcohol or drugs, it is a lifetime struggle. It is a lifetime job to maintain sobriety because just one little incident in a day that went bad for you and you get that old stinking thinking back again. And before you know it, you have talked yourself into a trap again.

Bobby expressed an issue that is hidden from most of us.

**Bobby:** All the alcohol and drug facilities that homeless people use are all in the same area. You got to walk through drug dealers to go to your group. You got to walk through these drug dealers; you pass them at your front door to go back into the alcohol and drug-free community. Once you complete the program, they put you in your single-room occupancy housing, you got the drug dealers in there who are in disguise as recovering addicts. So pretty soon you are caught up in the web; it is just a revolving door...

Bev was 48 when she stepped into our offices to be interviewed. Her story is compelling because it illustrates the horrific downward spiral of addiction and, again, how difficult it is to stay in recovery. A native of California, she grew up in a "struggling working-class" family. Her father was in the military and worked civil service positions as a gun specialist. In 1967 she began using drugs, and in 1971 she quit high school although she was supposed to graduate that year. She married a preacher but divorced him in 1978 and moved to Portland in 1980. She worked for a nonprofit organization for a few years.

**Bev:** [Then I] ran off with an alcoholic fruit picker and went up to Washington and picked fruit. So that was my first experience with homelessness, because we lived in the orchards and picked fruit by day and drank and ate beans by night. I ran into a lot of the railroad people that could not tell you how to get from here to LA on Interstate 5, but they could tell you every train to take and that was really interesting to me.

Bev's boyfriend had become increasingly alcoholic and violent.

**Bev:** My family was very worried about me at that time, and when my elder brother died in 1983, I made him a promise that I would not go back to the street. For some reason, promises to dead people are kind of like a seal. I was able to keep that promise and not go back, and I started college.

Bev began training as a lab technician and landed a job. But this was the beginning of the AIDS crisis and she was afraid of working with blood so quit school.

**Bev:** That was my justification for leaving school, but it probably had more to do with I was in love and wanted to get married. Marriage plays a big part in my homelessness.

At the time, she was dabbling in drugs, married, and then bought a house with the help of her parents. Gradually she developed a "hefty" cocaine habit although she was working.

**Bev:** I had my own business as a contractor for law firms in the area and I would convert their manual billing system to a computerized system so that attorneys could bill without guessing. I did conversions and was making really good money. But my cocaine use got so out of hand that I freaked out and quit my job.

Bev sold her house, moved to Hawaii, and her drug use escalated to smoking crack cocaine.

**Bev:** It was more cocaine than ever; there was just tons of it.

To extricate herself from a dangerous lifestyle, she left Hawaii, moved in with her mother, and attended truck driving school. She stayed clean for two years but drifted back into using drugs and drinking. Our interviewer asked her if she was on methamphetamines at that time.

**Bev:** Yeah, snorting methamphetamines, drinking a lot…and then I tried to do a job but I was so hung over that I was never called back. I put myself in treatment.

She was again clean and sober for a while and met another man in an Alcoholics Anonymous meeting whom she married three weeks after meeting him. This marriage also ended up in a divorce, and she moved back to Oregon and from there to Port Angeles, Washington. The next man she became involved with introduced her to intravenous drugs and she began drinking again. Her drug of choice was methamphetamines and she described more chaos including losing jobs and selling off her possessions to support her habit until she finally ended up with nothing. She next became a heroin addict and to support her habit became a prostitute. For two years she lived in motels.

**Bev:** I went to jail a lot during this time.

She was arrested for "doing returns," shoplifting then returning the stolen merchandise for cash, as well as for passing bad checks.

*Sisters: During that time, from 1993 to 1995, you said you were living on the streets. How were you getting your basic needs met?*

**Bev:** I was shooting heroin and doing crime.

She hooked up with a man who was leaving prison, and then her parents bought her a van. They lived in the van and she worked several states making a living as a prostitute, and by shoplifting and passing bad checks. While escaping from an arrest, they ended up in South Central Los Angeles, again destitute and "sick as dogs" because they weren't able to support their addictions. Eventually her family bought them bus tickets to Portland, and she and her partner attempted suicide by overdosing. This attempt failed and they both were eventually arrested and ended up in jail for two months. She entered a program for addiction, landed a job, and an apartment. But her sobriety didn't last when she began smoking pot, lost her job, and then her husband left prison and started using methamphetamines again. After he left her, she started back on heroin, but at the time of our interview was in a methadone program. She was also living in Dignity Village with her two cats.

Not only did our narrators report dual diagnoses of addiction and mental health problems, but many had more than one addiction, or used whatever substance was cheapest and easiest to acquire. Or sometimes they moved back and forth from one addiction to another for various reasons.

**Silas:** Now that I don't drink, I use more hard drugs. Because when I was in Little Rock, you know, I'd pretty much kicked the hard drugs because I was drinking a lot, so I used the alcohol as a crutch to get off the hard drugs. And when I couldn't drink no more I thought, 'Well, I'll just smoke a little weed and that's it.' Well, that went fine for about a month and then I thought, 'Well, if I just do a little coke, you know, I won't get strung out like I have been before.' But, you know, everybody says that, 'Well, I can handle it.' You can't. It eventually brings you down all the way to the bottom and you end up on the streets with no friends, no family, homeless, you know. I wish I could blame my problems on society, but I can't.

You know, I just don't understand how I got in this situation. I really don't, I mean, it's like 'boom,' there it was. I can't blame my wife. I drove her crazy, I'm sure. All the drugs I do. Finally, she got sick of it, I guess. She couldn't take care of the kids properly because I was never there, taking all the money. But I didn't see it that way then. I thought it was all her fault. She was just a mean old bitch. But it was my fault. I'm supposed to be the man of the house and I wasn't. It took me a long time to come to that conclusion, to be able to say that. But I know now. You know, all my friends after my wife left me with the kids, you know, they all gave me anything I wanted. 'Oh, poor Silas, he got stuck with the kids. His sorry old wife ran off.' No. That sounds good but I guess a woman can only take so much after a while.

And now it's like, I've changed, I really have changed, but now it's too late. I mean, my sister's got my kids. I had my parental rights severed, because I couldn't give the welfare a clean UA (urine analysis) in Kansas. So now I'm at a point I don't know what to do. Don't know where to go. I sleep at the missions. Try to eat at them as little as possible because the food's terrible. Gives you food poisoning sometimes. But I'm thankful for what I do get out of those places, you know. And I thank them every time I eat there or whatever, you know, I'm polite.

*Sisters: In an ideal world, what would it look like to help you stop doing drugs?*

**Silas:** Have a nice apartment. Have an old beat-up pickup so that I can start another business. Have somebody that I can care about, you know. I think I was real female-dependent on my wife, you know. She was always there for me until she just got sick and tired.

*Sisters: And so would it take knowing that those things were there at the end of treatment, or would it take having those things before, for you to get into treatment?*

**Silas**: No, it wouldn't take that for me to get into treatment. Something to look forward to, you know. Just getting clean doesn't mean much to me because after I get clean, what then? What am I going to do then? Still gonna be on the street miserable. You know? I'd go to a treatment center if I could go and they'd let me in. But I go and they give you a mile long of red tape. But if I was in prison, though, I could get right in. So what's it going to take? For me to get in bad trouble with the law and then I'll get some help? You see where I'm coming from?

*Sisters: Can you explain that some more? Like what kind of red tape?*

**Silas**: Well, we have a waiting list or you got to go check in Transition Projects, Inc. (TPI) and then come to outpatient treatment twice a week. Well, I'm still on the street. I'm still around the drugs, so I'm going to do the drugs. I'm not going to make it to the outpatient treatment because I'm too busy getting high. Then TPI is going to throw me out when they UA (urine analysis) me, and I'm back on the street.

I've lost a fortune. I've had everything. I've owned homes, cars, trucks. I used to collect checks for two or three thousand dollars a couple of times a week. And now I'm picking up aluminum cans in Portland, Oregon. I probably know five people in this whole town. No family. I'm like a lost soul. I need to do something. I don't know what.

Robin was another narrator who spoke eloquently about the all-consuming nature of drug addiction.

**Robin**: It has affected every part of my life. It has affected my family; it has affected every relationship I have with my family. It has affected my ability to give them the things they need. Every aspect of my life has been affected by drugs. No one can use heroin and say that any part of their life is not affected by it because heroin becomes the number one thing in your life. I do not care, you could sit there and say, 'Well, I love my kids,' and this is bullshit. It is coming before your kids, it is coming before your own health. I mean, you can take a heroin addict who is sick and he will say, 'Okay, I got twenty dollars, I'm gonna go get some heroin and get well, or I'm gonna go get this medicine that I know will fix me from having to have my finger chopped off if I let it go too long'…even though he knows that if he lets it go too long they might have to chop his finger off, he is going to go buy that dope. So if they say they will not, they are lying. So it affects every part of your life.

Sarah spoke to our interviewer about her experiences with alcoholism and homelessness, reflecting on how both impacted her health.

**Sarah**: Well, this winter I got a pretty bad cold, which was unavoidable, sleeping outdoors, breathing in that cold air, half the time your shoes being wet from being in the rain even if where you are sleeping is dry. Once your shoes and everything gets wet and they do not dry out, you end up getting sick. So yeah, it affects your health, and then when you cannot stay cleaned up all the times, just all those things add up.

*Sisters: And how is it trying to take care of yourself when you are…?*

**Sarah**: Well, when I get to drinking that much I really do not care as much as if I am indoors, here and there, and staying sober I care a lot more about everything. Every time I have been homeless I have been drinking. By homeless I mean on the streets, not like how I am now—like couch-surfing, staying with family—but outdoors. I felt there is nothing else to do, I might as well go get out and hide in some bush or under a bridge. Some of the people out there do not drink, but there is nothing else to do, you have nowhere to call home.

*Sisters: And can you talk some more about that, the relationship between homelessness and drinking or doing drugs as you do not have anything else to do?*

**Sarah**: Every time I have been on the streets that is all I have ever done, and the people I hung around, it is all they ever did, pretty much. We would do it and we were trying to figure out a way how to get some more; they just kind of go hand-in-hand, I guess.

Erick, who was recovering from pneumonia, joked about needing a new body, but his situation wasn't funny.

**Erick**: If only God could give me a new body, I'd be happy. Because with all the drugs and alcohol I've done in my lifetime, my body's worn out. I've got hepatitis C, nerve damage in this whole right leg. I've got tendonitis in my leg. I've got a slipped disc in my lower back. I've got cross vertebrae in my neck with a pinched nerve. My body's worn out.

*Sisters: You attribute it to the drugs and alcohol?*

**Erick**: Yeah, and plus I've got two broken jaws with arthritis in them, this one guy I was hanging with hit me like this twice, broke them twice, and then I went back to them and we started doing drugs again and he pistol whipped me, hit me here and back here. And when he hit me back here he made me have seizures, so I'm fighting with that too at the same time.

*Sisters: He hit you with a handgun?*

**Erick**: Yeah.

*Sisters: And you've had seizures ever since?*

**Erick**: Yep.

*Sisters: When was that?*

**Erick**: I got hit in '96.

*Sisters: Here in town?*

**Erick**: No, California, Long Beach. So, I stay away from Long Beach now.

A number of narrators mentioned that drugs and alcohol took away the pain of their experiences and helped pass the time. Denise and her interviewer were talking about how the general population distances themselves from the homeless, imagining that it could never happen to them, or that homeless people are bums.

**Denise**: [They think,] 'That person must be a bum, lazy, stupid, or on drugs.' Basically, most of the people on the streets are on drugs, not all of them by any means. But I found that it was a lot easier to get through a cold, snowy night on drugs because it makes your body numb, you do not feel the cold as bad. Plus on the really cold nights I had to just keep walking all night or I would freeze to death so I had speed to keep me moving.

People just do not realize that it is hard to get off the street. You are stereotyped and automatically people think that, 'Oh she could've done something to prevent it. She doesn't have to be out there on the street if she doesn't want to.' And it is true there are a lot of resources here in Portland, I think it is one of the better cities for that. Of course, there is more homelessness than most cities, but if you do not know about services, they cannot do you any good. Most often there are very long waiting lists and then you tend to get discouraged and do your drug of choice again or whatever it is. And then people steal to eat and steal for warm clothing and then they end up in jail, and once you are in jail it is hard to get housing.

Then there is this other thing I encountered. After I got clean and I was still on the street and I was trying to get help—I was trying to get into a drug treatment because that is the easiest way to get into housing. My real problem has always been depression. I used drugs to try to medicate my depression, but the underlying mental illness is a lot bigger thing for me than the drug use. The mental illness drove me to drug use and you cannot get help for that anymore, so you have to say you are a drug addict even if you are really not…But I encountered that even [when] I was clean and I would try and I was calling these drug treatment programs and you could not get in unless you had used in the last three to five days. That is really backwards because there are people out there that do not use drugs, they are just out there because they have had a series of bad luck and it is hard to get back in because it is a catch-22.

Brian, who was an alcoholic, was asked by his interviewer why people on the street drank.

**Brian**: I guess to forget. I was brought up drinking. My dad was a cop, but it was acceptable. I'm sure if you do a survey of how many people out here drink, you'll come up with a large number, probably ninety-five percent. A typical day is you wake up at the mission, go to Labor Ready [an employment agency] to get work. But there is no work right now, so the library gets packed full of homeless people trying to stay warm. On Sunday when the library closes at five o'clock, then I have nothing to do. You can go to Blanchet House for a dollar. Blanchet House is open from two to six on Sunday. You can go to church at the mission and have dinner at seven thirty.

In his interview, Allen, who was a drug addict and alcoholic, was discussing his latest relapse and his lifetime struggle with addiction.

*Sisters: What is it you started using again?*

**Allen**: Opiates, pain pills, drinking. A little of this, a little of that, mainly pain pills and drinking. Misery was back again, you know.

*Sisters: What does that mean?*

**Allen**: The self-imprisonment. Once you start using, it's kind of like setting off, starting a fire. It just builds and builds and builds and builds. But the sad part about it, I knew it. I knew what was going to happen. It got to a point where every payday would come and I'm, like, paycheck out for drugs. And that's when I went to the mission.

*Sisters: When you talk about self-inflicted prison, could you explain that a little more? What do you mean when you say that?*

**Allen**: Well, it's kind of like it's worse than regular prison. It's a prison inside yourself. You can't stop using. You live for drugs. Your thinking is centered around your addiction and how you're going to get more and how you're going to get the next buzz. What scam are you going to have to pull today to get high or who are you going to have to lie to, to get another buzz? I was the type of person that I would steal your wallet, and I'd help you look for it and ask you if there's a reward. It's crazy. It's just not being able to stop. It is horrible. It's crazy. It's insanity, of course. It's the worst thing that's ever happened to me, my drug addiction mood.

---

Interviewer's Journal Excerpt:

*This interview was full of theoretical constructs and larger themes of capitalist exploitation and the drug war and its effects on homelessness. At times, I felt lost due to his extreme intelligence and references to some theorists whom I have no knowledge of. I was quite pleased with all of this, but do have to admit that I could have interrupted to redirect him to a stronger focus on homelessness in general and in concrete terms. But in reality, I was quite interested in what he had to say. He spoke for almost two hours!*

*I was also quite happy to have conversations about his drug use, which he was relatively open to. I must admit that we had some conversation about this before the interview where I expressed my concern that I felt like this topic was difficult to be open about, but that it should be open because I was not there to judge anyone and it is an important aspect of people's experience. My previous knowledge of this person's past encouraged me to have this conversation and initiate a discussion about drug use. It went pretty well...although still he spoke much in theory, but also in concrete experience. I think that this theoretical talk is part of who he is, as in the past in our conversations he speaks on these terms. He also studied anthropology and philosophy, so go figure!*

Photographer: Jeremy Johnson

Photographer: Dan Newth

# Chapter 11

*I do not think God wants us to be homeless*

## Spirituality

---

*Faith is not making religious-sounding noises in the daytime. It is asking your innermost self questions at night—and then getting up and going to work.*

—Mary Jean Irion

I'm a more faithful woman for all my relationships with people on the street for going on thirty-five years. I have said out loud many times that as a society, we're spiritually bereft. But on the street, in the cafe, in an SRO (single room occupancy hotel), in the shelter, and in the Downtown Chapel, I could never say that about people in Old Town.

It's not that these spiritual people walk in the door spouting Bible verses or talking about Christ; it's that they walk in with the knowledge that there's a power greater than them, and that's how they get through their lives. Other people would have called 911 when some of these men and women walked through their door. Instead, I sat in their presence. They are prophets.

I knew Louise, who would start washing clothes in the sink in her hotel room and forget, flooding the room below and infuriating the desk manager. Or she'd come into the cafe with tears in her eyes for "all the lies women have ever been told." She was often under the influence, she got run over—that was eventually how she died—yet in all this confusion, there was a person who believed, who saw the miracle of being human, and shared that vision with all of us. Anybody else looking at her would have said she's a drunken, kleptomaniac Okie. But to me she walked through the neighborhood with grace.

You see it in every chapter, like the vets who come into Sisters from out of the woods… they are not thinking of themselves. They don't live their lives that way anymore. It's about gracing/blessing other human beings. When push comes to shove in this society, there will come an end to our national greed. When it does, it is the people on the street who will know how to comfort the rest of us and remind us of what's really important. And if that's not spirituality, I don't know what is.

—Genny

Many interviewees related that a Higher Power had saved their lives, carried them through a dangerous event, kept them safe, or helped them with recovery.

**Christopher**: I don't worry because I have a guardian angel. The good Lord takes care of me. [As] long as I don't get stupid, I don't break no laws, I am okay. I have been told to stay out of trouble by a very big spirit, *very* big spirit, and I am spiritually inclined.

While the majority described their faith as a source of strength, several admitted that their faith had been weakened by their experiences with homelessness. As one man said, "I am not impressed with Him right now."

**Tony**: Being homeless definitely affects you. Spiritually, sometimes I just feel bankrupt, down. You just keep on trying. What else can you do?

A Vietnam-era veteran with the Marine Corps whose fiancé had died the previous year explained that his circumstances sometimes overcame his faith.

**Andrew**: I still believe in God, but at times it perhaps is a little difficult. Homelessness puts a strain on everything, including your spiritual faith.

Tyler was a narrator who described suffering from depression and mentioned also that being homeless had diminished his connection with a Higher Power.

*Sisters: So when you look at the consequences again of having experienced homelessness, such as being in a depressed state or wanting to take your life, how has your spiritual health been since you've been out here?*

**Tyler**: Rocky.

*Sisters: Why?*

**Tyler**: Mule looking up at the sky and going, 'Why me God?' That really about sums it up.

*Sisters: Do you ask that question?*

**Tyler**: Sometimes. Sometimes as a joke, sometimes just out of frustration, but I do ask that question.

For some of our narrators, particularly those with addictions, prayer and faith were their last hope for getting off drugs and the street. And for some, recovery helped them discover spiritual aspects in themselves that had become dormant.

Tony was a drug addict struggling with his recovery and described his drug use as "pure madness" as he talked about the price he paid for his addictions. He panhandled for money and was taking steps to get clean so that he could return to his home state of Oklahoma.

**Tony**: I'm going to go to NA (Narcotics Anonymous) and ask them for some help. And just pray. I'm gonna pray like I do when I'm standing out there with that sign and people are giving me money. I'm gonna pray that those people will help me get off the street to start with. And I think they will.

*Sisters: And how has prayer and your faith been affected by your experience?*

**Tony**: None. I've been just really blessed, I feel, because I'm hardly ever broke. I mean I just feel like I'm always blessed. But I pray all day. You know, God please do this, God please do that. I don't know if it works or not, but it makes me feel better.

Another surprising aspect of our conversations was how often our narrators expressed gratitude for things large and small. We heard often about the generosity of their fellow homeless people and appreciation for this fact.

**Judy**: [Becoming homeless] made me look into the way I deal with God; every single day I walk with God. Every single day I talk to God. You know, I thank God for my blessings. I thank God for the air I breathe. I thank God for the lessons I learn. I thank God for inspirational people coming back on my path every single day.

### Christian Evangelism on the Streets

A note about what could possibly be misinterpreted as a Christian bias in this chapter: while some of our narrators spoke about other religions, this chapter reflects the fact that most spoke about Christianity. Beyond the obvious reason that Americans largely identify as Christian, there are several reasons for this Christian emphasis that are particular to the low-income and homeless community. Many services for people on the streets, such as meal kitchens, feeds, and drop-in centers are Christian-based, and traditionally (but not always) require church service as part of receiving services.

Additionally, there are charismatic, evangelical Christian "street churches" in poor communities all over America that offer a warm place to sit and a bite to eat for those willing to participate in a religious service. Those willing to convert will find a supportive community that may eventually help with an apartment, furniture, utilities, and employment. Although many of our narrators expressed bitterness over what they perceived as conditional help, many others expressed that the welcoming atmosphere and "forgiveness" inherent in charismatic Christian sects was very welcome.

It is also true that the major substance abuse recovery programs require participants to rely on a Higher Power, and although they can choose their "Power," our community speaks of a strong Christian influence there as well. Because many low-income housing programs and other social services are now linked to recovery programs, Christianity has become part of the daily environment on the streets.

*Sisters: How has your relationship with God been impacted by your experiences with homelessness?*

**Judy**: Oh, just beautifully. I said this the first time I got here, I said, 'I feel like I was sent here.'

*Sisters: To Portland?*

**Judy**: Yes, I was sent here to Portland because I've been trying to get back here since 1995.

*Sisters: So why Portland?*

**Judy**: I don't know. I honestly don't know, but when I first came to Portland, I had a connection. I still have that connection.

*Sisters: A spiritual connection with the town?*

**Judy**: A spiritual connection with the town, the people I was meeting, the things I was doing.

Besides believing in a spiritual connection, we often heard our narrators describe their relationship with a Higher Power as a source of strength. Many also described how becoming homeless had strengthened their faith. In fact, the topic of faith and gratitude being strengthened by adversity was heard often.

**Robbie**: My sponsor is the Creator, you know, because I can always talk to Him 24/7. I can always ask Him for help. People will let you down, but He's always there.

During his interview, Bill was asked how his spirituality helped him deal with being homeless.

**Bill**: It's hard to explain. It gives me hope and it makes me more apt to not care about society's views on me. Because I'm just going by what God tells me to do and God doesn't care about what society thinks about homelessness and what society thinks about me. God only cares about what I think about Him. And I'm just following His path. If He wants me to become a functioning part of society, then I will. If He does not want me to, if He wants me to continue being homeless and traveling and things like that, then that's what I'm going to do. It doesn't concern me anymore.

Like Bill, Robin described his relationship with God in intimate terms.

*Sisters: Now that you're homeless, how do you look at life?*

**Robin**: God and I have an understanding. I don't worry too much about tomorrow because I feel like somehow He's going to make something happen. And it's true. I used to worry a lot back in the years of what will I do tomorrow. What would I do next week? How is this going to work? But, yeah, there's a little thought before you go to sleep at night, but now I have a comfort. I know the next day something is going to happen, so I'm gonna be all right. And it does. The day falls into place. I guess with my near-death experiences…like even with my broken neck. I was told if I had the operation I would be paralyzed from the neck down. [Before the surgery] I had called for a preacher to come talk to me to see what would happen. How I could set things right in case I didn't make it through the operation? And he said only I knew if I was right with God…I figured by me forgiving [the person who had injured him], I'd be forgiven.

And I woke up a couple of days later. The operation was through. I'm not paralyzed now 'cause I started doing pushups and stuff off the walls. I honestly feel that there is a God and it's not the deeds that you do or what you don't do, I think it's how you live. You know, what you have really in your heart that counts and it all balances.

Along with finding a source of strength in their faith, many reported they felt protected and watched over by God or a Higher Power, and that their faith and this sense of protection made them feel less alone and vulnerable.

**Jerome:** I mean there's somebody up there telling me that they're watching over me. I can feel it. I know God's up there. But now it's like inside myself I have a friend. It's something other than me. It's my friend inside me, and I think it's the Lord. Actually, I know it's the Lord. He knows what you need. And if it wasn't for Him, I wouldn't be here getting the help that I need or I wouldn't have that plan. I have a plan and the only person that's gonna help me with my plan is the Lord. And most of these places that help you out around here, Union Gospel Mission, Portland Rescue Mission…all those kind of places say prayers. Feeding under the bridge, feeding in the park, feeding over here, feeding over there [describing Christian groups that distribute food and minister to homeless people]. They walk down the street handing out thermals and a little pamphlet or a little booklet of scriptures of the Lord's word and [asking] do you want Christ in your life? I mean, it's your God. I mean, if you don't have your God in your life, then you're pretty much…I don't know what the word is. I don't want to say confused, but you're not getting the whole picture. You're just getting part of a piece. Because it's scary. You don't know what to do. You think you're all alone but actually you're not.

*Sisters: So you're telling me that homelessness made you more aware of your spirituality or religious outlook?*

**Jerome:** Kind of. I'm getting to know the Lord a little bit better than I had. I mean before I never even picked up a Bible. I never even felt that feeling. It was like I was all alone inside. But He's telling me don't worry about it. Keep on doing what you're doing and I'm going to help you. I'm going to hold your hand.

When Angie was interviewed, she had been clean and sober for three years after being addicted to heroin and cocaine for twenty-seven years. She grew up in Portland in an upper-middle class family, with her grandfather a preacher. When she was 13 her parents divorced, her brother and sister went to live with her father, and she remained with her mother who became an alcoholic and eventually a drug addict. She was married before she finished high school and had a baby at 17. At 20, she was divorced with three children. She worked construction jobs but then began having health problems after an intestinal bypass surgery. Her life started going downhill from there.

**Angie:** Shortly after I quit working construction I met somebody that, like I said, my self-esteem is way down under the worm somewhere, and I met somebody that just was so suave and slick, and the next thing I know I'm working the street and I'm addicted.

*Sisters: And what were you addicted to at that time?*

**Angie:** Heroin. And my life is kind of a blur from that point on.

*Sisters: Do you remember very much about those years?*

**Angie:** Thank God, no. I almost got killed several times. I had guns held to my head two times.

*Sisters: How did you support your habit during that time?*

**Angie:** Worked the street. I stole. I haven't done that for about five years because I got real sick for a long time. I've got chronic severe asthma. I've got arthritis. I've got acid reflux real bad. Every time I went to the doctor I got a new diagnosis. I've got hep. C [hepatitis C]now. I've been just really sick.

With prostitution, health problems that included several strokes, and addiction, her life became chaotic and dangerous. During these years, her children lived with her mother although she was still also an addict. Eventually she entered a methadone program, but the daily trips to the clinic became a burden and she asked God's help to quit methadone.

**Angie:** And just one day I was on the bus [enroute to the methadone clinic]. One day, I said 'I'm not doing it.' I said, 'Lord, I know you wanted this and I'm ready.' I said, 'The only way it can happen is if I don't get sick. I'm leaving it in your hands.' I didn't get sick.

*Sisters: What do you mean? You didn't experience withdrawal symptoms?*

**Angie:** I did not have withdrawals. And I slept for two weeks, which is something you don't do. I kept on waking up every day thinking 'I'm going to be sick today.' I wasn't.

*Sisters: So you didn't have to go through a rehab program or anything? You did this all on your own? That sounds like a miracle to me.*

**Angie:** Oh, it has to be. I had tried getting off methadone at fifty milligrams for years and years before and wished I could die…

*Sisters: Really? It was so awful?*

**Angie**: It's beyond awful. Every bone, tissue, cell, everything in your whole body hurts for months and months and months. Finally, I just went back on it, you know. I went back on heroin because I couldn't take it. And this time when I said it, I meant it. I'm leaving it in Your hands. If I get sick, I can't do it. Don't let me get sick. I didn't. And even the doctors are amazed to this day because I did not get sick.

We also heard our narrators describe how living on the streets had brought about a spiritual awakening.

Bernie described how his situation eventually brought him closer to his Native American roots.

**Bernie**: Spirituality was part of it and I got closer to my culture because my father was Indian, my mother, she was Irish. And my mother used to talk about the IRA (Irish Republican Army) and the old soldiers and sing old war songs and stuff. And my dad, he is ashamed of being Native American because I guess it was not cool back then. He was a warrant officer in the army at the time, he was ashamed of being Native American, never taught me anything about my culture. So when I went to NARA (Native American Rehabilitation Association) I learned about my culture and the ways of my culture. Spirituality is part of it too; it is a real spiritual program.

*Sisters: And what do you feel is the importance of spirituality?*

**Bernie**: Spirituality? Because you got to believe in something, you know, does not matter what it is, you got to believe in something. It is just like you got to have your dreams, because without your dreams you're lost.

*Sisters: And how is your spirituality affected by your experience of homelessness?*

**Bernie**: It got me through what I got through. There has got to be a Higher Power out there or something.

Will was another narrator in a recovery program that helped him regain his sense of self and also brought about a spiritual awakening. His interviewer asked him about how his homelessness caused him to lose then regain his spirituality.

**Will**: Well, I knew that in order to get recovery and get off the streets that I needed to get in touch with the spiritual side because if you have that [faith] you cannot have an I-do-not-care attitude because it makes you care, it makes you want to do the right thing.

*Sisters: And how does that I-do-not-care attitude relate to homelessness?*

**Will**: Sometimes you get in such a rut being on the street. I experienced that the last time I was on the street, which was for a longer period of time. You feel like you have dug yourself down so deep that you have no real way back and so you can either fret about it or you can just say, 'I don't care anymore, this is the hand I've been dealt and that's it.' And a lot of times you will see some homeless people and just by the look on their faces, you can tell they have given up. They just do not care any more, they have resigned themselves to the fact that they are always going to be homeless. You are spiritually bankrupt and once that happens, then your morals pretty much go out the window because you just do not care about yourself. You sure do not care about anybody else…That, to me, is the fuck-it syndrome, or the short serenity prayer.

*Sisters: How do you mean?*

**Will**: Do you know what the serenity prayer is? It is a prayer that everybody in recovery learns at one time or another, it is, 'God grant me the serenity to accept things I cannot change, to change the things I can, and the wisdom to know the difference.' And the short serenity prayer is 'fuck it.' You cannot have them both. You cannot be in both places. And you can take the long way, which is the serenity prayer, or you can go the short serenity prayer, but it leads you back into what you have always done, and I guarantee it is going to lead you right back to homelessness.

Typically, missions that offer meals and shelter to homeless or poor people conduct services before a meal is served. Our narrators gave them mixed reviews. Either they appreciated the missions' emphasis on religion or they questioned if it was truly Christian charity to demand attendance at a service in order to sleep or eat a meal.

**Roger**: I've sat in on the things where you got to listen to the little religious bit and then get the meal, yeah. I've done those.

*Sisters: How is that experience?*

**Roger**: It's alright. It's what you make of it, you know? I think it's a little controlling. If they really loved you, they'd give you the food and then, by showing their love, someone might want to actually listen and be receptive to what they have to say. Instead of being held a captive audience for a morsel of food.

Sometimes, even Christian believers among our narrators expressed dissatisfaction over the religious recruitment policies of missions.

**Pete**: I do not want people preaching to me. I go to church because I want to go to church. I read the Bible daily before I go to work because I want to learn more about the Bible. I want to learn more about the Lord because the Lord is my life. But to force someone to sit through a church service before they eat—that is not right and I see that every night.

Violet, who jokingly said she was raised devoutly "Protestant Catholic," agreed.

**Violet**: And that's why I definitely don't like the missions. I don't like people forcing religion on me, for one thing. And for some reason, if you're homeless or you're poor, they think you don't know God. Which is the furthest from the truth than most people realize because almost everyone that I know that is homeless out here, especially here in Dignity Village, they are true Christians because we all believe in God. I mean, some mornings we have prayer meetings. We read out of the Bible every day. Sometimes we sing songs. And if He was here today, you can believe that He wouldn't be sitting in some of these churches. He would be down the street at the pool hall playing pool with everybody. Because that's who He talked to. He talked to the poor and the homeless and the people that needed Him. But you have to do that when you're in a mission, you know, you have to sit there and listen to 'em cram it down your throat that you gotta be better than what you are: 'Christ doesn't like you if you're not this way.' So, I just don't deal with that. I prefer not to have it crammed down my throat. If I want to go to church, I go to church.

On the other hand, some narrators specifically went to a mission for the sermon and, in fact, found it personally meaningful.

**Bjorn**: Number one, it is nondenominational, so there is no recruitment. They are not trying to convert anybody. I like that. I like the fact that generally what you hear from the podium is testimony rather than preaching. They do have guest churches come in, they do have ordained ministers that will come in sometimes and they will preach a sermon, but even a lot of them are alumni [formerly homeless or addicted]. That is one of the reasons they bring their church guy down there is because they passed through those doors sometime in the past themselves, and they have not forgotten. So they know who they are talking to. But most of the time it is testimony and it is people with experiences just like us who have found a way out through Christianity, through Jesus Christ. I am not that deep into it, but I do believe in a Higher Power and hearing the Gospel and hearing any kind of miracles in somebody's life. I do not care how they got on the right path, however they did it and whether it was Buddhism or Christianity, Judaism, it does not matter as long as they are doing it. That is the important thing. And that is encouraging. It is sort of like the kind of messages you hear in an AA meeting…'This is what I used to be like and this is what I'm like today.'

Tobias was another of many narrators who credited a mission with introducing him to religious teachings.

*Sisters: One thing you mentioned is that you feel that God watches over you. Tell me a little more about your faith.*

**Tobias**: I never used to read the Bible. I went to the Portland Rescue Mission and learned about the spiritual world. I heard it; it made sense to me. But, [inaudible] always told me that if you're down on your luck, turn to your savior Jesus Christ. That's what I turned to.

*Sisters: When did that happen, when you turned?*

**Tobias:** Thirteen years ago when I went to Portland Rescue Mission. They turned me around. Because God will never leave us. He will never forsake us. He will always be with us. It's there for you, you just have to open the door.

Trent was asked whether he got what he needed while living on the streets, as in accessing services.

**Trent:** Yes. God always gives me what I need. Not always what I want. And the timing is sometimes rotten, but it's all in God's time, not mine. And I do attend church there at Salvation Army every week because I believe that they house me and they feed me and I like to worship God with them. I mean, that seems right to me.

*Sisters: You're not required to attend service to stay there?*

**Trent:** No.

*Sisters: But it feels right to you?*

Trent: Yes it does. They do a very short, maybe ten minute [service] before a meal. Very short and a prayer and that's it. But I do read the Bible more, and a gal there gave me a Bible. It's not a King James Version, which is what I prefer, but I read it anyway. I like to do that daily, although I don't always do it.

Many times we heard that a person's faith or relationship with God was all that kept him or her going through hard times on the streets. Iris was asked about the effects of sleeping on the streets and in parked cars.

**Iris:** I lost my esteem, I lost…oh, I just lost everything. I did not want to be myself, but I kept on going to that Rescue Mission, to that church over there at night and keeping my faith. That is what kept me going. That is what is keeping me going, my faith in God. He knows and I know where I am at, and I just take one day at a time. But being out there at night, up and down anywhere around the bridges, sleeping out there with cardboard and different things like that. So my experience just being homeless, being down here, you got to stand and wait in line all through the day, wherever you go. And the people [the general public] just, they turn around and cuss you. They have not seen you before in your life and they approach you this way. I just keep on going; I just do not let it bother me.

I wasn't very strong when I was inside a permanent residence because I knew I was safe. I knew that I had nothing to worry about. But I know on the streets that is not the same. You gotta watch your back; you gotta watch out for yourself, you gotta take care of yourself. Before you can help anybody else. I am a very spiritual person. I ask for help through my days, my nights. I go to church whenever I can. I mean I even go to the Union Gospel Mission when I can to eat because they have a sermon before the meal.

*Sisters: Do you go there because of the sermon? Do you always agree with it, sometimes agree with it?*

**Iris**: I have an open mind. I did not judge.

*Sisters: You make yourself available to the experience and let it happen?*

**Iris**: And then sometimes I go up to the Rescue Mission, because they also have a sermon before dinner, and even before breakfast. I have been there once for breakfast and I have listened to the sermon, and when I can't get to church I read my Bible myself.

*Sisters: You carry your Bible around?*

**Iris**: Yes.

*Sisters: Really. Do you read a lot?*

**Iris**: I read when I can.

No matter how many people a homeless person runs into during a normal day, no matter if he or she lives on the streets with a partner or friend, it is still a dangerous and lonely life. This loneliness is inherent in being an outsider in society and in not being valued and even reviled because of your poverty.

Ryan, 44, explained the solace of his faith.

**Ryan**: Mother raised me, regardless how much I struggled, she always told me, 'God will make it better.' I have been believing that all my life, and He has never let me down.

*Sisters: And you were saying before we started this interview that the things you have been through have actually made you a better person, a stronger person.*

**Ryan**: A stronger person because this is something that I had to earn the right to sit here and do this interview. Years ago I did not even want to be here, be on this planet. It made me humble myself and it made me be more appreciative of the small things in life. I have a personal relationship with Him every day, and it helps me out a lot.

I'm a person that believes in it and I totally believe in God or whatever some people would call it. I know that there's somebody up there that does love us, and I know that He watches out for us. And it doesn't matter what you call Him, but He's there. And as long as I know that and as long as I believe that, I know I'm gonna make it.

Noah, 54, described his faith while living on the streets.

**Noah**: I pray more because you're not taking so many things for granted because it's been harder for you. So I think I turn to God more because I was spiritual anyway. I have a relationship with a Higher Power. One thing I learned is not to take so many things for granted. When you've never had hard times, you don't know what it's like to be like this. All of a sudden when you don't have things anymore, you learn to appreciate things that were just always there.

**Clay:** Spirituality is the only thing that is keeping me going. If I did not have God on my side, I think I'd have given up a long time ago. But I figured if Moses walked through the desert for forty years, I can stay upright in Portland for a month.

Aaron, a native of Ohio, was in our office on his twenty-fifth birthday. A former machinist, he had experienced homelessness on and off. One of his experiences was that he became involved in a religious cult that preyed on the homeless.

**Aaron:** They started talking about having a community. It was in my opinion, a little bit cultish. It was their way or no way. They didn't want you to go to a church, like First Baptist Church up on the corner. It [the services] was like at their house. Then they started wanting us to put all of our earnings into a pot. We would have to go to his wife and ask permission if we wanted anything, and she would, like, take it out. Because they said it's a way to keep people accountable so that you're not going out drinking or whatever and plus, it's the community's money. It's not your money, it's for everyone.

*Sisters: But one person had control over it all?*

**Aaron:** Right, and they wanted to save up and buy a bigger home to expand the community because they were picking up people. And also, I found out those type of people kind of prey on the homeless. Because you know you're at rock bottom when you're homeless and anything sounds good. Like if they say, 'You can crash at my place, no charge. There's a shower. You can shower whenever you want. We'll help you get a job.'

And everyone's looking for religion. You have two types of people out there. You have the people that turn real religious, like asking God to help them because they're homeless. And you have the people that are like real rebellious and 'Screw all this. God made me this way, and God's not here for me.'

When I started, they wanted to push us to go out with them and street preach. We preached to everyone because the square, [in downtown Portland] it's open, but the people that would come up were the homeless people. Then they would bring them back trying to expand the community. Get them jobs. But of course they want everything in a big pot for the whole community.

*Sisters: Did they talk about if they got a new house, would you be part owner of that house, or they would own the house?*

**Aaron:** Whoever it got financed through. Because the man who started his ministry as they refer to it as, he doesn't work. He expects everyone else to work and pay. He says that's his way, like his faith, and God is providing because if he provides us a place to stay, then that's how God's providing rent. He sometimes said things like, 'I don't need to work because I have strong men here that can go out and work. I'm doing God's work.' And we're expected to give them all the money which paid for their rent and their vehicles, their gas, everything.

*Sisters: Did you do that while you lived there?*

**Aaron**: Well yeah, actually I fell for it because I was looking for new friends. I was out here, didn't know very many people. I come from a Christian background, so I wanted to get established in a church or some kind of Christian organization. Everything sounds legit when they first start talking to you, then they start putting the little twists and turns the deeper that you get into it and the more that they trust you. Because they don't want to scare you off at first.

Aaron lived with the cult for two months before moving on. His interviewer asked him how his experiences on the street impacted his spirituality.

**Aaron**: I still believe in God, but I think that it's pretty much what you do with your life. A lot of people blame God or think that God is gonna deliver them. I believe in God, but I think it's one of those situations that you got to pick it up and you gotta do it yourself. I mean, He might be there spiritually or whatever, but He's not gonna give you a job. You're gonna have to go out and look for it. He's not gonna let some stranger just walk up to you and 'Hey, I gotta job for you.' You gotta go out and do it. You gotta go out and find your own place. You gotta keep your job. You gotta day by day do your thing.

A number of our narrators expressed spiritual beliefs although they were not active in a church or spiritual community. Bert was originally from Wichita and explained that his homelessness began after a devastating divorce. His marriage broke up in 1997 after he discovered his wife was having an affair with his brother. They had been married for fourteen years and were parents to four children.

**Bert**: I just left everything, just let her have everything.

I put my whole heart into that relationship and it really tore me up.

Bert's father died when he was 8 in a work-related accident, and his mother raised him and his five siblings while working at a meat packing plant. He said that the death of his father always haunted him, and he grew up "just kind of lonely, not having a father. And everybody else I went to school with had their dad, and I just felt really cheated I guess."

He was rebellious in his childhood and began drinking and using drugs, then quit school in tenth grade, but later obtained a GED. Until his divorce, he worked as an auto mechanic. During the divorce, his wife sold all his work tools, worth about twenty thousand dollars. The lack of these tools has been a barrier for him finding another mechanic's position since mechanics are required to bring their own tools to work. After the divorce, he moved to Kansas City.

**Bert**: And that's when I started drinking. I started drinking and smoking crack cocaine just to try to hide that pain.

He was sleeping outdoors during this time and working at short-term jobs. After about three years of using crack, he went into a rehab program and stayed clean for nine months, then resumed drinking, but not crack. He then started traveling around the country hitchhiking or traveling by bus. During his interview, he discussed the problems of living on the streets such as coping with bad weather and having his belongings stolen—he'd been robbed three times in the previous summer and was in the process of obtaining new identification. His interviewer asked him if had ever ridden the rails.

**Bert**: I have a few times, but I didn't like it.

*Sisters: Why didn't you like that?*

**Bert**: It was just kind of scary because—

*Sisters: Did you have to jump on and jump off and sneak?*

**Bert**: Yeah. And I always worry about breaking my leg trying to get off that train. Yeah, because they [moving trains] jerk back and forth and they hop up and down and they go sideways all at once. And I've met a few people…they've got gangs now. They have had for years on the trains. Freight Train Riders of America, that's what they call them. They'll steal your stuff and throw you off the train, literally.

*Sisters: Is it dangerous to be homeless?*

**Bert**: I think so.

*Sisters: How do you keep safe?*

**Bert**: Just depend on God.

*Sisters: Do you believe in God?*

**Bert**: Sure I do.

*Sisters: Is He watching out for you?*

**Bert**: Sure, He does every day. Yeah, that's about the only thing I really have to hold on to, you know. I always have believed in Him. And I think He keeps me safe every day. He's done it for this many years.

---

Interviewer's Journal Excerpt:

*I am very excited to discover that, thus far, every single participant in this project is interested in further involvement. Each individual has been really passionate about this project and their contribution to it. Individuals bring a variety of skills and interests, but primarily folks have stated that they want to do whatever is needed to help.*

*In addition, I feel that I have already begun to build relationships with participants.*

---

*There is one woman who I mentioned a few weeks ago, who I've been able to talk with at least once a week. There is a nice rapport building between us. What makes this experience particularly exciting is that this woman is someone I didn't think I could connect with at all. She had a lot of violent things to say in her interview. It's exciting to me that a relationship is building. She is someone who does not trust many people (as she told me herself) and she has expressed trusting me.*

*When I saw her last, she was sitting across from the cafe rolling a cigarette. I went over to chat with her. When I had to leave, I told her to try to stay warm. She asked me to pray for her and then asked, "Do you pray?" I said, "No, I don't pray...but I'll pray for you." She thanked me, smiled, and we hugged goodbye.*

Photographer: Terry Prather

Photographer: Laura Brown

# Chapter 12
## Chapter Twelve

*People do not like to be forgotten*

# Relating to Society and
# the Homeless Community

---

*There can be hope for a society which acts as one big family, not as many separate ones.*

—Anwar el Sadat

When we were founding Sisters, Sandy and I asked people in Old Town what they wanted, and they said, "We need a community gathering spot where we can be social, check in with one another, and talk about the things that matter in our lives and our world." It's a testimony to what Dorothy Day said: "We have all known the long loneliness and we have learned that the only solution is love and that love comes with community." Customers tell us, "If I don't come to Sisters, it's just me looking at the four walls of my hotel." Folks who have been living under a bridge or in a shelter together with eighty other people and then move to an SRO or place of their own are abruptly separated from the only community they know. It becomes even more important to have gathering spots; not social services, but a "third place" to go be human beings together.

As for relationships on the street, they mirror relationships anywhere in society. Sexism is alive and well. Domestic violence and racism occur. All the violence in the larger society walks through the door of the cafe. Don't romanticize skid row. That being said, in a lot of skid rows the historic tolerance of people's differences has disappeared in the process of gentrification. It's more than tolerance; in any skid row bar you might have had the Native American men, the African-Americans, a white woman with a patch over her eye, lesbians—and they all knew each other's names. The common disenfranchisement from the larger society they shared was core.

At Sisters we say that building relationship is the purpose of our organization. It's not just because it's the right thing to do; it's because it's the first thing, the meta-thing to do. Every story in this chapter relates to the nicest complement Sisters has ever gotten: "I'm not invisible in Sisters."

—Genny

Jared was a young man who had been homeless on and off since he was 14. He expressed a sentiment that we heard frequently—how the unkempt and unclean among the homeless community fueled the assumption that all homeless people are degenerates. Like many of our narrators, he resented being labeled and judged by society because of these stereotypes.

**Jared**: It was kind of like you are nobody. Your appearance has a lot to do with it. There are a lot of homeless people who have long straggly beards, stringy hair. It was kind of like being an ex-con; people looked at you differently, like you are a nobody, or you're not worth hiring, you are not worth taking a chance on. It was hard to find a job. It still is, that is why I am working with *street roots*, [selling a street newspaper that promotes self-help and empowerment among people living in poverty], because I could not find a job.

Warren echoed Jared's opinion of how the habits and behaviors of some in the homeless community cause problems for the majority.

**Warren**: I can't say that the city, the state, country is to blame, because they're really not. It's our own actions as a group of people. Homeless people are people too. It just takes a few to screw it up for everybody.

*Sisters: What do you mean?*

**Warren**: Campsites. Not keeping them clean. Okay, if you're in a neighborhood where you can see the look on the people's faces, kind of like, 'Oh, man, look at that guy pushing a shopping cart.' Why bring so much attention to yourself? Now I've seen people with shopping carts just majorly overloaded with all kinds of knick-knacks, bric-a-brac, and bullshit tied onto it, where it looks like the guy's really trying to build an automobile out of it. And do they really need all that? I mean, having three sets of clothes is one thing and having thirty sets of clothes is another. There are places that you wash your clothes. There are places where you can get a change of clothing almost every day, if you really want to. Why bring so much attention to the fact that you're homeless?

*Sisters: Why do you think they do collect so many things?*

**Warren**: That one I never really figured out. Another man's junk is another man's treasure. Maybe it's because they don't have something stable like a home. Maybe that's just in their nature. Maybe they just collect things.

*Sisters: So you think that homeless people shouldn't call attention to themselves?*

**Warren**: Not as much as some do. There are different groups of homeless people. There are the people that plain don't really care about working, that can get by however they get by. There are the homeless people who are thieves. There are the ones that are drug addicts, alcoholics. There are people with mental problems. There are people with relationship problems. Everybody has problems.

Warren went on to describe a recent incident. He'd been camping at a schoolyard with other homeless people for three weeks, and every morning the janitor would wake them, telling them when it was time to leave.

**Warren**: I mean we weren't on a first-name basis or anything, but there was a nodding acquaintance there, where he knew that we were there. It was all good because we kept the place clean. But, apparently, somebody jimmied some hinges on a door, and somebody left a cooker [drug paraphernalia] in the porta-potty, and those are just things that you don't do. You don't go ripping off where you're staying. You don't rip off, period. If it's not yours, it's not yours.

*Sisters: So they were trying to get into the school to steal something?*

**Warren**: I think they were trying to get into the janitor's stash of pop cans.

*Sisters: And they left a drug cooker in the porta-potty?*

**Warren**: Yeah, in the porta-potty. So those two things made it to where it's not cool for anybody to be there now. I mean this was really convenient because it was within short walking distance to a neighborhood place called St. Francis where people eat, and that's kind of a hub for a lot of people. It's a place for us to congregate. It's like our home. But, even there, people get careless. I mean it's no secret that there has been drug activity and alcohol activity around the premises of St. Francis off and on for years. But when you can walk through a park where kids are most likely to play sometime and find empty containers that had drugs in them at one time or may even still have needles, that's not right. A parent shouldn't have to worry about going to a park with their child, and the child going, 'Gee, Mommy, what's this?' That's not cool.

Warren explained that he'd had his belongings and his identification stolen.

**Warren**: That's another issue I've never understood. As a group of people in the city of Portland [homeless people], why steal from one another? Why steal at all? But stealing from one another is even lower than stealing at all, because it's like we're all in this together.

In fact, a number of narrators complained about being ripped off by other homeless people. One 54-year-old veteran described how he had his belongings stolen from his camper and truck by homeless people.

**Daniel:** I do not know why homeless got to steal from homeless. Well, I know why: because they are easy targets. You take a homeless person, they have not got the money to get burglar alarms. I have had stuff ripped off so many times from me it is pathetic, and I know it is the homeless doing it.

Personal safety concerns were expressed in many of our conversations, and both young and old narrators confided that they were afraid of other people on the street. Jason was 35 and had been in Portland one month at the time of our interview.

*Sisters: How did it feel being new to town?*

**Jason:** It was kind of iffy. I was wondering what kind of people were sleeping under that bridge with me.

You always worry about things like that. We have certain people that make being homeless a lifetime habit or something. That is what they want or something, but it is not for me. You see them under there drinking this, that, and the other, doing their little hooplas. As long as they stay where they are at and everything, everything is fine. But it still makes it a little rough to sleep because you just do not know where they are sitting; if they are crazy or they are going to stab you in your sleep, or kill you over your shoes. You always have that thought in the back of your mind. You do not sleep very well because of it.

At times it seemed that people who were newly homeless had keen insights into the homeless population and the issues that surround them. Aiden, who had been homeless about five months, offered this perception:

**Aiden:** You are going to have homeless [people] just because they want to be homeless. That is what they prefer. But the people that I think are trying not to be, that are trying to get off the streets, several that have families out there as well. They have a mass, homeless people here. It is not one hundred people, it is not a thousand people, it is probably several thousand people. You see people disappear often into the woodwork. Everybody has someplace they go throw a mat down, but you know what? I will tell you, there are a lot of mats being thrown down at a lot of different places and I think that is why people have not recognized how big the homeless problem is here. It is because the city has so dispersed people that they just go to numerous places so they do not get harassed.

Later he expressed his concern about the most vulnerable on the streets.

**Aiden:** There are a lot of mentally sick people in this town that are wandering around not able to take care of themselves. I know Reagan opened the doors and let this happen awhile back. They are nuts. They have no business walking around the streets by themselves, and I think it is an issue that needs to be looked at. I feel worse for them than I do for myself.

There are identifiable subgroups among people on the streets. Alexander, an African-American who rides freight trains throughout the country, makes distinctions between the broader classification of homeless people and tramps.

**Alexander**: Just because I am homeless does not mean that I want to be around a bunch of homeless people. There is a big difference between what everyone calls 'a homeless person' and 'a tramp.' Tramps are your hitchhikers and train riders, the type of people who like to get out and do something. We are not dependent on the mission. We will go out and we will do day-labor work. We will go out and work for somebody. We will go home and flash a sign off the freeway. We will panhandle. We will go pick up cans. We will hustle. We will actually try to take care of ourselves. A homeless person is something that we call 'a home guard,' and he is wandering from one mission to the next place that serves lunch, to this other place over here that will give them clothes, then go back to the mission again. They are caught in a vicious cycle, and they do not seem to be in any hurry to try to get out of that vicious cycle. There is a big difference between the two.

*Sisters: Are tramps and home guards instantly recognizable?*

**Alexander**: Yeah.

*Sisters: Are they different?*

**Alexander**: Oh, yeah! Very much so.

*Sisters: So, the tramp is the one who is working or hustling or always bettering their situation and not depending on services?*

**Alexander**: Right…uses services because he really wants to or he just absolutely has to. Smart tramps try to stay out of the little circuits as much as possible. Let's face it. It is much easier to panhandle or recycle cans or fly signs or anything like that when you are out someplace where there is not a bunch of people trying to do the same thing.

*Sisters: So it is not to your advantage to be in the same places where everyone else is?*

**Alexander**: Right…most of us real tramps, we might come down and hang out with them, party a little bit…but we usually try to get away from all of those people. Can you imagine having to stake out the McDonald's dumpster like, two hours ahead of time because there are twenty other people waiting on the hamburgers to get thrown out? You have to go scuffling. I see that all the time.

Train riders just generally do not get along with home guards very well and we just pretty much try to stay away from them as best we can. It is not really a prejudicial thing, it is that if the mission was to shut down they would probably starve.

*Sisters: So they are dependent?*

**Alexander:** Yeah, they are actually really dependent on services. And you run into a lot of drama in these missions, lot of drama. You are scared to pull out your pack of cigarettes and light one because one hundred people will say 'Let me have a cigarette, man,' and it is like a mob. You get tired of that, and not to mention the cops do target homeless people. And usually anyplace that you find a mission or soup kitchen, usually they are always located in the worst part of town where there are a million cops, and there are dope fiends everywhere, and everybody does not like to be around all that.

Later he described more distinctions among homeless people, some who are homeless by choice, and some who have lost jobs and are thus forced into homelessness.

**Alexander:** The ones that arrive here by choice, they do not really count, but there are a lot of homeless out who have run into financial problems and lost their jobs, and it is a vicious cycle. A lot of people get depressed about it and then they start to drink over it and then they start to get high over it and then the next day they are just out there. Drugs are a big issue with homelessness. There are a lot of people who are homeless because they cannot find their way out of the dope house.

And then there is a lot of camaraderie between the homeless people, especially locals in towns. The home guards that I talked about get out there and start meeting other people that had similar things happen to them, and they get to talking and develop friendships. And then you find out that a lot of these people are not all that bad.

[The media and society paint the homeless as a] 'bunch of bums, a bunch of good-for-nothings.' But once you develop friendships, you realize that a lot of homeless people are intelligent and don't deserve the stereotypes. You find yourself in another, entirely different society, and a lot of people get into these situations and do not want to go back into the mainstream, tax-paying type of life because they find that their best friends are homeless people.

*Sisters: So they are finding they have more in common with these other people who are down and out; the very ones society has said are not worth anything?*

**Alexander:** Right, right.

*Sisters: What do you think about that? Does that make sense to you?*

**Alexander:** It does make sense to me, it really does. People who find themselves into the homeless culture and they start to come into the realization, 'I have been working for twenty years, hard, paying taxes and struggling to pay these bills and make ends meet. Basically, the only thing that separated me from these people in the street is that I actually did have a home to go to. I was just as broke as they are.'

*Sisters: Yeah? Because they were paying bills and in debt?*

**Alexander**: Right. A lot of people get out there and a lightbulb goes off: 'I have been doing it this wrong way. I have been working to be broke.'

*Sisters: Working to be broke?*

**Alexander**: Right. So why not just let it all go…all of that responsibility and worry and heartache and just keep things simple? There is not really much difference between us and the average nine-to-five stiff; he is just working to be broke most of the time.

We heard from some who preferred to be loners.

**Terry**: I don't try to get too close to anybody because I've run across so many people…I've had my stuff stolen three times this summer.

Sol grew up in Minnesota and left home when he was 17. Except for four years when he was housed, at the time of his interview he had been homeless for almost twenty years. He traveled by freight train and hitchhiking, and although he had recently returned from visiting his mother in Minnesota, he travels and lives alone.

**Sol**: You usually do not run across somebody who is going to travel with you. Sometimes you do, but most homeless people, unless you have a significant other, are single, live to themselves.

*Sisters: What was that like, traveling alone?*

**Sol**: It is fun. I am not tied down to anybody. Sometimes it is fun.

His interviewer asked him if his family had always known where he was, and he replied that for a long time they did not know his whereabouts.

*Sisters: Was that on purpose that you did not tell them?*

**Sol**: [When you're] homeless it is hard to keep in touch. You do not have an address or anything. You are just kind of lost.

Sol explained that he had long-standing problems with drugs and alcohol, had sustained himself through criminal activity and eating from dumpsters, but now is doing better since he collects SSI and SSD benefits. He had been diagnosed with a mental illness and was on the Oregon Health Plan, which paid for his medication. Later in the interview, the subject of Camp Dignity [later called Dignity Village] came up. Sol dismissed its concept.

**Sol**: I think it is a place where people go and feel sorry for themselves. Everybody can get comfortable in their little zone and feel sorry for themselves.

In some interviews our narrators were asked how their opinions of homeless people changed once they became homeless themselves.

**Dustin**: Sad.

*Sisters: Before or since you became homeless?*

**Dustin:** I've always been a person, since I was adopted at 4, I've always been a person in touch with the person who didn't have something. Even when I used to run away from home, they would find me in the projects or across the railroad tracks at a bum's shack or something because I knew them people would tell me the truth about life. It wasn't plastic-coated. It's real. It's as real as you can get when you're that low, and a person who's down there has nothing to lie to you about, really. They're going to tell you straight up what life is about, how it is.

Sam was living at Dignity Village at the time of our study. He told his story to one of the three interviewers who lived at the village for four March days and nights, sleeping in a villager's unheated hut at night, and by day interviewing people in the community room, the bus, or in the cars they were camping in. He explained his role at the homeless camp.

**Sam:** I volunteered assisting with donations, and I do security from time to time, pick up the trash, and kind of clean up sometimes.

*Sisters: What makes you volunteer here?*

**Sam:** Well, for one thing, it is better than sitting around and doing nothing if I could make it cleaner or a little safer. I'm not going out making any money anyway, so I am going to try and help out.

*Sisters: Is there a closeness here? Is there a community here? Or is it more just a bunch of people kind of pitching tents here?*

**Sam:** Well both, I think. There is a community here for the most part, but for whatever reason, there are people who come in and pitch their tent who are not really a part of the community. There are some people here that run around and try and start arguments that pit people against each other, all the bickering.

Some narrators described how they noticed that a portion of people on the streets had become accustomed to, or were complacent about their situation.

**Janeen:** I am looking at some of these people down here and somehow feel sorry for some of them because I guess they just feel comfortable being homeless. That is all they are used to; that is all they know how to do, is be homeless. Most of these women do not want to be homeless. No way. It is dangerous because we are women, for one.

Generosity among the homeless community was also a common theme expressed in interviews. Arnold was new to homelessness and had moved to Dignity Village from the Oregon coast. Once at the camp, he immediately set to work building structures and making improvements. He described the atmosphere of Dignity Village.

**Arnold**: People share even if they only got a little. They share pretty much what they have. It is pretty pleasant and it is friendly. I think I only saw one little heated incident, but it was handled. A bunch of the villagers here got together and they worked with each other and got these two people apart.

Another theme was having a "running partner," usually someone of the same gender with whom you camped, cooked, and went canning, someone whom you protected and who protected you, someone you could leave your pack with, drink with, and trust.

Aaron, 25, a native of Ohio and a former machinist, moved to Portland to start over. When interviewed, he was camping in the city limits with a small group because he believed in safety in numbers. He interacted mostly with the younger people on the streets. His interviewer asked him if he spent time at this camp during the day.

**Aaron**: No, you don't want to do that.

*Sisters: Because you'll mess up your spot?*

**Aaron**: Well that, and plus some people can, like, follow you back because there's more people out during the day. Once you find a spot, you kind of want to keep it to yourself, because other people will try to take over or kick you out. There are a lot of possibilities that can happen to you. Once you find one, you gotta kind of guard it and be careful not to let other new people coming into town, like, follow you back. And that's why you don't leave your stuff back at your place, because some people can stake it out, and if you leave your bag, they'll go and rip you off or take your stuff.

*Sisters: So how many people are sleeping there?*

**Aaron**: Usually four to five of us.

*Sisters: If you didn't come back there tonight, would they be wondering about you?*

**Aaron**: Yeah, yeah. Once you get your, like, squat partners or a partner or whatever, usually you're…I won't say 24/7, but you kind of keep tabs on each other and make sure everyone's cool, you know. Because a lot of people out here, like if you're homeless, a lot of transients and that type people, they don't have family, and if something happened to them, it could be days, weeks until someone figures out what happens to them. So, like, once you get a partner, usually you keep pretty close tabs on each other to make sure that everyone's okay and what's going on. Like if you're gonna leave town, you better tell them, because it's a community. I found out that street people and street kids and stuff like that, they got their packs. I don't want to say like gangs, but pretty much that's what you get into.

*Sisters: So of the people that you're camping with now, would you consider them to be friends?*

**Aaron**: Mm hmm, yeah.

*Sisters: Good friends or strong friends?*

**Aaron**: I wouldn't leave my bag there, that type of thing, 'cause it's still, you don't know. Like a lot of situations, one minute they can be fine, but there's a lot of drug use out there, and they can come back and totally be a different person moment to moment. So, if they're sober, they can be cool, but if they shoot up or something and come back, they could be a totally different person. But of course when they come down or get off or whatever, they're back to themselves.

But it's a different world out there than what I pictured it. Because when people think of homeless, they think of like the old guy smelling, wanting booze all the time, sitting on the corner passed-out type thing. And it's not like that at all. I would say probably fifteen to twenty percent are like that. The rest of them, they might have a drug problem or an addiction, but it's more or less falling on bad times. And then when you get into the homeless situation, there's a lot of drugs out there, and you find out where they are, and there's a lot of peer pressure. Like, 'Man, you're down on your luck man; screw it all, here. Here you go.'

*Sisters: So you're saying that homelessness can cause drug issues?*

**Aaron**: Exactly.

*Sisters: And you said you don't use drugs or alcohol. Not at all?*

**Aaron**: I drink an occasional beer, but I go to the bar. I don't go buy a six-pack and go back to the squat and try and get drunk.

Everyone says that when you're homeless, it's just because you're running from responsibility. And that's true. I believe that some of the street kids, it's a big adventure and some people like that lifestyle. But it isn't really running from responsibility. You still have responsibility when you're homeless. You have to show up. It's kind of like a herd. During the day, you'll see the same people hitting up all the missions. It's kind of like a big family. If you stay in there for a while, people get to know you. And, it's like a big herd going mission to mission. You know, you just do this cycle throughout the day. So you aren't just doing whatever you want, you know?

*Sisters: Right, you're on a schedule. Do you feel like you're part of that family now?*

**Aaron**: I'm getting there. I don't have a nickname. That's a good thing. I think that once you get a nickname, you've been out there for a while.

*Sisters: You think it's a good thing you don't have a nickname?*

**Aaron**: Yeah, the street name. So at least I'm not that deep into it. But, I am getting to know a lot of them. I've been out there for a while and they're starting to get to know me. I mean, it's kind of cool in a way, but it's also kind of scary because like I said, once they start to know you by your name, they start asking you for stuff and whatever. Because, it's kind of funny, a lot of us don't try to bum stuff off of the people going down the street, the nine-to-fivers. We try to help each other out. If someone gets a pack of cigarettes, when you're waiting in line for a mission, you go hand out probably five or six cigarettes to some people that you know. A lot of people say homeless people are stingy and they're always begging for this and that. There are a lot of people that spange [ask for spare change] out there, but there's a lot of them that do the Labor Ready thing. Like me, I do Labor Ready here and there. I like to get some cash. You know, a lot of them would hustle too. What I mean by hustle, it's not like hustling someone out of something, like hustle can also mean that you're trying to get a job. There's this one guy that just goes around and he asks if semi drivers and people that are doing deliveries need help to unload the back of trucks. And, they'll throw him twenty bucks after an hour's worth of work.

Aaron explained that he tried to do things independently from other people on the street such as eating at fast-food restaurants, and not strictly relying on the missions for services, or staying in the same neighborhood all the time. He was asked how he thought society saw him.

**Aaron**: That's a good question because I've really noticed that if you're in between, it's a little bit harder. If you're homeless but you don't look it, you kind of get shunned from the homeless side of it, and then on the other hand, when people find out that you're homeless but you don't look it, they think something's up and they're more suspicious in helping you.

He then described how he stayed clean, still had his teeth, and didn't use drugs.

**Aaron**: I have noticed, though, that sometimes you gotta play the role. If you need something, I don't want to say you want to play the system, but sometimes you gotta dirty yourself up to get stuff, to play the role of homeless. And, you can play the role of being clean-cut and having the nine-to-five job. It depends on what spectrum you're trying to get.

*Sisters: So you still have the freedom to move between those worlds. You can go into McDonald's and then you can go the other way also, where as a lot of homeless people don't have that option. I mean, once you've lost your teeth, you know, you don't really have that option.*

**Aaron**: Exactly.

*Sisters: So, what's your self-image like now compared to what it was a year and a half ago?*

**Aaron**: I don't look down on the less fortunate people like I used to. Like I said, if I came across someone like that, I would just be like, 'Go get your booze. Here's fifty cents for the cause,' that type of attitude. But now I know that sometimes if you don't want to give someone change because you feel like they are in drug use or alcoholic or whatever, go buy them a cup of coffee. You know what I'm saying? It does help. I've been out there in the morning and wanting a cup of coffee. If someone just goes out and buys you a little twelve-ounce, dollar-fifty coffee, it makes your day.

Aaron described the categories of young people he sees on the street.

**Aaron:** This is what I came up with: this is the three categories of the kids out there. There's the true street kids, the transient kids like the ones that are from Portland that are on the streets, that's been there for years. They know the ins and outs of Portland. They got their nicknames, their street names, and that's all that they go by. They call themselves literally, 'the family.' Then there's the transients, the ones that just go all over the United States and they stop in. They got some buddies here, like some of the street kids that are permanently here, they know each other, but they just, like, move on. They go up through Seattle then back down through California, go out to New York, go down to Florida. Those are the migrating transient kids.

*Sisters: And how do they travel? Trains?*

**Aaron:** Trains or hitchhiking is the preferred way. Or if they come across some money, if their parents throw them some cash, they'll go Greyhound. But then there's the third. Then there's the wanna-bes. The kids that are still at home but they'll come out and hang with the street kids. They act like they're homeless on the weekend, like weekend warriors. But then when it gets too rough, they run home.

*Sisters: Do you have similar categories for people who aren't kids that are homeless? Let's look at reasons for homelessness maybe. You talked about there are people out there with drug and alcohol issues, people who are just down on their luck.*

**Aaron:** Yes, there's quite a few categories that you could come up with for the adults. There's the people that like it. That's their lifestyle. Almost kind of like if you're institutionalized in prison and you've been in prison for a long time, you just get used to someone telling you when to do it, how to do it, and you just get almost brainwashed. There's that type of people that like it because that's the way that they are. There's the people that are down on their luck. There's the people that are in addictions that they can't break and it just totally breaks them and they just deteriorate into homelessness. Then there's also a lot of people that are not crazy enough to be institutionalized, but they're not stable enough to hold a job or something, so they're homeless back and forth using the missions or whatever. Then there's also the people kind of like the kids, the transient adults, that just…I guess they started out when they were kids doing it, train hoppers, and they just go around city to city, just on a big adventure all their life. And then there's also the ones that are out there that are just out of prison like parolees. They don't have much when they come out.

If there was one statement that we heard most often during the course of this project, it is that homelessness can happen to anyone. Or as many narrators said, "A lot of people are only one paycheck away from being homeless themselves." Narrators pointed not only to their own lives, but to professionals who had lost everything because of an addiction, to women who left middle-class comfort to escape abuse, or to whole families who ended up on the streets after both adults lost their jobs.

We also heard that society doesn't understand the causes of homelessness. John was asked what he wanted people to understand about being homeless.

**John:** That there are various reasons. It is not just one reason why people are homeless. It could be mental illness, could be physical disabilities, it could be a variety of things. And it is not like a lot of society thinks, where they are just lazy, they just want to get off, or live off welfare or Social Security.

Another comment often heard was that they felt forgotten or overlooked by society at large. We also heard that homelessness cannot be solved by people who only understand it from a distance.

**Erin:** America's just not paying as much attention to their own people.

**Fred:** In order to really understand homelessness and accept homelessness, you or someone close to you would have to have experienced it. People donate money; that is their way of feeling good. They just send a check every month but it would be more valuable and more worthwhile to come down here and [talk to people] as you [interviewers] are doing.

**Lyle:** It goes back to richer and poorer. You know, the division is getting greater all the time. You're either in poverty or you're rich. The middle class aren't really around any more.

Reid, 35, was asked how homelessness affects society.

**Reid:** I think a lot of society just tries to turn a blind eye to it. Like I sleep in the park and you see all these people jogging by in the one-hundred-dollar Nike suits saying, 'Hey look at this bum over here.' It is not like I have a choice to sleep under the bridge…A lot of people just feel that we are an eyesore to the city…There should be no reason in the world that a city of this population should have a homeless problem.

Grant, a self-described "tramp," has opted out of contemporary society, preferring the freedom of his homeless lifestyle. He believes that in society in general, there is little incentive to try and change the system.

**Grant:** The majority of the people are just a herd of sheep. Most of them are too busy trying to hold down that nine-to-five and keep up with the bills and take care of their family and chase the American Dream to be worried with it, to even give it a thought.

Many narrators noted apathy toward homelessness in society at large.

**Austin:** Being homeless is not fun, so let's keep trying to get people off the streets.

*Sisters: Is that how you feel about homelessness?*

**Austin:** It's not the best thing, no. People say 'I walked home in the rain.' Well, you can go home, get dry under a warm blanket. I have to cuddle up wet with my blanket, ya know? It hasn't bothered me, but now that summer is over, it's bothering me. It would sure be nice to see someone care about the homeless. I haven't seen it myself.

Several of our narrators commented that the United States has its own caste system.

**Duncan:** [Homeless people are the lowest caste because] their voice is not heard.

Carlos was asked how homelessness was affecting society.

**Carlos:** It is starting to affect society in the fact that the only solutions that a lot of communities are coming up with are to criminalize homeless people. That affects a community because once you criminalize somebody, that limits their options for work and for becoming productive citizens in the future. Or even if it is something they do such as sleep on a sidewalk or in the forest or in their car or truck, it is temporary. But being criminalized kind of destroys your future because a lot of employers look at whether or not you have been convicted of a crime. I know a lot of people now are starting up a campaign saying homelessness is not a crime. It is not, really, because anybody can become homeless. I have had many, many people in the community say that homelessness is just one paycheck away for them, from sheriffs to schoolteachers to everyone…

It [homelessness] is becoming a very negative aspect of our culture. It is a drag on our resources. It has broken up families, the family structure, early death for a lot of them. There are a lot of negative impacts to society because we allow homelessness to continue. When I was a kid we never saw as many homeless people as we do now. If they could focus on this and solve this problem then I think they would have a better community.

Carlos echoed what Mark said about a caste system, and said what is needed is a society without a hierarchal structure, where communities are working together in partnership.

**Carlos:** We are suffering from ancient ideas and terms of how we should be, and the people climbing the ladder to be an elite are forgetting about the people at the bottom.

Frank, a Vietnam-era veteran, thought factors that led to homelessness were inflation, low wages, and a lack of unions.

**Frank:** I think a lot of society doesn't want to think that it [homelessness] exists, like it's not really there, and it can't happen to them. What I understand, the average person, if they didn't have an income for two months, they'd lose everything they have.

*Sisters: How do you think society deals with this issue?*

**Frank:** I think they ignore it a lot.

---

*Sisters: What leads you to believe they ignore it?*

**Frank**: Oh! There are an awful lot of homeless people out there that are not choosing to be that way. I know that there are a lot of services out there. But I know if I were to try and set my tent up in some nice neighborhood somewhere, it would last about thirty seconds. They certainly do not want to see something like that right across their fence.

*Sisters: So it is a certain kind of denial of that reality?*

**Frank**: Yeah…If I can go find someplace where nobody knows I am back there, they will never mess with me and nobody seems to care. I learned how to kind of camouflage my camp and my trail.

Narrators commonly complained that housed people misunderstood or labeled them. Rick moved to Portland from Detroit after his partner asked him to leave. He decided to start over in a different part of the country. He chose Portland because he believed the city was particularly attractive and the climate relatively mild. He had suffered from panic attacks and was becoming stabilized on medication provided by the Oregon Health Plan. During the interview, he described how he was embarrassed to be living on the street because of how other people saw him.

**Rick**: The embarrassment was just that I knew that people had these stereotypes and that you get these pity stares. And I just wanted to approach people sometimes and say, you know, 'Don't pity me; I feel better now than I have in years.' I was having such a great time and I am so glad that I took the steps and had the courage to do what I have done regardless of my circumstances. And then I am still young enough to really build a new life for myself. I am 34 now, which if you were to ask me when I was 21, I would have thought [34] was too old to do it. But I still feel pretty youthful. I think even though it sounds silly, the [reality television] show "Survivor" actually helped. I like that show and I thought when I moved out here, 'Treat this like a game,' and the game was like a scavenger hunt. Find out where the shelters are. Find out where to get food. Find out where you can loiter and where you cannot. Find out where the public bathrooms are; find out where there is shelter; find the library when the weather is bad. I just kind of turned it into a game.

Janine, 43 and the mother of three adult children, had grown up in Long Beach, California, then lived in Southern Oregon. Raised by a mentally ill mother, she explained that she had lived in poverty throughout her life. She moved to Portland from a small town in Southern Oregon, hoping to find work. Like many of the women we interviewed, her history included hardship and abuse, and a rape that occurred when she was 15.

**Janine**: Actually I have lived in poverty all my life, raised our kids in poverty, low-wage jobs, welfare, unemployment and also Social Security, and so homelessness has been a chronic, recurring thing in my life and my kids' lives. Until I moved to Portland, I never really thought about my homeless situations as being homeless. I am from Southern Oregon, which is very rural, and you were just scrounging around. Maybe you lived in someone's shack out back or whatever. Or camped in one of the campgrounds or lived in your car or a tent for a while, and that is pretty common down there. The level of poverty and the unemployment rate is pretty hard down there.

There are not a lot of jobs, so it is so common. We really do not think about it as homelessness, but just as getting by.

Janine went on to explain that she had mental health problems and that living homeless in Portland was more traumatic than being homeless in a rural area where there is more of a sense of community.

**Janine**: There was more the sense of being isolated and being ostracized from the mainstream community here. I really felt violated. [I] was only able to cling to sanity because of a few supports such as Sisters Of The Road and working for *street roots*, where I found dignity and respect, despite my circumstances. Then I found people that I could talk to, that were not as crazy as me…and not so completely disconnected from the community at large.

It took Janine three years to receive SSI benefits for her mental health problems after being fired from a series of jobs. She described a number of traumatic experiences she'd suffered.

**Janine**: Actually, when I was raped that was very traumatic, and I'd much prefer to be raped than become homeless, any day.

*Sisters: Do you want to talk more about that? I mean, that is a pretty amazing statement.*

**Janine**: When somebody rapes you they physically violate you in a sexual manner, you get over that, you can compartmentalize, 'Well, this is a sexual predator.' You can see that it is not you, that it is this person's [the rapist's] problem, right? But when you become homeless, everybody is judging you that you are no good, you have failed, you are lazy. It is all these judgments on you, and you begin to question everything you have ever done and how you got here. Am I lazy? I question everything and my value as a person. Where, when I am raped, my value as a person is not in question, just my vulnerability as a woman. I would much rather be raped than become homeless.

Janine went on to relate how a violent mentally ill woman on the streets had tormented her and other homeless women, even causing one woman to land in the hospital with her injuries. A large and powerful woman, she beat Janine several times and also knifed people. Desperate, Janine reported her to the police who talked with her tormenter.

**Janine**: [But] even though I had evidence that I had been assaulted, they did not take it serious and treat it as assault. And even though I had told them that I wanted to press charges, they just basically treated it as a nonissue and just a hassle as far as they were concerned.

She described how she kept watching for her assailant but hadn't seen her in a while. Janine went on to make another analogy about homelessness.

**Janine:** I have never been domestically abused, but you hear people talking about domestic abuse and how it accelerates from verbal abuse, and by the time it gets to the physical abuse, you are so demoralized psychologically from the verbal and psychological abuse, that you really do not have the strength of mind to be able to deal with the physical abuse. And that is exactly what homelessness is like. It is like being emotionally and psychologically abused by everyone. Someone might not say something to you [that is] degrading, but if they cannot look you in the eye just like they did a week ago when you were not homeless, you got the message loud and clear. These people look around you, under you, over you; they will not look at you and all of a sudden you are invisible. You are a walking ghost.

Janine also pointed out the subcultures among people on the streets.

**Janine:** There is a culture when you are poor and you have been poor all your life. And there are subcultures here in the city of street life, and then even within the street life there is a subculture of the people who use drugs, and there is a subculture of people who use alcohol, and there is a subculture of people who do not use any. For all these groups of poor people there are certain very cohesive kinds of rules, things like, 'Don't rock the boat,' 'Don't speak up.' Nobody really wants to hear it anyway. You can lie to the system but you can still call yourself an honest person. You do not lie to an individual. Honesty is a high value amongst poor people and yet people outside our culture do not realize that we are willing to steal because we have to in many cases.

Janine described how she had heard a homeless man describe other homeless people as predatory.

**Janine:** And I was thinking that all the time that I lived down here, the only people [besides the woman already described] I ever had to be afraid of was the police.

She went on to make a distinction between people on the street who were mentally ill and needed to be avoided and true predators.

Janine also explained that not getting ripped off by homeless people was mostly a matter of common sense.

**Janine:** And I did not steal a goddamn nickel from somebody if I could avoid it. In fact, I have ended up working at *street roots* because I will not panhandle. But, again I am one of those rare poor people that has these high values and principles, where it came from, God only knows. For instance, poor people network a lot, they share. If somebody comes along and gives you a bunch of sandwiches and you only need a couple of the sandwiches, you take them and you leave the rest where someone else will find them. Nothing is wasted, you share everything; you share information. A lot of business people and so on bitch about homeless people standing on the street talking to each other and stuff and loitering. Hell, that is the best thing they do. They are telling each other where to get things and they are networking and that is [called] loitering. It is one of the best things going on in Portland for the homeless people.

She also described acts of kindness she'd witnessed on the street, such as people helping families or women with children.

**Janine**: When you become poor and you have not always been poor, generally whatever family you have left behind and that are still doing okay, they have pretty much given up on you. By the time you have really hit the streets, you have worn out your welcome. You have asked for too much help, you are too needy. A lot of poor people do not have family but they form their own families. There is a high value of family [on the streets] but it is self-formed families. I know that a lot of people see poor people as isolated people with no connection, no values or anything like that, and instead I say, 'You know what? Considering the circumstances they have, poor people have high moral values on a lot of things.' It may not be understood from outside the system, but from inside the system, our kinds of values are very logical and effective means for getting by in our culture. You would be walking along somewhere and you see a blanket and stuff sitting somewhere, you leave it alone. And somebody who does take somebody else's blanket is going to get shit for it. That is not acceptable. You do not take people's stuff.

Janine describes an incident on a bus involving a homeless woman who was mentally ill, smelled, carried a bunch of bags, and wore "funky" clothes.

**Janine**: And there were a couple of young guys across from her and they started making snide remarks about her, about how she smelled, and the bus driver actually piped in and said she does stink and she should get off the bus. I mean, it is so socially acceptable to degrade homeless people. And you cannot be experiencing that kind of degradation from other human beings and not end up feeling, inside of you, totally, violently hated, unwanted and assaulted.

Interviewer's Journal Excerpt:

*Today was quite a day! My first interview was with a young woman who had just recently given up her three-year-old daughter because of her homelessness. Her reasoning was that she wanted her daughter to have a better life that was not on the streets. With immense bravery and emotion, she shared this story with me. She came to tears at one point where we took just a moment (she didn't want more time) to collect herself. I must admit that her emotion brought much emotion to myself as well. That moment that we took was good for both of us.*

*At one point in the interview, she talked about selling the paper* street roots *and having people walk by without any response, or say that they weren't able to when at the same time she would be hearing change jingle in their pockets. I wanted to ask something about this without being accusatory or judgmental. I was interested to know why she felt like she deserved someone else's money, but didn't want to offend her. It goes to the theme of responsibility and where people are taking responsibility for themselves around their experience with homelessness.*

*Beyond that, the rest of the interview was great. She had many ideas for solutions and changes, mostly centered around a warm place for people to be during the daytime by using old buildings that were standing empty. I feel like I asked good questions, probed and clarified where necessary, and overall had a good experience.*

Photographer: Dan Newth

# Chapter 13
## Chapter Thirteen

*No one is really asking for any handouts.*
*We are just asking to feel like we are human.*

## Dealing with the Services Available

---

*The more we take the welfare of others to heart and work for their benefit, the more benefit we derive for ourselves. This is a fact we can see. And the more selfish we remain and self-centered, the more selfish our way of life is, the lonelier we feel and the more miserable. This is also a fact we can see.*

—the Dalai Lama

Since the day we opened, our customers have said that a no-cost way to hugely improve the services they receive is just treating them with dignity and respect. When they go to the root of the problem, of course, they see that social service line workers get the lowest pay in the agency. Also, they see that line workers don't make the policies that decide how customers are treated. They also notice that policies aren't often reevaluated to make sure they still serve their purpose and are working equally for everyone.

One of the biggest tricks in the book is to put people through hoops and give them nothing in the end. "They asked me to fill out paperwork, a resumé, prove residency, and I did all those things; and I was six months at the Glisan Street shelter and six months at the Clark Center, but then I was sleeping on the street again." This is not a morality issue, whether someone deserves, has earned, or can afford their housing. If we don't go to the root of the problem and make a political decision in this country to adequately address the need, we'll hear these stories over and over—how people have jumped the hoops but were still homeless because enough low-income housing just doesn't exist; it's a mirage.

—Genny

*Sisters: How are the services around here?*

**Vincent**: In a word? They suck.

*Sisters: Got that.*

**Vincent**: I mean, I pay hell every time I need a blanket or especially big things or bedrolls. Sleeping bags. You know, I wound up going to Portland Rescue Mission to get the two that I have now.

*Sisters: Two bedrolls?*

**Vincent**: Yeah. And they got holes in them…the zippers don't zip up. And, you know, nobody seems to care whether or not you freeze at night.

*Sisters: And by nobody, whom do you mean?*

**Vincent**: I mean the people that offer services. Especially for the people that are allergic to wool blankets, like I am. I went into the majority of them in one day and told them that I was allergic to wool blankets. They were like, 'We don't care; here's a blanket. Take it or leave it.' You know, they have the attitude, 'Well, you're homeless. You don't know what the hell you want.' Therefore, 'We're not homeless and we know what you need.'

*Sisters: So they think that they know what you need?*

**Vincent**: Exactly. I've been trying for six months to get a damn tent. No luck.

Frequently heard complaints were: being forced to wait in lines for meals and services, and that shelter stays weren't long enough. Rarely were our narrators able to end their homelessness in a week, three months, or even in six months as mandated by various programs. Warren described a common sight: people lining up at a mission, trying to obtain shelter for the night.

**Warren**: I have seen guys start lining up down there as early as five thirty, six o'clock at night, in the rain. So there they are standing out in the rain, getting soaked…and then they let you in at eight thirty. Once it's full, it's full. That's it. You get turned away. Why can't we have a little bit of sensibility about this? Why do we have to stand there and get wet? Then you're going to go in, and you're going to get woken up at five in the morning anyway and get put out in the cold. That's not necessarily laziness or anything, but that's one luxury that homeless people do not have usually. I mean it's a lucky person that can find a campsite that the police don't know about or that they are not going to ferret out for any reason, where you could sleep the day away if you felt like it.

Another complaint was that missions and other systems used a lottery system to select people because they had more people needing beds than beds available. Jason had been in Portland a month at the time of our interview.

**Jason**: I have played the lotto since I have been here, if you know what I mean by that. Over at the mission they have a lotto because they have closed their overflow to where you cannot get a mat or something like that on the floor. They only have a limited amount of beds—I believe it is forty or something like that—so it is first come, first served. If they do not draw your number, you do not get a bed, so you are out on the street. I even had friends of mine giving me their numbers to go with the number that I drew, and I still could not get in. If you have sixty or seventy people trying to bid for these beds, it is almost a lost cause—kind of discouraging.

A few minutes later in this interview, Jason broached a topic that we'd heard before: often people are so desperate for shelter that they'll use a pretense or fake symptoms to be admitted to a program or shelter.

**Jason**: I have been to everybody pretty much, even went to a mental health unit and tried to lay a line on them just to try to get a bed. I know that sounds kind of cheesy, but you know it's something I actually tried because a friend of mine told me about it. He suggested that I act real nuts or depressed, but they just did not go for that. They did not think I was crazy enough. Every resource and every avenue that I have tried so far has denied me or told me that there is a waiting list of seven weeks to seven months. That does not help me at all right now. Seven weeks down the road, who knows where I am going to be?

He also brought up a subject that is not often voiced in public—dissatisfaction both with the quality of care given by nonprofit agencies and how they allocate funds.

**Jason**: You look at some of these places. They charge you eight bucks a night. It is kind of crazy. I thought they were nonprofit organizations. They make millions of dollars, but yet they cannot get somebody a free bed. I do not understand how that works. They make millions of dollars on what they sell in their stores, and they are supposed to be helping people, but yet they are not. They are not helping the homeless, they are helping themselves, and that is the way I see it.

*Sisters: What about getting your basic needs met? How has it been for food here?*

**Jason**: Food has been the only thing that I can really say [is] good…you are not going to go hungry. But food does not help you when it is raining outside. It does a little bit I guess, but I would much rather have a roof over my head than something in my belly.

*Sisters: Why?*

**Jason**: Have you ever spent a night out when it is raining?

*Sisters: Tell me about it.*

**Jason**: Oh! It is cold, it is miserable, you freeze to death and there are only a few places you can go where the police do not really harass you about where you are sleeping and those places are normally where there is a lot of wind and this, that, and the other thing. And if you do not have something over your head, it is going to be a rough night for you. Walking pneumonia is not my idea of a fun time. I'd much rather be a little hungry than sick.

Later in this interview he was asked to distinguish a hand up from a handout.

**Jason**: I have worked hard and I have definitely helped a lot of people in my day, and that is all I am asking back. I am not asking for somebody to give me a job or a place to stay. I will work for mine. I will earn my keep. They [homeless services] will give the person who just got out of prison an apartment, but I need help for a week and I cannot get a room.

George prefers the freedom of riding the rails over leading an ordinary life, and has spent time in many U.S. cities. He usually camps wherever he is.

**George**: I hate missions. I do not go to missions. There are a couple around in the nation that I like, but most of the missions are really not worth your time to go in, and you are usually better off camping out.

*Sisters: How come?*

**George**: Lot of idiots around them, and a lot of missions are kind of crooked. They get much better donations than the type of stuff that they give us; that is a fact.

*Sisters: What are they?*

**George**: Salvation Army is good for it. That is why they call it the 'Starvation Army.' They are good for that all over the country…you could donate them steaks; they will feed us rice and beans. It is a fact.

Later in the interview he added another reason to distrust the missions.

**George**: Nowadays a lot of these missions are collaborating with the local law enforcement as far as allowing them to come in at night and run warrant checks and things like that on the list of people that are staying in there. It is a good way of getting arrested if you are being looked for by somebody. So, it is in [people's] best interest to stay out of them.

Robbie grew up in Mississippi and was one of seventeen children. He described his family farm and picking cotton as a child. He eventually settled in North Carolina where he worked at a food processing plant for eight years. When the plant closed he moved to Portland, and had been in town four months at the time of his interview. Robbie explained that he had not worked for about fifteen years because of problems with diabetes, permanent injuries from a car accident, and three surgeries. He receives disability benefits, which amount to four hundred ninety dollars per month, although before he moved his benefit payments were higher and his cost of living lower. Out of his check he sends his college-age daughter and 16-year-old son about half of his income. He had been staying at a mission each night because he could not find affordable housing. It was his first experience with homelessness, and his research into affordable housing was discouraging, especially when one housing program had a five-year waiting list. He disagreed with the missions' policies of not allowing people in until late in the evening, then asking them to leave early in the morning.

Robbie's chief complaint about the missions' policy was that they seemed hypocritical.

**Robbie**: If you love me and care about me, then why do you let me stand out here in this rain? You know I ain't got nowhere else to go. Does that make sense? That don't make no sense. Know what I'm saying? It really don't. They should be able to let people come in and—just like today, it's raining, right? Seems like they ought to just let people come in out the rain. Just like over to the missions, if it's raining, they let you stand out there till ten, ten thirty, eleven o'clock at night, pouring down rain. I feel like if you have any kind of feelings for people, you will let people come in out this rain. I would. Wouldn't you?

Another aspect of hypocrisy that Julian, a Muslim and a former veteran, complained about is that Christianity is forced upon you as being the only faith there is. Not all missions have a policy that one must sit through a religious service before a meal, but many of the larger ones do.

**Julian**: If you do not sit in the service you will not be fed. You cannot wait outside till the service is over and then come in when they serve dinner, because they will not let you in. I thank God for having a roof over my head, but then, like I said, they push you out at five in the morning and then you're walking the pavement all day, trying to get a place to eat.

Narrators described how homeless people could find basic services but not a means for escaping their situation. We heard about how a certain stagnation can set in when all they do is stay in shelters and roam around town after free meals.

*Sisters: What was it like being in the missions?*

**Art**: It was depressing, like I said, you got these guys, and you just see that they're not going anywhere.

*Sisters: They never left?*

**Art**: They never left. I have been to a lot of places where I see people like that. For the life of me I want to tell them, 'Get up, move, move.'

Another issue that came up was that some organizations, particularly those that offer recovery programs, require clients to work or volunteer in return for services. However, though the addicted clients are working, they are not learning skills that can help them take their next steps out of homelessness and poverty.

During Frank's interview he was asked about the drawbacks of the recovery program that he had been part of.

**Frank**: There's definitely some holes there. The idea and mission statement is all good, but, the problem there is that they are taking advantage of people that have nothing else. They are getting forty-hours-a-week's work out of them. The counseling is limited. You spend as much time in their church as you do in counseling. It's always done mostly with interns. So, what they did for me is introduce me to that fact that there is what AA refers to as a Higher Power. I did what was available, but I didn't really progress. It was easy to substitute one addiction for another. I became a workaholic. I went through their program several times. When I went to work I did the same thing. I found a place I could hide from my internal problems. The other thing is, they keep you. It's a progressive cycle; the people that do shine and do a good job there, you're not really given any tools to do something else. Once you want to leave, they trap you into staying with them. [Recovering addicts and alcoholics] become employed with them, work for very low wages, with no chance of increase. You stay at the pay you're hired at.

We heard complaints about too many rules and restrictions in organizations. Some narrators complained that the penalties for breaking rules were too severe and recovery programs that included housing had no room for mistakes. If someone relapses, his or her lodging is terminated.

Another opinion we heard was that those experiencing homelessness resented feeling like a marketable commodity. Many people found it difficult to trust the motives of organizations and their staffs because they earned a living by providing services for the homeless community, especially those that are not perceived as trying to end homelessness. One narrator called such organizations "poverty pimps."

**Samuel**: They have commercialized homelessness. They have made it an industry. It is a moneymaking thing now, and it is destroying people's lives. It is destroying people's opportunity to live a productive life again because of that reason. It is all about the money.

Narrators expressed how they often felt powerless. Case managers who should be there to help them are overworked and impersonal, and have no will or time to create a plan to end their homelessness that includes the narrators' experience and ideas.

**Nicholas**: I think that the agencies right now don't take enough feedback from the clients that they are serving; they have the attitude that, 'We know how to do this. We are providing you the service, so just shut up and consume it.' And they are really not availing themselves of the tremendous resources within their client base.

We were amazed at the length of time people spent on waiting lists for services, medical attention, and housing. Some of our narrators had been trying to gain Social Security or disability benefits for two or three years and longer. One man had been on a list for housing for thirteen months. Consequently, our narrators said they felt frustrated, disillusioned, and "bounced around," and sometimes gave up on acquiring benefits or housing.

Rodney had applied for SSI and also for General Assistance benefits, which are meant to cover basic needs until the SSI benefits come through. His interviewer asked him about this process.

**Rodney:** That is what I am working for now, the GA. I will know within the end of the month, yeah probably by the end of the month, because they sent the paper back one time before and said, 'Oh, we ain't got enough information.' I said, 'Well, you got all the information I know, I can't give you anymore that I don't know.' And so she sent it back and I have not had an answer back, but it will be coming. I just got a feeling it will be coming.

*Sisters: When was the first time you applied?*

**Rodney:** About a year and a half ago. And I am still fighting for it.

We discovered that there are many ways for people to fall between the cracks when dealing with social services or governmental agencies. Joann, who had a complicated medical history, ran into problems when she was released from a facility.

**Joann:** Well, I was supposed to move out and all of a sudden they don't have my meds anymore. It's been a whole month now and I've been trying to get my meds and I still haven't gotten them. They have a med room. But all of a sudden they've got one pill and I'm taking twelve a day, six in the morning and six at night. I'm like, 'What's this?' You know? I'm supposed to be taking high blood pressure [medication] because my blood pressure's been, like, through the roof. And I'm supposed to take three for my blood pressure, three for my bipolar, my asthma. I've got chronic severe asthma. I mean, there are so many pills.

*Sisters: And you're not getting them? And you don't know why and nobody can explain it to you?*

**Joann:** No. They kept on saying, 'Well, we'll get the nurse on it.' I'm still waiting for meds.

We also heard narrators who had given up on frequenting missions and accessing other social service organizations. We asked Ambrose which services he accessed.

**Ambrose:** I do not really use any services down here anymore. I do not even want to deal with them. I do not even want to talk with them anymore. I go to Blanchet [House] and I eat. I come to Sisters Of The Road and eat and that is it.

*Sisters: Why do you go there?*

**Ambrose:** I love you guys. It is the one place where I am not being persecuted. I feel comfortable and wanted and cared about.

A surprising number of our narrators refused to stay in shelters and instead camped outdoors permanently or while working on other options for housing. Their reasons varied—they found them unsafe, unsanitary, overcrowded, and difficult to sleep in because of the close proximity of a stranger snoring a few feet away. We also heard from narrators that the quality of food was sometimes poor, and several reported incidences of food poisoning.

We asked Gena if she preferred to stay in shelters.

**Gena:** They are nasty places, they are.

*Sisters: How so?*

**Gena:** I just believe they are, just like the food they served me. I found lots of stuff in food that I got from them. [One of the missions is] the only good place they have that serves food. All the other places give you garbage.

*Sisters: What makes [that one] good?*

**Gena:** It is like real food.

*Sisters: How are you treated there?*

**Gena:** With respect. Like the other day at [a women's drop-in center]. I went there to get some tampons and I did not come on time, so they were snippy. They are like, "You got to wait till tomorrow." They give out tampons and hygiene and stuff, clothes, but I just did not make it on time, so I could not even get a tampon. I was bleeding real bad…and I do not want to bleed on myself. It was nasty because when I am out here, I do take care of myself. I do not get nasty like people out here. I always find some place to take a shower: at my mother's, my sister's. And that is why I do not stay in the shelters because everybody is gross.

*Sisters: Where do you go for showers and hygiene stuff besides your mother's and sister's?*

**Gena:** I will visit places that give you that stuff, churches and other places the women can go. I went to [a mission] the other day. They hooked me up. They gave me blankets and everything, they probably would have hooked me up with the food box, but I do not know what I'd do with it, I couldn't carry a huge box of food down the street.

And I did not have no place to put it, no place to cook it. That is why I go to these places that feed.

*Sisters: How are you treated [there]?*

**Gena:** They are real nice to me, but I am pretty sure they could be mean because this one guy, he got real pissed because I guess they would not help him. So he had a heart attack. He blew up at them.

Because homeless people are often treated as if they are invisible or worse, they have a hyperawareness of other people's attitudes toward them. An interviewer asked one man about how he was treated in a program he was enrolled in.

**Eddie**: Well, there they treat you like a person, they value your feelings in everything, and even when they know you are homeless. They do not just shove you aside.

It was clear that the attitude of staff in the various public and private organizations made a huge difference in how a homeless person felt about utilizing their services. We asked Lisa about her experience in staying at a shelter for women.

**Lisa**: Everybody has been really good to me. I have never been around so many females at once, but it is working. I feel good about myself today.

Nick also had words of praise for how caseworkers' warmth and concern can break down so many barriers.

**Nick**: You know when they ask you questions about your personal self, I think it shows they care about you more. Because if you're out here you really just pay attention to someone's attitude. A lot of them [people experiencing homelessness] want to be talked to and shared with, shake their hand or even hug them. It would be nice if some of these organizations and places could get more personal with them instead of looking at them just as homeless people.

*Sisters: Do you feel like you get looked at like that?*

**Nick**: Of course! You see it and you feel it too.

We also heard about some counselors and caseworkers that were allies and took their roles seriously. A man described his counselor as "persistent," and another narrator mentioned his caseworker's tenaciousness in getting him needed services. Yet another narrator described how weekly meetings with his counselor, which involved goal setting, made all the difference in his recovery.

It is often small policies and gestures that make a difference in a homeless person's day. Betsy discussed a church that offers meals and hospitality.

**Betsy**: It is a good place. The food is not bad. They treat you good, and you can get seconds and it is not like a lot of these sloppy places around here. They are nice and friendly. The lady that works there likes me and my friend, so she will hook us up with whatever we need.

Diane was staying in a shelter at the time of her interview. She commented on the need for more public restrooms, then described her recent experiences in temporary housing.

**Diane**: [This shelter] is okay, there are three toilets. You may have to wait, but it will be like living at home—you have to wait till the rest of your family gets through using the bathroom. And there are three showers, and when it is crowded I am not waiting and standing in line, so I omit that [taking a shower], thinking that maybe later if I ever wake up, that can happen. But anyhow, from what I have seen—I just came here yesterday—I observed and felt you are treated with courtesy, dignity, respect. They want to serve you, which makes me really comfortable. And they are trying to do that for all the ladies to be comfortable and be treated in a decent, ladylike manner. To be served your coffee you do not have to go do it yourself, push, crowd, shout, like other places, yell, say bad words, start hitting each other because you are frustrated, people butting in front of you. I mean, all the atrocious, gross, rude things that happen at most anyplace else. So this is dignity and that is good.

Alicia was involved with an organization that works with people who are sleeping outdoors to help them find permanent housing. Her interviewer asked about her experiences.

**Alicia**: Wonderful. They are angels. I swear God sent them to me and my mother. They are our miracle. They gave us hope, which is something we have not had in over a year. I will never be able to thank them enough, never, never. They gave us a chance, that is the one word that would help [homeless] people out here, you know, just give them a chance. All they need is a real kick-start. Yes, some are going to fail, but you are also going to be helping out a lot more. Like the shelters out here, they kick you out early in the morning, you cannot come back till later—what are you supposed to do all day? The people that can work, they should go out and look for a job or whatever, go to the employment scene or whatever. But people like me, I am in a wheelchair and I do not work. The cold is very detrimental to my illness, it hurts me bad, and, you know, being kicked out like that, and the only hospice unit, the only shelter that has a hospice unit, has twenty-seven stairs, no elevator.

Women, who sometimes spoke frankly about the physical dangers of life on the streets, seemed especially grateful for the respite of a shelter where they felt safe, cared for, and listened to. Brianna was accessing a women's drop-in center, and described how a worker there served her coffee, and how that small gesture spoke volumes about the policies there.

**Brianna**: They definitely care about everybody.

*Sisters: So, they had you sit down and they brought your coffee?*

**Brianna**: Yeah, coffee and doughnuts and I am going, 'Wow!' They have a place where you can just sit, if you want to just sit for a couple of hours. You could take a book and sit. That is really important to people that are on the street, sitting and not being chased off or harassed, or have somebody trying to buy something from you or sell something to you.

Kathy, who suffers from mental illness and is in recovery, described the rapport she had developed with her counselor.

**Kathy**: There are a couple of ladies, but there is one in particular I really like. And she has been really good with me, because when I first got here I had bought some beer, and I was explaining to her that I had problems and I was feeling suicidal. I was very depressed with the situation that I was in, and she told me a place to go where I can get my medication—I take Paxil for depression. I told her that I was carrying beer around with me and I was struggling with the fact that I wanted to drink it, but I knew that it could cause me more problems. And so she let me give her the beer and she got rid of it for me so I was not packing it around and struggling within myself with this beer in my bag anymore. And she just is always really nice to me when I go there, you know, she makes me feel like I am a human being and not just another bum.

*Sisters: Right, that is a big deal. How does she make you feel like a human being?*

**Kathy**: It is because she acts like she is happy to see me every time she does see me, and she knows about my situation as well as most of my story. And she has been calling for me to find my daughter and help me to get myself together. I do not know; she just is really nice to me.

It is obvious to see how these sorts of relationships can help bridge the gap between hope and despair. Our narrators also especially appreciated it when they felt like the people who were helping them were not judging them.

Mimi, who had been enrolled in a youth program, mentioned several staff members by name, along with pouring out effusive praise for them.

**Mimi**: I did not get judged by nobody. I got treated with respect and if it was not for Greenhouse (a Salvation Army program for homeless youth) standing behind me, I would have probably ended up in jail for a long time. See, it was a prostitution charge. I think I learned a lot. Being where I am at now, my life has kind of changed around and I have got a full-time job up at *street roots*[delivering a nonprofit newspaper]. And I spend a lot more time with my daughter.

Besides meals and services that were offered in a humane manner, our narrators described comprehensive and long-term programs as being the most helpful. Tammy had lived for eight months in a housing program for women. At the time of our interview she was housed again, and we asked how the program and staff had helped her.

**Tammy**: They have really good staff. And there's a lot of volunteers there. There's very few other programs that I've known that have been as thorough as they are. What they do is, they first have you get established with counseling or drug and alcohol treatment—whatever you need first. Then they start working with your financial problems: how to get a job, how to keep the job. They have a lot of resources where they can help you with your criminal background for a job or for moving into a new place or whatever.

Tammy explained how helpful it was that in the final stage of the transitional program they charged only a third of her income for her one-room unit, which allowed her to reestablish a good rental history.

**Tammy:** And once they get you established financially, then they help you start looking for housing where you know that you'll be safe. Some of them [clients] go into halfway houses and some of them go into their own housing. Some go into shared housing. And they'll help with the move-in costs. They'll help with furniture. They'll help with beds and bedding and they send a lot of people to [missions] to get pots and pans and silverware and plates and sheets and towels. And they give them lots of vouchers for food for first moving in there. They do pretty much all of it.

Tammy went on to describe a vital part of the program—building a community among the women and staff.

**Tammy:** You can come back there for the dinners that they have once a month and that's just to say hi to old friends or just know that you're still a part of this group so you don't end up feeling like, 'Well, I'm out on my own now and nothing is going to help me.' They have a dinner once a month there and it's usually a themed dinner, like a Mexican dinner, or they had Oktoberfest there, they had a Halloween party there, they had a Christmas party, Thanksgiving, and you're allowed to come back and help them with cooking and help them to fix everything. They allow you to come back for counseling, if you still need it, to the same counselors that you were seeing before. And they help you with any resources that you might need; if you're a little low on food they give food boxes. They get a regular store of food once a week and it's very stocked. We've gone there once or twice. And they help you if you don't seem to be managing your money too well; they have money management classes and financial stability class. They teach you how to get a bank account. There's nothing that I couldn't get there, everything that we ever wanted, and so it was a neat experience after being out on the streets for so long. And technically I've been pretty much homeless since I was 16, so that was a really different experience. And the people really cared about you. They're willing to really stick their necks out for the girls that go there.

*Sisters: How important has it been to have that continuing support to maintain your housing?*

**Tammy:** Very important. Because even though we were off in our own little apartment, there was both of us [she was living with a partner at the time of her interview], but it was still nice to know that we had a connection with someone else that we could go to and say, 'Hey, I can't deal with this. I don't know if I can deal with paying the rent and living here when we're just getting to know one another.' Sometimes it got really stressful so I was always able to go back and say, 'I need some help.' And so it was very important to us to have someone on the outside; you're not cut off, you're not just out there on your own. And they'll help you for up to two years after you move out.

We've always found help when we've needed it and we've been very grateful that they were able to provide it for us, and then help us find the places that we needed to help us.

Two rehabilitation programs received high marks: an in-patient medical treatment center and a treatment program and clinic for Native Americans. Michelle, whose relapse caused her to lose her job as a nurse and her home 'in the wilderness,' entered the former to undergo an alcohol detox program. Before entering, she spent time living in her car, camping in the mountains, and fishing to feed herself.

**Michelle:** Just trying to survive and keep a roof over your head takes priority. It takes up all your energy and all your time. And as long as you keep moving from one shelter to another, you really cannot do anything more in your life, you are really kind of stuck because you are too busy trying to survive.

She also spoke highly of the staff members and the empathy she found at the detox center.

**Michelle:** I liked the fact that the people there were real. They had gone through a lot of things, they were all in recovery and they knew. You could go up and say something to them and they understood what you were saying. They did not look at you like you had three heads, and that is important because you need to know that there is somebody that can understand and relate to where you are coming from.

*Sisters: And what is important about that?*

**Michelle:** It is important because once you get there [into a detox program] a lot of people do not know where to go from there. They want help, but they do not know how to get help. And so [the detox center] is very good at plugging people into resources to get some help, to try and skirt them away from drug abuse or alcohol abuse and get them into a program. And when I hear people put it down—I hear people in AA do that—it upsets me because these people saved my life. If I had not gone there, I would not be sitting here, I was that bad. I would have been dead, so what I feel is that they need more places like [that]. Places where people can get the medical help that they need, the medication they need to get off alcohol, get off drugs, and then get mainstreamed back into some type of constructive living again. And that is what they do there, and I think that is a real important step in anybody's recovery, especially if you are genuinely looking for help. Those people will help you, they are very good people.

*Sisters: And how did you know that you were treated with respect there?*

**Michelle:** Oh, I am a nurse and I know when I am treated with respect and when I am not—the benefits of being a nurse. I was treated with a lot of respect there; they were just very supportive, very helpful, answered any questions I had. If they did not have the answer they said, 'I don't have the answer but I'll try and find out for you.' They respected the fact of what I was trying to do, and they did it with everybody, not just me. And I think that is just really vitally important because when you get in that position you lose your dignity, you lose your self-respect, you lose your self-worth. Your self-image is very important. By the time you get there [into detox] you are beating yourself up, you are already feeling pretty crummy about where you are at in life, and the last thing you need is somebody throwing you an anchor. You need people that help show you how you can get out of it, I think that is just vital because people do not know how to get help, or they are afraid to get help. Or, they just have lost all their self-worth and that is what drugs and alcohol will do to you. And that is why a lot of people who take drugs or drink end up committing suicide, because they do not know how to get help, or they are afraid to: 'Oh, I don't want to go to [detox], that place is really bad.' You better go [there] because it can save your life. Forget about what your neighbor thinks; go do it.

She then elaborated on the treatment she received.

**Michelle**: It was really important that they treated me with a lot of kindness, and they were very patient with me. I was pretty sick. I mean, I could not even hold a glass of water and they were trying to help me just to drink water. Being a nurse, there is a real, big issue in emergency rooms: people that come in under the influence and the way they are treated is really bad. And these people want help, need to get help, they are going to put the walls up at that point.

At the time of her interview Michelle was attending courses to become a drug and alcohol counselor.

**Michelle**: I love school, I absolutely love it, you know, and it just lights up my life. I love the campus life, I love everything about it, but the one thing I really love about it is I am doing something with my life. And hopefully, somewhere down the line, I am going to be able to help other people because that is my whole objective of going back to school, is to be able to get my degree to help people.

---

Interviewer's Journal Excerpt:
*I laughed out loud and cried today with these two interviews. My first was the one where I could not control my emotions, although I did maintain control during the interview with the narrator. It was with a 42-year-old man, who looked over 60. He has been homeless since 1998 and left the United States to live in Canada. His experience there was a lot better because he said that in Toronto, they treated homeless people much better than here. Here you get treated like a thing where over there you get treated like a human.*

---

He became homeless after he got lung cancer and went through chemotherapy. He had lost his job and had nowhere to turn. He couldn't get SSI or any assistance at all. When I asked him about his first night on the streets, he began to cry. At this point my emotions went up as well. He said that he didn't think he could talk more, but he did without me really having to push him. In fact, he talked for a long time about his experiences. His insights were incredible about the lack of caring and humanity out there for homeless people. He talked about the loneliness a lot, and how now it is especially difficult because he does not like the shelters, but doesn't want to camp out alone for fear that he might need to go to the hospital but he'd have no one there to help him. He kept saying how he was only rambling and getting off track in what he was saying, but I encouraged that everything he was saying was great and going to be quite helpful for this project.

After the interview was over, I told him he should try again to get some sort of Social Security or disability benefit, because I thought he would be eligible. He had worked all his life before his experience with homelessness. It seems so unfair that because he became sick he has not been able to get any help. After he left, I kind of lost it a bit talking with Shani and Genny about his situation. His loneliness and the lack of assistance for any real help just got to me in my heart at a place that I could not control. I let that out in some tears for a bit, which was good. It was great to have some support from the team. We brainstormed a bit about the need for more resources in the office, especially resources and advocates for people to be able to maneuver through the system for monthly benefits from the government.

The next interview, on the other hand, was with an amazing woman who had overcome her experience with homelessness through her knowledge and perseverance to maneuver through that same system that my first interviewee had nearly given up on. She was articulate in her analysis and gave great examples of how things are, how she got through it all, and how things could be improved. I was amazed at how much she had experienced in her life, especially since poverty has been her reality for all of it. Much of her analysis had to do with poverty in general, but the implications are far-reaching into homelessness, which she identified as a subculture of poverty with its own subcultures within that. The most incredible analysis that she made was how a rape she had experienced was less traumatic than becoming homeless. She also talked a lot about the mental health issues that she is dealing with and about those issues within the population of homeless people. I was so glad to be able to talk with her because she was so open about her life and especially the topic of mental health. I was a little nervous about how open and honest she was going to be, because I had known her when she had worked at street roots and knew of how she had fallen out of it. But there was no trouble with anything and the interview went great.

Photographer: Brynne Athens

# Chapter 14
## Chapter Fourteen

*Family are the people that care about you*

## Definition of Family

---

*God has…ordered things that we may learn to bear one another's burdens; for there is no man without his faults, none without his burden. None is sufficient unto himself; none is wise in himself; therefore, we must support one another, comfort, help, teach, and advise one another.*

—Thomas à Kempis

The first time I was introduced to family mapping was years ago when a Lewis and Clark student asked if she could interview some customers about their families. She'd sit with them, draw a circle, and have them tell her who the significant members of their families were. What surprised us is that Sisters landed on the majority of maps.

This is the reason we so passionately explain to people that we are not a social service organization, but a community organization. My experience with social services is that they are time-defined: you can have housing for twelve months, participate in a recovery program for six months, and access a food box once a month. But people need consistency in their lives, places they can go where people remember who they are, not just what need they have. Sisters welcomes you no matter what your needs are; and when your needs are addressed, you are still welcome in the cafe to tell others your story, enjoy an affordable meal, play cribbage over coffee, and continue to connect with people you've come to know, and who give meaning to your life.

If a traditional social service agency lands on a family map, once they're done with their job there's no need for you to walk back through their door, and it feels like divorce. That's why Sisters and other organizations where people feel like they're part of an ongoing, family-

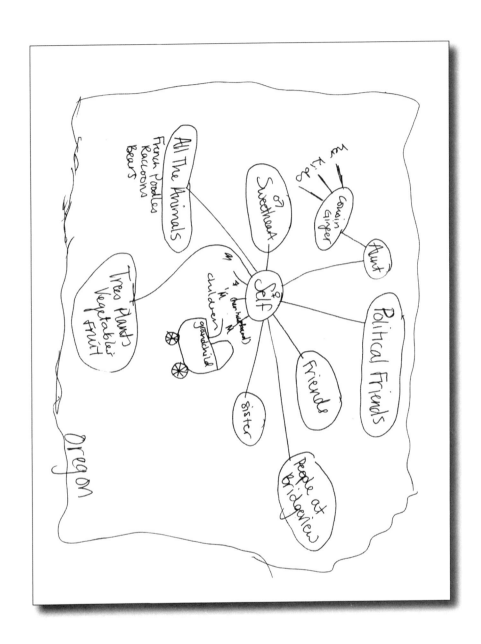

like connection made it onto the maps: JOIN, Rose Haven, Jean's Place. There was a woman who used to come to Sisters in the early days with her two little girls, and she came back recently for our holiday meal to say she was doing okay. She said, "You have our picture on the wall!" At that time in her life, we had made a critical difference to her and her daughters. She doesn't need us to solve her problems of poverty and homelessness, because she's done that. But she wants to check in, see their photo on the wall like anyone else who goes home for the holidays.

Having had that first family mapping experience at Sisters, I was not surprised this time when organizations landed there. What did surprise me was people's overwhelming feelings of loss and anger about the abuse they'd suffered from their families of origin, and sadness about the loss of the American Dream they had hoped for—a home with kids and a dog and cat in the yard. I was also surprised by those maps with a glaring absence of people or even organizations, instead only a stuffed animal or plant, or the word "me." It blew me away.

—Genny

Although the interviews were largely open-ended, there was a short list of standard questions that our narrators were asked during the course of their interviews: how they first came to be homeless, if they were housed at the time of the interview, and what their monthly income was, and where it came from. At the close of each interview, we asked, "What is your definition of family?" We gave them blank sheets of paper with a request to draw themselves in the middle of the page, and their current family all around them. These became the "family maps."

Narrators were often surprised or confused at the question, uncomfortable talking about their family, and unsure of their ability both to draw and to adequately depict their situations. Although the interviewers assured them that there was no standard definition of family or right or wrong way to create a family map, a number of narrators struggled with it, or simply could not bring themselves to draw one. But through probing and brainstorming, about four hundred narrators ended up drawing family maps or, in a few cases, dictating them to their interviewer. Many of the interviewers reported that the mapping process turned out to be the most emotional part of the interviews, and at times brought on tears. In these drawings and definitions, they created poignant, often heart-rending portrayals.

Perhaps because we encouraged narrators to define family based on their own truths instead of traditional interpretations, many described how a family is not necessarily comprised of biological relatives.

**Maria**: Families are those people who you love and who love you in turn and who take care of you. They do not necessarily have to be blood relatives.

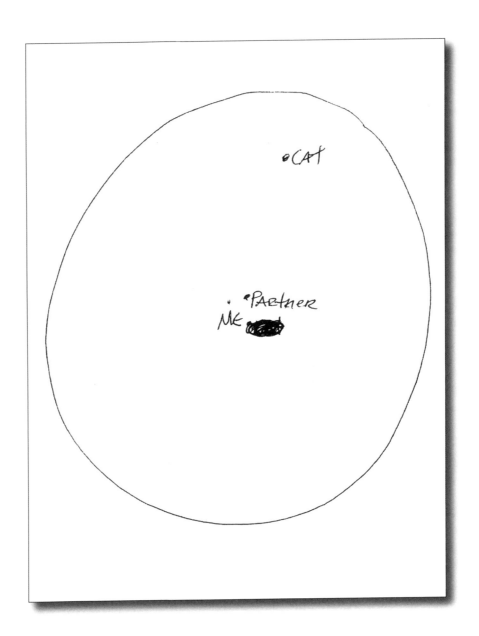

**Paul**: A family is things like brothers and sisters, people I respect, and who have respect and consideration for you, and then you have got to have that back for them. People who help one another out.

We seldom heard of families that are part of American myths, as depicted in paintings by Norman Rockwell; instead we often heard of estrangement, sadness, and dissolution. At times narrators' definitions of family were tainted by memories of dysfunctional or abusive families of origin.

**Liam**: I do not know what family is. I thought I did, but I do not, and a lot of people that tell you what family is, it is only their ideal, but not reality. Reality is different from idealism and there are some people who are so lonely they will tell you anything. I am not about to take and say what is the definition of family. I did not have a very good family life.

Sometimes the replies and family maps were whimsical and creative; and at times they were telling, such as when narrators drew cats and dogs on their family maps, or as was often the case, included community organizations such as AA and NA twelve-step groups, Sisters Of The Road, Northwest Pilot Project, JOIN, McDonald Center, *street roots*, Rose Haven, Downtown Chapel, and Dignity Village. On a few maps, these community organizations were the only "people" present.

One aspect of our narrators' answers was a longing for connection, constancy, and bonds to keep them safe. One narrator described family as people who "got your back," and another as, "a group that is supportive."

**Connor**: Well, family imparts stability. That is one reason I kept coming back here. My mother lives here, as does my sister, my nephew, my niece. Even though I am homeless here—I cannot stay with them because of my drinking problem—I can talk to them, call them up. I can visit.

**Jared**: Well, family, I think, is any group of people that have a little bit of unity, depend on each other. Some of my family is some of my closest friends because they have been there for me when I needed them. And I think that is what family is. It does not have to necessarily be blood.

Several narrators drew and described hypothetical families. Bernard, who had not been in a relationship for twenty years, described having a stable home in a safe community with his ideal family: two children and a partner.

**Bernard**: My partner, my wife, you know, is my best friend, my confidant, my lover, and if necessary, the planner, the decision maker. If I am not able to make the decision, she can do it, as long as it is the right one.

Bob described his idea of family.

**Bob**: Someone who is there for you whenever you need it, not necessarily for money, but sometimes for money if it becomes necessary. Someone who will listen to you even if they do not understand where you are coming from. Someone who will try to understand, not judge you. Someone who will do everything they can to help you. I would say unconditional love.

**Stan**: I'd like to have one someday. Now it's just a friend who is where I once lived, who is dealing with the same mental problems as me, and my mom and one other friend I trust.

Perhaps one reason defining family or creating a family map was so difficult for our narrators was because it brought into focus their isolation and estrangement from their biological families. At times, narrators refused to draw a family map or define their family because of discomfort, anger, or distress. Sometimes the activity brought up bitterness and hard feelings, as when one narrator described how her parents had insisted she was an unfit parent, and raised her children for a while when she was homeless.

**Lou**: When I needed them, they shit on me.

Another narrator explained why biological families do not always work.

**Gerald**: Family is supposed to help you out in your time of need or give you advice. But, in my experience, most of my family aren't that way. Some of them I might say are assholes. I got an aunt I haven't talked to in twelve years because she thinks I'm a bad person.

What became clear during interviews and was common to many of our narrators was their tenuous relationships with their biological families—more so than found in the general population. Additionally, a substantial number described themselves as loners. A man who had been on the street for most of his adult life spoke about being alone.

**Ed**: I don't have a family right now. I don't have anybody that I'm real close to.

There were a number of our family maps that contained only a depiction of the narrator, sometimes described as *me, myself,* and *I*. Sometimes the words *me* or *self* stood alone in the center of the page, the only word on the map.

Walt answered with the word *dysfunctional* when asked what family meant to him.

**Walt**: As a heroin addict you don't have many friends; they come and go—mostly go—which is good, because they want something from you that you probably don't want to give them.

During one session, an interviewer explained the family mapping project and how family didn't necessarily mean people you lived with, but those you relied on.

**Lawrence**: I rely on myself.

ME

Justin, 30, drew a pie chart to make it clear: eighteen percent of the pie was made up of street people and thirty-two percent was drawn as blood relatives, but half of the chart consisted of only him.

It was clear that many of our narrators' biological families had been impacted by drug and alcohol use, mental illness, criminal activity, and various forms of dysfunction. As Bonnie drew her family map, she didn't include her biological family. When her interviewer asked her if she saw members of her family often, she admitted she did not. "We are all spread out," was her simple explanation, but then she went on to reveal that it was impossible to get together with her family members without arguments ensuing and past grievances coming up.

Sammy drew a picture of a pig "taking a dump on his family."

**Sammy**: My ex-family, it don't mean anything. It means manure. It doesn't have any meaning to me. It's trash.

Allan explained his family in a similar way.

**Allan**: As far as family I can rely on and depend on, [there is] nobody.

I am open to the idea, but most of the people I consider friends have screwed me over once. Most of the people I used to call friends screwed me over at one point or another, so I eventually figured out the people I call friends now are going to do the same thing down the road; the only difference is I got to catch 'em before they do it.

Allan then drew a necklace with a heart full of daggers dripping blood onto an empty space below.

Franklin, who was 47, illustrated how when family ties unravel, a person is more vulnerable to homelessness. His parents were divorced when he was 10, and his mother raised him and his brother and sister while working as a waitress. He described his mother.

**Franklin**: Great woman. Big heart, sense of humor. We were number one.

His interviewer asked him if he was close to his mother who had died a few years earlier.

**Franklin**: Yes, and she held the family together. Since she's passed, the family has gone different ways. We don't do Christmas or anything.

Franklin was formerly married and has a son. He described how he and his wife gradually grew apart until their marriage ended when his wife began an affair with her boss at a company they both worked for.

**Franklin**: We had the whole American Dream: two dogs, a cat, a fish, a recliner with a big screen. I gave everything to them when I left. My lawyer told me to sell the house, but my boy said, 'Daddy, I don't want to move out of here.' So I just walked away. Took my truck and tools and TV.

Embarrassed by the affair, he left his job and found another one. He next moved in with a woman who was a meth addict. His security started slipping away when he lost his job and his girlfriend asked him to leave. He ended up living in his car at a rest stop on I-5. During his interview he described a subculture of about sixty homeless people who lived at the rest stop, many using drugs, some working as prostitutes for truckers who came through. Franklin explained that the group would pool their resources and access social services and charities in a nearby town. While living at the rest stop, he began living with another woman, also an addict, in her car. When she became abusive, he left her and hitchhiked into the city in search of social service agencies and shelter. During the breakup of his marriage, and while he was homeless, his family refused to help.

Franklin: I don't talk to my family. I've asked them for help and they have flat denied me so I'm pretty much disowned. It [family] doesn't mean anything to me right now. I think families in general are falling apart, like it says in the Bible.

*Sisters: I don't know what you mean.*

Franklin: I don't know what part, but it says towards the end times, families will fall apart. It seems like you hear a lot more about families not sticking together. This would not happen when I was younger. I wouldn't let my father be homeless, no matter what. I see kids today that don't give a shit, excuse my language. It's a mean generation of video games and whatever else they do. It's all about indulgence. There is no morality like there was when I was younger. Things aren't looking too good. That's the way it is.

*Sisters: I'm going to give you this sheet of paper and I want you to draw me a map or picture or diagram of what family means to you.*

Franklin: I'm done. It's nothing, nothing. I don't have any feelings about it at all. Don't have nothing. I've gotten very bitter. Family is supposed to help you when you need help. I've never been helped. I've been on my own since I was 16. I've never asked for help.

*Sisters: What do you think about your son?*

Franklin: Great kid. I think he's a good kid.

*Sisters: So, when you talk about family you tend to think about you and your son?*

Franklin: Well, I wouldn't call it family. We're working on it. He's a man now so we're more friends than a father-son relationship. He gives me advice more than I give him.

*Sisters: Is that bad?*

Franklin: No.

*Sisters: But there's nothing that you want to put down as a picture?*

Franklin: No.

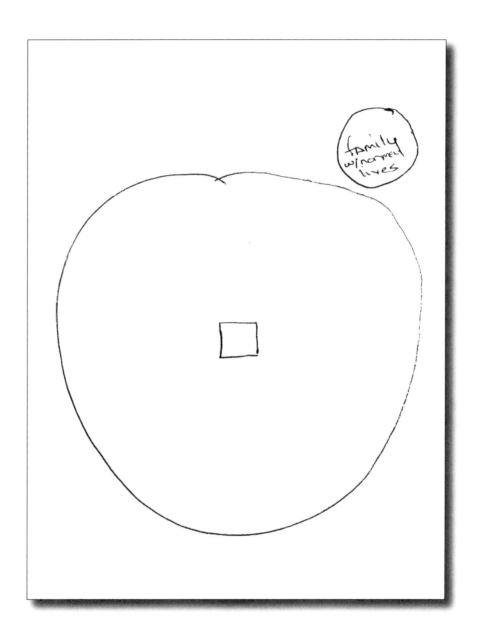

About half of our narrators could not separate their definition of family from their biological roots. Several family maps were intricate family trees, thorough and exacting. Others were literally geographical maps that depicted cities and states where relatives lived.

**Pete**: I think family is when you have blood relatives that help you during every time of crisis, as a means of support.

However, what stood out were the mixed emotions that narrators felt about the state of their family relations. We heard statements like, "Family means a lot right now," followed by contradictory expressions such as, "even though they're selfish, don't stick together, abandoned me, are not truthful, or judge me."

Sometimes a narrator included family members on their map even when they were estranged. Such was the case of Veronica, a recovering addict who created a family map that included her boyfriend, two old friends she had kept in touch with over the years, and one of her sisters, her daughter, and son, although they were estranged.

*Sisters: How do you define family?*

**Veronica**: God! That's a tough one.

*Sisters: Because it is more complicated than it seems.*

**Veronica**: Because family could be your best friends, especially if you do not have any family here. Family can obviously be your brothers and sisters, mother, father, grandparents, any of those. I do not know.

Another narrator, Bruce, explained to the interviewer, "Family is being together," that his brother is his only family, and he's the only person he won't take pills around, because it scares his brother badly.

John included his three daughters on his family map, along with friends from the street.

**John**: Family to me is close relatives. All your relatives I suppose, and then all your closest, your dependable friends. Friends that are not just fair-weather, but really, really good, long-term friendships I would consider as family.

The whole interview process was, for many of our narrators, a thoughtful exploration of their pasts, their situations, and the causes of their homelessness. Sometimes during these conversations, people reached profound realizations or entertained tentative answers. It was clear that many had already thought about the meaning of family in their lives, as in the case of Ethan, who was 28. This portion of his interview also illustrates the sort of probing that was sometimes necessary to elicit answers.

*Sisters: How do you see the word family? What does that mean to you?*

**Ethan**: I think of my immediate family right away.

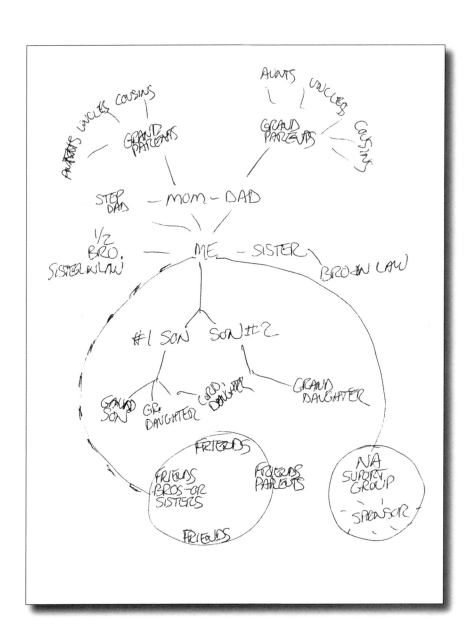

*Sisters: Your relatives?*

**Ethan**: Yeah. I'm kind of a loner. I wouldn't consider a friend a family member. A lot of street people form families. I'm away from that. I've just kind of avoided all that. A lot of people don't like their situation and need the comfort of others. It's safer to sleep in groups, which makes sense, but I'm just kind of off in my own world.

*Sisters: Do you have a girlfriend or anything?*

**Ethan**: No I don't. It would probably be a little easier if I did, I guess. But I'm not really into that right now. I'm enjoying being single right here at this time in my life. I've been single for a couple of years, and I'd kinda like to keep it that way. I guess I'm not good at relationships. I guess that's why.

*Sisters: Okay, if you were going to draw me a map of what family looks like to you…say you're right here [pointing to the middle of the page], who else is in your family? You can put anyone in there you want.*

**Ethan**: There's my mom.

*Sisters: Is there anybody closer to you than she is?*

**Ethan**: No, my mom. I've been closest to her for quite a few years now. There's my brother; I'd put him under my mom.

*Sisters: How about your son or daughter?*

**Ethan**: I haven't even seen my kid, so I can't throw him into the picture.

*Sisters: Anyone else?*

**Ethan**: I guess I consider my friend and her son, I guess I'll put them in there. They are pretty special to me.

*Sisters: Nobody in Portland?*

**Ethan**: No, I've got a few friends and stuff.

*Sisters: Aunts, uncles, or cousins or anything?*

**Ethan**: No.

*Sisters: Where's your dad?*

**Ethan**: Not even on there. Maybe someday we'll reconcile, I'll get older and want a father in my life, but, right now, I wouldn't. I don't know. This is a good thing to see. Maybe this is why I'm homeless. Maybe if I had more friends that I consider family, there would be more people to care about me, and more people for me to care about. It's a good thing to have people you care about. I've always been a loner, not much of a people person.

*Sisters: Thanks for doing that.*

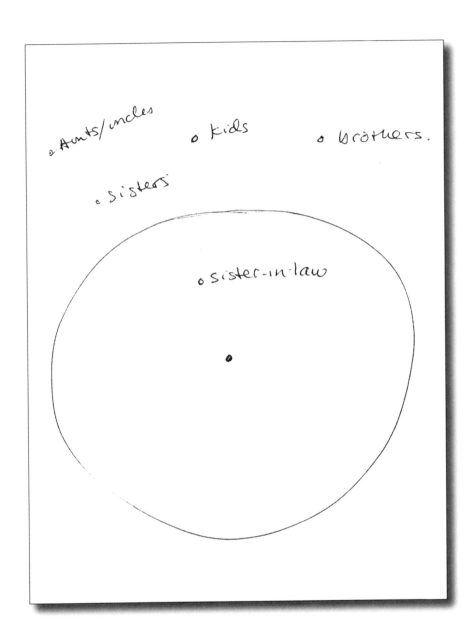

**Ethan**: There's not much on there.

*Sisters: Hey, there are people on there.*

Life on the streets often means making and keeping connections wherever one finds them. Narrators described how the bonds forged among other homeless people were sometimes the strongest they'd ever known. Lance described his family.

**Lance**: Well, my kids for one, a lot of people down here are too. I have family on the streets. A lot of the homeless people are my family. It is going to be hard for me to leave when I eventually leave, because they are my family. I have grown to love them.

**Stephen**: Before I became homeless, my definition was blood relatives. Now, my definition is people who care about you for who you are, and are there for you. It could be anyone, friends. Trusting, being honest, being real. Just loving one another.

Another narrator placed the people he called Mom, Dad, Brother, and Sister in the center of his family map, but in reality none were related to him by blood. He also sketched in fifty people who he described as his primary support group near the center, and five to six hundred in an outer circle, explaining that both groups were his extended street family.

**Thomas**: When you look at the overall picture as family, a family is anyone who is close enough to you, believes in what you believe and helps you at any cost, fight, [will] strive for what you believe in together. That's a family, whether it be one or one million.

**Alec**: Family is any group of people that have a little bit of unity, depend on each other. Some of my family are some of my closest friends, because they have been there for me when I needed them, and I think that is what family is; they do not have to necessarily be blood.

Ronny, who was a freight-train rider and had a daughter, commented:

**Ronny**: It does not really matter if they are actual, real family or not. Family is more of a togetherness. You could be family to me.

Pets are often an important source of comfort and stability in the life of a person experiencing homelessness. Tobias, who lives on the streets with his wife, Hope, spelled out the importance of his dog in his life, and the special importance of his dog's devotion to him.

**Tobias**: I've had J.D. since we got married, for ten years. He would rather sleep in a snowstorm with me, starving to death, than eat steak in front of a roaring fire with my wife. That's how much my dog loves me. Well, he loves my wife too. But I go like that [snapping] and he's there.

*Sisters: You're the one.*

**Tobias:** I'm the man. 'Who's your daddy now?' Sometimes I miss my animals more than I do my wife. And I hate to say it, but you know what, I gotta be honest. I'm just honest, that's all.

About one-tenth of our participating narrators included their spiritual or religious beliefs on their family maps. On their maps they wrote God, Jesus, or described a church as part of their family. Wendy drew her map and explained her definition.

**Wendy:** Oh! One more thing, because this is definitely to me family, number one—my God, and somewhere on the tree I would put the church as family. I regard them definitely as my family.

Maryann, 47, had been in Portland for two weeks when she was interviewed. She had a complicated past and mental health issues that led to her homelessness. She was fired from her job for refusing to work on the Sabbath. She claimed it was against her religion. Her interview revealed that her problems stemmed in part from an unstable work history and lack of references. While employed, she had owned a truck and a house. When she lost her job and was declared ineligible for unemployment benefits, she no longer could afford her mortgage payments. Her only option was to declare bankruptcy, which she refused to do because she claimed that too was against her religious principles.

After a series of misadventures in Nashville and New York, she ended up in Dallas where she became engaged to Alex, a homeless man she met there. From Dallas they traveled to Seattle, where Alex found work but Maryann was unable to find a job or stable housing. With regrets, she left Alex behind, and piled her belongings in a shopping cart, and started pushing it south along the highway. She walked most of the way between Seattle and Portland although she was given a few rides that helped her along.

**Maryann:** Alex was the first person I ever really truly loved because we sat down and talked about our childhoods. We talked about everything. We came to conclusions about society, and people, and religion, and when you can do that, you find your soul mate. They are your best friend, and you can talk to them about anything. He could tell me anything, about things he did on the job, good things and things that made him look bad and I still loved him because I understand.

If you cannot share everything in your life, they are not family. A lot of people in the shelter, now I can open up to them and talk to them like I do with Alex, and I feel like they are my family. They are people I can talk to.

As she drew her map she explained.

**Maryann:** This is God, all around me. He is my biggest family member, God and his son. Everybody in the whole world is my family, but there is this wall, and I call the wall 'the

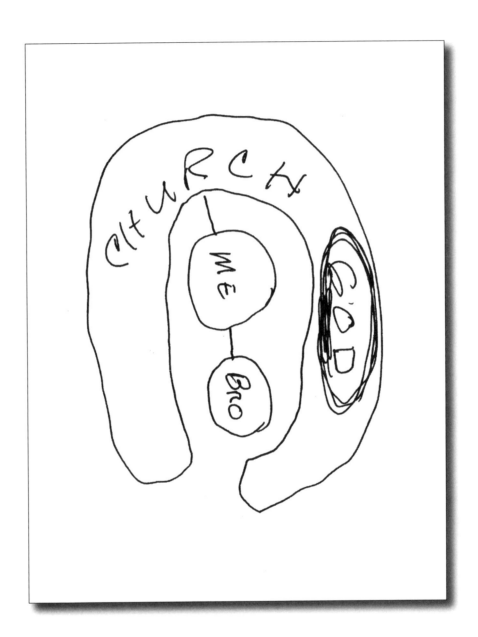

devil,' and there are little roads that go out here, and sometimes you can go through these roads and get out to these other people, and sometimes you cannot; they are little roads. Sometimes you could reach people out here, and sometimes you cannot, and it is just random as to whoever you can reach out to or not, but the devil cannot come between me and God, and this is the way I see me and my world.

Many of our narrators had abstract concepts for family, rather than specific people to be included. Their words reflected their hard lives and their need for belonging, comfort, and safety. Following are excerpts from narrators that express a range of definitions.

**Bryce:** Family is: compassion, trust, understanding and love, and a sense of hope that what you have of each of them will be passed on down the generations.

**Connie:** Family: those you care about and love, and you would do anything for each other.

**Mickey:** Family is when you come in the room and you feel welcomed; what you do matters; you are validated.

**Kelly:** Family: a grouping of people of all ages, shapes, and kinds, in support of one another. Once you have that, everything falls into place.

**Jan:** Family is anybody who is close to you, who you love and care about, and that you would do anything for. They won't ever leave.

**Louis:** Family: love, helping each other, caring, providing structure, including religion and morals to get you through your early years.

**Andy:** Family sticks together, loves each other, fends for each other, picks you up again.

**Margaret:** You're famous in your family! You all know each other and each other's business; you're close-knit.

**Susan:** The people who would die for you.

**Julie:** Close friends you can talk to, ask for help. They are there for you, and don't take advantage or hurt you. You don't have to say I love you.

**Kay:** It should be happiness and love unconditionally; it actually is misdirected anger, greed, dysfunction and chaos.

**Phyllis:** Family is bonded through thick and thin.

Sometimes expressions like *all God's children*, *the world*, *society*, or *earth* were included on a family map.

**Blaine:** Aren't we all brothers and sisters anyway?

Several family maps were faces grinning back at you, while some showed faces scowling. One woman placed Hollywood actors on hers, explaining that TV helped raise her. Another

included stuffed animals. Cops and even enemies were printed on several family maps; as one narrator wrote, "'cause there's good in everyone, some just need to be forgiven," while another noted, "people in corrections or police and mental health [staff] who work with you not against [you]." On another map a single word, *Mom*, appeared on the page. Several drew what looked like connecting atoms with two circles attached by a line. Inside the circles was written, *me and brother*, *wife and self*, or *self and God*.

Our narrators repeatedly stood outside of society's prescribed definition of family and found their own connections and meaning.

Grant, who was from California and visiting Portland, had first experienced homelessness when he lost his job at 21. He eventually became stabilized and finished college with a degree in elementary education, but he had been homeless on and off for the past twenty years.

**Grant**: I mean, most of my adult life has been in poverty and there have been several times when I was really close to it [homelessness], like getting General Assistance, where it just paid enough for rent and having to go to food lines. Even though I have not been homeless, recently I have been close to it or really dirt-poor. Most of my friends are homeless.

(Note: in order to qualify for our study, narrators had either experienced homelessness in their past, or were currently experiencing it. Their experiences included sleeping in cars, on others' couches, or in temporary housing linked to a job or social program, so while some narrators did not refer to themselves as having been "on-the-streets-homeless," they qualified as experiencing homelessness for our purposes.)

Grant explained that in his 20s, he was involved with drugs, and described himself as a "gutter punk," referring to his appearance: "spiky hair and safety pins all over the place." After living on the streets and in the margins of society, Grant became intensely involved in community organizing for issues concerning poor and homeless in Berkeley and Oakland. This included fundraising for a social service agency for people without stable housing, and peer counseling at a free clinic. He also held various jobs including working in a daycare center and collecting petition signatures. Grant has also survived over the years by selling plasma.

Toward the end of the session, we asked Grant how he would define family.

**Grant**: I guess I still look at it as there is a physical aspect, like who is your mother and your father. In my situation, I happen to know there are alternative definitions of family. I have got a mother and I got a dad and—well, I had a dad, he just died—and I got a brother and sister. When I hear the term 'family,' that is what I immediately think of. That's my family, though I am not that much in touch with them. But I also think there is a sense of family, kind of an alternate definition, like especially in Berkeley where you got alternative ways of

thinking. I definitely feel like the '80s family values are weird, because most of that family structure does not exist in a majority of cases.

Robin arrived homeless in Portland by a roundabout means. Robin's situation first became unstable after he was arrested in Southern California, fled the state, and moved to Colorado. He was working and in stable housing for several years, but then one of his jobs was causing too much stress and he began drinking to medicate his bipolar disorder symptoms, particularly depression. He quit that job, and saved money by camping on National Forest land for a number of months.

**Robin**: It was getting to be summertime, and I thought that if I could make it without paying rent for a couple of months then I would have enough money to clear my debt and find another place, which was the original plan. Once I started living in the woods, this plan changed quite a bit. I stopped drinking almost entirely. I was smoking quite a bit of pot up until that point in time, and I had stopped that almost entirely. I had no problems with my depression. I was living forty-five minutes outside of town, up at about nine thousand four hundred feet in the Rockies, next to a stream—probably some of the best days I have ever had in my life there. It was just incredibly healing.

Eventually, with winter coming on, he sold his mountain bike and traveled to California to visit his family. They bought him a bus ticket for Olympia, Washington. He ended up camping in Olympia and volunteering at a soup kitchen, then became involved in community organizing.

Next, he defined family for his interviewer.

**Robin**: Those people who have transcended the friendship relationship by becoming more an integral part of one's being, people who have become one's brothers and sisters and the mothers and fathers and grandfathers to which you were born.

He puzzled over his family map.

**Robin**: It is hard for me to do that, because I do not want to put myself in the center or the top or the bottom of anything, above or below anyone's name.

Evan, who was 27 when he was interviewed, began by saying that he had "a pretty strong family foundation growing up." Despite this background, and against his family's wishes, instead of attending college he moved to Alaska and worked onboard fishing boats. After two fishing seasons, he returned to Washington State and got married. However, his family life, which had become strained when he didn't go to college, became more so because of the marriage.

**Evan**: [The marriage] caused even more friction and problems in my family, and during that

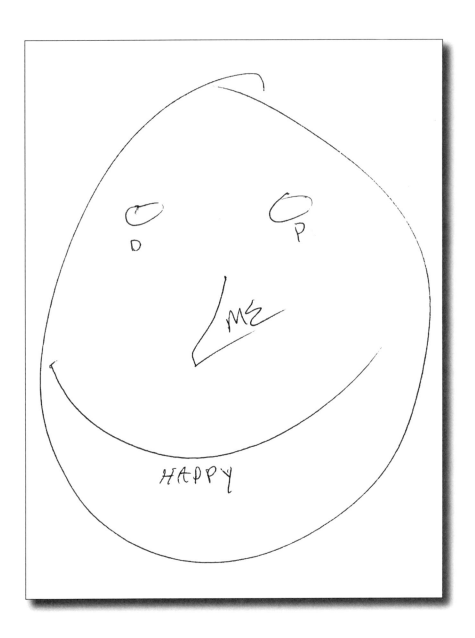

time a lot of my family started moving to Arizona. My brothers and sisters are at school, our grandparents are in Arizona, and the rest of my family started moving down to Arizona looking for jobs.

Then Evan discovered that his wife was cheating on him and, devastated, he left her.

Evan: So we got divorced and it just snowballed from there. I lost everything from that point.

The next few years of his life consisted of unemployment, temporary jobs, and living in missions and temporary housing in Portland and Eugene.

Toward the end of the interview he also defined family.

Evan: My relation[ship] with my family is a lot better than it was a few years ago. And I think family is really important because when it is all said and done, who you really have is your family. Now it is so sad because when you don't have anybody then you have depression, and perhaps disappointment and no courage. You know, family is there to give you everything that you miss when you are by yourself, when you are alone. This includes love, courage, support, self-esteem, confidence. They let you know when you are doing good, and in the same vein, when you are doing bad. That's what family is all about; relationship, commitment, honesty.

---

Interviewer's Journal Excerpt:
*She talked about wanting to change policies that take kids away from mothers who are homeless and that give them a very short time to change their situation and get their kids back. What was interesting about this was that the woman does not have any kids. It seemed significant to me that she devoted so much of her interview to a subject that did not directly affect her.*

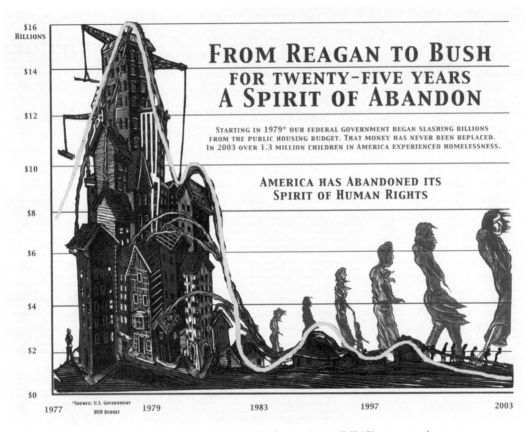

Artist: Art Hazelwood, for the Western Regional Advocacy Project (WRAP).  www.wraphome.org

*Read Sisters'* Voices from the Street *and the Western Regional Advocacy Project's* Without Housing: Decades of Federal Housing Cutbacks, Massive Homelessness, and Policy Failures. *Learn the answers to why so many people in the United States of America are dealing with homelessness and what it will take to end this national problem.*

—Genny Nelson

# Chapter 15

*Just give me a place where I can rest my legs*

## Solutions

---

*Homelessness is too common to be exceptional.*

—Dennis Culhane, University of Pennsylvania

Sisters has always believed that the people most intimately affected by a problem are those who need to be at the table to solve it. What you're about to read is evidence of this truth, and is only a small portion of a huge range of creative, practical, extravagant and simple solutions we collected in our database.

—Genny

Homeless people are experts on their situation.

The invitation to tell the world how to end this scourge seemed to exhilarate and lend hope to the participants. While a small minority professed to have no solutions for ending homelessness, most gave answers that were thoughtful, creative, practical, and often simple.

Our narrators certainly understood the difference between long- and short-term solutions. Many reflected that solutions must go beyond a turkey dinner on Thanksgiving and move toward immediate and systemic change in their situations.

**Boyd**: The days of people waiting in line for hours in the cold and rain to sleep on the floor ought to be numbered. Most shelters or systems limit their assistance to food, shelter, and clothing, just basic maintenance. They leave the rest to you or refer you to other forms of assistance usually resulting in some form of futility or runaround. Obviously, a better way can be found to help people and will bring about authentic, genuine, and more positive results. The homeless deserve, emphasize deserve, better. The world may not owe me or us a living, but our government or employers have no right to deny us opportunities or life, and yet they do. I encountered one poor fellow one time at a small Christian California shelter. He was in pain, distraught, not functional. His wife and children had been killed in an automobile accident. What is a guy like that to do? Where is he to go? He is not going up, he is not capable.

*Sisters: Why? Because he has been broken by his situation?*

**Boyd**: He has got to have a place where he can heal in dignity rather than out on the streets. This is something the society has got to get straight.

Janine saw solutions as part of a big picture, but at the same time expressed cynicism about the ability of a society to make these changes.

**Janine**: What we need to do is move towards more socialism in this country and that means to socialize medicine; a commitment on the community level for low-income, affordable housing; a commitment to better wages and a higher minimum wage, better working conditions, things like that. But the way that the system is working right now, I do not see that as something that is really going to happen. Our standard of living has become lower through the last couple of decades. The value of the minimum-wage dollar is much lower than it has been in previous decades and so we are not creating progress, but going backward at this point. And I just do not know how that can be resolved—the gap between the very poor and the very wealthy—it is widening not lessening. And I do not see any of those people who have power in our political system, which is people with the money, really being motivated to change that, so I do not know what the answer is there.

While our narrators were sometimes overwhelmed with the magnitude of the problem, almost everyone had at least one suggestion to ease or eradicate homelessness.

**Sandra**: The bottom line is we need more housing. I've been working in this part of town since 1976, and what we've always needed is more housing. What's happened is that we've gotten less housing. We have lost so much low-income housing and not replaced them [units]. I think we have been promised things that have not happened. The biggest problem is housing.

One important finding in our research was that people on the streets recognized the need for a new housing paradigm since the old model doesn't provide housing for everyone in need. Accordingly, while narrators mentioned solutions like more Section 8 housing vouchers or building SROs (single room occupancy hotels) or low-income apartments, just as often they looked beyond those traditional formulas.

Most often mentioned was affordable housing for people with low incomes.

**Gwen**: There is no more lower-income affordable housing, certainly we cannot afford it, certainly our government recognizes the need for it, certainly we [the government] spend a hell of a lot more money on things that give a lot less value, certainly I do not see any logical reason why we have lost all the low-income affordable housing.

We should have housing, but until we have that housing we need to provide better shelters that have longer term stays that end in transitional housing, where you leave the shelter to go into housing rather than back on the streets.

She went on to elaborate how the existing shelter system can be improved to move people into housing.

**Gwen**: Also [a shelter] that allows you to have a place to be during the day and to leave your belongings and just shower and so on, not just, you know, come in every night, hope you get a bed and out the door with your belongings in the morning. The shelters need services such as counselors that will help get you into housing and jobs and mental health programs and recovery programs and whatever your needs are, but to also have people who are working with their clients, listening to their clients and hearing their needs, their dreams, their hopes, instead of telling them what they have to do. Who in the hell wants to go into a program to be forced to do something you do not want to do?

Felicia was one of many narrators who fantasized about converting empty buildings to low-income housing but recognized why it probably wouldn't happen.

**Felicia**: Because, they are trying to either tear the buildings down and make parking lots out of them or make them into apartments for the rich people. Everything out here is going for the rich, not the poor, and there's a lot of poor people in Portland. And if you're a person who's ever been in jail or prison, you can't get on Section 8 or SRO because they go after your records. If you have a case record, they will not let you in them. And I don't think that's fair. I think it should be for anybody who needs it, instead of making all these places for the college kids and rich people. But, I don't think the city will do that. I think they *should*, but I don't think they *will*.

During his interview, Tony pointed out a building that stands across the street from an organization that offers food and services to the homeless.

**Tony**: [It was] ample to house every homeless person that you have in this entire town. You could just fill it with beds from one end to the other. I think the city is using it to house toilet paper and stuff like that, records of some sort. I think their toilet paper is more important than the people they have in this town because that is what I see.

Art, 51, made this suggestion about renovating buildings:

**Art:** Well, I definitely think that they need to take some of these buildings that are just sitting abandoned and decaying, and someone, whether it be the federal government or somebody, turn them into places for homeless people to be able to stay. Because there aren't enough facilities and they don't go far enough in giving a homeless person a place to lay his head down safely at night. I think the food is adequate in the city, but I don't think the housing is near what it should be.

Jason was 20, and although young, offered a far-reaching solution.

**Jason:** My solution to homelessness is, there's a lot of abandoned buildings across the nation. If you told all the homeless people, this is what we want you to do: 'We'll give you the building, but we want you guys to refurbish the building and make it habitable. We'll give you an apartment in exchange for that. And you are expected to upkeep it and clean it. While you're there, we want to see you try to better yourself, and we'll give you everything you need in order to do that.' That would end homelessness. That would end a dependency on some agencies. All homeless people would learn to be self-sufficient. They would be able to say, 'That place used to be a squalor over there and I helped fix it up. I helped fix up my place. And now I get to go to school and be somebody, somebody I want to be.' That's a big pride; we all need that kind of pride. If they just did that, it would end homelessness.

*Sisters: Are there any other things you could add?*

**Jason:** Although I don't do drugs anymore, I think they should legalize drugs because if they legalize drugs and prostitution and they tax the money on that, then there would be more money going into the government.

Related to the abandoned building solution was the suggestion that parcels of public land should be set aside for building subsidized and low-income housing and for campsites and tent cities.

Vincent was asked what he would do if he had the power to make changes and implement programs.

**Vincent:** I would first come up with a place totally separate from downtown. You know, in a woodsy-type area. Erect a big-ass building. Put beds in it, showers, kitchen to where everything would be available twenty-four hours a day, seven days a week. Have all the materials needed for the homeless to where they wouldn't need anything. You know, such as for the ones that do want to stay in, have enough bed space for the ones that would like to stay. For the ones that wouldn't, get tents, blankets, hand warmers, portable heaters for the camps, clothes, socks, and have it available for them.

*Sisters: So you're envisioning, in addition to the building, a campsite for people to pitch tents?*

**Vincent:** Yeah. I mean, why not? You know, it does not take a genius to sit down and figure where the campsite would be, where they want it. I mean, I'm sure there's plenty of spots here outside of town that would be big enough to support something like that.

*Sisters: Why would you place it outside of the urban area?*

**Vincent**: I think the reason that I would place it outside of the mainstream of town is to give everybody a break from the law enforcement. Give them a sense to where, 'Gee, all my shit's [belongings] still there.' You know it's not going to be messed with. As far as making reference to the wooded area, I know a lot of people that have come from living in the woods, literally, being thrust out here. Can't see a tree. Such as myself. I grew up in California so I'm used to seeing ninety-foot redwoods. I think it would be better to put them in a wooded environment just so that they wouldn't have to deal with the bullshit out here.

Many of our narrators had creative, detailed suggestions for temporary or transitional housing, and many emphasized the need for supportive services with them. Barb envisioned using land in the warehouse district to build a shelter system that reflected the needs of different types of people on the streets.

**Barb**: I'd build three, thousand-bed shelters with all the facilities you need, feeding and all that. One clean and sober shelter with help, all the help you need, job resources, whatever you need, [then] a party shelter that you can be kinda drunk. If you're stoned, whatever, but as long as you're clean and you're competent, [you'd] have that shelter with help.

*Sisters: Could you drink and use in the shelter?*

**Barb**: Not in the shelter but you could come in and you could stagger a little bit. You know, a little leeway. And then third would be for the shopping-cart bums and the hopeless. And then have the social services and resources for everybody who wants help to be able to 'Hey, you've got an appointment, be in this office.' 'What can we do for you today?' 'How can we help you with your Social Security?'

*Sisters: And what about the people who will never be able to take care of themselves? Could they stay in your shelter?*

**Barb**: Sure. That would be like the shopping-cart bum shelter and like a hospital shelter. Something that if you need help, lay down and somebody would watch them. Because there was a guy who went into diabetic seizure at Portland Rescue this morning and the ambulance had to come. I've heard stories of people just dying there. Just lay down on the mat and they're so sick and they just die and that's it. You could sleep next to somebody who is dying.

Many narrators mentioned tent cities as a solution to homelessness and voiced their support for Dignity Village, which was a fledgling community at the time our interviews were conducted.

**Deb**: We need places like Dignity Village. We do not need that place to shut down.

*Sisters: And what is it about Dignity Village that you like?*

**Deb**: It gives the homeless a chance, a place to lay their head at nighttime, so they do not have to sleep in doorways. Some of them still sleep in doorways, but a lot of them do go to Dignity Village and it is a good place.

**Sara**: I think this city could offer some kind of forums that they invite people to come and ask, 'You have been in the shelters, you have been living at SROs, what can we change about that?' I will say this to you, if Dignity Village would have been available at the time that I went to a shelter, I would have never been in that shelter, I would have been at Dignity Village. I would rather be in a collective of people working on their own empowerment than struggling alone just to survive on a day-to-day basis. And just knowing them in an hour [members of Dignity Village], I am not saying that they do not have problems, but I think that that kind of group, anybody who is willing to stick together, bond together and solve their own problems, has got a lot more power than [City Commissioner] Eric Sten does in his commissioner seat.

Rich, a resident of Dignity Village, suggested that the public needed to visit the village and that it generally needed to be more in the public eye.

**Rich**: To raise support and to raise awareness, I think periodically we should have open houses out here. An open house in the Village would be a good thing. And we'd use some of the better shelters and structures and what not. People can just open them up and people can come in there and see them and see the way people out here are living and what they're doing with the resources that come out here.

*Sisters: What kind of awareness do you want to raise?*

**Rich**: Well, I think it will be good for people to realize, 'Someday this could be me. I don't care what you think. This could be me. What kind of things would I want available to me?'

While almost all narrators believed that most people would leave the streets if they had the chance, many told us that there will always be a few people that do not fit in mainstream society, and that alternative housing would grant them the autonomy they required.

**Robin**: You cannot get rid of homelessness. You can't do it. And not everyone that's homeless is going to get out of it and join society. In fact, to be honest with you, I think it's an irrational demand that society places on people that society should be the end-all and be-all. Some people would be perfectly suited to not living in buildings, are not willing to work full-time, but would prefer to live in the woods or live in, like, maybe a tent city like Dignity Village. Obviously it would have to be on the east side of the river because the trend over here [west side of Portland] is to get rid of all the affordable housing. The gentrification process is the trend. That's very serious.

The city really needs to come to grips with the reality of the situation that you can't push the homeless out of town. A city needs to plan, not just on the basis of the business population or the middle class or the upper class. But since we're going to be planning this sort of stuff, we might as well set aside a quarantine zone on the other side of the river for low-income housing and Dignity Village. That would be very wise.

*Sisters: Do you see shelters included as part of the solution?*

**Robin**: I, for one, severely dislike shelters. TPI (Transition Projects, Inc.) is the only place I'll even go to because most shelters prey on the dispirited and demoralized people. But, you know, there are never going to be enough shelters.

*Sisters: Are you saying, even though you don't prefer shelters, let's provide shelter beds, let's provide low-income housing, and let's give Dignity Village a chance?*

**Robin**: Yes. Definitely. That would be wise. A city is comprised of the entire gambit, the entire spectrum of the human population, so it's completely irrational for a city to only plan along the ultraviolet and the blue end of the spectrum and to completely overlook or deliberately turn hostile against the infrared and the red and orange side of the spectrum. Because you're not going to get rid of us. As a body of people and as a class of society, we're not going to be gotten rid of. And so an enlightened and rational council would take all that into consideration and plan in such a manner as to make it so that all the different classes and all the different endeavors within the city would cooperate together or at least there wouldn't be hostility.

Many narrators suggested that people experiencing homelessness band together and combine resources in a community like Dignity Village.

**Bryan**: If you got forty or fifty people camping in one spot you have a pool of resources to draw on, especially if those people become part of your community. If there is that spirit of community involved—which I have been told exists at Dignity Village—people rely on one another and there is a pool of resources there, it is a real achievement.

*Sisters: So, that spirit of community brings its own resources?*

**Bryan**: Absolutely.

He suggested that in such a community, a person might be able to borrow money for bus fare and share food. But he explained that community extends beyond shared meals.

**Bryan**: Not to mention the intangible resource like the feeling that you get from being in a community again—you are not camped under a bridge by the river now, you have a place where you go to at night. It is a camp, it's a tent, but it is there. You do not have to take it down every day and put it on your back and take it to town. You leave there in the morning, you return there at night, you have people around, you have neighbors. How long has it been for a lot of these homeless people who have been on the streets for a long time since they had neighbors?

*Sisters: What is the importance of having neighbors?*

**Bryan**: A sense of community. People live together; that is one of the things that we have done since the beginning of time. We need to feel like we are part of something. We need to feel like we are associated with each other and that those associations are not necessarily meaningless.

*Sisters: So being part of something bigger? Would you advocate tent cities as a solution?*

**Bryan**: Absolutely. I not only advocate tent cities as a solution, I advocate tent cities in more numbers and closer to resources and closer to transportation. And they should be provided for people who not only have no choice, but also people who choose to live there and they should be self-governed. I do not think that it has been thought out enough to be legalized. I think the concept of it is vulgar to a lot of people, and I think that is why they have frowned on it and that is why they did not make it legal.

*Sisters: They are against tent cities because they are vulgar?*

**Bryan**: Yes, of course.

*Sisters: Do you mean it's vulgar based on aesthetic consideration?*

**Bryan**: Absolutely. You put a tent city somewhere and you are not going to have developers coming to you wanting to build two thousand units of condos right next door. People are not going to want to live there. They are not going to want to look down and see a bunch of people living in tents in their front yard. It does not work that way.

We also heard that multiple-family housing and shared housing were solutions that would end people's isolation along with their homelessness, allowing them to pool economic resources and form a support network.

**Lydia**: I think single-family homes are part of the ruination of our country.

**Pat**: If I was the boss of Portland, I would have fair housing but not SRO. Not the way it's being done.

*Sisters: What kind of housing are you envisioning?*

**Pat**: I would envision family-type housing. I don't know how we would get the families together, but there's gotta be a way. Like you screen everybody. You find people that are compatible and you put them in a house together. Grandmothers, young kids, single guys, single girls, whoever. Even with the people that have jobs and are making money, there is a huge loneliness going on in this country. People are lonely, isolated, no matter if you've just come off the street or if you're making forty grand a year. It's still a big problem.

Jay spoke of the isolation inherent in much of the current low-income housing.

**Jay:** I would get rid of all this SRO housing. This SRO thing is a mess. That SRO thing is a bunch of drunks living in single rooms. That's not helping anything. It's made it much worse. It's alienated people from each other. It's supporting drunks in free rooms. That's what it is. That is not good. That is not helping out.

*Sisters: How do they alienate people from each other?*

**Jay:** Just putting them in isolation like that. I had lunch the other day with an old, wise Indian who said the circle is broken. That's at the very core of the illness, the whole illness of our society is the circle of broken people and not connecting with people. You got to have programs to get people connected again. There's more connection with the people on the street, the street people, than there is when you get off the street. You go live in some neighborhood, you got less contact with people than you did when you were on the street. You go get a job in a warehouse, you don't meet people. The only place we have dancing and music is in bars.

A number of our narrators identified that before solutions can be put into place, the general public and policy makers need more education and awareness about the homeless community and the resources required to end their plight. They described also a need for accurate media coverage, more face-to-face meetings with policy makers, and generally having a bigger voice in the communities they lived in.

Narrators talked often about the need to change attitudes toward and stereotypes about people on the street. Kenneth, who at 74 was our oldest narrator, emphasized this point.

**Kenneth:** The people that have a nice house, a car, a good job, they look at people that are homeless like people that don't belong. They should try to help out people that are homeless just a little bit more. Give them the benefit of the doubt. Give them at least a chance to prove that they don't want to be homeless. They don't want to be cold and alone. They want a chance to have something, but people don't give them that chance. And it's just really sad when people aren't given that chance to show what they can do. Really is sad.

*Sisters: If you had a thirty-second or one-minute commercial spot that went out during the Super Bowl, what would you say to the world relative to homelessness?*

**Jordon:** I'd say if you've never been homeless and you need to understand it, just ask somebody that is homeless, and they'll explain it to you. Don't be scared to ask somebody because if you don't ask, you don't know. Homelessness is not really a disease; it's just a problem and it needs to be solved. That's what I'd say.

We also heard the need for compassion as a solution. Ray was asked what would end homelessness forever.

**Ray:** 'Love thy brother.' Until society, from top to bottom, decides that people are more important than televisions, they are more important than superhighways, they are more important than doggies, they are more important than doggy parks or fantastic-looking Pioneer Squares…when people are more important than that, then people will say, 'I love my brother. I cannot allow my brother to live under a bridge when I have a garage, when I have an extra room, when I have got five million dollars in the bank. My five million in the bank is not worth it to me anymore because I love my brother, and there is that old lady sleeping on a park bench out in the cold.' That is never going to happen, I am sorry to say it. It is sad, but it can be improved. I mean, someone has got to fight and I am willing to fight for that cause, but not by myself.

Benjamin replied to a question about what is needed to help homeless people achieve goals and stable housing.

**Benjamin:** First of all, the main, the most important thing that is needed to even start to pursue these goals is understanding by the general public. This means every average person that is living here in Portland, Oregon, or anywhere in America where people are homeless, they have to understand that a lot of people, the majority of people out here do not want to be homeless. And the first thing we have to do is bring our truth to the general public, [to] the person that frowns down on homelessness as, 'These are lazy people, these are all alcoholics, these are all drugs addicts, these are all criminals, prostitutes, whatever, who do not want the same things I want or will steal from me.'

And if they understand the truth about the homeless, the taxpayers will take care of them. [They] have to get that idea, that [false] conception, out of their mind. And, you know, one of the most bizarre things I have heard, and I thought it was kind of funny, but it was just such ignorance, is when I did that interview across the street with them kids at the college about homelessness, and the youngster asked me a legitimate question. He said, 'What do you feel about people who are in a residence [and are] concerned about homeless people moving into their neighborhood?' I answered, 'Look, we had homes before we were homeless; we lived in neighborhoods before we lost everything.' It would be different if he asked about people camping out in their neighborhoods or sleeping on their sidewalks. You know what I am saying?

Many narrators called for better leadership as a solution. This brand of leadership included asking people who are experiencing homelessness for short- and long-term solutions, implementing some of their ideas, and being instrumental in securing increased funding to eradicate homelessness.

Ambrose, a Native American activist, talked about this need for leadership along with compassion.

**Ambrose:** We need for a group of rich people, of lawyers and doctors and people who got money, that are secure where they are at, to step up to the plate and be human beings. Number one, be Americans, and number two say, 'Wow! Wait a minute here, I'm not buying the party line no more. I'm not buying any of it anymore; I want to know what is right and wrong.' There is an old, old saying that somebody said a long, long time ago and it is really the key to it all. It said, 'Love thy brother.' If you love that brother, you cannot beat him down, steal what rightfully is his, covet everything he has got, and take it away from him and hurt him. If you love him, you cannot do it.

We need heroes, people like Mr. Martin Luther King, Jr., and we need our government to quit killing them. Let them do some good because ultimately it is our government that suffers. When the country collapses, the rich people come down with it.

We heard often that solutions meant cooperation, involvement, and "everyone invited to the table."

**Craig:** I believe [a forum should include] also the concerned citizens, not just homeless people, but people that got a house and a regular twenty-year job, to be there. They are tired of seeing people pushing shopping carts down Burnside [Portland's main street] and instead of just ignoring them, they should face it.

Our narrators called on the federal, state, and city governments, along with individuals such as the governor, mayor, and city commissioners, to become involved in solutions. Several narrators also said that it was time to hold leaders accountable for the plight of homeless people.

Angela was in favor of community organizing and aggressive action as a solution to homelessness.

**Angela:** The first thing that comes to my mind is organize and raise demands and get pushy with the city. You know, get in their face more. But like I say, it's very hard to do when so much of your time is consumed with just getting your basic needs met. And maybe they do that here, but it'd be nice if there was a place where a homeless organization [had a] meeting place or front house and then flyers could go out to people for several days in advance and say, 'We're gonna have a meeting here.' And flyer the place where all the homeless people go for about a week before that and just flood people with this.

You know, raise your demands and let's get in the face of these officials who are gatekeepers to our buildings, and get what we need. And like I say, I haven't been that involved to really know if that's already going on or not. But if it isn't, I'd like to see it happen because we need a lot more than we're getting. And we need a lot more from the government. It shouldn't all come from religious organizations. For people like myself who get offended by having to cross that line to get certain things I need. I don't want to go into a religious organization for anything.

Steve, 51, was also in favor of community organizing.

**Steve:** I think it's important to get everybody together and have rallies. I am not talking rowdy rallies or anything, I am talking about peaceful rallies. I am talking about candle vigils, where it is peaceful. I am talking about organized security and getting all the homeless people together and having them [go] places, and have your speaker activists maybe in front of city hall or city council, wherever we need to go and say, 'We have had enough.' Get people organized to where they get lawyers [to represent them]. Get people together and say, 'Hey, we need this done. We need to open up these buildings or raise new facilities and whatever we need.' I think we need to work at it and not give up; stay on it because eventually we will get there. Just have faith, you know.

Pete, a 54-year-old veteran, suggested that homeless people in Portland and other cities need to organize and work for change, emulating the civil rights movement of the '60s.

**Pete:** The homeless have to get up here and start doing the same thing. This is a repeat of history; instead of the blacks now, it is going to be the homeless.

*Sisters: This is the same discrimination that the blacks went through?*

**Pete:** I think so. Just because of their status, which makes them more like homosexuals because that is more of a status, not race.

He went on to explain that the lawsuits that result from gay bashing and homeless rights will eventually change policies and laws.

**Pete:** And another thing we can do is get rid of the old politicians and get newer, younger politicians because when you become a politician [you] end up getting corrupted.

Jay, who we heard from earlier about the need for community, had an interesting perspective on who has the power in Portland to change things for the better:

**Jay:** The one-percenters are the people that change the mass.

*Sisters: The one-percenters? Can you explain that?*

**Jay:** People like yourself. The one percent that believes there can be a change. It's been proven in history—Gandhi, Mother Teresa, Martin Luther King, Jr., those people and the people that think like them. Like the peace movement in the '60s. They were the one percent that changed the one hundred percent.

*Sisters: One-percenters. I've never heard that expression. I like that. Who would be in that group?*

Jay: I think the Hawthorne people [referring to a Bohemian neighborhood], I think the north [part of Portland], the black people. The black people have been through all this. They've been through hell and they know what it's all about.

*Sisters: What about the Hawthorne people?*

Jay: I think there's a new wave of '60s people at Hawthorne that want peace, that want change. They want to use the power of democracy to work for change in this country. It's gotta be handed to them by somebody, and it's gotta be a direction that they can see. Like India would have never changed if Gandhi hadn't handed them the idea. I mean, it's just a pie in the sky until there's somebody standing up saying, 'You gotta do this.' Not just like idealism. Gotta be concrete.

A number of narrators mentioned the need for jobs or job training.

**Brit**: Employment is the answer to a homeless person.

A veteran who has worked in restaurants, among other jobs, talked to a local charity about help obtaining a food handler's card, which is a necessary requirement in the food service industry.

**Harold**: I think that would be a big help for a lot of people because if you go to work in that type of business, you need one. And sometimes it's hard to come with the ten dollars for one if you're not working at all. At least people could manage some part-time work, cooking or washing dishes.

As part of finding jobs for those living in poverty, Josh, who was 34, suggested that the government prioritize domestic spending, a popular suggestion.

**Josh**: Start cutting back our help to other countries; instead, make those opportunities available here at home. Create more jobs, more opportunities, more chances for school or more opportunity to learn a trade or to get at least a minimum-wage job. And an increase in our wage too; I mean, inflation is so completely out of control compared to what minimum wage is.

Many narrators mentioned the need to increase the minimum wage. Rich had apparently given this issue a lot of thought.

**Rich**: I believe that minimum wage should be about thirteen dollars an hour. Most people will have to pay at least four hundred dollars a month for a place to stay. But see, if you're making minimum wage or about six fifty an hour, you're talking about a thousand dollars a month (in wages). But see, right away the government takes twenty-five percent of that, so you're still living on about eight hundred bucks a month. That's about the same thing as I make on Social Security. For minimum wage. And it's real reasonable to say that most people have to pay at least four hundred dollars for rent. That leaves four hundred dollars for food and transportation. And you have to budget at least seventy-five dollars a week for food. Okay, so, seventy-five times four is about three hundred twenty for food. That only leaves eighty bucks for transportation. And that's not enough to own a vehicle. That's about enough for a bus pass. That's about it. If you're making minimum wage, I guess you can just about get by at six fifty an hour. But then you still need clothing and incidentals. You still come up short. Even at six fifty an hour.

Bo, 54, recommended more help in finding jobs and improving on current job-search programs.

**Bo**: Somebody helping you network with job leads rather than telling you 'You need these jobs; you need to go to these meetings.' We need to see more action from the people. Actual help from people who are helping the homeless.

*Sisters: So actual job leads. Not classes.*

**Bo**: Exactly. And more management experienced with helping homeless people rather than just doing it for the money or the name. Does that make sense?

Thomas, 44, envisioned a temporary service run by the City of Portland that hired homeless people.

**Thomas**: I don't know why they don't round up a bunch of homeless people and pay us money to go around and pick up trash. There's a tunnel at Labor Ready and it's always full of glass and paper; the city should take care of it, but it's been like that ever since I started there. It's nasty, needs to be taken care of. I don't think the city is trying to create jobs for the homeless people. There needs to be a temp service that the city runs.

*Sisters: What would that temp service be like? Would it be different than other temp agencies?*

**Thomas**: It would be beneficial to the city, manicure the city a little, clean it up. This is what community service is. Instead of sweeping floors for a private contractor, you could be sweeping floors for the city. You would think there would be plenty of things the city could have people doing.

Art echoed Thomas's idea and noted the need for flexibility when reintegrating people into the workforce.

**Art**: There should be some type of program set up where homeless people can go in and do something to earn some money, too. Whether it be cleaning up…just go around and clean up the city. There's gotta be some way to create some jobs for the homeless people because a lot of them have no skills, and a lot of them have been without work for so long that they don't have the stamina to do a regular job, so they need some kind of creative way just to earn some money.

Eighty-two of our narrators identified a day center as the number one need in Portland and described models found in other cities. The day center that was suggested would include a place to store belongings, escape the elements, gather with friends, use telephones and computers, and shower.

**Morgan**: They need a place for people to go in and get out of the day and the weather…I mean, just let them get in there and sit down and get out of the weather, get warmed up a little bit.

Along with other narrators, Greg, who was 40, believed that the homeless community should be involved in creating solutions.

**Greg**: Instead of giving money to the Portland Rescue Mission and Union Gospel Mission, let's get money to build our own day care center. Since there's plenty of the homeless, I bet we could do it ourselves, if we can get the funding. Like you said, lots of us are clean and sober; I bet we could build it from the ground up.

*Sisters: A lot of people we have interviewed have said we need a day center.*

**Greg**: You need something that's open twenty-three, twenty-four hours a day equipped with laundry and a TV. A nice big place. But let's open it up 24/7 so the person that's tired at three in the morning can come in maybe for a hot cup of coffee, just get out of the weather, take a nice hot shower, and be on his way.

In a sense, our narrators created a wish list of the small and large items needed to ease and end homelessness. Along with a day center, their wish list included: lockers, mail service, more public restrooms with access to them at all times of the day, more public drinking fountains, more access to legal representation, the ability to sleep legally in parks and public places, and a marketplace so that homeless people could sell crafts and products they make. Other solutions included, "A place where people listen to you," a special bus pass for homeless people, another camping site with bathrooms like Dignity Village, a sped-up SSI approval process with minimal red tape, free laundry facilities or work exchange for laundry privileges, and a reduction in red tape associated with receiving benefits, especially needed medication.

Suggestions for change covered mostly practical matters that meant the difference between living on the streets or being sheltered.

**Blair**: [Instead of losing your housing for a single infraction], three strikes and you're out if you're staying in transitional housing. If people are medicated legally, such as on methadone, they're allowed housing.

We heard that shelters need to build more bathrooms and showers, suggestions that shelters be built outside of the Old Town/Chinatown and downtown neighborhoods, and suggestions to allow camping on BLM (Bureau of Land Management) and other public lands. We heard suggestions to issue permits for panhandling and performing in public, and to legalize prostitution and drugs and sleeping in cars.

We also heard the need for more counselors and caseworkers and for establishing long-term relationships with them as a stabilizing force. One woman talked about needing more individual attention from counselors.

**Julia**: I think a closer look or closer contact with the individuals would help. Maybe to get the counselor to somehow get inside of the person. I mean to have that person open up or to convince them somehow to get some kind of help even though they do not want to get off the street. It is a lot like other programs for recovery.

Brenda also spoke of the need for more one-to-one counseling.

**Brenda**: I think it is very effective and somebody who is very sincere and very understanding, no matter what they say, no matter how they are reacting, to show them love. I think love has a lot to do with that, and I know it's a stressful job for counselors and caseworkers. Show them that somebody loves them. Maybe some of these people have had a rough life, a lot of neglect, lot of rejection.

Joe, who was 44, focused on the need for a caring support network of family and friends, saying that without it, "It is practically impossible to make it out of the gutter."

*Sisters: And so what is so important about having friends or family support in order to get out of the gutter, as you said?*

**Joe**: What is important is that they are established and a person needs a boost up. They need a real helping hand, a head start. You have got to have a place to go, to live, in order to find a job, in order to have an address, a phone number, in order to be clean, in order to have nice clothes or be presentable, to present yourself and your skills. It is a catch-22 situation; if you do not have that, you just go in circles. You got to have some kind of strong support as far as family or friends.

*Sisters: How do you compare the support that you get from family and friends versus the support that is out there through social services?*

**Joe**: Like night and day. Because they care about you and the people in facilities do not care about you or love you; you are just a number. With your family, you are a person with feelings.

Tom suggested that a program based on the twelve-step model be used to end homelessness, with an emphasis on mentoring.

---

**Tom:** Like they have Alcoholics Anonymous and Narcotics Anonymous groups to get people together, they should have Homeless Anonymous. Places where homeless people can meet, have coffee and doughnuts. Have somebody there, maybe one or two people who are activists or professional counselors. And then start the action there…have all these people talk about their problems.

I think people who have been homeless and now are out of it, they are happier, they have life. I believe that they can help other people just like an alcoholic who is doing good now, who has not drunk. The alcoholic who is suffering can relate with the alcoholic who is recovering; I think the homeless person can relate with the person who has been homeless. There could be some kind of bonding or connection.

Other narrators talked about how most of the services and shelters for the homeless are located within a few square blocks in downtown Portland, but that the few available jobs for unskilled workers are located in the outer edges of the city, causing a transportation nightmare. Bryan described how this difficulty sometimes meant finding places to camp because you're stranded in another part of town, or missing the free meals which are mostly available in the inner city.

**Bryan:** So to even apply for the job I have to have money that I do not have, and then to get back and forth from that job I have to have money that I do not have, and then I have to be able to eat until I get my first paycheck.

*Sisters: So, for the few openings there are, they are hard to get to?*

**Bryan:** If you really want to get extraordinarily reductionist about it, you [can] look at problems and the barriers that lie between the problem and the solution. The problem is unemployment, 'I have no income.' They can get jobs, many of them may be highly skilled, but how do they get to and from work? And what did they do? They are working all day, they have no money, they are eating at the missions. They are not going to get breakfast, they got to be to work by six in the morning. They are not going to get lunch. Yeah, they get a lunch break at noon, but can they make it back to the mission to eat? No. When they get off work, can they make it back to the mission to eat, probably not. Yes, they are going to get paid in two weeks and they will probably get a sizable paycheck, but how do you do strenuous work and fast for two weeks?

*Sisters: So, they will basically starve by the time the first paycheck comes?*

**Bryan:** The problem is you cannot do strenuous hard work for two weeks and not eat.

Bryan's proposed solution is as sharp as his analysis of the problem, suggesting that missions maintain a list of people who are working and travel around in a van and deliver sack lunches or to provide loans that cover lunches, for the first weeks of employment.

**Bryan**: After a few paychecks they are going to have enough money to get into an apartment, they are going to have enough money to get a car, but it is the first two weeks that is a killer. You have the transportation issue, you have the food issue. I think with those two things [taken care of] anyone can work.

He also made an intriguing observation about the psychological need for such a solution.

**Bryan**: Journeying away from services can be a lot more than inconvenient, it can be disconcerting. You do not know what is going on till you get back downtown. In a sense, downtown becomes your home while you are homeless. And any time you leave there, you are uncomfortable because you do not have that knowledge.

*Sisters: You can never leave?*

**Bryan**: Yeah, you do not want to; it is comfortable there. You can walk around downtown Portland and look at people, and you can play chess, and you can get all your meals, and you can stay here until you are very old and very fat and never have to worry about anything. Why leave?

*Sisters: You mean instead of traveling to the limits of the city where the jobs are?*

**Bryan**: Right. So for me, getting a good grip on what exists outside of downtown is very important.

Jay had creative ideas that stressed self-reliance.

**Jay**: We could set the poor people up, the homeless people, with rickshaws. They could taxi around the people with money. I'd set aside parcels of land where you raise food. We'd have parcels of land, serious parcels of land; we'd raise food on it. There would be jobs.

Gretchen had a practical idea for helping women who are pregnant and poor.

**Gretchen**: They expect you to be able to get yourself back on your feet and everything before your baby is born, but yet they only help you with cash after the baby is born. I mean, I always thought maybe they should help, like, a month or two before the baby is born, before the due date, because a lot of the pregnant women, if they had the money a month or two before, they would be able to be in an apartment by the time the baby is born. And the baby wouldn't be taken the moment it's born because they don't have a place to live. And I've seen a lot of my friends go through that, and I want to help them so bad. But I don't even have a place myself to help them.

Gretchen had another suggestion for welfare reform.

**Gretchen**: They don't help you with general relief if you don't have a disability. The only way you can receive General Assistance here is if you have a disability. And that's no good. 'Cause right now I don't have money. I cannot receive General Assistance for that reason. You know I don't have a disability. I don't want to get disability [benefits], because I can work.

**John**: One of the things I see as an option for homelessness, and this is my personal opinion, has to do with the armed services. You have a lot of former military, like myself; we are former marines [on the streets]. Have the armed services give us the opportunity to reenlist.

While several dozen narrators recommended cracking down on drug dealers as a solution, many others saw the system's tendency to direct resources chiefly at people with drug and alcohol problems as the problem. The focus on substance abusers often means women, families, or people without addiction issues don't qualify for programs.

**Francesca**: I think you have a lot of avenues, a lot of different resources here, but I think they are targeting just one particular scenario, and that is drinking and drugs. They figure everybody who is homeless is a drug addict or an alcoholic, and that is just not the case. I think they need to directly look at some of the people who are not. Some of the people are just having a tough time.

Randy, 44, was one of many narrators who commented that transitional housing needed to be available for everyone, not just those suffering from substance abuse.

**Randy**: I want to see this unfairness end. There is money allocated for homeless alcoholics and drug addicts, but there also needs to be money allocated just for homeless people. You know there is a difference. Right now, just to be homeless with no alcohol or drug problem, nine times out of ten, as long as you are down, you are going to be on these streets.

People suggested both large and small program changes, particularly to the food stamp program. Currently, food stamps or electronic food stamp benefit transfer cards (EBT cards) are usable for two purposes: to purchase unprepared food—which allows someone to buy a can of chicken from a grocery store but not a whole roasted chicken from their deli—or in exchange for a hot prepared meal from a USDA (United States Department of Agriculture)-approved meal site. Sisters Of The Road Cafe is currently the only such site in Portland and one of six approved in Oregon. (A meal and drink at Sisters costs only $1.50.)

One narrator addressed the need for more restaurants and cafes to accept food stamps.

**Lars**: I have been watching things at Sisters. Lots of times the guys come in they are so proud that they can use their food stamp card. And I heard one guy who was talking about the bartering say, 'Well, I might have to barter now, but I got this.' It gives them a sense of worth, sense of buying, purchasing power.

**Ron**: People should be able to get toilet paper, soap, deodorant, toothpaste, stuff like that with food stamps. You need it for hygiene. Whereas you could buy a soda pop or coffee, but can't buy necessities like that. They're more important than coffee. Talk about allocating the food stamps properly. If you went for a month without a shower, or a month without a Coke or a cup of coffee, which one is the most harmful?

Several narrators discussed providing people on the streets with the opportunity to work for essential needs, whether food, shelter, showers, or storage. Narrators often described the need to store backpacks and belongings. As one man said of carrying his bags, "It's like being a pack mule."

**Ansel**: Somehow there's got to be more setups for people to keep what you have. I mean, if you carry everything around with you constantly, if you go looking for a job with a backpack and stuff, that's not going to look good. Where do you leave your things so somebody doesn't steal them while you're going to obtain a position? Where do you keep your stuff that it's safe? That's a big thing for the homeless: some way for people to have public lockers available. Like Sisters Of The Road does its food, a way to barter for use of a locker, or a better cheap way. Maybe some organization could come up with a plan. I'm sure that would be helpful to a lot of people on the streets. [Note: a Portland organization, JOIN, has such a barter-for-storage policy.]

Other narrators mentioned barter programs or job programs that offered housing for work. Will, a 54-year-old veteran, suggested that the city create a program where homeless people clean public places in exchange for a small salary and food stamps.

**Will**: I think that is going to give them a little respect and dignity as well. 'I am doing something instead of just give me, give me, give me.' Because I think that is a bad thing. I think it is a bad habit to get into 'give me' type of stuff. You got to make the people work a little bit for it even though you are not really changing anything.

*Sisters: Is there some way that we can end homelessness for a great number of people?*

**Will**: Figure out ways to get them into trade schools, get them a GED or high school diploma, and when they get out have some kind of job waiting for them. That is the trouble with a lot of these schools now; they turn you loose and there are not jobs out there. And then where are you? Same place you started before.

Our narrators continually came up with small changes and answers that would make their lives more manageable and dignified.

Of all the organizations and nonprofit groups that interact with homeless people, the shelters received some of the lowest grades from our narrators. When asked for solutions, some narrators mentioned small considerations in the shelters such as extending hours, handing out more than one blanket, providing thicker mats, and generally considering the clients' comforts.

**Patrick**: I think individual cubes (cubicles). We'd like to have more time to ourselves, closed in, an individual cube, not on top of each other, in a close setting.

*Sisters: Like having individual spaces for each person?*

**Patrick**: Yeah. It should be closed in, so once you go to bed, you have a lock and you're by yourself. All you're doing is checking in the place there.

A woman of 25 had a simple request to make life better for those living in shelters.

**Elsa**: In the shelter you cannot cook. They should have at least a little microwave for you to warm up food, like snacks and stuff. Everybody could eat before they turn their light out and then can do a clean-up check before everybody goes to sleep.

Virtually all of our narrators described the need for shelter from the elements, and mentioned that in the rainy Northwest, the weather needs to be taken into more consideration when creating policies and programs.

**Michael**: Get people out of the weather and elements because this is not Orlando, Florida. I mean, if it's cold and wet here eight months out of the year and you're on the streets, God only knows what your health, immune system, your state of mind is. I mean, you wake up, you're already in a gloomy position, and you look up at the sky and it's just as gray and gloomy as the mood that you're in. Come on, that works against you. Now you're cold and you're wet on top of that. Duh, you haven't eaten. You maybe haven't bathed or whatever. You know, all that plays on a person.

One narrator who had worked in construction most of his life recommended:

**Earl**: Clothing and tools, allotments for something like that. A pair of work boots or a set of clothes to be able to look for work in.

Sometimes solutions seemed simple, but were not.

**Malcolm**: We need to get them out of this routine to get them back into circulation, into society.

**Holly**: I think that if everybody in this town would give up a dollar, that would be your solution right there.

The old Native American saying of 'Walk a mile in my moccasins' came up again and again during our talks. One man mentioned how friends had let him share their tent for three nights at Dignity Village.

**Shaun**: They were friends of mine, so they let me sleep in their tent just to give me a place to rest my head because they knew that I had been sleeping under these bridges for as long as they had, longer actually, but they have a lot of compassion. That is where you find the most compassionate people, [those] that are homeless; they understand it better than anybody. If you could take the mayor of this city and put the shoe on the other foot, make her sleep under the Steel Bridge out here for a night or two, I think there would be a lot of changes made, I really do. It would be a humbling experience because it has humbled me to the point that I am not used to it. I have to go with it; I have to bide my time and just go with it.

**Paul**: Now, if the people making the policy came down here and spent twenty-four hours in the streets with someone who lived in the streets, they would change the policy. I guarantee you they would change the policy because they would see what we are going through down here.

**Lance**: In order to really understand and accept homelessness, you or someone close to you would have experienced it. There are people that donate money; that is their way of feeling good. They just send a check, but a lot of times it would be more valuable and more worthwhile to come down here and do as you are doing and your other colleagues are doing here and really get into these peoples' lives. Ask 'Why are you here? What do you feel needs to be done as a society?' Because it does not have to be this way. What really gets me, makes me almost cry is when I see a young mother down here on the streets with her children.

A 48-year-old veteran put it this way:

**Zachary**: Until people who have experienced homelessness are at the table where solutions are being discussed, solutions will never be found.

At 48, Duane had a college education, had worked as a framer and carpenter, professional musician, and claimed many professional accomplishments. He had also begun using heroin to treat a back injury and when we met him was being treated with methadone.
He mused that some of his problems in life began in childhood.

**Duane**: My parents were divorced when I was 11. And that in a sense would be my first experience with homelessness because at that time I felt like I didn't have a home when I came home from school. It didn't feel like home once my real father had left. I grew up with many, many privileges; downhill skiing, music lessons, voice lessons, speech team, everything you can think of, I got to do. Including having a brand new Mustang to drive on dates for Friday nights when I was 17. And I started smoking marijuana and eating LSD when I was 15. I've had problems ever since my parents got divorced really. It hasn't stopped.

He and his partner, who has a master's degree in social work, had been living in an apartment that they managed. When it was sold, things went downhill fast.

**Duane**: We lost our housing and our income at the same time and got bad credit references out of it too, so that we couldn't find a place.

After briefly staying with relatives, he began selling *street roots* for income. They next moved to Dignity Village.

**Duane:** Because it represents an organized effort to address the problem by the people that are being affected.

He discussed how after being situated under a freeway underpass, the tent city was moved to the outskirts of town.

**Duane:** And so they moved us to another site. We had several options. What site do we wind up being pretty much forced and cornered into taking? The one right next to a leaf-composting operation that's putting some kind of bacteria in the air that's making a black mold on the inside of the tents. Several people have been in the hospital with respiratory problems, and it's all about the dust and the mold that's in the air. So they keep putting us in the really unhealthy situations that if we were white, middle-class people, we'd be suing them. They wouldn't dare put us there because they know that. But basically they're hoping that we are so disorganized, so dysfunctional, and so unhealthy that we'll never get around to suing them because we're just going to sort of fall apart, go away and die before we get around to it.

They keep making laws to oppress the homeless rather than laws to eliminate homelessness. In other words, these laws that you can't stand on the sidewalk or sit on the sidewalk or basically be anywhere for any length of time or you're going to be harassed. Now, if you're a white, middle-class-looking family and you're having your lunch, they obviously aren't going to bother you.

I'm just appalled that in this society, supposedly the richest society in the history of humanity, no one comes up and says, 'I've got an extra room in my house' or no one says, 'I've got enough money.' Why aren't all the people with a lot of money putting together housing for the homeless? It just seems to me to be symptomatic of some kind of real self-disgust and self-hatred. There's something really wrong with people here in our society. Something really deeply wrong that they cannot identify with their fellow humans. And something logically amiss that they think that it won't happen to them.

He also questioned the government agencies that are supposed to help homeless people.

**Duane:** I don't understand why the city or the federal government or the state government can't just take the unemployed population and, with the right kind of assistance, have them build their own shelters on lands owned by the state. I don't see what the big problem is except that it would undermine the landlord-tenant system. Because then people would feel like they had an option besides being enslaved to the minimum-wage job and paying the monthly rent.

*Sisters: What do you feel would help the homeless people the most?*

**Duane**: That's a wonderful question. What would help homeless the most would probably be to make illicit drugs legal, to control how they are made and distributed in an equitable and sensible way; to help direct people to make their own housing. People don't have to live in split-levels. We want to live in housing that's environmentally sustainable. So we don't really need the model that we have of the wooden house that's got five bedrooms and two garages and all that. We need small structures that are easy on the earth and easy to keep warm but that are safe and properly made. And there's no reason that can't be done. It's actually an insult to all of us that that isn't being done because it could be done as easily as anything else we're doing right now. Probably easier than most of what we're doing right now. And by affordable, I don't think people should even necessarily have to pay for housing. People want meaning in their life. Meaning comes from action, if you've studied existentialism.

*Sisters: And so when you talk about those changes that you think would be helpful, who do you feel has the power to make them?*

**Duane**: Well, I'm very much in favor of individual empowerment. I think that that's obviously the beginning and the end in terms of solutions for all these things. On the other hand, it's impossible to do much when laws are made to go against these movements towards self-realization and self-expression and taking care of oneself.

Basically, I don't think everybody should have to have a job; or if everybody has to have a job, people should be able to work twenty hours a week. Everybody should be able to work a little bit and contribute and be able to receive what they need to live in an equitable way. And by equitable, I mean that a poet should be able to have some time to write some poetry and share that poetry, and a musician to make music and so on. And these aren't, like, new ideas. These are ideas people have had for at least a couple of centuries.

Returning to ideas of self-sufficiency, Duane described the potential of tent cities like then-named Camp Dignity [now Dignity Village].

**Duane**: There's so much that Camp Dignity could do, and yet, because of the impoverishment and the social stigma and the way we've been pushed out to the edge of the city and so on, people are just plain isolated and incredibly depressed. I've been wondering when there's going to be a suicide at Camp Dignity. I mean, how long can people that are already at the end of their wits live in a nylon tent with forty-five-mile-an-hour winds and pounding rain and no heat and a heck of a lot of problems and bad memories. How do you expect them to sit there and sleep through the night and not think about killing themselves?

Neil was 44 when interviewed, and described how he first became homeless six years earlier when he was a bike messenger and his girlfriend left him because of his increasing drug use.

---

**Neil:** I was, I guess, probably a pretty typical story in that for many years ,I had a stable situation and found myself in a position of all of a sudden making a lot of money and choosing poor ways of spending it, which gradually became sort of a whirlpool of substance abuse and bad financial choices. It kind of dragged me out of stable housing situations and put me into a place where I was spending all of my time making money to spend on drugs and alcohol. It's probably a very common story. I could never bring myself to steal or anything like that to support my habit, but I am a finish carpenter by trade.

He went on to describe how he made good money, but spent most of it on a party lifestyle.

**Neil:** I would trade work for housing and partner up with buddies and stuff like that. Basically, your own expectations for your own housing situation deteriorate slowly over time to where you accept less and less adequate situations as being acceptable. And that is pretty much how that happened. Nothing happened just once, in one day, all of a sudden; it was like a gradual withdrawing from normalcy.

He tried various living situations that including camping outdoors, living in a home he rehabilitated in exchange for rent, couch-surfing, and then lived on a boat with two friends and sometimes worked for Labor Ready. He explained that he and his friends were able to obtain the best temporary jobs because they showed up at the job site clean, groomed, and without backpacks.

He and his best friend Ted managed to do their laundry once a week and keep up their personal grooming.

**Neil:** It is when you get into that continuing cycle of real poverty or where all your money is going to feed whatever nefarious behaviors you are engaging in that things really start to slide badly. And I think I can say with some truth that one of the reasons that Ted and I are clean right now is because we never really tumbled quite that far. We were always able to sort of hold our heads up a little bit, and not completely lose our self-worth. And that is a big issue when you are homeless and when you cannot find work. For me it is a huge one, because I come from an upper-middle-class Portland family, and even when I was at my worst situations, I would have to go show up with family members who are local TV personalities and relatively well-known people. And I could not go in there looking like Charles Manson on a bad day. And I was always able to sort of pull that off.

*Sisters: How?*

**Neil:** Just through ingenuity, and also because I never stole from the people who helped us in our living situation. I always kind of gave value for what we got. I would perform valuable service for our little housing situation. So we would get little privileges that a lot of people would not get, like we could go over to the main house and take a shower twice a week.

And this absolutely wonderful 85-year-old woman would let us into her house to go take a shower and get cleaned up. We would sit around and yak it up with her in the morning, and I really used to have a great time there. We never really lost sight of our essential humanity. A lot of people who find themselves in these kind of homeless strung-out states end up stealing for a living, for instance. So, not only do they eat up their soul doing that, but they are in and out of jail all the time because they are probably not very good at it, and they look like hell and people, when they see them come in [a store], they think, 'This guy is not here to purchase.'

Neil eventually kicked heroin on his own, then learned he had hepatitis C and relapsed. He tried rehab, and tried living in a van until his father finally helped him establish himself in a studio apartment. Once housed, he was able to find part-time carpentry work. At the time of the interview, he had been clean for four months for the first time in four years.

**Neil**: One of the things that I want to emphasize is that if there are things that allowed me to overcome my situation, they came from inside me. They did not come from services, they did not come from programs, they did not come from well-meaning social-worker types or anything like that. So if there is something that you can build in someone, if you wanted to design a program that works for people, you got to design a program that builds their self-esteem and makes them feel like they are capable of contributing to society instead of being a drag on it.

Neil's main suggestion for solving homelessness was to create an apprentice program so that people can learn trades.

**Neil**: It is hard to feel good about yourself if you are not earning your own keep. I think it really is the biggest single thing because a lot of these people have never had a shot at it, never. They have always had pizza delivery jobs. The reason that I was a bike messenger was because I wanted to be a bike messenger, just not because I could not be a finish carpenter. I just wanted to do that job for a while, and it was the most fun job I ever had.

*Sisters: Is there anything that you would like to see different? Could you talk about any solutions or changes you would make?*

**Neil**: I would like to see clean, respectable transitional housing, and not so judgmental about being clean and sober, [where] if you are trying, then you win. If you are sincere about trying, even if you screw up occasionally, you do not get thrown back out to the wolves again.

*Sisters: Where [now] if you relapse at all, they throw you out of your housing?*

**Neil**: Exactly. They will throw you out, and I am talking about the very basic level of their sleeping at the mission, maybe even in overflow. I understand that these things are difficult, expensive issues for communities to deal with. And I think we have got a large population of homeless people who should really be at least in some kind of supervised medication program where every day they have to show up at a place and take whatever psychotropic meds they need, or whatever keeps them from shouting at their fingernails through the course of the day.

*Sisters: So, we need some way to keep homeless people stabilized on their medication?*

**Neil**: Yeah, that is, not every homeless person needs medication.

He went on to explain that he had two friends who committed suicide by hanging themselves out of despair over their addictions. They had tried to enter a treatment program but were refused.

**Neil**: As long as we are talking about things that make a change in people's lives, if you can get folks into stable housing that they do not get kicked out of for relapsing a couple of times, that is a big issue because probably a large percentage are not going to succeed first time around the track. If you just throw them to the wolves, then they will be starting from ground zero again. I am not saying there should not be consequences, but you should not lose your housing, because the housing is important to staying clean.

Bernie is an Osage Indian, originally from Oklahoma. He formerly lived in Kansas with his wife and children, and owned a small air conditioning and refrigeration repair business. He described his descent into homelessness.

**Bernie**: Things were starting to click, we were starting to make it, and then one day, I just woke up and she was wanting a divorce. Next thing I knew she was hauling the kids off to grandmother and grandfather's, and she did not come back home. So I was left with the house and I consequently could not afford it by myself. So I let it go back; I declared bankruptcy on my small business and moved down here. I have been just trying to get it together, and then I got tired of the streets, got tired of the hustle and the bustle, got tired of having to run the scams, to make money out there. So what I did is went back to detox and dried out, and went to a drug rehab called NARA (Native American Rehabilitation Association) and did two months inpatient there.

Bernie explained that he had been clean and sober for eleven months, relapsed, and was evicted from his transitional housing. He was on the streets again for three and a half months, then went into detox and started his recovery cycle again.

Bernie believed solutions needed to be centered on self-sufficiency.

**Bernie**: [Services and free meals] make it a little too easy for a person on the street.

*Sisters: How do you mean?*

**Bernie**: Well, you could stay on the streets, just do your hustle forever out here and not have to worry about eating food because it is available. The only thing you have to worry about is shelter in the wintertime. I think a perfect situation would be that they go ahead and give the homeless some land and divide it off into communal sections, and let them raise their own crops to be self-sufficient, kind of like Blanchet House does on their farm.

*Sisters: Why do you feel that self-sufficiency like that is important?*

**Bernie**: Self-sufficiency gives you self-respect and dignity back. You lose your self-respect and dignity when somebody is just handing it to you. Now, when you have to work for it, it means a lot to you, makes you feel good.

*Sisters: How is that different than what is out there right now?*

**Bernie**: If you are an addict and an alcoholic, all you have to do is hustle and somebody else is going to feed you. Why even bother to come off the streets unless you are tired of that way of living? I just got tired of that way of living. I want a life.

He also described how for many homeless people, having their driver's license revoked or suspended was a huge barrier to finding and keeping employment and resuming their former lives. He suggested a special program to help poor people get their licenses again. Like other narrators, he complained that when he steps outside his door in the Old Town/Chinatown neighborhood, he's approached by drug dealers and prostitutes.

**Bernie**: If you are going to have transitional housing, a clean and sober house, do not put it right smack in the hood where all the drugs and alcohol and abusive crime goes on.

*Sisters: And how do you feel that affects your sobriety?*

**Bernie**: If I was in a bad mood or having a bad day and somebody offered me some free drugs and alcohol out there, I might take it without thinking. Then I would be on the downhill trail again. Drugs and alcohol are everywhere, but you would have to go looking for it if you were in a nice, clean neighborhood, and you would have to know where the dealer was because he is not going to be standing down on the street corner and saying, 'Hey, are you looking?'

Bernie also described the transitional housing at NARA outside the city as serene and recommended more rural opportunities for people in recovery and homeless people.

**Bernie**: [Living in the country] gives you time to think; you do not have to deal with the hustle and bustle of the city. No pressures.

He also proposed ideas for making the everyday lives of homeless people more comfortable.

**Bernie**: Public bathrooms ought to be more accessible. Parks ought to be open twenty-four hours. They are shutting them down, and parks are for the public, as long as you are not abusing it, like littering it all up. And most tramps that I see out there, they are not tearing a place up; they respect the place because that is where they are living on the outside.

Bernie also mentioned the importance of creating housing and assistance that is not linked to a substance abuse problem.

**Bernie**: I was talking to a homeless person yesterday, and he was going to go out and get drunk purposely so he could go to Hooper [a detox center], so he could get back in the system and get back into housing. He was going to take his income tax check, go out and blow it all, and get loaded so he could get back into the system to get housing, and those are wrong reasons. That is the way it works. It is a shame it works that way, but that is the way it works.

The mentally handicapped need to be helped a lot more than what they are now, because it just seems like they are lost people, you know, like the untouchables in India. They are kind of their own tribe, and nobody wants anything to do with them because the budget has been cut and they have got nowhere to go. They wander in the streets. It is a shame.

More government money towards the homeless instead of putting it in the defense budget. I hate to be like a '60s radical, but let us have more peace and not as much war. Let's put more money for social programs, just take care of our own. Let us not go over there, start pecking into other people's business like Israel and the Palestinians. Let us take care of our country, get our country back where it should be.

*Sisters: And what kind of social programs would you want to see?*

**Bernie**: Not much. See the mental health programs get back up. I would like to see them [mentally ill people] get some housing. I would like to see them getting some help, some therapy, get them back on their meds or whatever it takes. I think what would be ideal is like a community, and handicapped and mentally incapable people, like forty acres or so with little cottages where you can learn how to live on your own. And have people showing them how to do it. That would be awesome because their teacher would work with them and be patient with them. And on the other homeless situation, I would like to see more housing available and more shelters available and communal living and being self-sufficient. And when it comes down to the programs of handing out benefits, I would like to see people be made to work for it because it is too easy right now to play the system. Maybe you have to get out and maybe fix potholes in the roads and stuff like that.

*Sisters: In exchange for...?*

**Bernie**: Yeah, in exchange for your benefits. And that way you would maybe clean up the waters in the streams where we have been dumping for the last fifty years. I would like to see them out planting trees where we have raped our forests. Let us get back in this together and make this a better world to live in. That is what it is going to take; it is going to take togetherness because we cannot do it on our own.

*Sisters: And are there any other solutions?*

**Bernie:** Yeah, let's leave politics out of these programs too, because it takes somebody to lobby for these programs. Somebody has to go to Congress and lobby for them before they get voted in. I think they just should be automatically voted in and just take care of the situation without having to go through the bureaucratic bullshit to do it.

*Sisters: If you had influence over the government and how it affects people who are experiencing homelessness, what would you want to accomplish?*

**Bernie:** I would want to accomplish unity between the government and the homeless people. Let us not have this, like, stigma. If you are homeless, you do not have a voice in society… so I think it needs to come down to unity. And be open-minded, give them a chance to voice their opinion because they do have the right, and this is America; this is the way it is supposed to be.

*Sisters: And what is important to you about unity?*

**Bernie:** Because one person cannot do it alone. It takes everybody to work together to get something accomplished.

In addition to the many innovative and intelligent solutions we heard from our narrators, we also heard that they felt like an underutilized resource and that they were voiceless. Ben was asked if there was anything he believed was important to tell the world.

**Ben:** Just, give them [people on the streets] some sort of hope, the hope that it's not all lost. And people to talk to. Somebody to talk to that will listen 'cause they're not fools. They're out on the street and they've been shunned by everybody. To have somebody sit down and talk to you, but not unless they really meant it; us street people are so wise we can read right through it.

Finally, Ellen, 44, was asked:

*Sisters: If you had the world stage and could offer one thing about your experience with homelessness, what would you want people to know?*

**Ellen:** That homelessness is not unsolvable, and that with cooperation, compassion, and understanding, there is a solution.

---

Interviewer's Journal Excerpt:
*The first narrator had many good ideas for solutions, which seemed to come to him just as he was speaking. It was so much that we did not hit all of the topics on the category sheet, but his interview was still very rich with information. He developed this idea for a support group called Homeless Anonymous where people could come together and offer support to one another for their situations. He said it would be good for this group to include formerly*

*homeless and currently homeless individuals so people could get ideas about how to get out of their situation. He broke it down very well by including the ideas of having recovered homeless and recovering homeless come together and have sponsors for people. It was very much coming from a place of years of being in recovery services. He said it was extremely important to have love and feel like you are being listened to when the decision is made to get out of the homeless situation. He also noted the importance of people organizing themselves more and coming together to say that they are not going to take this situation anymore. He said that people should take over Waterfront Park, sleep there at night, and have their own security but be gone by five in the morning. I found this interesting because he noted the importance of nonviolence and making an attempt to work with the system in order to get what is needed for people.*

*He talked about being gay and being homeless and the need to hide it in some situations. He talked about privacy issues and not wanting to shower and sleep so close to so many other men. This caused him to spend many nights outdoors for sleep. He talked a lot about the mentally "unstable" people around him and that he had fear at times that they may snap. He felt that it was necessary to have special separate facilities to really help those people.*

Photographer: Brynne Athens

Photographer: Brynne Athens

# Chapter 16

*I just keep moving forward*

## Dreams and Hope for the Future

---

*I like the dreams of the future better than the history of the past.*

—Thomas Jefferson

It's especially important to say here that it's really hard to dream when you're living on the street 24/7 and all your energy is used up on your safety and how you're going to get your next basic need met. I remember a woman in our job-training program walking into Sisters before the cafe was open. She had come in from the shelter where she had stayed the night before, and had a look on her face that said "beat down, without, disgusted, and angry," because someone in the shelter had stolen the only washcloth she had. How do you even began to hope when you know that most people in the city you live in have a linen closet full of washcloths, and the only one you had was stolen by another homeless person? It's hard to have hopes and dreams when you're invisible.

What is it, at what point do you lose the ability to dream? We did interview people with dreams—some were humble, and some were grandiose. In a culture where there's so much available to some, for the people who don't get to avail themselves of it, hopes and dreams won't necessarily look the same. Maybe it's that people on the streets don't have the time to reflect on their experience. When they do, their reflections could be helpful to us all.

—Genny

During the interviews, our narrators were asked where they saw themselves in five years. For some, their answers were precise and detailed, but for others their goals were hazy or they simply had no concrete plans for the future. We listened to narrators who claimed they didn't know what the future held because they were most concerned with immediate matters.

**Devon**: Hopefully, just being happy for once in my life, because I have not been happy in a long time. You know, just being productive, moving forward.

**Craig**: I just want to work, any job. I don't care if it's a dishwashing job, but I just want the simple things in life. At one time I was a pretty sought-after basketball player. And I had a very bright, bright future, and that was all wiped away. I had big ideas. I could have gone far in life, there is no doubt in my mind about that. And, I've just come to the realization that I've accepted the fact that that's all gone, and I just want the simple things in life.

At least half the narrators speculated that their futures were going to be easier than their present, would include more stability and some kind of housing. Again, these hopes were often modest, with many claiming all they needed was a studio apartment with a bathroom and a place to do their own cooking.

**Keith**: Probably I could deal with a studio apartment with just me and [my partner]. That is big enough for us. She has got a neck and back injury, and we're in the cold a lot. It freezes her back up, and it is just not cool. I want, like, a place where we can go, we can lock our door, we can feel safe, we can turn the heater on and not have to worry about sixty other people around us and what they are doing, or who is going to come back drunk, and who is going to act stupid, and where you are going to basically lay your head down comfortably next time.

Our narrators dreamed large and small, vague and well-defined. Peter was in the Submarine Corps and Merchant Marines and had owned his own accounting business. He spoke wistfully of owning a violin again. He had played for thirty years and as a boy had dreamed of playing in an orchestra, his dreams interrupted by getting drafted.

**Peter**: If I got back on my feet, I would get back to music, but that seems to be, for the moment, out of reach.

One man described building a small home that he could live in. Others described plans for finishing or returning to school, moving back to their hometown or home state, getting into treatment or staying clean and sober, and obtaining SSI or other benefits so they had the security of a modest income.

Some of our narrators' hopes for the future sounded realistic, sometimes they seemed grandiose. Bill was asked about his goals.

**Bill**: Every time somebody asks that question, I can't help to say I want to be the President of the United States.

*Sisters: What would you do?*

**Bill**: I would try to make everything better.

More modest achievements were Regan's hope.

**Regan**: Well, I want to get my book written. I have some long-term goals. I want to revamp the educational system to give kids a better chance to grow up with healthier futures and outcomes. But, you know, I need to take small steps first. I need to get myself stable first, then become part of the community, and then start making changes through my community involvement.

It was clear that the majority of our narrators gave a lot of thought to the future, and it was equally clear that they were not always sure about the path or steps to secure it. Tom, while discussing the options for his future, which included going back to school or becoming a truck driver, confessed he wasn't sure which type of career he wanted to pursue because "there's so much out there."

**Tom**: I'd like to get up in the morning and feel good about myself and halfway enjoy my job and make enough money so I can pay my rent and all that. I can do anything, really. I'm not particular, you know what I mean? Nothing really bothers me that much. I've hitchhiked around the country and done a lot of things. Being homeless is like going in a circle. It's no good. You've gotta move on and you've gotta progress, produce. You could lose your mind out here.

For our narrators who had been homeless for a number of years, when imagining the future, first came the understanding that they could no longer cope with living on the streets. For many this was a daunting realization because they had so often enjoyed the freedom of the road or the streets, or had simply become accustomed to their daily routine or become demoralized by their situation. Thus, breaking out seemed impossible. Sometimes narrators realized that they could not physically deal with the rigors of the streets because they were aging, had too many physical ailments to contend with, or were finding the streets ever more dangerous. Or, like Curtis, 37, they came to understand that they were changing and didn't belong on the streets any more.

**Curtis**: I want more now. I don't want to be homeless anymore. I am at my age now where I am getting tired. I want to get out of the streets, and I want to have a place, you know. Now I am old enough where I know what I want. And I guess it took me that many years to realize it. And, I don't want to be on the streets. It's not because they are rough or different; it's just that I guess I am different.

And for some of our narrators, the future might never come. At 52, Michael, who has lung disease, was asked where he saw himself in five or ten years.

**Michael**: I don't expect to be alive in ten years.

Often our narrators explained that there were a series of small steps that needed to happen before they could plan for a larger future, such as obtaining their state identification card or getting a driver's license. Some narrators described their first step off the street as obtaining a GED. When looking ahead, a portion of our narrators planned to enroll in college or obtain job training. A surprising number were interested in a career in computers.

Several of our narrators described getting their children back from relatives or foster care. Or, before they could move forward they needed to clear up legal affairs and business from the past—outstanding debts, fines, warrants, and obligations. Sometimes future plans needed to be put on hold until the narrator could regain his or her health or strength.

Jim, whose terms of parole required him to look for work, was asked where he saw himself in five years.

**Jim**: I can't think about five years from now. The reason why, I'll tell you the truth, number one, I got to worry about getting through this day before any other day. This day right here matters to me, then I'll worry about tomorrow when it comes.

*Sisters: What do you have to cope with today?*

**Jim**: Not much. Not much at all; I cope with thinking about where I'm gonna get help. About my spelling, filling out applications. I know it's dangling over my head.

At the heart of our narrators' longing was a desire for safety, security, and a more fulfilling lifestyle. Raymond, who had lived a fairly middle-class lifestyle before experiencing homelessness, expressed this in his interview.

**Raymond**: I am going to buy a home or something, somewhere they can never throw me out of again. It's been a very difficult experience. You know, I used to drive by [homeless people on the street] in my car and think, 'Oh, those people! Why don't they get a job?' Well, I know why, because they are too dirty, there is nowhere to take a shower, and if there is, they are full. They don't have decent enough clothes to go look for a job, and if an employer finds out that you are homeless, they aren't going to hire you in most cases. They are not sympathetic to that sort of thing. So, it's rough out there.

Almost all our narrators who had dreams of the future described how their future would be shaped by a job, career, or a stable source of income.

**Ted**: I see myself in five years having a career with computers because I like them. I see myself as finally being able to keep myself in a job that I am not going to take and quit after a month or two months or six months. Hopefully, I will be at the point in my life where I can actually start having something to show for what I am doing, and by that I am talking about material stuff, relationships, friends, family and maybe having a house, car. I have never visualized what would happen in the future if I did not do something. Now I am learning that, and I am almost ninety-nine percent sure it will happen.

Nathan, a 54-year-old veteran, replied to the question of where he saw himself in five years.

**Nathan**: I do not know. I see myself five years older…I would be looking at something like a regular, full-time job that I can depend on until I retire, which is going to be five years after that. I got to check with the VA on that one because when you turn 65, you get full benefits.

Jordon had described how he returned from Desert Storm and had gone on a long "hero's party." His hope for the future included:

**Jordon**: A warm body, someone to be there and…I want to keep giving back; honoring the memory of people that have done that for me, and honoring myself, showing myself respect, getting out of myself by helping others.

When Toby's interviewer asked him what his future would look like, he had this innovative solution.

**Toby**: Well, I have a personal desire for how I would want to live, but I will be the first to admit that it is not going to be for everybody. I love being on boats. I found a set of plans for an eighteen-foot boat that is eight feet wide and has about the interior space of maybe a Volkswagen van and a half. I have lived in a Volkswagen van before, I can do this. With a boat, you would have access to protein sources from the river or the ocean, although I am not sure I want them from the Columbia [River], but it also gives you mobility. It gives you a place where you can lock your stuff up, go in, get your job, do your job, come back to it. With a little kerosene stove in there, you have a cheap way of preparing your own food. While you are restricted to not having refrigerated food, you can do dried food, you can do canned food, and you can bring perishables home in small amounts and use them before they spoil. In the winter, you do not even have to worry about that.

Many of our narrators' stories ended with hopes for a brighter future. It was heartening to listen to these imagined futures where their lives were less chaotic, desperate, and unsafe. Where they were able to return to being the person they had once been or grow into the person they always dreamed they could be.

MaryJane, 40, was also asked where she saw herself in five years.

**MaryJane**: Well, hopefully, in five years I'll have a degree and a good job, a decent job. I don't really care too much about how much it pays. I don't care too much about the money. But, you know, I'd like to have a stable life. And then, I have a business that I want to start in addition to that. So, that's where I want to be in five years.

*Sisters: What's the business you want to start?*

**MaryJane**: I used to own a used bookstore many years ago. So, I'm going to start, like, a used bookstore, mini coffee shop, have artwork by local artists. And have a lot of alternative things in there, like alternative transportation you know. Alternative help, and things like that.

*Sisters: Oh wow! So kind of a resource place where people can go...*

**MaryJane**: Yeah, but have a complete bookstore because my reading is important to me, so I'd like to have all kinds of books there. You know, and just have it be a kind of quiet, peaceful place. I'm going to have a chi machine there, and have a chi room where people can go to relax. You know, and have a nice alternative health section. And just have the place be sort of a large variety and have a nice atmosphere.

Kimberly explained her dream of helping children.

**Kimberly**: My life dream has always been to have a home business. Since I am having a baby again, I am seriously considering going into some type of home daycare. It is something that I am familiar with, I have worked in state-run daycares back in Arkansas. So, I feel that it would be something that I would be capable of, and I would be able to have my children with me and maybe even turn it into a small school or something because I would like to homeschool my child. I feel that that one-on-one quality of an education is something that children in the public schools do not receive, that especially some children truly need.

Mark, 44, suffered from bipolar disorder and was a former nursing assistant. Raised in Florida, he described a childhood of instability, brushes with the legal system as a juvenile, and his brief incarceration as an adult. However, he said that his past and becoming homeless had strengthened him, including a jail term where he was jumped and beaten by six inmates.

**Mark**: And so I learned a lot of peace. I lost my fear. There's nothing that I really fear anymore. I have no reason to be scared. The only thing that scares me anymore is small fears like, I'm starting to wonder and starting to fear a little bit if am I ever going to get off the streets, you know? I fear that. It's like, how am I supposed to get a girlfriend because I'm on the streets, except for another homeless girl? And two homeless people is no better than one. And then I'm scared to get a girl pregnant because, I can't [in these circumstances].

*Sisters: What do you look forward to five years from now?*

**Mark**: I would like to be able to eventually take some drama classes at college. I would like to be able to take some vocal training because I do cartoon voices. I can imitate a lot of voices. And that's what I want to do for a career. I want to work for Will Vinton Studios or MGM or Warner Bros. or Pixar, for Disney. I want to do voices for kids' cartoons and programs. And so, hopefully, somewhere in the next five years I will maybe at least be going to school. And maybe be settled down with a woman I can curl up with at night that has a job and isn't scary or whatever. I just want a good woman and a place to live and be going to school, and working on the side when I'm not going to school, just so I can have the things I want and do the things I want. I got really used to it there for a while when I was with my girlfriend that died, being able to go bowling if I wanted to go, or go to the bar and shoot some pool, or spend the weekend at a motel somewhere just because I had enough money. Because she worked and I worked and everything was good. We had a brand new car that was in her name because I don't have a license, and I miss having those things.

*Sisters: Having a lot of choices?*

**Mark**: Yeah. Having a lot of choices and a lot I wanted to do, and I really miss that. But it's so hard to get back there that I don't know. I hope and pray that I'm back at least in a room for rent and going to school in five years. So that's my five-year goal basically.

Unlike Mark, some of our narrators claimed that they didn't have a positive outlook on the future, even when it was clear they'd given it significant thought. Christopher, who was 31, also described a chaotic childhood. His mother was in the military and he lived with various relatives when she was serving and was adopted when he was 10 by relatives who were fundamentalist Christians. As a juvenile he began shoplifting and running into trouble with the legal system. When interviewed he no longer had a relationship with his biological mother and brother or his adopted family and explained that he'd had problems with drugs, especially methamphetamines, which he began using at 20. He also had an ex-wife and a son from whom he is estranged. Christopher explained he'd been homeless previously, but that his most recent homelessness began two and a half years earlier after he was released from prison and had obtained a job and housing, but then a knee injury caused him to lose both. He was sleeping outdoors and was on a waiting list for temporary housing, and had outstanding warrants when interviewed.

*Sisters: Do you pretty much keep to yourself out there on the street?*

**Christopher**: Yeah. I'm the loner. I really am. Because you all are dangerous. You're dangerous. The next thing you know, I'm gonna start liking somebody and then they're just going to stab me in the back with my own knife. I mean, I've got an ex-wife to prove that, you know. I've got family to prove that. I got me and I don't even trust me. I trust God, but he's a real dick sometimes. You know? Your prayers are always answered even if the answer is no.

As the interview was winding to a close, he was asked where he saw himself in five years. His answer proved how these stories hold endless surprises and how sometimes our narrators have hopes that they cannot admit.

**Christopher**: Yesterday I would have said 'dead.'

*Sisters: And today?*

**Christopher**: I thought about it. I said I never planned to be here [on the streets], but then again, I never really planned. That's kinda how I got here. I guess I'm real shortsighted. But there's no way to say where I could see myself. I mean, I could say if I stay here, I'll probably be sticking a needle in my neck or dead or still homeless, but if I'm still homeless, I'll be sticking a needle in my neck like some junkie or in some other state doing something.

*Sisters: Is there a job you would like to have if you could? Say you could just pick it, what would you do?*

**Christopher**: I'd finish college and I'd be programming computers.

*Sisters: You seem like a smart guy.*

**Christopher**: I used to be.

*Sisters: Do you have access to any computers?*

**Christopher**: No. Just the ones at the library, but that's not good for anything except checking your e-mail. I want to write a book.

*Sisters: What would it be about?*

**Christopher**: I didn't bring the paper. It's kinda like *Sling Blade* with kind of a twist to it, but without a murder.

*Sisters: Fiction?*

**Christopher**: Yeah.

Christopher then described an elaborate storyline that included an uplifting ending.

*Sisters: Why don't you write it?*

**Christopher**: No computer access, no disk space…can't walk around with computer disks.

*Sisters: Could you e-mail it to yourself?*

**Christopher**: Only four megs maximum in my e-mail storage.

*Sisters: How about writing it out by hand?*

**Christopher**: Paper is very susceptible to water. I'd have to figure out something.

One recurring belief our narrators expressed was the need to be clean and sober to assure a reasonable future. In fact, it seemed that narrators who had been homeless for a long time or were dealing with recovery or addictions had the hardest time imagining their futures. Ned was asked about his goals and answered this way.

**Ned:** Self-sufficient for sure, and clean and sober.

*Sisters: And what needs to happen for those things to occur?*

**Ned**: A job and just my mental state probably of wanting those things. Ten years ago it was easy to go get a job and get that check and move into a place…but it is not as easy as it used to be.

Joe, 41, described a series of escapades, drunken incidents, and a generally chaotic lifestyle that led to his homelessness. However, when asked how he saw his future he replied:

**Joe**: I see myself getting a job. I see myself abstaining from alcohol. I don't know if I'll ever quit smoking.

*Sisters: How long have you been sober?*

**Joe**: Well, I just did twenty-two days. And then I went to a friend of mine's and we got drunk, and I just remembered why I hated it [drinking] again. This time I'm going on eight days. But, out of the last month I've only drank one time. I know that's the total downfall right there, always has been. I can spend two hundred dollars. It's not just the alcohol alone, it's the music, ya know?

*Sisters: It's the bar life?*

**Joe**: Right. That's what it is. I'm buying a guitar in Seattle, so I'm gonna start playing that thing. When I was getting into that, I started trying to get creative. I see myself in a couple of years not being homeless. I just don't want it no more.

Elliot, 44, had been homeless once for six months in his 30s and during several different periods following a divorce when he was 37. He had completed one year of college; had a dishonorable discharge from the army; briefly worked in a carnival and most recently for a publisher; was the father of a 9-year-old son; and was originally from Michigan.

After hearing about his most recent experiences with homelessness, his interviewer asked him to tell her something about his family background.

**Elliot**: Man, I'd rather not. Alcoholic father; drug-addicted mother; a lot of physical abuse.

His parents divorced when he was 12 or 13 and he went back and forth between them. At 16 he hitchhiked around the country for a month, and at 17 he left home for good and moved to Minneapolis. Despite the fact that he was employed and married, his life was far from stable. Elliot went on to describe some details of his drug use, including doing drugs with his mother and events that led to her death in 1993.

*Sisters: You were well out of the home. What'd she die of? Was it an overdose?*

**Elliot**: Well, we were both doing methamphetamine crank. But, I'd been around it all my life. So I got a quarter from a friend of mine and I went to her house and I gave her some of it. And, she did it. And this guy that lived upstairs had robbed some cocaine dealers and he came down to give us some cocaine. She did the cocaine on top of the crank, and she had a stroke. Then she had to learn how to walk and talk and eat all over again. And then about three years later, she just had a massive heart attack. I mean, her whole left side was immobilized. She couldn't function well, and about three years after that, she had a massive heart attack and died.

*Sisters: It sounds tragic.*

**Elliot:** Well, I used to feel really bad about it. But, nobody forced her to do it. We all make choices, but it sucked.

*Sisters: How many different kinds of alcohol treatment programs have you been in?*

**Elliot:** I don't know, seven or eight.

Elliot went on to explain that after more than ten years of wishing he was clean and sober, he finally achieved those goals after entering detox and getting involved with another rehabilitation program and twelve-step groups. He explained how things had changed for him.

**Elliot:** I used to stay clean for short periods of time—five, six, seven months a year. But I always went back to drinking. And then when I got here [to Portland], I was actually trying to kill myself, so I started doing heroin. And, I was just waiting for it to kill me and it wouldn't kill me and I just got sick and tired of it. I spent a week living in the park doing drugs every day and stuff. And then I got really sick, and then I went to Hooper.

*Sisters: That was how long ago?*

**Elliot:** About sixteen months ago.

*Sisters: Now, why were you trying to kill yourself?*

**Elliot:** I don't know. I was just fed up with everything.

*Sisters: You said that you had a problem with depression.*

**Elliot:** Oh yeah.

He then described how when he stops taking his medication his depression returns, and then talked more about his decision to stop drugs and alcohol.

**Elliot:** Well, it [using] used to be easy because I could always blame it on somebody else or something. But now, I've just finally come to realize I can't blame this on anybody else. Sometimes you have to take responsibility. I think that's most of it. It was just everything in general. Just coming to realize that I couldn't live like that anymore. Look, I was sick of being sick from the dope. I was sick of having nowhere to live. I was sick of being on the outside looking in. Man, I was just sick of being sick.

*Sisters: What do you do for cash?*

**Elliot**: I've learned how to work on computers a little bit, so sometimes I'll find computers that people have discarded or whatever and I'll be able to repair them. Then I'll sell them and make fifty bucks or whatever.

Elliot was also asked what he looked forward to in five years.

**Elliot**: I don't have a clue.

*Sisters: Let's say two years from now. What do you see as your next steps?*

**Elliot**: I really don't know. I don't, honestly. I'm kind of dealing with the depression and recovery stuff. I'm just kind of like stalled right now. I don't know. Sometimes it feels kind of hopeless, you know what I mean? Like stuck in a rut. So I really can't plan that far away like two years. I guess when I was younger, it wouldn't have been a problem, but now that I'm a little bit older, I'm not sure.

*Sisters: You're probably a bit more realistic now.*

**Elliot**: Yeah. And I would still like to be clean and not using. Working.

*Sisters: What kind of work would you like to do?*

**Elliot**: Something with computers, probably repair. Maybe a computer service place. I really don't have use for computers once I get them fixed. I don't. I'll take them apart and rebuild them. I can take them apart and put them together. You know, if they need a new sound card or a new video card, memory, whatever, I can do it.

Over and over we heard that our narrators had simple dreams and needs. We heard narrators say they just needed a "roof over my head," "my own apartment," or "maybe a decent place to live where I can do my own cooking." They often didn't mention recreational needs except for an occasional wish to "be able to go catch a movie or something every now and then."

Benjamin, 54, was asked about his goals for the future.

**Benjamin**: A little room like this [referring to the room the interview took place in], a little black-and-white television, an FM radio, and some job to pay for it. And as long as I got my books and library card, and my cat purring, a plate full of milk, I just would be okay. I would like to get a new woman, like to take her out to dinner and maybe a movie now and again, but women need more attention than that. I guess that's about it.

*Sisters: That's not too much.*

**Benjamin**: I just, I don't know why people need all these things. Can't take them with you on the train.

Reggie also had modest dreams.

**Reggie**: I've been looking for a job from the beginning. I have been looking for a job because I wanted three things I've been praying for. I've been praying for a job and a place to stay.

*Sisters: And what's the third thing?*

**Reggie**: A woman. I wanted those three things.

Greg explained his plans:

**Greg**: I am having a little trouble dealing overall with my life. The paper, *street roots* puts a few dollars a day in my pocket, so I can go to McDonald's and have an Egg McMuffin if I want instead of eating stale pastry down at Blanchet House. But they do what they can do with what they got, and thank you people for doing that. But now I am getting spoiled again, now I want to be able to get my own place where I can cook my own bacon and eggs, where I can do it my way. Or I could go out and get a couple of new pairs of jeans. I would like to get a pair of nice, new, rugged work boots. Live like a normal human being. I mean, you are going for some classy-looking woman and asking her for a date and say, 'By the way, you got any money on you?'

Brandon wanted a little bit more also.

**Brandon**: I would just like to be in my own place; it does not have to be a house or anything. I'd just like my own bedroom or a studio apartment. I would like to be working in a kitchen instead of a garage. I do not care about making a whole bunch of money, but I would like to be making enough where I am taking care of my rent, my travel, like bus tickets and whatnot, and have a little money left over to where I can start buying my groceries.

Our narrators' dreams, sometimes expressed wistfully, were often about normalcy or a lifestyle many people take for granted. Brian, 46, was also asked the question about where he saw himself in five years.

**Brian**: I really don't know. I'm hoping I'm not out on the streets like I am now.

*Sisters: You are hoping? What would you like to see? Paint a picture of what you would like your life to be.*

**Brian**: I would like to go to work and get my own place, start getting back with my family and seeing my kids. I just think it would be great to call my kids and say, 'Come over and spend the weekend or the night,' or something like that. I'd just like to have my family back.

Many of our narrators talked about how they felt stranded in Portland because they could not break out of their cycle of homelessness and poverty to take their next step. For some, this was doubly frustrating because they wanted to return to their home state, hometown, or family.

**Larry:** I want to get back…I want to get the hell up out of here. I want to go back to Montana. I have not been back to Montana in almost three years. I miss home. I miss the snow. I miss the cold.

A surprising number of people, when asked about their futures, talked about working in service to mankind and helping the homeless community. Several narrators mentioned that they'd like to open a cafe like Sisters Of The Road to feed the homeless. Some narrators explained that they could be effective helping others because they knew what it was like firsthand to grow up in an abusive family or to grow up on the streets. One woman who was a domestic abuse survivor talked about counseling other women who were abused, and another woman wanted to work with homeless people using the skills she'd learned navigating the system. One narrator had helped other homeless people fill out forms necessary to obtain welfare benefits and spoke of expanding that into a service. At least a dozen narrators wanted to be drug and alcohol counselors.

Simone, who said she wanted a dual career as a business owner and drug and alcohol counselor, was asked why she chose that field.

**Simone:** Well, I have a lot of life experience, and I think that will be helpful. I have a lot of compassion. I don't think people choose to be addicts. They don't say, 'Yeah, I wanna grow up and be a drug addict.' You know, people have disabilities and a lot of mental illnesses, I think partly because of a lot of external pressures in their lives. And I think that a lot of times we have individual illnesses, but our communities are also as sick and they need to be healed. Every dollar that you spend on these things saves communities seven dollars later. But people don't really realize that. And you save lives when you help people get treatment. Everybody that's alive has some kind of problem. Nobody is perfect. We tend to think, 'Oh, it doesn't affect us if this person can't get help.' Well, it does affect us. It affects us all. You know, when people can't get health care and treatment, and don't have food to eat. And when kids go to school hungry, that's going to have an effect on us all.

Ryan, who was in recovery, explained to his interviewer that he wanted to return to school.

**Ryan:** I think I want to be a counselor because Lord knows I have enough problems in my head and made it through most of them to where I might be able to help some other people. Money is not really an important issue to me, material things or whatever. I want a job to where it would be fulfilling. I feel that helping people, making a difference, is where I would be happy. I am still kind of scared, I am still kind of thinking that, 'Oh, you can't do that,' but I am going to give a shot at it. I am going to try it. But I'm taking it slow right now and just concentrating on recovery before I get there.

When Kevin, who was 60, spoke of the future, he talked about what he could give.

**Kevin:** [I imagine myself] helping people. Not a lot money involved in it, but at this point in my life I am not really worried about how much money I make. I am worried about the end result. When I prepare to go to bed at night, if I did the right things, I feel good about myself.

Homelessness has always been around, and it will probably always be around, but if there's one thing that I can do before I die, I would love to donate either a big farm or something and go, 'Here, this is for the homeless.' You know, a ranch or a building or a couple of buildings where it would just be for the homeless.

*Sisters: What kind of effect would that have on the homeless in Portland?*

**Kevin:** Well, hopefully it would cut down all the illegal camping and this, that, and the other—all the people that are sleeping in doorways.

Another narrator, Jennifer, also dreamed of creating a place for homeless people based on a day center where she had volunteered in Eugene, Oregon.

**Jennifer:** Someday…I have this dream. I would love to buy a big building with lots and lots of rooms. Yeah, I'll have rules and regulations. I mean, there have to be some otherwise it's just total chaos. But…someday, hopefully, if it ever, ever, ever happens, that's what I would like to do. To where I can help all types whether you're single, you're married, with or without kids, or you have a partner or not a partner, and whether you're a gay couple or you're a lesbian couple or you're a heterosexual couple. I want to be able to help everyone. I know that's kinda far out there, but that's what it should be. I mean it really, really, honestly—that's the way it should be.

Rickie had another innovative plan for helping the homeless community.

**Rickie:** Myself, I aspire to do something about it [homelessness]. There are two things I'm going to do. I'm going to put together a band, which I'm doing right now, and the proceeds from that band (and the main theme of that band) are going to help homeless people. And this is what God wants me to do. I firmly believe this is what God wants me to do is to get into a situation where I can do like what you're doing [referring to the research project]. Because I'm out here. I have seen what these agencies are like. I have seen the changes that need to be made. I don't really know how I'm going to influence these agencies or anything at this point. It's going to take numbers to be able to do this. It's going to take petitions and voters and things like that to be able to change the policies and the views that society in general has on homelessness. But, I intend to do something about it. But the main goal I have right now is to get myself in a situation as to where I am able to help, because it's kinda hard to help people when you need help yourself.

Justin, 30, had been living in his car for about a year before he was interviewed in Portland.

He started drinking and smoking pot as a boy, had left home at 15, was an alcoholic, and was on a waiting list for temporary housing.

**Justin**: At one time I was gonna be a psychologist, and I kinda goofed that off too.

*Sisters: When was that?*

**Justin**: I was 18. I took some community college [courses]. I was looking for a career. After all my experience in institutions—I spent most of my childhood in foster homes—so I got a feel for it and thought, well, I'd like to help someone else out. I started taking classes but I got hooked up with partying. I never completed anything and so here I am at 30 years old with no career. I see guys out here that are 70 doing what I'm doing and that scares the shit out of me. So I'm doing whatever I can to change that. I don't want to be that guy.

Justin went on to explain that his main goal was to live in an apartment. He was asked about his goals for the next five years.

**Justin**: I hope to be able to have a career and maybe a family and start buying a house.

*Sisters: How do you go about that?*

**Justin**: A career? Well, I've been looking into community college and grants and stuff like that for welding or something that I know I'm gonna want to do for a while. Up to this point in my life, I've done so many jobs I don't know what I want to do. I haven't even made up my mind. But, if I do something and I like it, I usually stick with it. Everything's been so mixed up in the last year, I don't know what I'm gonna do. I know I believe in God, and I got faith that He has a plan of some sort for me.

*Sisters: I get the feeling you've changed recently in some ways.*

**Justin**: I have.

*Sisters: How would you describe that change?*

**Justin**: I guess I've gotten a lot more serious about life and about what I want. I've been thinking long and hard about what I need to do.

*Sisters: How did you live before?*

**Justin**: Going job to job and partying. Going through women like they were beers. Not caring. Didn't really care until I woke up and I was 30 going, 'Wow, where the hell am I?'

*Sisters: Turning 30 made a difference?*

**Justin**: Yeah. Shit, half my life's over now. I might live another thirty to forty years if I'm lucky. I would like to die knowing I did something good, or at least a good half of my life. I would like to have a couple kids. In order to do that I got to get my shit together and have a job.

*Sisters: Why do you want kids?*

**Justin:** I love kids. I got eighteen nieces and nephews. I like teaching them. I taught my nephew how to fish. It was neat. Now he's 16 and he's like, 'You want to go fishing?' He's a fishing buddy. And my nieces, I put them on a horse for the first time. That's kinda neat to do. I'm a great-uncle now. That made me feel old. My niece is 20, she had a kid. I'm getting old quick. I just want to accomplish something in my life. Maybe I can help some people out or be a volunteer somewhere.

*Sisters: What kind of place would you like to volunteer?*

**Justin:** Probably a drug program or something. But I need to make the decision to quit smoking pot and drinking. Even in a homeless shelter, serving food. Maybe I can make a difference. I'd like to accomplish something in my life, not do it halfway. It would be nice to have the picket fence and all that. If it doesn't happen, it doesn't happen. But, I'd like to at least have a goal to work towards. You got a lot of time to think when you're on the streets.

---

Interviewer's Journal Excerpt:

*My second interview showed up right on time. He was a soft-spoken man in his 30s, who had a long history of drug and alcohol addiction related to years of homelessness. Much of his homelessness was traveling around the country, living in "hippie houses" and following the Grateful Dead. He is now in recovery, living at the Estate, and waiting to go into inpatient treatment. At many points in the interview, he seemed so sad and defeated that I was surprised that after the interview was over, he was laughing and thanking me for talking with him. I also noticed how my energy level just drops after lunch; it wasn't even the heat since it was raining today. I need to keep a cup of coffee ready for me for those afternoon interviews as well as in the morning.*

*He talked a lot about not feeling like a part of society and made the connection to the media and how everything in society is focused on how much money you have. He said that it seemed that you don't exist unless you are buying something.*

Photographer: Buddy Bee Anthony

Photographer: Alan Shipley

# Chapter 17
## Chapter Seventeen

*I learned there is much wisdom and*
*a staggering amount of pain walking around our streets*

## Insights from Interviewers

*I think we may safely trust a good deal more than we do.*

—Henry David Thoreau

We've been following our narrators' lives and stories throughout this book, trying to connect the small dots that make up a larger picture of what it is like to be homeless today, and what solutions and insights can be learned from these stories. But of course there is another side of the story: the interviewers who spent hours in small rooms talking with mostly strangers about the intimate details of their lives.

Marla described her role as an interviewer this way:

**Marla**: It is my privilege to ask homeless people in Portland about the reasons for their homelessness, the realities of their day-to-day lives, their dreams for the future, and the roadblocks keeping them from their dreams. Once a week for three hours the little green room at *crossroads'* office is reserved for me and one person who has experienced homelessness. I have permission—in fact—the responsibility, to ask that person questions that would never be allowed in polite society.

The green room has become my secret garden. It is in this room I get to make real connections with real people. There is no talk of the weather or sporting events. There is much talk about human reactions to the reality of life on this planet. There's talk of homelessness and despair, of joy and discovery, of spirituality, health, and attitude, and how homelessness affects everything in a person's life. I suspect the people who tell me their stories are changed in some way by the telling. I know I am changed by the listening.

In the beginning of this research project three women—Shani, Orion, and Layla—were hired as interviewers to listen to and talk with narrators in coffeehouses and restaurants. Eventually the project moved into offices for more privacy. In addition, they spent four days and three nights at Dignity Village conducting interviews and sleeping in a hut belonging to one of the residents. All three women had bachelor's degrees, one had her master's, and one had personal experience with homelessness. Fara, attending Portland State University for a master's of social work, also conducted some of the early interviews. When funding ran low, due in part from the fallout of 9/11, Megan, Marla, John, Liam, and Sandy were brought in as volunteers to finish the interviews. Megan was taking a yearlong sabbatical from her undergraduate studies at Brown University in order to get hands-on experience in community organizing. Marla was a middle-class, stay-at-home mom whose kids were becoming more independent; Liam was a volunteer prep cook in our cafe and lived in the neighborhood; John was a volunteer waiter in Sisters and a retired psychologist; and Sandy, who became interested while she was interviewing Genny for another media project, came on board for the last few months of interviews.

Jamie, our project associate, was our technical guru. He knew what equipment to buy, he found or created the necessary software, trained every interviewer, and was available for daily mentoring, all to ensure the success of the project. Jamie provided valuable moral support to all of our interviewers, and was often the assurance of safety in the office when a narrator came in too drunk, drug induced, or specifically angry with women.

Genny, project director and cofounder of Sisters, and Judith, our project consultant, developed and implemented a training curriculum for project staff and volunteers. Judith was responsible for ensuring consistency in the interviews, providing advice and insight to the project director early on, and collaborating on a how-to manual. Genny met regularly with the interviewers to deal with issues that arose, monitored their methods, read their journals, and helped them debrief when an interview was particularly difficult. There were also weekly team meetings where problems were hashed out and feelings aired.

One aspect of the project was that each interviewer was asked to keep a journal about his or her experiences. These journals became part of the record of the project, were referred to during meetings, and helped the interviewers sort out complicated emotions and insights gained during the workday.

Fara addressed a common struggle for the interviewers: keeping narrators on track.

**Fara:** The major difficulty I had during the interview was in keeping the narrator focused on homelessness issues and experiences. He kept bringing the conversation back around to his addiction and recovery. I didn't want to cut him off or make him feel that what he had to say was unimportant. I had to keep saying, 'This is really interesting, but would you mind if we shift gears a little because I have a lot I want to ask you,' or something to that effect.

In another entry Fara muses about a man's need to distinguish himself from other people on the streets, and the role of the research in changing people's perceptions.

**Fara**: He kept saying that he didn't know if what he had to say was relevant because it wasn't representative of most homeless people's stories. I felt, however, [and expressed to him], that it was precisely because his story was so unique that it needed to be heard. It is stories like his that break stereotypes about homeless people. He was a highly educated, skilled, and experienced man from a middle or upper middle-class background who has been struggling with homelessness off and on for seven years. It was interesting to see how important it was for this man to constantly separate himself from what he called 'most homeless people' whom he identified as criminals, mentally ill, and addicts. He seemed to be struggling immensely with having that label [homeless] when he feels that it carries so many negative connotations that do not apply to him.

Writing in the journal was therapeutic.

**Fara**: Today's interview was very emotional [for both parties]. The woman I spoke with had a long, tragic story and broke down several times. It was a challenge for me not to get overwhelmed with my own emotions. I have a hard time watching someone cry.

Another big issue for me was dealing with the narrator's extremely hateful and racist views. I felt the need to interrupt this violence but was paralyzed. My biggest concern was I didn't want to stop her story, and these views were part of that story and who she is. I didn't want to make her feel like she had to censor herself at all. After the fact, I was so glad that I resisted the urge to interrupt this violence because it was a significant part of the narrative. So, I tried to just listen and understand where she was coming from—how her views were shaped by her experiences. As challenging as this was for me, I found that I was starting to gain insight into the reasons for her hatred. She mentioned several times the injustice she experiences in being refused basic assistance while refugees are guaranteed immediate assistance. She feels betrayed by her country and has turned this into anger towards the foreign people being helped by this unfair system. She had also gotten into conflict with two administrators in a welfare office, who happened to be African-American. These types of experiences are what added fuel to her racist views. These compounded the already powerful anger that she carries with her from her years of experience living on the streets.

The interviewers used their journals when they needed to vent or to reflect on narrators who had led particularly tragic lives.

**Fara**: Today's story was awful. This woman has had so many tragedies in her life and yet she has so much strength. She has a strong desire to reach out to other women in her situation to help them learn from her experiences. One disturbing reaction that I had to her narrative was that several times I felt like she sounded like a child. Something about how and what she was saying made me feel like she was a child in a woman's body. First this made me feel sad for her, and then I felt awful for feeling that way. I guess it just seemed like because her life was so awful, she responded to little things the way a child would. She experiences great joy in little things that often adults are too busy, preoccupied or whatever, to enjoy. This childlike quality is certainly something not to pity at all, but rather to envy. She was overjoyed by this opportunity to share her story. She says she's been waiting for many years to speak out and have someone really listen. It felt amazing to be part of something that was making that possible for her.

The journals were also helpful to sort out emotions and strategize ways to react or behave in future interviews.

**Fara**: Today I had my first experience during an interview where I wanted to do therapy with the narrator. I had a tough time trying to resist this urge. The woman I interviewed was talking about her childhood and how she had it really easy compared to other women she knows. She talked about the abuse many women suffer and how she was lucky. Then she said something like, 'Well, you know my brother and father were real curious, never having a girl in the house before, so, you know, they experimented a little, but nothing too bad. My mother took care of it within the family so it never got outside. She told me nothing bad happened and that it wasn't so bad that it would affect me as an adult or anything, so I've been real lucky.' Hearing this woman minimize and rationalize her abuse was difficult. I knew that this was her coping strategy, but it was hard to hear her justify what happened. I wanted her to be able to claim her abuse and say that she didn't deserve it. I wondered whether this need was for me or for her. Why did it bother me so much? I did, however, resist the urge to be her therapist, and I simply let her tell her story, as I'm supposed to do. It definitely made me really sad though, and it took awhile to get back into the swing of the interview.

One of our original interviewers, Layla, used her journal to reflect on the intense feelings the interviewing process could tap. A few of Layla's journal entries illustrated how she related her personal experiences to those of the narrator.

**Layla**: [The narrator] noted that he has a severe panic/anxiety disorder, especially when he is around large groups of people. He said that is why he likes sleeping in his truck, but at the same time, it makes him lonely. He said that after a job-related accident he had in 1997, he hasn't been the same emotionally or physically. He said that the panic attacks have occurred since that time. Although his account of the accident did not seem traumatic, from what he said it sounded like it was a traumatic experience that he did not fully recover from. When he talked about this, I found tears welling up in my eyes, as it reminded me of my father who had a severe car accident when I was in high school and really never recovered from it mentally. Especially as he talked about the importance of his kids and how much he wants to do for them, it reminded me a lot of my dad and made me feel really sad. I did my best to control it and he did not seem to notice.

Two highly emotional interviews were often conducted in a single day.

**Layla:** The first interview was with a man dealing with a lot of mental health stuff around depression. He talked about his kids and how he didn't want them to see him in his depressed state. This made him cry, which he later noted that he rarely does, but felt comfortable to open up with me. When he began to tear up, I did also because of some similar issues that I am dealing with [in] my family right now.

> The second interview was with a Native American man who has been out of prison since July after serving twenty years. His story was heart wrenching as he has spent pretty much all of his adult life incarcerated and is now homeless. Although he did have housing at the Everett Hotel, he decided to leave it because he got married to a woman who is also homeless. He said that he didn't want to be staying in a comfortable place while knowing that his wife was on the streets unsafe. This was a recurring theme in his interview, that there is a strong need for a place where couples can be housed.

Layla wrote about an inspiring interview and the all-important process of building trust with narrators.

**Layla:** My interview was with an amazing woman who was so open and honest about her experience with domestic violence [many instances] and drugs, and all of her experiences with homelessness. It was my first interview with a woman who talked about trading sex for a place to stay for a night. During our break I thanked her for being so open with me and told her how much I appreciated it. This seemed to make her even more open after the break to talk about things.

The journal entries also gave another layer of depth to the interviews when viewed alongside them. In one, Layla describes meeting with a woman who is the mother of a woman with a chronic health problem. Mother and daughter moved to Portland together hoping for a better life. Layla's journal reveals other aspects of their situation, and shows the creative lengths interviewers sometimes went to meet with narrators.

**Layla:** I came into the office in the morning and my interview had not shown up. Her daughter, who was being interviewed by Orion, passed the message along that [my interview] was at home and just couldn't make it to the office because she has lupus and was sick. She was very disappointed that we couldn't do the interview that day because we had rescheduled a few times already. After discussing it with Jamie and Orion, we decided that if she was up to it,

I could do the interview at her apartment building. We talked in the lobby of the building, which was a bit distracting with people coming in and out of the building, but it still went really well.

Her story is unique and a true demonstration of the failure of the social service system in California. Her daughter had a severe accident after being diagnosed with cancer, and there was nowhere they could go. They lived on the streets of San Francisco for over fifteen months. They moved up to Portland after they heard that Portland had good services for people experiencing homelessness. She was quite emotional during the whole thing and I kept trying to help her focus on the positive place that they are at now. Through JOIN, they are in a studio apartment downtown. She is still extremely frustrated because she cannot get work or even get food stamps, because she had no ID after the first days of being in Portland when a police officer confiscated their belongings because they were in a 'stolen' shopping cart. The police have no record of their things. So she is waiting for her birth certificate to arrive so she can get ID in Oregon, then she can start looking for work. Her story was very intense, because it is a clear example of someone [a family] who has fallen through the huge cracks in the system.

Layla, like Fara, also journaled about her desire to counsel some narrators.

**Layla:** He has basically used drugs very heavily all of his adult life. Throughout his interview, he talked about his desire to get off drugs and get off the streets. But he does not feel that there would be anything to look forward to afterward because after treatment one is left without housing and back in the same place where he was when he started. He lost his wife and kids and feels like he has nothing really to look forward to. I must admit that I felt like I wanted to figure something out to help this person, especially as he was talking genuinely about the desire to get clean.

Many times Layla and the other interviewers found themselves feeling righteously angry about the injustices narrators were forced to choose between.

**Layla:** I must admit that my emotions get heightened every single time I hear someone say that jail would be an alternative to their homelessness, because then they would have a place out of the cold. Especially hearing this from someone who has been in the system for so long makes me so angry. His questioning of why the system is set up the way it is was so fresh, like it was running through his mind right then and [he] was trying to piece it together with me in the interview.

Another journal entry reflected on how patterns emerged during the interviews, and also how hard it was to not get emotionally tangled in people's stories.

**Layla:** Both of the interviews today were with people who are in recovery. It was interesting because the two of them noted a similar peculiarity about the system that is supposedly set up to help folks who are homeless and in recovery. Why is it that these recovery places and SROs (single room occupancy units) that house folks in recovery are located in places where when you walk out the door you are bombarded by dealers and temptations? Why is it that when you look out your window you can see people shooting dope into their veins and see the places where you yourself used to do your drugs? It just doesn't make sense if the system is really trying to help people. They both also noted the fact that drugs and alcohol are used as a means to escape the pain they are experiencing in their lives.

Of the two, the woman I interviewed walked in with her boyfriend and 1-year-old daughter. I wished that we had a space for them to hang out and wait, but in our small office it would have been difficult. So the man and the baby went on their way back to the Salvation Army where they have a childcare room. This interview was quite intense. There were many points where she was yelling and crying. The woman was extremely angry about her situation, which seemed rightfully so as she told me of her life. She has been homeless since she was 14 years old. She had been moved from one foster home to another before that time where she had experienced a lot of physical and sexual abuse. She ran away at 14, came to Portland from rural Eastern Oregon, then moved to San Francisco. When she got to San Francisco, she said that there were no services out there to assist a young teenager. She turned to prostitution to get her basic needs met. After a while of prostituting, she turned to drugs to heal her pain and found herself in a deep addiction. Now with her daughter she had found success in recovery. But that is the only success that she identified since after she had graduated from recovery she was left with nowhere to go, so she and her boyfriend moved back up to Portland in hopes of creating a new and better life with her daughter, [of] whom she said that she doesn't know who the father is. She has only been in Portland for two days and is already frustrated with the process of trying to get government assistance as far as Aid to Families with Dependent Children. All the while she was talking, I was doing my best to maintain some sort of emotional control, because her story made me angry that she had gone through so much, truly feeling that she was trying but was getting nowhere. I also had to fight that urge of trying to help her and advocate for her, although I did direct her to some resources that I knew of and someone who I know is an advocate for homeless families.

At certain points in the interview she kept calling me 'sweetheart' and 'honey,' in some ways making me feel like she was angry at me. Especially because at one point she talked about how at certain agencies they have people there who don't know anything about homelessness and have just graduated from college and then take condescending attitudes with people who are homeless trying to get help. She connected this with why she likes Sisters and wanted more places like Sisters because there are people there who have experienced homelessness and remember where they came from. Deep down I don't think she was angry with me, and she said that after one heated comment that she made. It seemed that she was just extremely emotional in sharing her thoughts and opinions.

Orion often wrote after a long day of listening to narrators and dealing with other work-related issues.

**Orion:** The theme for today's interviews seems to be 'denial,' which I say without judgment, but rather with bemused interest. My morning interview was with a youthful man in his mid-thirties who answered my initial question about his background in regard to losing his housing with, 'I went to prison and lost everything.' Okay, I've heard that before, and it sounded very plausible. But later on, when I wanted more details about exactly what he had lost when he went to prison, he thought about it for a while, and finally admitted that he just used that line to placate people when they asked him why he was homeless. It was an easy answer that everyone could relate to, he said, and they were satisfied and ceased with their questioning. It had become second nature for him to answer that way. But when he thought about it, he said he had never had anything to lose to begin with. He was a neglected child, a homeless teen, a military dropout, and then homeless and living in his van and engaging in survival theft at the time he was incarcerated.

I have to say, if we weren't in the context of an in-depth, very personal interview, 'I lost everything when I went to prison' may have satisfied my casual inquiry. It is a credit to our interview format that deeper patterns and causal relationships are slowly revealed, peeled back like the layers of an onion in the course of the session.

Another of Orion's journal entries reflects the difficulties of dealing with the narrators' traumas and how unsettling being a listener can be.

**Orion:** My interview today was with a woman who has had a very hard life. Instead of crying, like many people do, she laughed sarcastically. I felt kind of cold, and like I couldn't breathe, like holding in so much pain rubbed off on me somehow in listening to it. I don't know which is worse, this, or being sad with somebody in an interview. The latter is more immediately upsetting, but less so in the long run, perhaps. If we can cry about it and come out laughing at the end, like some of the women I have talked with, I am exhausted, but at least feel human.

This journal entry follows, showing the range of people an interviewer might encounter in a single day.

**Orion:** My afternoon interview was with a Gulf War vet with some very serious emotional problems from the experience of killing and coming to like it. He also developed quite the alcohol problem from being in the marines, as it is heavily embedded in the culture and the environment, and the military does not seem to be addressing it. This has come up in many interviews, the culture of substance abuse in the military; just yesterday, a man was telling me about keggers (beer parties) thrown by his superior officers. He is in recovery now, but it's very hard for him, harder than his military service ever was, he says.

Anyway, he is very intelligent and self-aware but full of self-abuse, and kept asking me if he was talking too much, or sounded stupid, or was 'killing me' with his talking. I kept assuring him no, but at one point decided to pause to tell him that it seemed like he was recreating his whole self at this time of his life, and the person I saw before me today was that new person he's creating, not some 'screwup,' like he kept asserting. He seemed to really listen to that, and thanked me genuinely, and I think it helped for the rest of the interview.

I don't usually insert my editorial comments into interviews, and certainly not editorial comments about people themselves, but it seemed like his tremendous self-doubt was hindering his ability to talk freely, or to feel okay about talking. He told me at the end that he felt thankful for the chance to talk and be open, and that he was the one that owed me. 'Oh, no, it is I who feels grateful that people are generous enough to come in and share their experience with a complete stranger, in such an honest and genuine fashion. I'm just glad I can receive it,' I said.

And I meant it! I felt very honored by his candidness, just the way I did this morning, and yesterday, with the other people I talked to. But at the same moment, I felt guilty, thinking about all the complaining I have done about people rambling on, all the anger I have felt toward them and their rambling. This is a conflict I deal with almost every day, feeling at once thankful and full of love towards the amazing people I talk to, and feeling burnt out and angry and desperate about the work being too much. I feel guilty at being angry, so I'm afraid I'll internalize the anger and get sad.

At times the journals expressed the problems with the process itself—equipment that failed, narrators who didn't show up, or interviews that ran late. In the beginning of the program when a narrator didn't show, the interviewer was often forced to scour the neighborhood for his or her replacement.

**Orion**: My interview did not show, so I waited around hoping someone would walk in so I wouldn't have to wander the streets. Someone did finally come in, but then he had to run get his stuff, so we didn't start until eleven o'clock. This made the whole day late, and the team needed the back room for the meeting, and everything got all fucked up. Pressure, from all freakin' angles!

The interview was stressful, too, because this man does not want to be found for very legitimate reasons and has joined the underground freight-hopping society to stay hidden. Consequently, we had to stop the recording a number of times to discuss things off-recording, and to have conversations about what we could talk about when the recorder turned back on. We stopped the recorder about three times, once for over half an hour. Before I turned it back on, we worked out everything we would and would not bring up, and what he should say if I touched on something too sensitive. I stopped the recorder myself once to ask him if I could continue with a line of questioning before doing so. As a result, he came to trust me, and told me many things that enrich my knowledge as a researcher, though they are not on recording. I will not mention here the things that are not on recording in a direct fashion, as I promised.

Of all things that tear him up, the worst is that because he can never rejoin society, he cannot live with his little girl 'and be a real daddy.' He sends her postcards and money all the time and visits her briefly and under wraps. He showed me her picture and we talked about her awhile, and we both cried a little. I was so sad for him, a life in exile.

He told me a lot of things about riding the freights, about the freight community, about how it functions as an underground society for people who are purposely lost. Riding the freights, he says, represents absolute freedom for him and others. Since 1997, he has crisscrossed the U.S. uncountable times, always on the go, always in the shadow economy. He won't stay in shelters, because many of them allow the police in whenever they want, to run warrants on whomever. He referred to the 'Starvation Army' as being the worst, taking the good donations and leaving shit for homeless people. He talked about the best and the worst rail lines, how to handle yard bulls (security guards), how to ride 'units' (freight cars), and close calls he's had with injuries while hopping.

Orion and other interviewers were sometimes able to talk with two people who were partners or married, although interviews were conducted with each of them separately. In a journal entry, she described a couple who were heroin addicts that could not get into detox because they couldn't enter together. The woman was four months' pregnant and using heroin.

**Orion**: They had come to Portland to get help and start anew, and all they found was more heroin than ever, an endless supply of needles, and no help for them. He was so depressed; he didn't know what they would do. 'I'm gonna kick,' he pledged, 'but not now...' He explained to me that to kick, you have to have a safe place to stay for a week, and food to eat. Another man today told me that, too, that it just isn't safe or possible to kick on the street. So without housing, and without Hooper [detox center], this couple felt hopeless.

He said he was going to take the money from the interview and go get a hit. Apparently, seven and a half dollars is just enough for a hit of heroin. Some days on this job it feels like 'power to the people,' but some days it feels just like watching a drowning man.

On a more hopeful note she began another entry.

**Orion**: Yesterday I had two great interviews, a woman in the morning and her husband in the afternoon; today I had the same setup, a woman in the morning and her husband later. What made the interviews 'feel-good' was not only the friendly demeanor of the interviewees and the resultant pleasure I had in meeting them, but also the love the couples expressed for each other. Usually, I hear so many sad stories, especially about family. If people are going to tear up or cry, it is most often when talking about parents who don't want them, siblings they don't know anymore, or children they had taken away from them. When people have a loved one in their daily lives, they have so much more sparkle and happiness, and to talk about that person often alleviates the sadness of the rest of their familial breakdown.

The woman I interviewed this morning spoke of her sweetheart with such tenderness, and listed her status as 'married,' because they are emotionally, if not legally, yet. When I interviewed him later, he drew a family map with an outline of the country, with an 'X' marking him here in Portland, and another 'X' far, far off in Ohio marking his family. Next to that he wrote in very careful cursive, 'I haven't seen my family in almost five years. I miss them very much. Thank God I've got my wife.' I tried not to tear up when I saw the map. I also had a moment earlier in the interview when I started to tear up, because after telling me all the ways they rely on each other and love one another, he said he thought sometimes they shouldn't be together. I was surprised, and asked, 'Why?' Because he's worried it will hold her back from getting off the streets, or vice versa, he said. I thought about how much they love each other, and it made me so sad that the streets are so hard on love, ripping people apart who might be just fine if it weren't for the stress and pressure of the street.

Yesterday I had the same feeling listening to the couple speak about their situation together. Although they count themselves as married, they cannot get legally married, or she will lose her SSI. She is very disabled, no doubt about it, with many physical handicaps from being beat up badly in the past, including seizures, and with a low IQ. But they say they will take her benefits from her if she marries, because he should be supporting her. He, a homeless man working minimum wage, is supposed to support both of them, pay their rent, etc. It makes me so angry. And, although her SSI payee (the person responsible for budgeting her money) is supposed to help her get housing on the first of the month, under no circumstances may he live with her, or she will lose her housing. They assume he is 'using her.' The system is so paternalistic and degrading.

This job continues to be very tiring, and the days are long. Even after the interviews are done, this journaling, and downloading, and rewriting the forms takes so much time that no day is just eight hours. Lunch is often hurried and laced with work stuff, unless we leave the office. This office is loud, crowded, distracting, and hard to work in sometimes. But, I am still excited to have such a meaningful job, and the people I interview are often excited about the project, which rubs off on me. Work fills my mind. When I get home, I need to not think about work sometimes. In those cases, I reach for a book and sometimes read all evening.

We used to have friends over more, but often now we're too tired. In the absence of friends, books are an important escape.

Once Orion questioned some of the things that were said in an interview with a mentally ill man, along with her own doubts about her performance.

**Orion**: But I have to ask myself, was it worth it? Here it is, almost nine at night, and with me very, very tired, and we have an interview with a potentially insane person. Thing is, I found it impossible to make the call to end the interview, as I almost always do. With someone as highly functioning as him, the insanity of the interview is understood mostly only in retrospect. It creeps up on you, and the valuable information and beautiful quotes are strung out like breadcrumbs along a twisted path. It was like trying to grab a potholder in the eye of a hurricane.

Interview Quote of the Day: 'The streets are an entity whose sole purpose is to eat you alive, from the inside out.'

After an interview that lasted more than three hours, Orion continued.

**Orion**: Is it okay to get out of work so late, and not finish until I'm hungry and my stomach is upset? No. But is it okay to skip a fascinating discussion on the oppressive paternal system of controlling people's incomes that I'm sure we'll use in the book? Definitely not. And, it's like, maybe if I cut him off about other stuff, we could have gotten to that sooner. But, wading through stories is tricky, because you never know where a story will take someone. It's like Shani says, sometimes stories led nowhere, and sometimes they led to gold. It's frustrating.

My morning interview was with a really cool lady who has had a very hard life. Her interview ran long, too, and even though we were late getting done, I made a point of staying and chatting after the recorder was off, asking her if she was okay, etc. Her interview had been hard on her emotionally, and the family mapping made her sadder, so I wanted to be sure I didn't send her out depressed. I ended up sending her out laughing, and when she saw her friend in the lobby, I invited both of them outside to take silly pictures of them together, which resulted in uproarious laughter by all.

She was one of the few women to talk frankly about doing 'dates.' She was talking about how easy it was to get drugs when you're a woman, especially a somewhat attractive woman, 'and to get dates, everything. That's how women survive down here…it's an easy way of making money. You can't get a job, can't get a house.' She told me about a friend who is staying in motels doing dates when she's not sleeping in the Salvation Army, because she can't get bus tickets to go out of downtown to look for work, and it's much easier to go to the bar and pick up a date.

She said she did dates herself when she got to Portland two months ago, to make money for shelter, etc. But after she got together with her boyfriend, she quit, because 'it would break his poor little heart,' and she cares a lot for him.

Marla came into the project as a volunteer.

**Marla**: Tough interview. Guy wanted to cooperate. Wanted to tell his story. But I think too many drugs and tough breaks made it hard to tell his story in a coherent fashion. Man whose mother died when he was 3 and father took him to an orphanage after her funeral. Jail time at 15½, homeless on and off since he was 8. Vietnam vet. This man is ready to be taken to the Lord. He feels like this world has nothing left to offer him. He hopes to pass his time peacefully out of jail. But his liver is damaged. He's 50 and has been told he has three years to live. That seems to be fine with him.

The journal entries sometimes found the interviewers second-guessing themselves about what had just transpired during the session.

**Marla**: Abuse from father and later her first husband came up. I didn't try to connect that to her homelessness. A connection? Should I have gotten her talking about her childhood? Is someone's childhood always connected to their homelessness?

All our interviewers felt bonded to the research project and all found the experience profoundly moving, and often transforming.

**Marla**: Once again I found myself feeling love for the person I interviewed. During all my interviews to date, I have been very interested to hear their stories. Hearing about their pain has not been difficult for me. I expect everyone has a painful story to tell. I can hear it without taking it on—so far.

A week after an interview was conducted, Marla wrote about the experience:

**Marla**: It's been a week, so the particulars are not as clear, but the impression is crystal clear. I was sitting at the table with a man. This man has no attachment to earthly goods. All his needs are met. He is content with his life—seemed more content than most people I know. He had compassion for people, but he doesn't need people for happiness.

He walks lightly on the earth. He causes no pollution from a vehicle or heating a home. He makes very little garbage. He consumes few resources. He salvages cans and bottles from the garbage and gets them recycled. He cleans up after himself.

He makes his own way in the world. He eats at Sisters; he lives in the moment. He doesn't see himself as a doer in his life. Oh, but if I could have a small piece of that…

He sees his lot in life as a homeless person who picks up bottles and cans. He said some people were meant to be lawyers, etc. He was meant to do what he does. And he was content with that. He said that for people who are homeless who don't want to be, it must be very difficult. But he's at peace.

Another journal entry finds her reflecting on a difficult session.

**Marla:** This interview was very hard [his reaction to life was violence]…I'm sure he had a troubled childhood, but I didn't pry. Why? Lack of confidence he would tell me the truth? Lack of interest? Discomfort with his lack of interest? I don't know.

I carry a backpack with me here. My purse is in my backpack. I leave it near the door. This is the first interview I felt uncomfortable leaving it in the room when I stepped out. I felt like he could have easily grabbed my wallet. He would have and not looked back. If I were homeless, he is the kind of person I would be afraid of.

After describing a woman with a childhood of physical and sexual abuse, and then noting her drug addiction, Marla wrote:

**Marla:** I haven't interviewed anyone yet who was clean and sober right after a program. Those who are clean and sober, came to that place in their own time, their own way. She made a good quote about not being able to change until you want to. If you're doing it for your children or a relationship, it won't work. Have to do it for yourself.

And another interview brought out these emotions:

**Marla:** I feel sad. I don't know if the sadness is from the interview or from my life, but it's palpable. Wow. That's my literary comment. This guy really moved me. His homelessness has all been around drug addiction. He understands the beast; yet he keeps falling. And this is a good man. That sounds offensive. Who am I to say? But I felt energy coming off him that made me feel safe and happy to have had the chance to meet him. Anyway, I'm thankful for having had the opportunity to spend three hours with this man. I feel uplifted.

The journals were an opportunity to sort through their experiences and also name what had happened.

**Marla:** Didn't have a lot of confidence in much of what he said. I think he's been lying all his life in what he thought was necessary for survival. The lies or drugs or blocking out pain makes it difficult for him to remember the truth.

In another entry she muses on the spirituality of the streets.

**Marla:** It strikes me how some of the people I interview have this faith when it looks to the casual observer as though God has let them down. But these people have a much clearer sense of what is needed. The people in my life seem much more confused about necessities versus desires.

The journals also recorded anger and despair.

**Marla:** Whoa. Hardest one yet. Had to debrief with Jamie and Genny. Still left very distraught, sobbed in car on way home. School bus full of middle-schoolers stared. Wonder what they thought?

---

Several hours have passed. I feel the hangover from the combination of a crying jag and tears left uncried. I could let them go right now, but I'm at my son's baseball game. It might freak some people out. I'll put on my happy face or just keep a low profile.

One of Marla's journal entries reflected a narrator's insight and Marla's optimism for her.

**Marla**: This woman had been homeless for four months because she fled an abusive husband. She had been with him twenty-plus years. He started doing things that were worrisome two years into the relationship. The last three were really bad. She left when she did because she was certain her husband would eventually—and sooner rather than later—kill her. I was struck by her courage, her fear, her journey. She proved to me what I badly wanted to know—people are homeless due to circumstances somewhat beyond their control.

She went to a pawnshop and hocked pieces of jewelry he had given her. She got three hundred and seventy-five dollars. She carries the receipt and showed it to me. She bought a Greyhound ticket to Portland from her hometown in the Southwest. She had never traveled by bus, only by car or plane. She didn't have the road-weary look so many homeless people do. Her entrance into homelessness marked her liberation.

She amused me with the story about her parting. She had come into a bonus at work and had tried to placate her husband by buying him toys—electronics, CDs, movies. When she left she gave everything away to the neighbor children. Then she sprayed all of his clothes and furniture with perfume he liked her to wear. She said he would never see her again, but he was going to smell her for a long time. I loved the way she took control. He had been keeping her out of control for a long time. She had the last word.

She cried quite a bit. She's still in the middle of her grief. She feels a loss of her material possessions, especially the things that were given to her by family and friends. She wonders if she didn't get thrust into this situation to learn that she was too attached to things.

She started her journey to Portland with four suitcases containing everything she deemed necessary. Each time she changed buses, she reevaluated what was essential and weeded out a suitcase full of 'essentials' at each stop. One of the more shocking things she said was the hot rollers made it all the way to Portland, where they were gifted to the woman cleaning the Greyhound restroom, along with designer suits and shoes, cosmetics, and a suitcase. The brave traveler left the restroom with a backpack. Four suitcases full of essentials littered her path.

When I met her she was without makeup. Her hair was its original color and had dried without aid of electricity. She was beautiful. She had the most magnificent blue eyes. And the remarkable thing is she could see how beautiful she was. She had come from a community where big hair and extreme cosmetics were the norm. And she could see how her true, unadorned self was beautiful and radiant.

She cried some more, but her sad story didn't make me sad. I wondered briefly why I didn't cry. I still wonder. Maybe because I've heard a number of stories now. I wasn't numb to her story; I listened with compassion. I was able to try to imagine her pain…but I wasn't sad. I think I was too excited about her future to be sad. She was finally free. And Portland was taking pretty good care of her.

After a difficult interview with a developmentally disabled man Marla simply wrote, "I tried."

Here is another entry:

**Marla**: Once again I am awestruck. Another extremely intelligent narrator. She feels lucky for her freedom. She appreciates being able to sleep until she's ready to get up. She has time to read. She gets videos from the library. She goes to free screenings. She eats okay. She seems more content than most people I know on the gerbil wheel.

The common denominator theory holds through one more interview—she had a very difficult childhood. Her father was physically and emotionally abusive to her and her mother.

At the end of a journal entry in large letters Marla wrote:

**Marla**: What the hell is wrong with us?

It was clear that many of the narrators left a haunting presence in the interviewer's memory. Megan, who joined the project as a volunteer while on sabbatical from college, wrote about a woman she had talked with that day.

**Megan**: She was a lovely interview. Maybe I'm tied up more in the beauty of the words or the strength of connection I feel with the person sitting across from me—but I loved this woman because tears clung to her eyes through most of the interview and she looked through that watery cloud with intense feeling. She talked on about the little things that pull homeless people down. 'I'm tired,' she said. 'I'm tired.' And her whole face spoke it.

Most of the homeless people I talked to in that place said how tired they were; they would say this, 'I'm tired,' and that phrase now seemed so different to me. Students used to say it—they were tired because they stayed up late writing a paper, but that is not tired at all. I am sure, for that sort of sleeplessness is chosen, it is a self-made sacrifice. Students might have strange night patterns when they want to cram many interests into their lives, but the tired I saw couldn't always return to the realm of dreams, the grand comfort of a stable, solid bed, private room, free of uncertainty. And although I could never fully understand that horror—a daily search for a place for sleep—I, too, knew what it meant to be without rest.

When I heard the phrase, 'I'm tired,' that was usually said with white eyes, falling jaw, often with no words at all, it was the kind of sentence that ripped into despair, 'I'm tired,

I'm tired.' I was not homeless; I had no experience with homelessness. I was only too aware of the frame of my ceiling. I was swallowed into the thoughts that run and keep you feeling worn in the morning. And I was flattened by those people who told me this: 'I'm tired,' because they told me with so much absence, they said it as if there was no sleep.

Like other interviewers, Megan's journals also reflected her frustration.

**Megan**: Interviewed another Tom today and just couldn't crack him. He didn't want to talk about himself. We couldn't go there. He had these monologues about homelessness and positive thinking and voting…'Get off your ass and vote.'

Liam was a volunteer at Sisters and had experience with homelessness. John was also a volunteer at Sisters and a retired psychology professor. In an interview with the author, Liam observed recurring patterns in the interviews.

**Liam**: What came up in the interviews was that, 'Nobody looks at me, like I don't exist. Nobody hears what I say, I'm invisible, I'm not even here. So when somebody is just sitting there listening to me, I really feel like I'm a human being.'

John noticed a pattern of fragile social networks.

**John**: People need stable childhoods plus a web of relationships that last. But if you are uprooted, like in the army or whatever, or if a marriage ends, you are cast adrift. But the point is, if you have links with other people, you are able to call them up.

After the research or interview portion of the project was over, several of the interviewers left Portland. To catch up with them and those still in town, a questionnaire was distributed to solicit the interviewers' memories and impressions of the project.

Megan conducted about twenty interviews while volunteering with the project.

*Sisters: What did you learn about homelessness that surprised you?*

**Megan**: I learned about drug addiction. People told me the same story—with different characters, and different back-stories—that they'd been forced into rehab clinics, used as soon as the program was over [or during the program], and only quit when they reached some sort of 'rock bottom.' Someone they loved died of an overdose, they almost died of an overdose, or for some reason they looked around themselves and felt an extreme disgust and had to quit.

    I was also surprised to learn that army or navy brats were typical in the homeless community because they moved around so frequently and didn't have a secure community to support themselves. [It was revealed] that homelessness often starts as a wanderlust [often involving drugs] that turns permanent.

*Sisters: How has working on this project changed you or affected your outlook about homelessness?*

**Megan**: I think I wasn't as aware of the patterns of homelessness before this project. I didn't know that there was a pretty predictable cycle of living on and off the street. It's made me realize that this type of work is both incredibly fulfilling and incredibly draining. I love collecting these stories, but I couldn't do it full-time. I would leave an interview barely able to order a sandwich at the restaurant down the street.

*Sisters: Did you reach any conclusions about the causes of homelessness?*

**Megan**: I actually think it taught me to be less naïve about homelessness—that there are so many problems that feed into this one issue. When we say 'homeless,' it seems that homelessness is just about a lack of housing, but it's more than that. It's about being forgotten and neglected by mainstream society. It's about sleeplessness—when you are homeless there's no real sleep. It's the struggle against uselessness—when you are homeless and jobless, it's difficult to feel productive. Often it's about drug addiction.

I think I was aware of those interconnected issues before, at least in a general sense, but I didn't realize that that means homelessness is one tangled mess of issues that are not so easily solved with community organizing or even public policy. I mean, a lot of solving homelessness would have to be about healing folks in a very full way. How do you create public policy that teaches social skills? How do you create community organizations that create supportive families for folks, that provide not only emotional support but financial support?

For a few months while I was working on the project I was unemployed. I'd recently left college; I had very little money. I was experiencing panic attacks. I couldn't sleep at night. And I was closer to that world of homelessness than I'd ever been before. I was only at its edges, but the chaos screamed at me. It was wild and terrifying. In those months when I got close to the terror of homelessness, I realized that I would have been the interviewee if not for my parents and my privilege.

Among the many benefits Megan said she gained from working on the project, this one stands out:

**Megan**: In those moments of true connection or learning, I gained the joy of doing work that felt raw and pure—the work of sharing stories with intention and yearning.

Layla conducted interviews until the end of June 2002, and along with Shani, Orion, and Fara, did the bulk of the interviews.

**Layla**: There were many memorable interviews. Each one was so unique and full of insight and surprises. The Vietnam vet who told me that heroin is an incredibly good painkiller and not only for physical pain, but emotional and mental pain as well. I can still see his eyes.

*Sisters: What did you learn about homelessness that surprised you?*

**Layla**: What I learned that surprised me most was how cruel mainstream society and social services can be. It alarms me that social service agencies fool themselves that they are helping people. I am alarmed that government agencies continue to fund programs that are a revolving door for homeless people, while also completely dehumanizing them into believing that they are the cause of their homelessness.

*Sisters: How did you personally benefit from being involved in this project?*

**Layla**: I grew as a person in my ability to listen without judgment. I became stronger in processing trauma—my own and other people's. I found my voice. I was able to critically analyze the work and help the project evolve into something attainable.

Orion conducted interviews alongside Layla, Shani, and Fara until June 2002.

*Sisters: Was there a single interview that was particularly memorable or moving?*

**Orion**: Several people told me that it was the first time they'd told anyone the things they were telling me, especially people who talked about histories with abuse. I wrote about especially moving interviews in my journal as a way to deal with my emotions about them.

She also recalled a particularly painful interview.

**Orion**: I remember one woman who told me about how she was going through the recycling bins on the street she used to live on, and one of her ex-neighbors called the police. They said she was stealing, stealing their unwanted bottles and cans, in the very neighborhood she was a homeowner in for a dozen years. The policeman put this frail woman into a 'pain hold' and broke both her arms. She said, 'Do you know what it is like being on the street in winter, with two broken arms, and you can't even wipe yourself?' I'll never forget the agony and shame on her face as she remembered the betrayal of her old neighborhood.

*Sisters: Were you ever frightened or uncomfortable when interviewing someone?*

**Orion**: I wasn't frightened, but with a couple of mentally ill people I got 'ungrounded' and found it hard to keep doing the interview. I had to discontinue two or three because it just wasn't productive. A couple times, men persistently hit on me, and that made my job harder; but when I asked them to stop, they did. But I don't ever remember being afraid…

*Sisters: What did you learn about homelessness that surprised you?*

**Orion**: I learned that people who lose their housing stay in their home neighborhoods more often than I thought, camping in parks, etc. I learned that people often felt so paralyzed by fear and shame when they were in the process of losing their housing, that it made it hard for them to fight for it, and that those desolate feelings made it even harder to fight to regain it. Our culture is very hard on the self-worth of those of us who can't always pull ourselves up by our proverbial bootstraps.

*Sisters: What did you learn about homelessness that alarmed you?*

**Orion**: I was alarmed about some of the police brutality I heard about; for example, the 'pain holds' they are trained to use can break people's bones and cause other serious harm.

*Sisters: How has working on this project changed you or affected your outlook about homelessness?*

**Orion**: It's hard to talk about such a deep experience without sounding clichéd. But hearing the emotional experiences of so many people has deepened my compassion for us all, who, despite where we came from and what our paths are, still feel the same pain, loss, longing, hope, and love. The power and pathos of the stories brought home the same humanness in the gutter punk, the elderly street lady, and myself alike.

Shani was our first hired interviewer, beginning her work in October 2001.

*Sisters: Was there a single interview that was particularly memorable or moving?*

Shani remembered one woman who was a little uncomfortable talking to her in the beginning but opened up.

**Shani**: [In the interview] I learned something about my history and what I think about when certain words come up. I asked her where she was raised and she darted off telling her life story quickly. And in that process she told me rather matter-of-factly that 'at 11 years old I was sold by my mother.' My mind kind of stopped. Did I hear 'sold'? And then my mind went to chores. Was she sold for chores? Because when I was 11, I was doing chores. When she broke for breath, I asked her what she meant. Her reply was that she was sold by her mother to her mother's drug lord. Her and her mother had always lived in hotel rooms and she had never lived in a house. That took the wind out of me. It was a very big realization about the protection of children in this culture.

She was 36 and had a partner, and they slept under the bridge. She was trying to get off crack. And she was also trying to stop prostituting because she had a boyfriend who didn't really like it. You can understand that, but there are a lot of couples out there who go through this process of needing money and the woman having the ability to make money quickly… and they were in love and they were really trying. It was memorable mostly because I learned that I come with my own perceptions, presumptions, and assumptions. And it knocked the wind out of me to learn that she was sold to a drug lord at 11. It's unimaginable.

There was also another memorable interview, a blonde-haired woman who wasn't currently homeless. Tobacco, I found almost necessary in my job for people to feel comfortable sitting with me. We would take a smoke break and at that point, I wish I would have had the tape running because they opened up more to me while sitting casually outside the building than they did while in the office.

So this woman named every problem on the streets. Named it all the way down the line. I was very impressed with the way she was able to articulate and had thought about what she would say about the problems that existed. We went out and had a cigarette and she got a little friendlier. And we went back after smoking a cigarette, having a bit of a free conversation, and finished the interview. Now two hours had passed, and in the very last ten minutes I asked her, 'Is there anything I left out that you'd like to talk about?' And she told me the story about her father being the Grand Poobah of the KKK (Ku Klux Klan) of a small town where everyone knows everyone. And this was back in the fifties. So at the time, child abuse and sexual abuse were not really discussed or taken care of. She told me the story of how she had put a gun in her underpants and waited for her father to come, and when he came home he asked her to get up. She did not. He yanked her up and she pulled out the gun and shot him in the heart. And she went to prison. She felt that the judicial system was punishing her for not protecting her.

Now that was my first interview of the day. And she just knocked me out with one punch. And what do you do? You literally have been knocked out like you're in a boxing ring. There's stars going above your head, you can't see straight, you're nauseous and hurt. I had this breakdown at work; I felt like I had been punched because her description of the story affected me. I had a great interview with her, and it just knocked me out. So I didn't do another interview that day because I would not have been able to give the next person the right amount of time and energy to listen to their story.

*Sisters: What did you learn about homelessness that alarmed you?*

**Shani**: The sheer numbers. There is nowhere to go. There are people flying signs [displaying signs asking for help] on every corner. The threat of violence on the streets. The fragility of people out there and the violence perpetuated against them through the system by not giving them basic rights. A freakin' shower would be nice once in a while. There's so much scheduling of people on the streets…all that stuff is so intense, how in hell can you ever straighten your life out when you have to get place to place to place just to get your basic needs met—that's alarming. And theft in the homeless community is outrageous! It should be the biggest faux pas on the street to steal from your brother, your tribe. There should be no theft going on.

*Sisters: How has working on this project changed you or affected your outlook about homelessness?*

**Shani**: I think I had a pretty good outlook from my own experiences and experiences of others from being in the community. Working at Sisters Of The Road changed me. I worked on myself there every day, and that changed me.

*Sisters: Did you reach any conclusions about the causes of homelessness?*

**Shani:** I think there is a strong case to show that a trauma within a familial group is more often a catalyst to an experience of homelessness. Trauma can be a divorce, loss of a job, injured on the job, or there is a death. There is some pivotal point in a person's life that can change people instantly and can cause people to have to seek shelter. Addiction can be included in the trauma of a familial group and addiction is exasperated by the experience of homelessness, because mind-altering states are much more pleasant than the dreary, wet muck that you have to wade through every day. I think the length of obtaining and the logistical matters of getting SSI and SSD income are unreasonable for people who need funding. I think PTSD has a lot to do with the veterans I talked to. And not wanting to be part of the system; there is an anarchist side to squatters; people at Dignity Village; people living in vans, cars, Winnebagos—not wanting to participate in the system, not wanting to work six days a week to pay the rent, to pay the bills, to buy some food. Another cause of homelessness in my own life and experience and in others you talk to is the nomad experience. Living in my van is not that hard…I think a lot of people like to travel, especially the young ones on the trains and the old ones on the trains.

*Sisters: Did you reach any conclusion about the solutions for homelessness?*

**Shani:** I think the only solution is organizing people in the community. That's the first step. The decriminalization of people living outdoors would be a good public policy. So there's a lot of systemic change that needs to be done. Also, mental health issues need a lot of funding to help people, and I'm all for socialization of medicine.

A solution that would help would be a day shelter that has phones, showers, day beds, child care, storage facilities—all the basic things you're going to need—and is also like a community center. I think it's vitally important in a place where it rains nine months out of the year. Somewhere to go inside besides the library.

*Sisters: How did you personally benefit from being involved in this project?*

**Shani:** I just cannot say enough about my experiences working with Sisters Of The Road as a barter worker, Cafe floor manager, and as a field researcher (interviewer).

*Sisters: Was there a single interview that was particularly memorable or moving?*

**Sandy:** So many. One guy who was a meth addict really touched me. He was so alone in the world; so unwanted. He was just trying to survive and had so little love. I also was touched by a diabetic who could not get his disease under control as a homeless person, so his cycle just continued. I felt for the woman who was a prostitute, along with her daughter, to pay for their drug habits. And the alcoholic woman who went between two men she loathed because they gave her a place to sleep. Or the teenager who told me all about the meth business and about the street family who took him in. I remember the guy who spent every day in the downtown library, reading a book a day and sleeping in a parking structure.

*Sisters: What did you learn about homelessness that alarmed you?*

**Sandy**: That the cycle is so hard to break. For example, I'd never realized that if you don't have teeth, you can't get a job. If you don't have an address or e-mail or phone number, how do you get a job?

Marla was among the later wave of volunteer interviewers.

*Sisters: What did you learn about homelessness that surprised you?*

**Marla**: I learned something I didn't want to know. I learned that a lot of people are homeless because of mental illness or addiction or a truly horrible childhood. I didn't want that to be the truth. I wanted to be able to go around and tell my friends that it could happen to me, it could happen to them. Because if the middle and upper class are vulnerable, if the homeless population is really us fallen on hard times, I could convince people to feel compassion, to help, to check their judgments. But the reality I saw was many people were homeless because they were not like me. They had truly horrible childhoods, or they were addicts, or they were mentally ill, or any combination of the above. This does not make the need for compassion and help any less, it just makes it more difficult to sell. The middle and upper class can still believe with some accuracy that it couldn't happen to them. They're wrong. It could happen to any one of them or their children, but it probably won't. And they know it.

*Sisters: Did you reach any conclusions about the solutions for homelessness?*

**Marla**: The interventions have to occur as early in a person's life as possible.

During the work of writing the book, well after the interviews were completed, Sisters spoke with the interviewers again.

**John**: Sometimes it's a choice and sometimes it's the way of life you're brought up in. And that way of life is, you're always living on the edge, and your only hope is the lottery. And you're never going to get out of it.

**Liam**: But then it gives you freedom to be generous, because it's going to be gone tomorrow, anyway.

**Marla**: And that generosity always took me aback, that 'I don't have enough money for food for the whole week, but I have money today so I'll buy all my friends lunch. And I don't have cigarettes Wednesday, but I have cigarettes today, so I'll give them to all my friends.' I really loved the people who the first thing they did when they got a pack of cigarettes was went and gave them to all the people they'd been bumming off of.

*Sisters: That was mentioned a lot—the amazing amount of generosity on the streets.*

**Marla:** I personally reacted very negatively to the guy who, when I asked him what brand he smoked, it was 'O.P.'s [other people's]' and when I asked him how many he shared when he got a pack, and he said, 'none. They're mine.' I wanted to say, 'Alright, the interview's over! You're out of here!'

*Sisters: Some of the younger women interviewers (wrote in their journals) about men who sexually harassed them. Do you remember the narrator who was in jail for rape and assault, and he said it was all the women's fault that he was in jail?*

**Marla:** Yes, there was a guy I didn't respond emotionally to. He said that all women were cruel and unusual beasts. He was really angry, because 'women get all the advantages because they got a little slit between their legs.' He was seething towards women, but I didn't feel threatened by him. However, I did excuse myself long enough to tell Jamie what was going on and ask him to stay close and attentive in case I needed help.

**Orion:** The[re was a] guy who said, 'all women are all the same, you just shake 'em upside down and some smiles are bigger than others.' I'll never forget that. I just kept saying to myself, 'how can the world be so ugly and horrible?' That was my little mantra.

*Sisters: Is your world view different now that you've worked on this project?*

**Marla:** Yes, but I wouldn't allow it to get negative. I was really pleased with my capacity to feel love for all, with the exception of two narrators. I really enjoyed that aspect of it, that I can just open my heart and we can have this exchange, and I may not understand you, our lives are very different maybe, but I can listen.

Marla was asked by the author what she had gained from the experience of being an interviewer.

**Marla:** This was by far the best job I've ever had. I learned that I have the capacity to listen with an open heart to a wide variety of people. I learned that I can have compassion for almost anyone. I learned there is much wisdom and a staggering amount of pain walking around our streets. I became more committed than ever to meet everyone on the street, housed or not, with a sincere smile and direct eye contact.

My dad drank and smoked himself into an early grave but maintained his job and was always kind. I am eternally grateful that my dad was a 'good' alcoholic. He took care of his family to the end; it could have played out differently. This project showed me exactly how it could have played out.

I have always been appreciative of the roof over my head and the food in my belly. This project made me more so. When I think of the homeless people sleeping under a bridge on a cold, rainy night, there are faces. I see Mike's face most often. I don't want Mike to be cold.

Photographer: Brynne Athens

Photographer: Alan Shipley

# Epilogue

*I have been struggling*

## Changes in Lives of Narrators after the Interviews

Natural questions after reading this book include how is the situation now and how are the individual narrators? With just a broad awareness of national life in the last few years the reader can respond to the first with certainty that the situation is worse. Health care, employment, overall state of the economy…the list goes on; the factors that contribute to homelessness and poverty have worsened. An appendix is included to help the reader find the references to substantiate this claim for themselves.

As for the narrators, Orion (one of the original interviewers) recently met with many of the original narrators and asked how things have changed and what their current circumstances are. We have intentionally given these interviews only the lightest of editorial touches. Names have been changed to protect privacy and no effort has been made to connect the names with narrations included earlier in the book.

### George

George, 54, volunteers every day in Sisters' office to earn his meals since he broke his leg last year and could not work in the cafe. He was one of the PhotoVoice photographers.

*Sisters: We interviewed you in January 2003. What has life been like since the time of the interview?*

**George**: Things have changed. For a couple of years I worked in the afternoon and mornings in the cafe, but I was still kind of uncertain as to what I wanted to do with myself. Now I have ambition. I don't have the same habits. I didn't used to realize that I could take my shoes off when I slept at night, and now I just take them off and relax.

*Sisters: What does that mean that you sleep without your shoes on now?*

**George**: When you live on the street, you live minute by minute and calculate a plan for meeting your daily needs and not disrupt people who are going to work in the morning, not disrupt society. Now I've found a way to be around people, around society and relax. I have ambition now to get off the street. I can reenter society, maybe get a 9–5 again. I enjoy life, take in concerts, watch TV, instead of worrying where I'll be tomorrow. I have my basic needs fulfilled with myself mentally. With Sisters, I know I have a place to go where I'm welcome, and it's a daily change in lifestyle. At soup lines, there's no compelling reason to socialize. At Sisters I can socialize with people and find things to talk about, open up and discuss.

I have more clarity, I'm feeling different, not so hazed. Not that before I was hazed or blurred around the edges, but maybe my reality was hazing others. I'm an open person, there are no hidden doors here, I'm not causing problems or anything, but maybe I was naïve and was hazing others. Now I'm certain I'm not disturbing others, whether homeless or not homeless.

Homelessness has got to go with me. It has become my livelihood, I'm afraid to say—being out here since I was 17 and growing up that way, since I was legal drinking age. I had conformed to living on the streets, and with Sisters there has been a gradual change. There's been a gradual mental consciousness adjustment to me getting inside now. I'm still George, I just have more clarity, more appearance, an easier breathable space.

## Mary Anne

Mary Anne uses a walker and suffers from multiple disabilities. Although she qualifies for Sisters' disability program, she prefers the barter program, wiping down chairs and those counters that she can comfortably reach in exchange for her meals.

*Sisters: How have things changed for you since you did your interview in August 2003?*

**Mary Anne**: My friend and I used to sneak out of Harbor Lights shelter early to work at Sisters. We sneaked out so we could avoid gossip and 'elements.' I hated staying there, mostly because of my injuries and I had to pack my stuff around during the day. Now I'm staying with a friend in a Section 8 apartment.

*Sisters: Are you couch-surfing or on the lease?*

**Mary Anne**: I'm not on the lease, and I wouldn't want to be. I wouldn't want to be because of the 'elements,' and the theft—the theft is really bad. At least it's a place to sleep. I have an appointment with JOIN tomorrow [an agency that gets people into apartments]. I left Dignity Village because of the cold. I came here to Sisters today because I'm under doctor's orders to drink thirty-two ounces of iced tea with lemon, to keep my lungs clearer. I've been fighting a cold and the flu. I take echinacea every two days.

*Sisters: So you lived at Dignity Village after the original interview?*

**Mary Anne**: Yeah. The main reason I left was the cold. I told my friend, 'Dignity Village was one of the better chapters of my life.' I was with sixty rebels with a different cause, and life was never dull! There were so many personalities. They built me a house there. It had an interesting design. It was all built out of pallets. It had a bunk bed made out of pallets, away from rats and water. I don't like public housing, and I don't intend to go back. I lived in the North Towers and that was awful, worst place I ever lived. I don't like Section 8.

*Sisters: Why are you going to JOIN tomorrow?*

**Mary Anne**: I have an old pending unemployment case. He [the worker at JOIN] is going to help me with some papers. A year from this month, I will apply for retirement. I canceled my application for disability because I was mad. I said, 'You're not even trying, asking me stupid questions, not even to do with my injuries.'

*Sisters: What injuries?*

**Mary Anne**: I was assaulted in 1999 by a man hired by the county to take our belongings and sell them to the thrift store.

*Sisters: Where were you living?*

**Mary Anne**: I co-owned a house with the man I was taking care of. The house was my payment for caretaking. That's what he wanted too, so that if he died before I died, I would always have a home. And while he was in the hospital, the city and the county were fighting over the house before he even died. So they hired this man [to clear out the house] and I tried to stop him and they were paying him three thousand dollars, and you know how desperate people can get, people on the street. He hurt me bad. I later found out he was wanted for attempted murder and was out on his own recognizance. He tortured me. He poked holes in my face [she points to multiple scars on her cheeks and temples] and bit a hole in my face. He tried to poke through my temple but I turned my head and he couldn't do it. I am still going through Post-traumatic Stress Disorder.

JOIN will pay a deposit [on an apartment] but I have to show an income, so I'm trying to get unemployment. I was working full time at the time of my injuries. I'm trying to work with an ombudsman. I have a lawsuit pending over the co-ownership rights. I'm going for my house back. I had to go to tenant-landlord court, and that isn't right. I was an owner. They have to give me a house of equal or greater value.

*Sisters: Overall, how would you say your situation is now, since we interviewed you?*

**Mary Anne**: I'm just about to put it all together. My physical ability is better. All this housing,

I've got to where I accepted it. I've got the strategy in place now but it will take them knowing someone's watching. I want [this worker] at JOIN to type out paperwork for me. That man [hired by the county to clear out her house] tried to pull my eyes out of my head and he did permanent damage and that's frustrating to me. My breathing is better, I have more power in my lungs. My weak breathing allowed people to give me flack before. I have one year until retirement and Medicaid owes me, I worked forty-seven long years. Unemployment will give me money to survive for a year and a half. They owe me seven years of back pay for unemployment.

*Sisters: What kind of income are you living on right now?*

**Mary Anne**: None! I'm living on no money right now. I'm resourceful. I last worked in October 2002. Do you know how I survived nine months in my apartment? I had a roommate, a girl on the street, but she left [when I lost my job]. She thought the burden of the rent would fall on her; I tried to tell her, 'I'll take care of myself!' but she left. I had five hundred and fifty dollars a month to pay, so I worked the phone books all day long. I called churches, groups, fraternal organizations, and they sponsored me!

*Sisters: What is your housing like now? Is it stable, or shaky?*

**Mary Anne**: It is very shaky. I shower at JOIN because I am not supposed to use the water at my friend's apartment. The landlord knows I'm there, but I'm not supposed to be sleeping there. He's kind of rolling with it.

## Jose Luis

Jose Luis often cheerfully works for his meals in Sisters' cafe, always carrying a duct-taped, dog-eared Bible with him and always wanting a hug.

*Sisters: We did the interview four years ago, March 2002. Since then, are things different for you?*

**Jose Luis**: My situation is different. I am more speaking English. God helps me every day. My life…I'm okay, I'm healthy. I'm working sometimes at festivals, under the Burnside Bridge, at the Plaid Pantry [where day laborers congregate waiting for contractors, etc., to pick them up for jobs].

*Sisters: What else has changed for you besides speaking more English?*

**Jose Luis**: My change is that I have humility. I help people because I have money sometimes, I like to give them a dollar. Because they're the same homeless. I like to help everybody.

*Sisters: Where are you sleeping?*

**Jose Luis**: I'm sleeping in Clark Center.

*Sisters: Where were you sleeping in 2002 when we did the interview?*

**Jose Luis**: Sometimes in the streets, TPI, Clark Center, back and forth, back and forth. Sometimes I got a room. My sleeping situation is the same. But maybe the future will change because I'm waiting for papers so I can work in a restaurant because I need to save some money in the bank.

*Sisters: What papers?*

**Jose Luis**: Residency papers. I'm looking at to go to school, maybe community college, for to speak English, writing and reading. In 2002 I'm not speaking English very good, but much better now, radio, tapes, memorize, practice with people, people at Sisters, repeat, repeat, repeat. I use the Internet and library. I have a library card. With papers, it is much better for me. Maybe I can find a woman, one woman for my whole life. I pray for God it is coming, God helps me. I like understanding the Bible. I go to the Salvation Army. Maybe I'm more spiritual now. I like helping people like the Bible says. People need a normal life, no use drugs, no use violence. They need a God, peace in their heart.

*Sisters: Who is helping you get your papers?*

**Jose Luis**: My brother in Chicago. He's living here fifty years, since he was a child. My nephews, I call them Chicanos.

*Sisters: Mexican Americans?*

**Jose Luis**: Yes, Chicanos. He has very good English. But I no like living with him together. I like Portland. People know me here, especially Sisters Of The Road. Everybody's family at Sisters. Everybody's wonderful here.


Stephen

*Sisters: Your interview was in November 2001; that was a long time ago.*

**Stephen**: I was the first. I was the first person interviewed.

*Sisters: Wow. Has much changed in your life since the interview was done?*

**Stephen**: Sisters Of The Road has been a catalyst since my interview was done. I've been on boards, on numerous committees. I have skills in community organizing and am able to not only help the community but help myself to understand what's going on with me. Before I was just confused.

*Sisters: What do you mean, 'going on?'*

**Stephen**: I suffer from Post-traumatic Stress Disorder and depression. Being able to get out of myself and communicate with other people and understand when my depression or anything else happened to me. I have a community that supports me and I support them. Sisters Of The Road and active community organizing have allowed me to get out of that, and get proactive helping others, which helps me.

*Sisters: What committees and boards have you been serving on?*

**Stephen**: Sisters' Board of Directors and Development Committee; the Neighborhood Safety Committee of the Old Town Chinatown Association; I was temporarily on the Communications Committee for the *Town Crier*, the paper for my neighborhood association in Old Town Chinatown, mostly doing distribution and making contacts; I've been on the Board of the Old Town Chinatown Neighborhood Association for four years and I'm ready to be a former member in March when my term's over. I'm looking forward to getting into something else to stay busy and active in the community.

Community organizing has changed me, to realize I have to humble myself. I'm no better or no worse than anyone else. I'm helping people to help themselves. Like helping women on the street realize they are lovable and can love themselves. And children need to be children! There's so much crisis, abuse, trauma, and women and children need the reminder that they are lovable. It was a woman who abused me as a child, and there was no program for her. I'm trying to do something that wasn't done sixty years ago.

*Sisters: How's your financial situation?*

**Stephen**: It's the same since 2001. When I got SSD in 1971, I didn't know it would be so complicated at first, yet it's simplified through the years and I've been able to budget my money and help others do the same. My health is a little more extreme since 2001. I lost a lot of muscle mass in my lower legs. I went from a cane to a walker to a wheelchair. So even with the disability advancing, I can be a productive member of society.

*Sisters: What disability do you have?*

**Stephen**: Spinal stenosis and degenerative disk disease of the pelvis and spine. And arthritis, osteo and rheumatoid. Amongst other stuff, like hep C; I have a whole laundry list of stuff wrong with me!

*Sisters: Is some of this from your military service?*

**Stephen**: The PTSD, yeah, and tinnitus, ringing in the ears. Depression is part of it. The physical trauma is more from childhood.

*Sisters: What else is new since 2001?*

**Stephen**: I hooked up with my childhood sweetheart. She's been married for twenty-six years. We e-mail daily. So romance is back in my life.

*Sisters: But she's married?*

---

**Stephen**: Well, romance as a friend. I've always been in love with her, but I know my place. Number one is whatever makes her happy. So I'm still an eligible bachelor. It disturbs me that I do so much in the community but I usually shut down relationships when they start. When I'm helping a woman I don't want it to be a conflict of interest, so I deny myself carnal activities.

*Sisters: So, are you saying that the women you are around most of the time are women down here on the street that need help? What about women that you might be on an equal footing with, that you could have a relationship with?*

**Stephen**: What I need for myself is a stable woman who is self-sufficient but has no baggage to carry into a relationship. A strong woman like you or Genny. There are a lot of broken people out there. I've learned my boundaries. The last thing I want to do is hurt someone. I never married because I knew I'd hurt someone. It's so hard to get into a relationship when you don't know how to relate. Alcohol was the main thing. I've been clean twice, [each time] over ten years. This time I've been clean over fifteen years. I got in recovery the first time when I was 28. Now I'm 53.

*Sisters: That's great, congratulations! So, has your living situation changed since 2001?*

**Stephen**: It's the same, [a Section 8 alcohol and drug-free housing].

*Sisters: Do you like it?*

**Stephen**: As a bachelor, it's okay. I could use more space. It seems like I placed myself in a life of poverty, and I'm enjoying it! I'm humbling myself every day. When I get in line at Sisters, people say, 'Go ahead.' I say 'No, I'll wait, I'm no better or no worse than anybody.' And I have my 'children' on the streets who call me papa, grandpa. And I didn't have to have one of 'em! In January, my godson turned 5.

*Sisters: So that is a big change in your life since 2001, having a godson?*

**Stephen**: Yes! He's the love of my life. He's taught me more about unconditional love than anyone. Children are that way. He has the best of both worlds, being multicultural and multiracial. He's handsome, smart, he already knows computers, already reads.

*Sisters: How often do you see him?*

**Stephen**: As often as I can. He will always be in my life. He's my little buddy.

William

*Sisters: We first interviewed you in November 2001. What has changed for you since then?*

**William**: Actually there's nothing changed. It's the same thing.

*Sisters: How about your health?*

**William**: I got diabetes in December 2005 and then got cured of it. I had it for a year.

*Sisters: How did you cure it?*

**William**: I don't know. Take care of myself, I guess. It's gone.

*Sisters: How about your living situation?*

**William**: Same.

*Sisters: Has your income changed?*

**William**: Well, since I've taken that last interview, my income raised to almost seven hundred dollars a month.

*Sisters: That's great. How did it raise?*

**William**: I got hooked up at Aging and Disability. I'm on Social Security now. They eliminated my Medicare. Aging and Disability pays it now; I'm still covered.

*Sisters: What changes has the extra money made in your life? Any?*

**William**: Not really. Like I said, I'm a constant. I don't spend no more, don't save no more neither!

*Sisters: How about your personal life?*

**William**: Had a girlfriend in 2004, now I don't have one. But it's okay, I'm learning to cope.

*Sisters: So what keeps you coming back to Sisters? I see you every day.*

**William**: The beans!

*Sisters: The beans?!*

**William**: Exactly right! Plus, I like the camaraderie, the people here.

*Sisters: How old are you?*

**William**: [long pause]

*Sisters: Have I finally run into a question you don't want to answer?*

**William**: No, no. I'm 62 years old.

*Sisters: You should be proud.*

**William**: I am! I'm proud I'm still alive! With all the things I used to do!

Carlos

*Sisters: We interviewed you a long time ago, December 2001. What is different in your life since then?*

**Carlos**: I have a new perspective on humanity, on how we look upon each other in classism. I have a new hatred of humanity.

*Sisters: Hatred, wow. Did something happen to you?*

**Carlos**: I have a new perspective on how those 'with' treat those 'without.' I love people, but I hate the person.

*Sisters: What person?*

**Carlos**: It could be anyone.

*Sisters: What else has changed? Your living situation?*

**Carlos**: I moved to Gresham to have my own apartment.

*Sisters: Do you like your apartment better?*

**Carlos**: Oh yeah!

*Sisters: Congratulations.*

**Carlos**: Thanks. But it's fucking expensive. I'm still living on a meager income. Hell yeah, it's a struggle.

*Sisters: Is your financial situation the same?*

**Carlos**: [At the time of the interview] I was working here at Sisters and at a bar. Now that bar is a video gaming place. I got better money then, I was working two jobs. It's gotten harder since the time of the interview. But I'm happy, and that's what's important. I enjoy my job.

*Sisters: That's not often something you hear people say about their job. What job is that?*

**Carlos**: Social service outreach.

*Sisters: So you're helping people?*

**Carlos**: Yes.

*Sisters: So, you like helping people, but you hate humanity?*

**Carlos**: [I hate] the characteristics of a person. How we as a people…when you look at some people who believe they are better than you, or that the world owes them something because of something, the characteristic is, 'I want this because you owe it to me, not because I need it but because it's there and you have to give it to me.' Infantile behavior.

*Sisters: Are you talking about people on the street, or…?*

**Carlos**: Not just people on the street. It's a problem in me also.

*Sisters: So, does having your own apartment ease the stress?*

**Carlos**: Yes. Solitude is important. I can shut the door.

*Sisters: How old are you?*

**Carlos:** I'll be 38 next month.

*Sisters: What are your hopes for the future?*

**Carlos:** My health. I don't ask for much. I want more though. I earn everything I have.

*Sisters: And your job?*

**Carlos:** I did manual labor since I was 14. This job is different, working with people. It's the hardest job I've ever had. I've worked with chemicals, been set on fire, I used to recycle paint. [In this job] every person has a different personality every day, everyone. They're not in the same realm. Something might blow them off: their check didn't come in, their husband might have left them. They're not in the same headspace, their personality changes. How they're treated is how I get treated. Getting cursed at, vented to two hours every day, but it's not their fault. I'm more than content. It's an honor and a privilege to serve, I believe. I wouldn't call them my clients, I'd call them my guests, and it's my privilege to serve them.

*Sisters: How long have you been at this job?*

**Carlos:** Three years and four months.

*Sisters: After all those manual labor jobs, what brought you to the social services?*

**Carlos:** I love self-sufficiency, I love to work. When I left work, I was forced to leave for medical reasons. I had seizures. I believe it was the chemicals from the paint. I had a psychiatrist and everything. I knew I would be homeless. I was forced to live on my retirement. When I left [that early job] I was 28 years old. I never knew about unemployment, I never knew I was eligible. I tried to get Social Security, food stamps, but I couldn't get anything until I spent my nest egg. I had to spend it. It was twenty-thousand dollars I had saved.

## Joe

I put off interviewing Joe because he can be very volatile and he makes me nervous. But as we sat down I saw that he's doing much better.

*Sisters: It's been five years since we interviewed you, April 2002. What has changed in your life?*

**Joe:** What has changed in my life is I've watched a lot of people in downtown Portland getting heavy into drugs. A lot of people come to me and ask, 'How can I get off the street?' I send them to Central City Concern, which helps people with housing and to get off the street so they can get into treatment. The police are respecting me for that. Because they asked me, 'Why don't you get yourself off the street?' And I said 'I'll get off, but right now I'm trying to help some people down here get off.' I was at the ___ building, but I had a seizure and got put out. I'm going through ___ program to get housing right now. Once I do, I'll still come to Sisters to help out.

Right now I cook to feed people at the park. I fix plates of leftover food and bring them to people who are too sick to come out. Meals on heels. People call me the protector because I protect others. If I can't protect them, I can't protect myself. All my kids came in from out of state on Thanksgiving. I miss them. But then I had a seizure in front of Downtown Chapel and was in the emergency room on Christmas, and I missed them.

*Sisters: You couldn't get to them on Christmas because you were in the hospital?*

Joe: That's right. They left. I have a doctor in the Old Town Clinic who is trying to get my medication right. I went through a treatment center for drugs and alcohol. They are treating me right because I thought I'd have to leave after I touched someone while I was having a seizure. I didn't hit him. But the staff was afraid of me; they thought I'd be violent. This man was a small man, I'm much, much bigger, and he was afraid because I was so loud. If you notice, my voice is calm and collected now because I'm on medication. I'm very focused on things around me.

*Sisters: Yes you are very calm.*

Joe: Thank you.

*Sisters: What other changes have been going on for you in these last five years?*

Joe: With the new Max [light rail] line going in, I'm seeing some changes. There's new businesses, a lot of clubs have opened down here, and I've watched them open and close. And in the Pearl District, they're putting up apartment complexes. Are they for the homeless, or for rich people? They are expensive apartments. Like when they closed Burger King over here [on the edge of the Pearl District]. It was a good restaurant for people. But people were selling drugs, and some of the management too. They weren't keeping it clean. The State forced them to close. And like the Tacoma Cafe, it closed too. This [Sisters] is now the only cafe where people can eat when they hardly have any money.

It's getting hard for people, and why do they want to sell their food stamps? They want drugs. It's a bad system. I'd wait until they get housing, only give them a little money until then. And they are selling their [food stamp] card and then canceling their PIN. Then those people they sold it to come back with violence, wanting their money back. Two nights ago two girls got stabbed over here. A black girl was stabbed over by the light rail under the bridge by the Portland Rescue Mission. I'm afraid the Rescue Mission will shut down. It will bring a lot of people to the street. They are running very low on money. I went there the night before last and all they had was oatmeal, and the chapel was not very full.

*Sisters: So, you're clean now?*

Joe: Yes. That's a very good change. My mind is focused on making other people feel this way, get their life together too. There's a lot of new faces down here, getting sold bunk.

*Sisters: Bunk?*

**Joe:** Bunk, bad drugs. They're coming back with knives and guns to get their money back. Women are coming down here to sell their bodies. Why? Leave it alone! If you wanna come down proper, come and do something proper for the community. Like when Sisters' [barter workers] come sweep the sidewalk. Why not do the whole block? This is Sisters' corner! Do the whole block. This is a restaurant for people who care. And you're the only one helping others now. The Tacoma Cafe closed. They didn't have people who volunteered their time. When you volunteer, you're doing it for love, making it a higher priority than your job. People will put it down [that they worked at Sisters] as a reference when they go to get a busing job. They'll call us and ask us for a reference.

*Sisters: So where are you living now?*

**Joe:** At the ___ Building. The people working there said, 'We're tired of seeing you on the street. When we were on the street, you were here with us. You're still here. We don't want to see you behind bars. We'll help you get off the street.' I'm still drawing portraits of people. I drew a portrait of every person at [the treatment center]. I watch people very closely so I can draw a very detailed portrait of them. I use thousands of little dots, with different colors, to make a portrait.

*Sisters: How long did you live there?*

**Joe:** Three and a half weeks.

*Sisters: So you are out of treatment and living at the ___ Building now?*

**Joe:** That's right.

*Sisters: How long are you allowed to stay there?*

**Joe:** Over a year, until they find you a place.

*Sisters: How is your financial situation since 2002? Has it changed?*

**Joe:** My disability came up. Every year it comes up twenty dollars. I'm my own payee now. Every time I go in a treatment facility, I give them my check. Then, by the time you graduate from treatment, you have some money saved up and you can get an apartment. I got a letter from HAP (the Housing Authority of Portland) just today; I was reading it when you came and asked me to do this interview [hands over letter].

*Sisters: It says you're number six hundred and two on a Section 8 waiting list of three thousand people. That's pretty good. Congratulations.*

**Joe:** I get my mail at Sisters. Other than Sisters, I have no mailing address. When I moved to [treatment], you returned my mail and I got cut off of food stamps. But when I got out of treatment, I got them back again. Now I can get my mail here again. I got my medical card, my Section 8 letter. They lowered my food stamps to ten dollars when my SSI went up.

*Sisters: Do you think you are going to stay clean this time?*

**Joe**: Yes.

*Sisters: Why?*

**Joe**: This time was the first time I tried it. I've been helping others get into it, and they come back and say thank you. It was someone I had helped, who came and drug me off the corner and took me to the ___ building. They knew me there because we were on the street together. Now they got themselves clean, and they were glad to see me. They wanted me back there. I tried to go through the Rescue Mission and I couldn't. I was clean for three weeks when I went there and asked for help. They said no because I take phenobarbital, and to them it's a narcotic, even though it's for seizures.

*Sisters: Even though it's prescription? It seems to be doing you a lot of good. That doesn't make any sense to me.*

**Joe**: Thank you! I need it. You can see I'm focused, I'm calm, I'm on a downward level. I need it three times a day. Before I was taking phenobarbital, Dilantin, and Tegretol twice a day. I slept all day. I went to Emmanuel [Hospital] and they dropped it down, actually. At the ___ Building I take it only when I need it now.

*Sisters: How old are you now?*

**Joe**: I'm a 51-year-old man.

*Sisters: How's your personal life?*

**Joe**: Single. By myself. I got a new life getting started, I'm proud of that. Thanks for Sisters. I would like to come back to Sisters and cook.


Charles

Charles has been an incredibly active member of Dignity Village for years and the public face of the Village in many ways, meeting with community groups, giving tours, and representing the Village all over the city.

*Sisters: So, we interviewed you in March 2002. Do you remember what was happening then? I bet a lot has changed.*

**Charles**: I had just gotten to Dignity Village in December of 2001. That's when I first got out there. In March 2002 I first started working for outreach [public outreach coordinator] for the Village. I've almost spent five years working out there, all for naught.

*Sisters: All for naught?*

**Charles**: I'm no longer anything at the Village. I just do security two hours a week. I'm no longer chairman, I'm no longer a member.

*Sisters: Wow. But you still live there?*

**Charles**: Yes.

*Sisters: What happened?*

**Charles**: I'm not really sure. I was forced to resign.

*Sisters: Wow. So what does that mean, you're not a member?*

**Charles**: I can't vote, can't do nothing. Seems kind of weird, all those years I put in time and energy into something like that. I wouldn't have minded if they came and asked me to resign. But they didn't do it like that. They did it backhanded. There are very few originals there.

*Sisters: The original members of Dignity Village?*

**Charles**: Yeah. Lots of things are changing. I'll see before I say anything whether it's good or bad change. But it's not the same as the original fight. It's a shame. It's not where we came from.

*Sisters: What do you mean, the 'original fight'?*

**Charles**: The fight to get off the street, out from under the bridges. The only fight we have now is to sign leases. People aren't sure which way to go.

*Sisters: What do you mean? Which way to go with what?*

**Charles**: Instead of doing things recycled and writing grants for money, they're moving toward getting a phone bank set up to get money. It's different. We were always 'hands up, not hands out.'

*Sisters: Is this phone bank 'hands out'?*

**Charles**: I'm not sure how it's going to work. If it's going to individuals with a lot of money, maybe it will be okay. If it's going to the City [Portland], I don't know.

*Sisters: Oh, so this is not like people at the Village working for some company's phone bank on site; this is a phone bank where Villagers call and ask for money for Dignity?*

**Charles**: Right. And there's other things in progress like selling roses on the side of the road to make income, and those things are okay, if it's the fruits of our labor. Now, if it was a phone bank like a charity hiring us to call out and raise money for them, that would be okay. But we'll see how it goes.

*Sisters: So, you've had a lot of roles at the Village since 2002, right?*

**Charles**: I was Treasurer 2002, 2003, 2004. I was elected and was Chairman in 2005, 2006.

*Sisters: Have those leadership roles affected your psyche, your life?*

---

**Charles**: I'm not sure, I haven't digested it all. I have the same philosophy, 'Give me a few days and I'll get over it.' Someone, a friend, said 'You won't get over it, you'll get around it,' and that's probably true. You wake up and it's a new day, and that's what counts. Yesterday doesn't count. When you get up in the morning you say to God, 'What do you want me to do today?' It's better than getting up and cursing God. I'm not against all changes. The Village will grow from this, so things like this won't ever happen again.

*Sisters: Things like…?*

**Charles**: How they forced me to resign.

*Sisters: But have these last five years changed your personality; have you learned skills?*

**Charles**: Well, yes. I have learned things I never knew. I've learned computers, I learned the web site, I didn't know how to do it before. Pictures, all that. I've been helping Kwamba with the media tool kit. We just did a tool for people coming into the Village. It was all directed, filmed, and acted by the Village for intake [purposes] by the Village. It was for Kwamba, for Heather for her doctorate degree in psychology. We spent the last, over a year working on that. It was fun because we got to learn how to do a storyboard, film, writing, rewrites, going back and dubbing in the voices. It's interesting; it's all been a learning process. Hopefully it's made me stronger.

*Sisters: Has your health changed since 2002?*

**Charles**: Worse. Now I have arthritis in all my joints. I still have high blood pressure, high cholesterol, emphysema, pain on top of my legs and back. I'm in constant chronic pain. It's another thing life deals you, and you have to learn to live with it.

*Sisters: Do you have medical care?*

**Charles**: I'm one of the few left who still have the Oregon Health Plan.

*Sisters: You mean, since they cut it so drastically?*

**Charles**: Yeah. I'm fortunate because I couldn't afford my medicine otherwise.

*Sisters: Didn't you say you came into Portland this morning to pick up your meds?*

**Charles**: Yeah, I have to pick up my meds after this interview. I try to do more than one thing if I come into town. I've been doing that for twenty, thirty years.

*Sisters: You mean dealing with illness?*

**Charles**: No, combining trips. I've been dealing with illness since 1984. They don't know what's going on. They just keep taking tests and more tests.

*Sisters: Have your finances changed since 2002?*

**Charles**: I actually make a little bit more. I've been doing surveys, taking them. I've been fortunate; I've gotten three checks so far. Not a lot, but the biggest one was thirty dollars. That's thirty dollars more than I had yesterday.

*Sisters: What do you use your income for?*

**Charles:** Bus fare. Because I don't smoke anymore. I stopped three years ago in March. So I don't have that expense anymore.

*Sisters: Congratulations.*

**Charles:** Yeah, I did it for health reasons. Other than that, I did it because my doctor said she was gonna kick the shit out of me. And she could, too!

*Sisters: She must care about you.*

**Charles:** Yeah, I have good doctors.

*Sisters: What is new in your personal life?*

**Charles:** Last year my boyfriend got married to some girl. We'd only been together for seventeen years! Well, I shouldn't say 'some girl,' I've known her for seventeen years, too.

*Sisters: I'm sorry.*

**Charles:** It's okay. It hasn't changed us any; we're still close friends. Of course, I was at the wedding! Why would there be a change? He just got married so that when he dies, she can inherit his land and things. They said vows years ago but this way she can get benefits. He's gettin' up there. He's 65.

*Sisters: How about your pets? You used to be close to them.*

**Charles:** I still have a dog, Zags, and my cat, Zacat. Now I have more cats only because they've chosen me. I have Willow, Cream, Namaste, and four new ones.

*Sisters: Will you keep living at the Village?*

**Charles:** For a while. I don't know how long, but a while. Hopefully I will get my SSD soon. I've only been trying since 2001.

*Sisters: What is holding it up?*

**Charles:** The judge. The lawyers keep saying they are hoping it is going to be soon. They are hoping this year. I can live on eleven hundred a month.

*Sisters: Is that how much it will be?*

**Charles:** Yes. Especially with back pay, I can live on that.

*Sisters: What else is new? What about your family?*

**Charles:** In the Village there are more people again. We're building. We're getting ready for our big move in March.

*Sisters: You're not leaving your site at Sunderland Yard, are you?*

**Charles**: Part of it. We're losing part of it, reconfiguring. We're opening up the fence and going farther north. It's one hundred and twenty-six feet wide and three hundred and ninety four feet long.

*Sisters: Wow, that's exciting. And it's interesting that when I asked you about your family, you told me about the Village.*

**Charles**: Well, yeah. And my sister still sends me phone cards so I can keep in touch. She doesn't do e-mail; that would be easiest.

Kevin

*Sisters: We did your interview in October 2003. Do you remember what was going on for you then, and what has changed?*

**Kevin**: I remember I was sitting over in the cafe, and someone said they got seven dollars for doing an interview. I thought, 'I can do that.' I came over and scheduled my appointment. I missed my first appointment, but luckily the interviewer had missed that day too, so I rescheduled.

*Sisters: So, what has changed since that time?*

**Kevin**: I've been through a lot of hard work. Because I first volunteered in the cafe, and then became a member of the Sisters Board of Directors, then an on-call employee, and now a full-time employee.

*Sisters: You forgot 'a photographer for the PhotoVoice project.'*

**Kevin**: Yeah.

*Sisters: When did you become a full-time employee?*

**Kevin**: In August, on my birthday. That was a good birthday present.

*Sisters: Were you homeless in 2003 when you did the interview?*

**Kevin**: Yes I was. It was 2004, early 2005 when I got housing. I'd been on their list for four years.

*Sisters: What list?*

**Kevin**: HAP (Housing Authority of Portland). I just moved out of HAP housing yesterday. I rent a real apartment now. Well, a duplex. Still, it's nice.

*Sisters: Congratulations. How does it feel?*

**Kevin**: Nice, but also kind of scary. It's a lot of responsibility. With HAP, if you lose your job, you don't have to pay rent that month. With this, if I fail at my job and you decide to fire me, I lose my apartment. I'm stuck. This is my first time in about eleven years where I've been responsible for something other than, 'where will I sleep tonight?' With HAP, I'm not responsible for paying the rent if I don't have a job. It's kind of scary.

*Sisters: How's your family?*

**Kevin**: My dad was sick for a while. It looks like he's recovering from that. I'm closest to my father, so that was the worst feeling. Even when I was homeless, it was a rock. My dad was a normal person, a person who cared for me and was always there. Seeing him less than immortal was a big shock.

*Sisters: Are you in touch more with your family since you got housed?*

**Kevin**: No. I've noticed I'm still a bit antisocial. I have a roommate, and oftentimes I sit in my room hoping he doesn't knock on the door. I don't want to talk. I don't think I was that way that much before.

*Sisters: Before you were homeless?*

**Kevin**: Yes.

*Sisters: Have all your accomplishments since that time changed you?*

**Kevin**: I wouldn't say that I've had an increase in confidence. It sounds weird—I haven't had an increase in confidence, but I've reached the point where I've realized that's gonna have to happen. It sounds bizarre. And I find myself noticing girls more often.

*Sisters: Why?*

**Kevin**: When you're homeless, it's kind of hard to date. So yeah, it sounds bizarre, but…

*Sisters: It doesn't sound bizarre to me at all. Part of changing your identity is realizing the next way that you need to change, right?*

**Kevin**: Yeah, I guess so.

*Sisters: Not changing your identity, but changing it, tweaking it.*

**Kevin**: Right. I'm not as good at tweaking it, though!

*Sisters: So, has your financial situation changed?*

**Kevin**: Drastically, yes. In 2003, my mantra was, 'I don't need a good job, I need a job.' Now I have a decent job with health insurance, and my mantra now is, 'Now I need a living wage.' It sounds rotten, ungrateful, I know…

*Sisters: No it doesn't. It's good that you have identified what you want to strive for. What more would it take an hour, to be a living wage?*

**Kevin**: Three fifty an hour. But I feel much better about everything in life.

---

*Sisters: What are your hopes, now?*

**Kevin**: Well, I became a reverend since 2003. I'm thinking of going back to college. It sounds silly, but I took an online test to challenge a master's in military science. Not a big test, like two thousand questions. I passed with a ninety-six percent. Maybe military science is the degree for me! I'm not sure there is a college locally that offers one, but it would be ironic working here and having one. It's not exactly the place you'd expect a military science degree.

*Sisters: What else has changed? How's your health?*

**Kevin**: It hasn't changed much. But I noticed I care more about it now. I'm more interested in it.

*Sisters: How old are you now?*

**Kevin**: 36. My back aches once in a while.


## Agnes

*Sisters: So, what has changed in your life since the interview in March 2004?*

**Agnes**: I was staying in the Salvation Army, on the street, in at 8 p.m. out at 7 a.m. type of thing. Now I'm at the Royal Palm. I'm still in a shelter, still waiting for housing. I haven't been in the Royal Palm all that time. I was in Central City Concern (CCC) from 2005 to 2006, housing through the CEP program, but I screwed it up. The CCC program is housing, a type of government grant. CCC is the type of place where you're in treatment, required to go to groups, have a counselor.

*Sisters: How did you screw it up?*

**Agnes**: I ended up having a warrant and I didn't see my caseworker. I ended up thrown out of the program, evicted.

*Sisters: And you consider the Royal Palm a shelter?*

**Agnes**: Yeah, I'm in a dorm. It's through Cascadia Mental Health; the Old Town Chinatown one got me in there.

*Sisters: Is it better than the Salvation Army?*

**Agnes**: The Salvation Army was much more cleaner and more monitored, as far as staff supervising people. There weren't as many mental health people. The Royal Palm is for mental health people. But this is better because I don't have to get up and stay on the street all day, and food is provided so I don't have to stand in food lines. Plus my clothing is provided.

*Sisters: Has your financial situation changed?*

**Agnes**: Yeah, I got a warrant in 2005 and didn't find out about it until 2006, and they took my Social Security because of the warrant. Because they said they were aiding and abetting me if they continued to give me money. Just now I'm supposed to get a check after eight months. I'm waiting on it now.

*Sisters: How have you survived since then?*

**Agnes**: Shelters. Food. Sisters Of The Road. I was on the street for a while. I ended up with a concussion. Remember when I had that neck brace before? I had a concussion. I got into an altercation with a man.

*Sisters: An altercation about what?*

**Agnes**: Because we were smoking crack and drinking alcohol. They all think that just because you're smoking crack you want sex—that they go hand in hand.

*Sisters: That's—*

**Agnes**: Disgusting, isn't it? So degrading. Sickening. I can't believe some of the stuff I'm doing now on crack. I did heroin for twenty-three years and I never did the crap I'm doing now. What's wrong with you, Agnes?! It's my life. I'm putting my life on the line, and my freedom too.

*Sisters: Are you clean now?*

**Agnes**: No. I'm still chippin'.

*Sisters: Chippin'?*

**Agnes**: Chippin'. Like you have a rock but you don't smoke it all, you chip away at it.

*Sisters: Would you get kicked out of your housing if they knew you weren't clean?*

**Agnes**: No, not unless they found it on the premises. I can do it outside the premises if I can control and maintain myself. They ask you to stay out of the common areas if you are high or drunk. It's a wet house. It's a mental illness place, you know. I had to be evaluated and everything. It took me two months to get in. I was out here with a concussion and the muscles on my neck sprained. I'm just lucky that's all that happened. I could have had my neck broken!

*Sisters: What was your diagnosis?*

**Agnes**: PTSD. Suicidal tendencies. Severe dependency on drugs. I have quite a long history. I've been using heroin since the age of 7. I started out like everyone else, a love child in the '60s, peace, love, and all that crap, and it progressed. I've done everything there is to do, except for those new contractions of uppers-lowers-hallucinogens, whatever they call those, and I am not interested in those! I hope and pray that this crack thing falls off. I'm 53 years old; I'm too old for this crap.

*Sisters: What do you mean, 'falls off'?*

**Agnes**: I've been exchanging one drug for another; the methadone keeps me safe from heroin. I hope I don't want crack anymore. I can't white knuckle it. I can't go without it. I can't quit until it's inside of me to quit. Treatment can't make me quit.

*Sisters: Are those diagnoses new?*

**Agnes**: No. I just had to evaluate that part of my disabilities to get in.

*Sisters: How about your family? Has that changed since March 2004?*

**Agnes**: Today is my daughter's birthday; she's 33. I lost track of her; I don't know how to get a hold of her. I prayed a little while ago for her. I pray that she heard me, in my heart and in my spirit. I have a son that's working, and I hear he's a good dad to his little girl. My youngest daughter is in boot camp and she's struggling. She has too much energy and ends up getting in trouble. She won't talk to me. Her grandparents and her dad poisoned her against me. I have a sister in California, and I also lost track of her. She's ten years older than me. I wonder if she's still alive. I'd hate to someday try and get a hold of her and find out she has passed away. That would be horrible.

I've finally come to the understanding that me and my husband are definitely over. I went wacky in 2004 [until] here recently. I got myself in trouble. I got a Driving While Under the Influence in Clackamas [County], and a Stolen Vehicle and Possession in Multnomah County. I didn't care. I almost willed myself to death. I ended up very sick on the street. My hep C kicked in, I couldn't go through anymore. Thank God I'm over the hump. I think about him a lot, too much. Twenty-three years, I feel those were the best years of my life. Most of the time he was in prison and I was waiting. He wasn't there when my daughter was born. I waited and waited on him; I kept thinking he would change. He's clean now and in NA, and he's judging me because I'm on methadone. I don't know what he said to my youngest daughter, but it's bad enough she doesn't want to talk to me. So now I got court stuff, probation, hoops. I have to do twelve months of probation, a victim assessment, a diversion, a DNA swab. Now I'm a felon; 53 and now I'm a felon! It don't make sense.

*Sisters: I'm sorry.*

**Agnes**: I know. I did it to myself; I'm mad at myself. Nothing can be done. I have to try to undo it. I'm self-sabotaging, it's self-inflicted. Since I was so sick, my immune system is depleted. Today is a good day, but sometimes I feel bad. When I feel good, I think, 'How long before I feel bad?' It's ass-backwards, but I'm waitin' to feel bad! Life is ass-backwards, so why not my health? I always feel like I'm being judged. I think that's why I'm always so put together.

Brent

Brent's face is extremely deformed. He told me a story when he first sat down about going out to a buffet for his birthday last week and having a little girl turn around in line and see him and scream and drop her plate; later, a little boy eating with his family said, "Look at that man's face!" and his dad slapped him, which made Brent feel awful.

*Sisters: We originally interviewed you in December 2001. You were one of the first! What has changed since then?*

**Brent**: They just put me through a four-day medical protocol with an IV for drugs for pain. You know you're in trouble when the internist says, 'Is it okay if we just try to control the spikes in your pain?' It's fun when they take a baseball-sized tumor out of your head. We're coming up on an auspicious anniversary; not only is it my birthday, but I'm coming up on the anniversary of the diagnosis of my condition, when I was a child, which shocked my parents because they were told I had a fifty-fifty chance of being okay.

*Sisters: You found out on your birthday?*

**Brent**: Yeah.

*Sisters: Wow. What is your condition?*

**Brent**: Basal cell carcinoma, nevus syndrome. I get to go in for surgery in two days. They did a biopsy over my right ear and found it's positive, so I get to go in Thursday and have them hack away at it. The fun part is, I have to have it done awake.

*Sisters: Awake? Why?*

**Brent**: Because they can't see it with the naked eye. They have to cut it, freeze it, put it on a slide and read it. Then they start over if it [cancer] is still there. There's an hour and a half between each time. My mom said, 'You're not gonna end up like your father, are you?' He lost both ears.

*Sisters: So this is hereditary?*

**Brent**: Mmm-hmm. We can trace it through five generations of our family. I've had forty years, six types of cancer, and sixteen hundred eighty operations.

*Sisters: Wait, did you say sixteen hundred and eighty?*

**Brent**: Yep. As one doctor said, I've had more plastic surgeries than Michael Jackson, and I still look more like me!

*Sisters: What else has changed in your life?*

**Brent**: Well, we're no longer managing the apartment.

*Sisters: You and your wife?*

**Brent**: Girlfriend! We're not married. That would complicate matters even more. If we got married, the money she gets paid by the state for taking care of her mom would count against my SSI, basically eliminate it. Now we live in a three-bedroom house out in Aloha where she spends all her time taking care of her mom. We used to spend more time with the grandkids; I think it makes her a little sad. But now they're out at the coast.

*Sisters: Your grandkids?*

**Brent**: Hers. I'm just Grandpa Brent. That's one good thing that did happen on my birthday: she found out her youngest is expecting.

*Sisters: Congratulations. How long have you been together?*

**Brent**: Ten years. So we've lived out there four years now. It's a nice neighborhood, nice and quiet, compared to our old neighborhood. We're out of the apartments and into a house now.

*Sisters: Do you own?*

**Brent**: No, we rent. And now we have three puppies in the family that are probably going to a new home.

*Sisters: Has your financial situation changed?*

**Brent**: Not really. It's the same income. We got more bills now. It used to be, when we were managing the apartments, we didn't worry about rent, just utilities. But now most of our money goes to rent and utilities. I guess it's the price we pay for more time to ourselves and not being called by people twenty-four hours a day.

*Sisters: How old are you Brent?*

**Brent**: I turned 42 on Monday.

*Sisters: Happy birthday! What else has changed for you?*

**Brent**: I have more medical abnormalities. They found…in 2002, I was in my house, and I grabbed a coffeepot, poured coffee, put it back, and my arm locked. I found out that I have bone spurs in my arm, and if I turn my forearm just right, they lock and dislocate my elbow. The doctor said they'd do more harm taking them out. He said, 'Just be careful with it.'

*Sisters: But, if pouring a cup of coffee isn't within the realm of 'careful'…*

**Brent**: Yeah. I still do heavy lifting, too. We've moved [my girlfriend's] older son, like, three times now. And I get stuck with the heavy stuff. That was one thing we used to do at Sisters. We were on a baseball team here.

*Sisters: How long ago was that?*

**Brent**: At least twenty years! Let's just say I can remember when Sisters had breakfast in the morning and lunch in the afternoon! I mean, I've seen so much staff come and go from this place. It's amazing how things change and move on.

*Sisters: Were you homeless in the old days at Sisters?*

**Brent**: Yep. I was homeless for ten years. That was back when TPI didn't have bunk beds, they only had cots. I could tell you horror stories. [Proceeds to tell a horror story about the hospital repeatedly sending him back to the shelter one night in between two surgeries because the state wouldn't pay for a hospital bed for that one night, and how he almost died of 108° fever]. I have to be in the new OHSU (Oregon Health and Science University) building next week. I drive to the Max [train], and walk to the streetcar to get there for my surgery.

*Sisters: You can navigate all that public transit after surgery?*

**Brent**: Oh yeah. Two weeks ago my neighbor took me to the emergency room at OHSU because I had a sharp pain in my head. That was before they removed the tumor. They gave me enough Dilaudid in the emergency room to put down a horse. The first thing they asked me was, 'You're not driving, are you?' I said no. I took the bus, the Max, and walked just under a mile the rest of the way home. I can make it under twenty-five minutes on foot.

*Sisters: Wow, you're tough, Brent.*

**Brent**: Then there's something I don't really like to talk about. I nearly lost my dad. I got rather stupid. I got called one night and they said he was going into surgery; they have to do stuff on his arteries. I thought, I'm sixteen hundred miles from home; if something happens I won't find out until later. I was in pain, I still had the tumor in my head. I snapped. I got stupid.

*Sisters: What do you mean, 'got stupid?'*

**Brent**: I overdosed. Methadone, morphine, Nortriptolene, and Dimazapan, a sleep agent. I don't remember this, but somehow I got from the transit center to St. Vincent's [hospital]. Apparently I was screaming so much in the ICU that when [my girlfriend] came to see me, the nurses said I didn't want to see anyone. She reminds me of that fact for the last ten months now.

*Sisters: Reminds you—*

**Brent**: That I overdosed. You take physical pain like that, and throw emotional pain on top of it, and I just overloaded. I have friends that say, 'If your life weren't chaotic, you wouldn't know what to do!' My life is never calm.

*Sisters: Do you like it that way?*

**Brent**: Not entirely. If the state came and took [my girlfriend's] mom away, we'd lose our house.

She's frustrated and it's getting worse. There's not much we can do. She has Alzheimer's and dementia. Just after we did the interview [in 2001], [my girlfriend's] mother's mother died and we had to drive down there. We can show her mom pictures of the funeral and of her mom in the coffin, and she has no recollection of it.

*Sisters: So living with that adds considerable chaos to your life?*

**Brent**: Oh yeah! Now we have a chain on our door. She's gone out of the house twice when I've not been at home and she's gone into the street. I was at doctor's appointments last week and I was on the train on my way home, just coming out of the tunnel, when I got a voice message from [my girlfriend] telling me to come home. [My girlfriend's mother] was down the street six houses away trying to talk a neighbor into taking her back to California. Yeah. Tonight I get to go home and strengthen the playpen for the puppies. When you're up all night with pain, it's challenging.

*Sisters: Is your dad okay?*

**Brent**: Yeah. [My girlfriend's] convinced she's got both me and my dad with one foot in the grave and one foot on a banana peel. Both of us.


Kyle

*Sisters: What's new since October 2003?*

**Kyle**: Let's see. In a way, not a lot; in another way, quite a bit. At the time of the interview, I was homeless. Three weeks later I was housed. I was already employed here [at Sisters] through AARP, coding the research. That was true at the time of the interview. So I wound up in Section 8 housing, which was a blessing. Because at the time Jamie [Sisters' previous research staff] left, AARP wanted to haul me off the assignment. And because I was in subsidized housing, I was able to say, 'It's the wrong time to leave these people, they need stability right now.' So I was able to stay because I didn't need the rent.

*Sisters: Are you still in the same housing?*

**Kyle**: Yes. It's been convenient. After the project ended—the coding side anyway—I felt no ambition to get a job. Then I realized I was old enough to retire. I didn't retire on a lot because it was an early retirement, a few hundred less a month. So Sisters was my last job. That was nice. It was a nice way to end my clerking career. But it's hard to get a job when you're older. It's a lot of work to get a job. Because of the environment of the Pacific Northwest, you need a bachelor's degree for clerking. So I'm undereducated. People come here to live because it's a great place to live. That's why I came here. Because it's not Minnesota!

*Sisters: How old are you now?*

**Kyle**: 63. So, retirement is a change. And then people decided through the ballot, the Constitution—I'm not sure how—they cut the money for social services. The Oregon Health Plan got cut back. I'm blind in my left eye because OHP Standard won't cover cataract surgery. They'll cover cataract care, but not cataract surgery. The doctor said, 'What do they mean care—they'll give you a cane?'

*Sisters: Man. When did you lose your vision?*

**Kyle**: The first symptom I noticed was in summer of 2003, but I wasn't blind for about another year and a half.

*Sisters: So that's a big change since the time of the first interview.*

**Kyle**: Yes. In theory, someday the VA will do the surgery because I am a zero-compensation disabled vet. They will also perform a hernia operation I've needed for a while, which OHP won't cover either. And if you don't pay your premium, you will lose it and never get it back. If you have zero income, you pay zero, but I have a retirement income.

*Sisters: So what is holding the VA up?*

**Kyle**: It hasn't happened; it's been months. The VA is not trying to be incompetent. There are just so many people. A lot of people don't have insurance, but a lot of people were in the army. It's not fun, but I don't feel wronged. And I am going in for a pre-op session next week for the hernia. Apparently there is less demand for hernias than for eyeballs! So I was on a waiting list for months, and then, the most dramatic thing happened, my fibrulation occurred. I had always had a heart murmur, but I developed one of the frequent consequences of heart murmurs, atrial fibrillation. Because of that, my cardiologist decided I should have surgery. Somehow or other, he got a surgeon to perform it pro bono. I'm still stunned. Fifteen years ago it [would have] cost thirty thousand dollars. Today, I don't know how much. There's been a geometric increase in prices. That was just over two months ago. Now I can go back to life to the extent I'm able to.

*Sisters: Congratulations.*

**Kyle**: It's not a matter of congratulations really. I consider myself incredibly lucky, incredibly blessed. I still get dizzy thinking of it. OHP covered my hospitalization. Because of the fibrulation, I was in the emergency room three times in October. They covered all of that, including all the tests. They just won't cover the surgery. They don't cover surgeries anymore. They covered the MRIs, echocardiograms, CAT scans, all of which cost more than the eye surgery [would]. I gather it was because it was all done through the ER. They won't cover it through doctors' referrals. I don't really know, I'm inferring.

*Sisters: Do you feel different?*

**Kyle**: Oh yeah. I'm not fully back yet, not as strong as I was before. It's pretty…they cut your sternum and rib cage open, pull your chest apart, slice your heart up, a machine pushes your blood around. It is 'nontrivial,' as my sister likes to say! Apparently I'm recovering very well. Sometimes it takes up to a year to bounce back.

*Sisters: How about your medications, are they paid for?*

**Kyle**: Yeah, OHP pays. They don't do some, but they haven't said no to the ones I need. Now I'm a cyborg! They couldn't repair my valve, so they replaced it with something metallic. I can hear it click. It takes some adjustment to hearing myself click. It's hard to fall asleep sometimes, listening to myself click. Your heart isn't supposed to do that! I had hoped the valve could be repaired, but it couldn't. The tube was severely damaged by going to the dentist.

*Sisters: The dentist?! I have a dentist appointment later today.*

**Kyle**: This part is all in the original interview, so you don't need to write this part down: they were putting dentures in, pulling teeth, and they found a pocket of streptococcus which lost their home and wandered my blood looking for a home. And they found my heart a beautiful place to make a home. Their waste products ate through the…like a tent has support ropes? They ate through the support ropes of my heart. But that is all in the original interview.

*Sisters: Wow. So has anything else changed since 2003 besides serious surgery?*

**Kyle**: No, I'm pretty stable in my retirement. I got HDTV (high-definition television). You can get it over the air, you don't have to get cable. It's incredible. And some day, I'll have two eyes to see it!

Johnny

*Sisters: We did the interview over five years ago, in January 2002. What has changed for you since then?*

**Johnny**: I've got permanent housing. Knock on wood.

*Sisters: Why knock on wood?*

**Johnny**: I ended up going to the bank on the fifth of February and leaving the bank, coming down here to Sisters and finding it closed for the day, but I saw a couple of my friends and we talked a bit and walked up to Pioneer Square, and I ended up passing out in the bathroom.

*Sisters: Why did you pass out?*

**Johnny**: I had a blood clot in my lungs and didn't know it.

*Sisters: Why did you have a blood clot?*

**Johnny**: I'm prone to throw blood clots. I have a rare disease.

*Sisters: What's that?*

**Johnny**: It's called Factor V Leiden Disorder. [fvleiden.org says Factor V Leiden is the most common hereditary blood coagulation disorder in the United States, present in 5% of the Caucasian population and 1.2% of the African-American population.]

*Sisters: When did you find out?*

**Johnny**: I knew I had a disorder. I'd been on medical all this time. The blood clot broke apart from my leg and traveled up into my lungs. I kinda knew it might do that.

*Sisters: Did you get housing because of your illness?*

**Johnny**: No, thanks to some friends I have permanent housing. In 2002, I was fighting for SSI and SSD, which I got in May 2004.

*Sisters: Congratulations! That's a big change since 2002. How has it changed your life?*

**Johnny**: Well, one of the changes is I'm not on the street anymore.

*Sisters: How about in other ways? Has it helped with your health?*

**Johnny**: Yes. It's 360°-help. Basically, a 360°-turn from being out in the Village [Dignity Village], cold, wet, in the rain.

*Sisters: How else has it impacted you?*

**Johnny**: It's impacted me making friends. Having a phone I can actually use without being on a five- or ten-minute time, having to go down to the public library and use computers, having to fight for bus fare.

*Sisters: So you can afford bus fare and things better now?*

**Johnny**: Yes.

*Sisters: So your income went up?*

**Johnny**: Yes. I get a monthly check, two actually.

*Sisters: From your SSI and SSD?*

**Johnny**: Yes.

*Sisters: At the time of the first interview, what were you living on?*

**Johnny**: Food stamps, unemployment when I could get it, and donations. I also worked part-time.

*Sisters: Do you work now?*

**Johnny**: No, I do not. I am not cleared by my doctor to go back to work yet.

*Sisters: What else has changed? Anything?*

**Johnny**: I'm living with some family. I'm living with my half-sister and my nieces and nephews and great-nephews and a great-niece, and another great-nephew is on the way.

*Sisters: Wow! How is that? Is that less lonely, or a little chaotic, or...?*

**Johnny**: It's good. It's a little more chaotic, a little bit, but it gives me more freedom than being on a bus that only runs once every hour or so, or every half hour. I have a couple of different ways of getting back and forth to home, different buses. And I have laundry facilities and other things, you know.

*Sisters: Is it easier to live?*

**Johnny**: Mmm-hmm. And my leg is getting better all the time. I was still on crutches in 2002, and a walker, and a wheelchair, and a cane. I had ankle surgery in 2001 from an injury, I broke it four and a half years previous to ankle surgery. You remember, don't you, you interviewed me, I believe?

*Sisters: Yes indeed, I remember. I remember.*

Photographer: Brynne Athens

*In here there are no strangers, just friends we've never met*

## Sisters Of The Road

Much has been written about Sisters Of The Road and how the cafe works. We thought this bit from one of the interviews described it best.

**Darren**: Yes! I've asked people that just come in or get off the bus, [and they say] 'Where can I eat at? Sir, can I have a couple of dollars for something to eat?'

I said, 'Well, bud, you don't need any money…go to Sisters Of The Road, up here. And, uh, before you eat, I'm gonna tell ya, you can pay cash, you can pay with food stamps, or, sir, before you decide to eat, why don't you volunteer? Why don't you ask if you can serve the water and the coffee and lemonade? Or, carry the trays, or pick up the trays when people leave, bus the tables. Or wait on people.' I said, 'Why'n'tcha earn a little bit? Because you'll come out way ahead. Just from working, like, an hour, an hour and a half, or an hour and three-quarters, you'll get twelve dollars on your books. That way, you can come back tomorrow, and the whole week; you cannot eat up twelve dollars in the whole week! Your meals are only a dollar and a quarter, and your drinks are only twenty-five cents.'

'And if you want to, you can find a buddy or something like that, if you want to buy them lunch, another homeless person lunch, they'll put it right on that tab, right on that ticket. You sign for it. You work an hour and three-quarters, you get twelve dollars on your books for being helpful. You help serve other people, plus you get something to eat, and it works out, that way. Be kind to someone, and they'll be kind to you.'

And so far I've known three different people started working for Sisters Of The Road during the day to volunteer their time.

*Sisters: Three people that you've referred there?*

**Darren**: Yes, yes.

*Sisters: So you can, I mean, you get money on your books, but you're also doing something good for someone else?*

**Darren**: Well, it's not money, it's credit.

*Sisters: Credit, right.*

**Darren**: Bartering. Yeah, yeah. My first day was twelve dollars. My second day was twenty-four; my third day was thirty-six.

*Sisters: Wow.*

**Darren**: So, I know that, if uh…I don't need food stamps. I wanted to tell them, at the food stamp office, 'One monkey don't stop no show.' Because there's enough food around here in the evening, there's enough places that will feed something to eat, that I don't need food stamps.

*Sisters: You're not dependent.*

**Darren**: Right! And at Sisters Of The Road, they're open between ten and two-thirty. I've got enough money on the books that I can feed myself, or feed anybody else that might be hungry.

*Sisters: So you don't have to be dependent, because you can go do that.*

**Darren**: That's right. All it was…the only thing that irritated me, mentally, that uh, it kind of just twisted me, was the runaround. And it seemed like a game that they're playin'. See, they want to get you hung up in the system.

*Sisters: You mean the food stamps and the—*

**Darren**: The food stamp office and the bus tickets, the job force, the Workforce, and stuff like that. One hand's patting the other hand. So it's like one big glove; you got four fingers and a thumb, and all the organizations belong to the palm of the hand, belong to the wrist. And one's making sure the other finger gets their portion of whatever you're doing.

*Sisters: So, they're all milking the same…*

**Darren**: Yes, the same system.

*Sisters: The same pool.*

**Darren**: Yes. So uh…

*Sisters: It sounds like with the barter at Sisters Of The Road, that—*

**Darren**: That's the best thing that's happened.

*Sisters: The best thing?*

**Darren**: That's the best thing that I've ran across in my life. As far as homeless shelters go? There oughta be more places like that.

---

*Sisters: Why?*

**Darren**: Because it gives an individual…I felt good after. I just went up there, and the cook asked me, says, 'Buddy, could you help us? We're shorthanded.' I says, 'Well, sure! What do ya need?' He says, 'We need you to work on the steam tables, putting the food on the plate.' And he says uh, 'We're running beans and rice, we're running cornbread, we're running scallop potatoes. Whatever the order calls for, put this, just take one spoon, and put it on the plate, and set it up on the counter up here, and someone else who's gonna serve the food, will put it out.' He says, 'Do that for us, will you?' And I says, 'Why, sure!'

So I felt good; I felt that I accomplished something within myself. I had my dignity back. I felt good. And I felt better after I got done eating, too! I finally had something I could pay a meal for!

*Sisters: Right on!*

**Darren**: A little bit of labor got me a meal. And it got me more than a meal. It got me quite a few days' meals. So, that's what they should have. And I think that'd stop a lot of shoplifting.

*Sisters: Shoplifting of food, you mean?*

**Darren**: Yes. Yes.

Photographer: Brynne Athens

Appendix B

## Idiom

---

**13th step**: this is the step after the 12th where people go to AA meetings to pick up people from the opposite sex

**bad tramp**: someone on the streets who will cheat and steal from you

**boosting**: stealing; shoplifting

**bunk**: bad drugs; intentionally diluted or falsified illegal drugs

**camp robber**: someone who steals people's stuff from their camps

**cellie**: cell mate in jail

**chasing the bag**: getting drugs out on the streets

**chippin'**: using small bits of a crack rock to extend its use.

**classification**: when you first get into jail, they give you a probation-like time where they see how you get along in their system

**closed custody**: when you only get ten or twenty minutes out of your cell during the day

**con's code of ethics**: prison ethics

**cooker**: drug paraphernalia

**criminal system**: the government

**fence**: somebody who will buy stolen merchandise

**fire it**: doing drugs through IV

**flophouse**: a place where a bunch of people sleep in one room

**flyin' a sign**: holding up a cardboard sign on an on-ramp or busy street to get money; (e.g., "Homeless Vet, Need Help" or "Traveling—anything will help")

**fortified wine**: Mad Dog or Thunderbird or other wines with a high alcohol content

**Gs**: grands, or thousands of dollars

**get some Act-Right**: do right by people

**get whoop**: being sold fake drugs

**good tramp**: a good citizen who helps out others who are on the streets

**hoin' it**: prostituting

**home guards**: homeless people who stay in one town and utilize the services circuit

**jacked up**: to be asked for name and ID by a police officer

**nut check**: getting an SSI check because of mental health issues

**porch robber**: someone who takes people's cans straight from their recycling on their porch or in their backyards

**roofless**: another term for homeless

**rubber tramp**: someone who sleeps in a vehicle

**running partner**: your partner on the streets who watches your back and who spends most time with you

**Sally tramp**: a tramp who goes to Salvation Army and tells them they have family or an emergency in another state so that the Salvation Army will give a bus ticket to go to the next destination the tramp wants to visit

**SO**: significant other

**SOS (shit over shingles)**: gravy with meat or sausage over toast or biscuits

**spanging**: asking for spare change

**Spring Fever**: when people are not as dependent on their recovery programs for housing because it is not as harsh to stay outside, so they relapse into using drugs

**stinkin' thinkin'**: bad thinking—recovery language when you are thinking bad thoughts

**squat/squatter**: a squatter camps or stays illegally somewhere; a squat is where they stay

**sweep**: police ordering homeless persons to vacate the premises, followed by removal of their possessions

**taxing**: when on the streets, people take things from one another as a "tax" for being on the streets

---

**tootin'**: snorting drugs through the nose

**tramp**: homeless person who is self-sufficient, who will hustle, do day-labor, panhandle, and fly signs to make money

**units**: locomotives

**yard bulls**: railroad security guards

Photographer: Alan Shipley

Photographer: Brynne Athens

# Appendix C

## Suggested Sources for Continued Investigation

Many organizations and government agencies offer excellent resources related to topics addressed in this book. Below is a list of only a few of those we have found particularly relevant.

### Documents

Excellent reference articles and insights into the project are available on the Gray Sunshine Publishing web site:
>    www.graysunshine.com/pages/tidbitsv.html

History of Sisters Of The Road:
>    www.netraising.net/images/sisters/Sisters_25th_Book.pdf

The Oregon Center for Public Policy's 2006 Report: "Who's Getting Ahead? Opportunity in a Growing Economy":
>    www.ocpp.org

Western Regional Advocacy Project (WRAP) report:
>    www.wraphome.org/wh_press_kit/index.html

### Local Links

Affordable Housing Now (AHN):
>    www.cdnportland.org/ahn.html

Coalition for a Livable Future:
>    www.clfuture.org

Dignity Village: the web site has been unstable fairly often in the last couple of years. When it is up, the site has good information.
www.dignityvillage.org
This article from Tolerance.org provides a nice history of Dignity Village: "Village Maintains Its Dignity—and Its Land":
www.tolerance.org/news/article_tol.jsp?id=959

JOIN:
www.joinpdx.com

Northwest Constitutional Rights Center:
www.nwcrc.org

Sisters Of The Road:
www.sistersoftheroad.org

*street roots*:
www.streetroots.org/index.php

Oregon Statewide Links

Oregon Center for Public Policy:
www.ocpp.org

Oregon Food Bank:
www.oregonfoodbank.org

Oregon Hunger Relief Taskforce:
www.oregonhunger.org

National Links

American Bar Association on Homelessness and Poverty:
www.abanet.org/homeless/home.htm

Joint Center for Housing Studies:
www.jchs.harvard.edu

National Center on Family Homelessness:
www.familyhomelessness.org

National Coalition for the Homeless:
www.nationalhomeless.org

National Law Center on Homelessness and Poverty:
www.nlchp.org

Share our Strength (SOS):
www.strength.org

Urban Institute:
www.urban.org

Western Regional Advocacy Project (WRAP):
www.wraphome.org

Artist: Victor Guschov

# Glossary

**AA**: Alcoholics Anonymous

**ACLU**: American Civil Liberties Union

**Adult and Family Services**: the Children, Adult, and Family Services Division of the Oregon Department of Human Services deals with food stamps, vocational rehabilitation services, foster homes, employment training services, and other supportive resources

**Agent Orange**: an herbicide used for defoliation during the Vietnam War; its release of dioxins has caused severe bodily harm to those who served in the war

**ASPCA**: American Society for the Prevention of Cruelty to Animals

**AWOL**: absent without leave (a military term)

**bipolar disorder**: an affective disorder causing the sufferer to have prolonged periods of depression interspersed with bouts of mania

**Blanchet House**: The Blanchet House of Hospitality, a service providing food, job referrals, and temporary shelter in Portland, Oregon

**BLM**: Bureau of Land Management, a federal government department responsible for the management of public land

**Catholic Worker**: the Catholic Worker Movement, founded by Dorothy Day and Peter Maurin in 1933, practices the works of mercy in their houses of hospitality and farming communes and devotes itself to direct action against violence in any form

**CEP**: Community Engagement Program is housing and support services for homeless adults; operated by Central City Concern

**CETA**: Comprehensive Employment and Training Act

**CHIERS**: Central City Concern Hooper Inebriate Emergency Response Service, an outreach van belonging to Hooper (*see below*); it finds inebriated people and brings them to the treatment center.

**Clark Center**: run by Transition Projects Inc; is a shelter for men

**CO**: conscientious objector or commanding officer

**day center**: a facility that allows people experiencing homelessness to be there during the day, often providing hygiene facilities, phone and mail services, and other resources

**Dignity Village**: a tent city on unused public land within the city limits of Portland, Oregon

**Downtown Chapel**: a parish of St. Vincent de Paul; has a hospitality center with snacks, sleeping bags and clothing, hygiene services (including foot care and haircuts), and transportation aid; a food pantry that hands out bags of food; and a cafe serving food once a week

**Eagle Scout**: a boy scout who has achieved the highest rank

**electronic food stamp benefit transfer card (EBT)**: a card that serves the same purpose as food stamps

**food stamps**: benefits that may be used in one of two ways: to purchase unprepared food from a store, or to buy a hot meal from a USDA-approved meal site

**Fred Meyer**: a chain of stores that sell groceries, clothing, and housewares

**functioning addict**: someone who is addicted to a drug, but can still maintain a job and take care of his or her basic needs

**GED**: general equivalency diploma

**General Assistance**: benefits that are meant to cover basic needs until the recipient receives SSI benefits

**Harbor Light**: a Salvation Army shelter

**Hawthorne neighborhood**: a bohemian neighborhood in Southeast Portland, Oregon

**Hep. C**: hepatitis C, an infection of the liver transmitted by contact with blood

**Hooper**: David C. Hooper Detoxification Center is a treatment facility for those with addictions

**Jean's Place**: a women's shelter operated by Transition Project Inc.

**JOIN**: an outreach program for homeless individuals and families

**Junior League**: an organization for women, which promotes volunteerism

**kleptomaniac**: one who experiences an obsessive need to steal

**Labor and Industries**: Bureau of Labor and Industries (BOLI), a government agency protecting workers' rights to equal nondiscriminatory treatment by their employers

---

**Labor Ready**: an employment agency

**Lewis and Clark**: Lewis and Clark College, located in Portland

**loitering**: standing about aimlessly on public property in violation of the law

**MAX**: Portland's light rail system

**McDonald Center**: a Holy Cross-run assisted living center

**Merchant Marines**: those who work aboard a country's commercial ships

**Methadone**: a narcotic that is not as addictive as heroin or morphine, often used as a substitute for other drugs for those in treatment for addiction

**minimum wage**: at the time of the interviews, Oregon's minimum wage was $6.50 an hour

**NA**: Narcotics Anonymous

**NARA**: Native American Rehabilitation Association, providing health services, education and drug treatment to Native Americans in a culturally relevant way

**National Coalition for Homeless Veterans (NCHV)**: a nonprofit organization striving to end veteran homelessness. It serves as a network for different community service organizations, and works with care providers and the government.

**National Coalition for the Homeless**: an advocacy group aimed at ending homelessness; provides a network for those experiencing homelessness now or in the past, organizations and service providers, and activists

**Northwest Pilot Project**: an agency providing housing services for people over age 55 who are homeless or at risk of becoming homeless

**NPR**: National Public Radio

**Old Town/Chinatown**: the part of downtown Portland where many services for people experiencing homelessness are located, including Sisters Of The Road

**Oregon Health Plan (OHP)**: a state-sponsored program for low-income residents

**Pioneer Square**: a community square in downtown Portland

**PO**: parole officer

**PTSD**: Post-traumatic Stress Disorder: a psychological disorder that affects those who have gone through or witnessed a highly traumatic event or circumstances, causing them to have difficulty sleeping, social phobias, flashbacks, anxiety, and other problems

**Rescue Mission**: the Portland Rescue Mission, a Christian organization providing a men's shelter

**Rose Haven**: information, referral, and advocacy services for homeless women and children

**Salvation Army Harbor Light:** Emergency shelter for single women and single women with children

**Salvation Army Safe Harbor**: beds for working men at $10 a night

**Section 8**: a rent assistance program that requires participants to 1) meet low-income guidelines, 2) pass a criminal background check, and 3) demonstrate that at least one person who will live in the house is a legal resident of the United States

**skid row**: a decrepit or shabby area, often inhabited by people experiencing homelessness

**SRO**: single room occupancy

**SSD**: Social Security disability insurance

**SSI**: supplemental security income

*street roots*: a nonprofit newspaper sold primarily on the street by people experiencing homelessness. Its content is oriented towards homelessness and social justice issues. When a person sells the paper, seventy cents of the dollar charge goes directly to the vendor.

**submarine corps**: those serving on submarines for the Navy Supply Corps, dealing with supply, logistics, support of fighters, fiscal issues, and contracting

**TB card**: a card proving that someone does not have tuberculosis, that shelters require

**Title 14**: Portland City code dealing with public order issues, specifically conduct prohibited on public property

**TPI**: Transition Projects, Inc., provides shelter for men and women for up to six weeks, transitional housing for up to four months, and support housing to help people build a rental history

**transitional housing**: aimed at assisting those who are ready to move out of emergency shelters

**Union Gospel Mission**: a Christian organization that hands out clothing, provides meals, and hosts an addiction recovery program

**USDA**: United States Department of Agriculture, manages and supports agriculture

**VA**: United States Department of Veterans Affairs; governs veterans' health and other benefits (such as burial, employment, and loans)

**XO**: executive officer

---

# Index